Between Principle and Practice
Human Rights in North-South Relations

Between Principle and Practice examines the human rights diplomacy of three prosperous industrial democracies with international reputations for protesting human rights abuses – Canada, the Netherlands, and Norway. David Gillies reveals that even these countries were seldom prepared to sacrifice short-run economic or political interests in order to protest gross and systematic human rights abuses beyond their borders.

Based on case studies of five Third World countries (Sri Lanka, the Philippines, China, Indonesia, and Suriname), Gillies explores the extent to which principles were followed in practice and shows that consistent, coordinated, and principled action is elusive even for countries that have a reputation for internationalism. He highlights the growing rift between the North Atlantic democracies and emerging Asian economic powers, the effectiveness of using aid sanctions to defend human rights, and the vicissitudes of human rights programming in emerging democracies.

On a theoretical level, Gillies examines the explanatory power of political realism and the scope available for ethical conduct in a world of states. Linking policy assertiveness with perceived costs to other national interests, he constructs a framework for analysing policy actions and applies it to his various case studies. He concludes that when it comes to human rights, the gap between principle and practice is still far too wide.

DAVID GILLIES is manager, developm
Aga Khan Foundation Canada.

D1227546

Between Principle and Practice

Human Rights in North-South Relations

DAVID GILLIES

McGill-Queen's University Press
Montreal & Kingston • London • Buffalo

© McGill-Queen's University Press 1996
ISBN 0-7735-1413-9 (cloth)
ISBN 0-7735-1414-7 (paper)

Legal deposit third quarter 1996
Bibliothèque nationale du Québec

Printed in Canada on acid-free paper

This book has been published with the help of a grant
from the Social Science Federation of Canada, using
funds provided by the Social Sciences and Humanities
Research Council of Canada.

McGill-Queen's University Press is grateful to the Canada
Council for support of its publishing program.

Canadian Cataloguing in Publication Data

Gillies, David, 1952–
     Between principle and practice: human rights in
     north-south relations
     Includes bibliographical references and index.
     ISBN 0-7735-1413-9 (bound) –
     ISBN 0-7735-1414-7 (pbk.)
     1. International relations. 2. Human rights. I. Title.
     JX1569.G54 1996   327   C-96-900073-1

Typeset in Sabon 10/12
by Caractéra inc., Quebec City

For Elizabeth and Arthur

Contents

Tables and Figures

FIGURES

Abbreviations

ACP	African-Caribbean-Pacific countries (Lomé Convention)
AFP	Armed Forces of the Philippines
AID	Agency for International Development (United States)
ASEAN	Association of Southeast Asian Nations
CAFGU	Critizens' Armed Forces Geographical Units
CCIC	Canadian Council for International Cooperation
CHDF	Civilian Home Defence Force
CIDA	Canadian International Development Agency
DAC	Development Assistance Committee (of OECD)
EC	European Community
EU	European Union
EDC	Export Development Corporation
EMJP	Ecumenical Movement for Justice and Peace
FLAG	Free Legal Aid Group
G7	Group of Seven (most-industrialized countries)
GNP	gross national product
ICHRDD	International Centre for Human Rights and Democratic Development
ICRC	International Committee of the Red Cross
IDRC	International Development Research Centre
IFI	international financial institution
IGGI	Inter-Governmental Group for Indonesia
IMF	International Monetary Fund
JVP	Janatha Vimukthi Peramuna
KMU	Kilusang Mayo Uno

LCL   less-concessional loans
MDC   Ministry of Development Cooperation (Norway)
MFN   most-favoured nation
NAFTA North American Free Trade Agreement
NATO   North Atlantic Treaty Organization
NDF   National Democratic Front
NEDA   National Economic and Development Authority
NFSW   National Federation of Sugar Workers
NGO   non-governmental organization
NORAD Norwegian Agency for Development Cooperation
NOVIB Netherlands Organization for International Development
       Cooperation
NPA   New People's Army
NRDF   Negros Rehabilitation and Development Fund
OAS   Organization of American States
ODA   official development assistance
OECD   Organization for Economic Cooperation and Development
PAHRA Philippines Alliance of Human Rights Advocates
PTA   Prevention of Terrorism Act
TFD   Task Force for Detainees
UNCHR United Nations Commission on Human Rights
UNDP   United Nations Development Programme
UNP   United National Party

Preface

Twenty years ago, human rights were peripheral to the foreign policy concerns of most Western democracies. Today they are a central theme in the policy rhetoric of all the OECD democracies. The passing of the Cold War and the turn to democracy in Latin America and in parts of Africa and Asia have prompted OECD donors to promote rights and democracy with confidence as keys to sustainable, market-based development.

A coherent foreign policy requires attention to the defence as well as the promotion of human rights. Based on the case studies of five countries, this book underlines the fact that consistent, coordinated, and principled action to defend human rights remains elusive even for nations such as Canada, the Netherlands, and Norway that have a reputation for humane internationalism. States are rarely willing to sacrifice immediate commercial or security interests to protest gross and systematic human rights violations. Trends that might prompt more assertive human rights policies are countered by signs of a growing rift between the OECD democracies and powerful emerging economies in Asia. Activists are thus still condemned to work in an international environment that is fundamentally inhospitable to human rights.

This book is primarily a historical study of the human rights diplomacy of three smaller Western powers during the mid- and late 1980s. This period was a turning point in international relations, marked by the demise of the Cold War, the acceleration of globalization, and new macroeconomic thinking premised on a diminished role for the state and an emphasis on the market as the engine of growth. The late 1980s were also marked by the spread of democracy and the rapid expansion of non-governmental organizations and citizens' initiatives worldwide. This prompted a growing importance to be attached to the concept of civil society in which citizens' initiatives generate "social capital" and the non-profit sector plays a dynamic role in setting and implementing social priorities. These seismic shifts in international relations and in the intellectual climate were soon registered in the rhetorical pronouncements of Canada, the Netherlands, and Norway. Much of the book is concerned with examining the extent to which policy principles that had been developed during the 1980s and early 1990s were played out in practice.

Four case studies (Sri Lanka, the Philippines, China, and Indonesia) examine Canadian, Dutch, and Norwegian relations with Asian countries, and one case study is placed in South America. Those on China and Indonesia illustrate the growing rift between the OECD democracies and emerging Asian economic powers. Several of the case studies also focus on political conditionality: using aid sanctions to defend human rights. The Dutch and Canadian responses to the Dili massacre in East Timor underline the limits of unilateral political conditionality. However, while a coordinated donor approach has the best chance of success, political conditionality remains a credible vehicle of human rights diplomacy. The real value of aid sanctions is in setting international standards when governments are judged to be culpable of gross and systematic human rights violations.

This book stems from a doctoral dissertation prepared for the Department of Political Science at McGill University. It has benefited from my later practical experience working for the International Centre for Human Rights and Democratic Development, a para-statal organization funded from Canada's aid budget. Rights are about real and sometimes desperate human struggles. So while I have taken the ideal of objectivity seriously, I hope that a sense of urgency and engagement has found its way onto these pages. Research and practice should inform each other. This book tries to bring these two solitudes in closer communion.

At McGill, Baldev Raj Nayar and Irving Brecher nurtured the gradual development of my interest in human rights and in this project. Cranford Pratt of the University of Toronto gave me valuable comments on earlier versions. This book is in good measure a reply to the patience and support of all three. In Europe, Professor Peter Baehr at Leiden University, Asbjorn Eide, director of the Norwegian Institute of Human Rights, and Dr Olav Stokke of the Norwegian Institute of

International Affairs, helped me find my way around the Dutch and Norwegian human rights communities.

Portions of this study have been read by Jack Donnelly in the United States; by Lakshman Marasinghe, Terry Keenleyside, Stephen Toope, Robert Miller, Peter-André Globensky, and Gerald Schmitz in Canada; by Peter Baehr and Herman Burgers in the Netherlands; and by aid officials in Norway. Marion Bloekpol and Inger Weibust translated Dutch and Norwegian material. Greg Firneau, a McGill University Law Faculty graduate, assisted me on the Indonesia case study. I have drawn heavily on the views of NGO staff and government officials, many of whom have preferred to remain anonymous. The interpretations are my own, however, and not necessarily those of any individual or institution cited in the text.

My deepest thanks to Marie for keeping faith in this project, and to our children, Malcolm and Hannah, for bringing joy and laughter. My thanks also to Philip Cercone of McGill-Queen's University Press for his initial encouragement to work on this book and to Joan McGilvray, Carlotta Lemieux, and Peter Blaney at McGill-Queen's Press for assistance with the editing and preparation of the text for publication. Any failings, whether of omission or commission, are my responsibility alone.

Ottawa, November 1995

PART ONE
Theory

1 Human Rights and Foreign Policy

Tiananmen Square, Dili, Halabjah, El Mozote, La Cantuta – these are places infamous for gross human rights abuses. By contrast, Canada, the Netherlands, and Norway are three prosperous industrial democracies with an international reputation for protesting such violence. How well deserved is their reputation? This study examines the human rights diplomacy of Canada, the Netherlands, and Norway in the Third World. It pays special attention to the linkage of human rights and development aid, because all three states have built bridges between these previously disconnected issues. To do this, the study draws on case material to compare each state's resolve to defend and promote human rights.

On 14 November 1991 the Netherlands announced that it would suspend its government-to-government aid to Indonesia following the 12 November killings of demonstrators at the Santa Cruz cemetery in Dili, East Timor. On 9 December 1991, Canada announced that it would suspend consideration of three Canadian International Development Agency (CIDA) projects for Indonesia in response to the Dili "incident." On 15 July 1989 the Group of Seven most-industrialized countries served notice at their Paris Summit that the World Bank would freeze new lending to China in the wake of economic uncertainties following the Tiananmen Square massacre.[1] In 1990 the World Bank reduced its activities in Zaire to a minimal core program, following Belgium's decision to cut bilateral aid to its former colony. On 26 November 1991 the World Bank announced in Paris that a Consultative Group of Donors for Kenya would withhold new loans for at least six months. Moreover, on 14 May 1992 the World Bank announced on behalf of the Consultative Group of Aid Donors for Malawi that the donor community would not approve us$74 million in new loans.[2]

Issues of good governance, human rights, and democratic pluralism played a part in each of these decisions. The denial or postponement of development aid is sometimes described as political conditionality. During the Cold War, most Organization for Economic Cooperation and Development (OECD) donors were not willing to link human rights to development aid. The United States was a controversial exception. In the 1980s, as this study will show, three small Western powers – Canada, the Netherlands, and Norway – each experimented with political conditionality. Since the collapse of the Berlin Wall in November 1989, a consensus has emerged among members of the OECD Development Assistance Committee (DAC) that development aid is an appropriate means by which to promote human rights and democratic development. The DAC donors also agree that in certain exceptional circumstances, aid spending should be linked to a recipient government's performance in respecting human rights, good governance, and democratic development.

The practical message of this book is that a coherent development aid policy requires consistent action to defend as well as to promote human rights. Political pressure to protect human rights is more controversial than using persuasion and technical support to promote fundamental freedoms and democratic pluralism.[3] The record of the three Western donors suggests that more consistent attention needs to be paid to the protection side of the human rights ledger, rhetoric notwithstanding. As a mechanism to prompt change, conditionality is a blunt sword; its real value is in setting international standards. Credible donors, such as Canada, the Netherlands, and Norway, can show leadership by a more consistent willingness to condition development assistance on respect for universal human rights.

MORAL CLAIMS OR NATIONAL INTERESTS?

International human rights pose problems for states. They imply duties beyond borders and thus conflict with other national interests. Realists and idealists differ profoundly on what scope there is for ethics in foreign policy.[4] Internationalism is "the idea that we both are and should be a part of a broader community than ... the nation state."[5] But this cosmopolitan impulse is tempered, in practice, by systemic constraints and national interests.[6] Nevertheless, self-interest is not the only force behind diplomacy. All states seek security, prosperity, and prestige. Some may have ethical goals beyond economic gain, national security, and international kudos. Canada, the Netherlands, and Norway have tried to promote global human rights. In the practice of foreign policy, the imperatives of realism and idealism need not be mutually exclusive. The challenge, as ever, is to advance internationalist objectives without damaging parochial foreign policy interests.

Realists of every complexion share three assumptions about the nature of world politics.[7] First, international relations are necessarily conflictual. They take place in an anarchical global society elevated just above a Hobbesian world by rudimentary procedures for settling disputes and managing conflict. Without a "common power to keep them all in awe," norms, rules, and principles may prove ineffective. States must therefore be self-reliant in generating and maintaining the conditions that ensure their survival and well-being. These uncertainties are a natural setting for conflict. Second, realists hold that groups are the essence of social reality. Groups reflect the tribal nature of *Homo sapiens*, and among human "conflict groups" competition is the characteristic mode of interaction.[8] Today, the tribe is the nation-state, and nationalism is tribal loyalty. Realists argue that nation-states are the dominant actors in the international system. Third, and arguably realism's keystone, is the belief that power is "the final arbiter of things political."[9] Hence, states' perpetual quest for power. This ceaseless struggle may stem from the self-help nature of the international system – Kenneth Waltz's "third image."[10] Or it may be the expression of a deeply rooted need for security, if, as Thucydides believed, "men are motivated by honour, greed, and above all, fear." Whatever the underlying motive, realists assume that politicians invariably "think and act in terms of interest defined as power."[11] This preoccupation with power and wealth is the rational response of states to the verities of international life.

Realists assume that the makers of foreign policy are rational actors relentlessly pursuing national interests.[12] In any contest among policy options, parochial interests invariably trump international idealism. Realist thinking underpins my central argument – that Western states will sustain an assertive human rights policy only when the costs are perceived to be low in terms of other national interests.[13] This claim has two sub-hypotheses – that in situations where "gross and persistent human rights violations" confront countervailing diplomatic or economic interests, states will be unassertive in their policy responses; and that nations will adopt assertive human rights policies only when they confront weak states or states where they have few vital economic or political interests.

The connection between assertive policies and perceived costs is best tested by choosing issues and cases which, on *prima facie* evidence, most likely would disprove realist assumptions. Human rights and development aid are internationalist concerns *par excellence*. A policy study of a group of states well known for its rhetorical projection of internationalism should illuminate the opportunities for, and the constraints to, the promotion of ethical interests in foreign policy.

Discussions of the linkage between human rights, development aid, and foreign policy turn on two issues: using aid as a punitive or coercive lever when gross human rights abuses prompt donors to reconsider their support to a repressive regime; and using aid as a reward to regimes that are taking steps to improve good governance, human rights, and political pluralism. Development aid can help build democratic institutions and foster the political voice of historically disadvantaged communities. The first strategy represents "negative conditionality" to defend human rights. The second strategy represents "positive conditionality," or "political aid," to promote human rights and democratic development.

The evidence in this book validates realist scepticism about the ethical conduct of states in defending human rights abroad. But it does not confirm the more extreme realist arguments.[14] The search for moral opportunity by Canada, the Netherlands, and Norway is most visible in the new agenda to *promote* human rights and democratic development, although, even here, the actions of these countries with regard to the Philippines and Sri Lanka emphasize the practical limits of an ethically driven agenda.

The next chapter describes an index to "measure" the human rights performance of developing countries and a hierarchy of human rights options to interpret Western policy. Western internationalists will favour low-cost, unassertive instruments with a bias towards using the United Nations in those cases where economic or geostrategic interests are involved. Where Western states resist assertive policies in cases of severe and enduring human rights violations, strategic and economic interests have submerged human rights in the policy calculus. This suggests a discordance between the severity of violations, donor rhetoric, and action.

This study's focus is thus empirical; namely, to examine through the lens of human rights the record of three Western middle powers in one facet of North-South relations. It is undertaken, however, with a broader purpose in mind. Scholars differ on the motives and behaviour of states in a self-help system. The "great debate" continues to pit realists against idealists even as the language of this intellectual divide takes on a new vocabulary. As international conditions have altered, the anarchy-versus-cooperation debate has splintered into newly labelled factions, such as "neorealism," "interdependence," "neoliberalism," "regime theory," and "liberal institutionalism."[15] Whatever the labels, at question here is whether ethics have a place in foreign policy and whether states have the duty to project moral values beyond their borders.[16] International human rights have been proclaimed as "the idea of our time."[17] They are claims that may well be as revolutionary for the international system today as John Locke's libertarian tracts were in seventeenth-century England.[18] Visions of a brave new world notwithstanding, there is, in practice, "an inescapable tension between human rights and foreign policy."[19] This tension, and the efforts of states to resolve it, is the subject of this study.

Is Canadian, Norwegian, and Dutch diplomacy likely to differ from the flawed and compromised performance of the Carter administration – when human rights were ostensibly "the soul" of U.S. foreign policy?[20] Can these states successfully integrate human rights into other aspects of their foreign policy as the basis of a consistent statecraft? Comparison becomes important here. Do common conceptions of their international role lead to common conduct? Or does Canada's alleged emergence as a "principal power" inhibit an assertive human rights policy?[21] Do the social democratic traditions of the Netherlands and Norway make for common policies, or are there significant differences in their response to international human rights issues?

As a field of inquiry, human rights have traditionally been the preserve of lawyers – a reflection of their juridical underpinnings and, until the Carter years, of the slim attention Western powers paid them. Since Jimmy Carter's presidency (1977–81), interest in international human rights has grown among political scientists in many Western states.[22] Understandably, attention has focused on the United States.[23] First, U.S. policy is controversial – some even say that it is contrary to the cause of global human rights.[24] Second, U.S. domestic opinion on human rights is polarized, and successive administrations have differed markedly in purpose and vision. Third, superpower status and global strategic and economic interests intrude decisively on ethical interests, making a consistent human rights policy perilous or impossible.

The United States therefore provides the starkest example of the "inescapable tensions" in human rights diplomacy. But focusing on the United States leaves much uncovered. After all, "if such a thing as a normal country exists, the United States is not it."[25] American human rights statecraft is often unilateral and markedly interventionist, but the traditions and capability of most Western states exclude this foreign policy style. What options are open to them? While there is a large U.S. literature, much less is known of other countries. The few non-

U.S. studies available focus on single states. Comparative studies are only now emerging.[26] Even less is known of the international human rights policies of a group of Western states. This book is a step towards filling that gap.

Promoting internationalism is important to Canada, the Netherlands, and Norway. These nations are less encumbered by global strategic troubles than the U.S. Gulliver and are less divided by a polarized domestic public. They should therefore be less compromised in their human rights statecraft. But each state is driven by economic and diplomatic interests in a state-centric world; in this respect, these internationalists are no different from the United States or any other country. A closer look at Dutch, Norwegian, and Canadian human rights action will help unravel debates about ethics in international relations.[27] Realists argue that international life allows little scope for ethics in the conduct of states. Not that statecraft need be amoral; quite the contrary. *Raison d'état* is not an abdication of morality, but simply the morality of statecraft.[28] The *dicta* of Machiavelli endure precisely because their appeals to restraint and prudence are so reasonable. Machiavellian statecraft is based on the morality of group instincts. It is less inclined to moralize or to take up evangelical causes (human rights?). Realism is anchored in the "is" of political life and steers clear of those troubling "oughts" that can drive the ship of state into dangerous waters.

Realist thinking reveals some of the premises to the Westphalian order and contemporary international law. One such pillar is non-intervention in the domestic affairs of sovereign states. In international law, the juridical personhood of states is a given, while that of individuals remains tenuous. Non-intervention requires that states be insensitive to the fate of individuals and groups beyond their borders. The logic is simple and compelling: "If sovereignty, then non-intervention."[29] Insensitivity to the fate of individuals and groups within state borders may be a necessary price to pay in the larger interest of order among states.[30]

The realist logic underpinning the contemporary state system, although dominant, is not immutable. There are other visions of world order. A Grotian conception of international conduct gained currency during the twentieth century.[31] The law of nations adds ethics to statecraft and extends, however weakly, the concept of a juridical personality to the individual. The U.N. International Bill of Rights is a Magna Carta for the rights of individuals everywhere. At the same time, international law has tried to define legitimate state behaviour. The Dutchman Grotius argued long ago that states have a moral personality in addition to their juridical status: "Independent states that are dealt with by international law ... have a moral nature identical with that of individuals, and with respect to one another they are in the same relation as that in which individuals stand to each other."[32] Grotian thinking resonates in those who now challenge the sharp line drawn between domestic and international justice and the restricted scope for ethical conduct perceived by realists.[33] Renewed claims for international distributive justice have focused on international human rights, on development aid, on the policies of international financial institutions, and on the North-South debate on a new international economic order.

In a recent assault on neorealism, David Lumsdaine has used the appearance and evolution of foreign aid to show how conceptions of international society have influenced the ruthless, uncaring logic of the international system.[34] Lumsdaine also underlines the importance of domestic political culture and attitudes towards the welfare state in fashioning economic aid to less-developed countries. The "aid policies of OECD nations were influenced persistently," he says, "over a period of 35 years by ideas and values drawn from the general ethical traditions and domestic political experiences of these countries."[35] In his reading, the "essential causes" of this "wholly novel development" lay not in the economic and political interests of donor countries but "in their implicit belief that only on the basis of a just international order ... was peace and prosperity possible."[36] Lumsdaine's larger argument is to show that moral vision does shape international politics.

Lawyers and activists say that the Universal Declaration of Human Rights has the status of customary international law and is a "common standard of achievement" by which to judge the legitimacy of political regimes.[37] By contrast, realists and libertarians argue that the bonds of a global collective sentiment are tenuous and that "the great majority persists in drawing a sharp distinction between the welfare of those who share their particular collective and the welfare of humanity."[38] Sceptics see the burgeoning law of international human rights as a weakness. Unlike the situation in economics, the logic of interdependence rarely applies. With the exception of refugee problems, state security and material well-being are only marginally affected by rights violations in distant lands. Moreover, human rights are global norms, not laws, and are profoundly weak at the level of compliance and enforcement. It is easy to see why. Beneath the appearance of consensus in a common vocabulary, deep ideological divisions work against a community of values and inhibit common action.[39]

This book tries to address how donors translate the principles linking human rights and development into effective practice. All three of the Western states in this study acknowledge that there is a link.

Effective practice requires policies appropriate to the diverse circumstances in which human rights violations arise, persist, or abate, and it requires sensitivity from the aid donors who are seeking to build democratic institutions in diverse political systems and cultures. In Canada, for example, the 1980s saw a flurry of government and parliamentary debate aimed at elevating human rights to "a fundamental and integral part of Canadian foreign policy."[40] The government then began to move beyond rhetoric in a series of practical steps to entrench human rights in Canada's foreign policy. Bureaucratic expansion has been matched by a certain degree of willingness to make hard choices. Government-to-government development aid has been suspended in cases of gross and systematic violations of human rights. Haiti is the clearest example. Aid to El Salvador and Guatemala was renewed in the mid-1980s, ostensibly to support a "redemocratization" process in both states.

Canadian thinking, particularly where human rights impinge on aid policy, has been shaped partly by the initiatives and practice of "like-minded states" such as the Netherlands and Norway. The Dutch were pioneers in linking human rights to development aid.[41] Norway, with guidelines conditioning aid on human rights performance, has led the effort to measure the human rights performance of aid recipients. All three states have taken steps to integrate human rights in foreign policy. But political life is full of examples of cosmetic institutional expansion masking status quo policies. Does the recent record of middle-power diplomacy match the bureaucratic frameworks now in place? How have the three states used the United Nations, international financial institutions, or bilateral diplomacy to respond to human rights violations? A closer investigation of the framework and conduct of Dutch and Norwegian international human rights' policy may provide some lessons for the Canadian policy makers who are trying to implement an ambitious human rights policy.

CHOOSING THE COUNTRY CASES

The Northern Cases: Middle Powers or Internationalists?

The middle powers are a second-tier group of Western states. On a number of indices of national power, such as gross national product (GNP) and military capability, they are placed behind the major industrialized states. They are sometimes grouped together by common international role conceptions, such as strong support of multilateral organizations and mediation in the settlement of international conflict.[42] Canada, Australia, Belgium, the Netherlands, and the Nordic states are generally agreed to be the principal Western middle powers. They are a relatively neglected group in international relations research.[43]

There is a compelling case for closer scrutiny of the foreign policies of the Western middle powers and a reassessment of their classic challenges. Accelerating interdependence requires more international coordination on economic, environmental, and security issues; but the great powers may be either unwilling or unable to exercise leadership, and the small states are too weak to play such a role.[44] Because some middle powers are internationalists, they are well placed to lead opinion on issues where international cooperation is imperative, such as promoting global peace and disarmament, protecting human rights, alleviating world poverty, achieving global food security, preserving the global environment, and supporting Third World demands for a more just international economic order. Bridge building is part of this internationalist tradition.[45] Middle powers also lead in certain "functional" niches where they have acknowledged skills and interests.[46] When many instruments of international cooperation are threatened, there is a special need for the "responsible radicalism" of the middle powers to fill the leadership vacuum created by the relative decline of U.S. hegemony.[47]

American unilateral policies have been singularly ineffective in altering the behaviour of many repressive regimes. Global economic and strategic imperatives compromise an ethical foreign policy; or (as under the Reagan administration from 1981 to 1989) they lead to convenient distinctions between friendly authoritarian regimes (Latin America) and unfriendly totalitarian regimes (the Socialist bloc minus China). Given this thinly veiled *realpolitik*, Western middle powers could be credible leaders in the defence of global human rights. They are less prone than the United States to messianic stridency, and they are more committed to multilateralism and are uniformly respected in the developing world.

Are the characteristics commonly invoked to identify middle powers sufficient? Assessments of international power and rank are problematic. As Wood admits, "defining what is meant by a middle power is a challenge that has always dogged discussion by both academic analysts and practitioners."[48] Wood relies on a single indicator, GNP, to define middle powers. He considers GNP the most tangible expression of international rank, one that "automatically captures aggregate economic power, wealth ... and to a substantial extent, military potential."[49] However, assessments of power and rank that avoid intangible factors are deficient insofar as perception and role may be equally significant in the classification of middle powers.

On the basis of GNP, Wood arrives at a list of some thirty middle powers. The virtue of this formula is parsimony. It has the added attraction of helping to identify a group of states that cut across the traditional North-South, East-West divide. But parsimony here is also a serious analytical weakness. Raw GNP, while pointing to a band of medium-ranked powers, says virtually nothing about their expected behaviour. There is nothing implicit in being categorized as a middle power that would lead one to expect policies of conciliation or internationalism. The rankings speak more to the possible roles and potential of this group than to their actual practice. There is little to suggest that many of Wood's proposed middle powers identify with this category more than with such traditional groupings as the Non-Aligned Movement, pan-Arabism, the Nordic group, NATO, or the European Union.

This is not to deny the importance of potential role shifts among new middle powers. The inclusion of newly industrialized countries such as Brazil, Mexico, and South Korea does capture significant changes in the international power hierarchy. And the East Europeans, loosened from their geopolitical moorings, might perhaps become mediators and human rights activists in the twenty-first century. Nonetheless, such a formulation is not credible now.[50] Wood's definition fails precisely because it does not consider "fuzzy" concepts such as national-role conception and the linkage between domestic political culture and foreign policy orientations. Moreover, some of the worst human rights violations occur in the developing world, and diverse ideologies and political systems so far have precluded a meaningful consensus among states on some human rights issues. In this field, North and South will often be at loggerheads.[51]

Recent scholarship has attempted to reformulate the middle-power concept to renew its operational value in a post–Cold War world in which economic issues are as important as security issues and in which the "technical and entrepreneurial capacities" of states provide the basis for "initiative-oriented" leadership in issue-specific contexts. In their examination of Australian and Canadian diplomacy, Cooper, Higgott, and Nossal describe Canada as playing a passive and "followership" role in security domains but as being able to exercise technical and entrepreneurial leadership in some economic and social arenas.[52] In the human rights arena, Canada has displayed significant technical flair in multilateral forums as a "facilitator" and "manager" in setting new agendas and building global norms. Children's rights and women's rights are two clear examples of Canadian leadership. On women's rights, Canada played a lead role in shaping and supporting the action plan that emerged from the third World Conference on Women, held in Nairobi in 1985. The building of a multilateral norm was subsequently reflected in CIDA's deepening commitment to women-in-development issues. Similarly, Canada has consistently shown mediation skills in, for example, helping the United Nations reconcile North-South differences surrounding the Convention on Children's Rights and the Vienna Declaration and action plan emerging from the second World Conference on Human Rights, held in 1993. Part of the burden of this book is to underscore that middle-power traditions of issue-specific leadership and coalition building are less consistently evident when it comes to defending human rights.

I have been using the terms "middle power" and "internationalist" interchangeably. Although the terms overlap, a sharper distinction is needed. "Internationalist" is a more accurate and appropriate label than "middle power" for the countries that are to be investigated.[53] If power is fungible, it is untenable to speak of "big," "little," and "medium" powers. Similarly, using GNP as an index confuses more than it clarifies. Some middle powers are mediators and internationalists; a great many are not. Few, in any case, form their foreign policy in accordance with some shared middle-power logic. Most have allegiances to regional, cultural, or ideological groupings that cut sharply across the broad constellation of middle powers. The term is simply too vague to be of much analytic use. Take Canada, for example. True, the concept of "middle power" and the early application of David Mitrany's "functional principle" are largely a Canadian contribution to international affairs, but is Canada a middle-rank power or an emerging "principal power"? And what of Norway? With a tiny population and a small but internationally competitive economy, is it best described as a minor middle power or as just another small, weak state? Whatever their differences (in geography, economy, alliances, and political culture) Canada, the Netherlands, Norway (and Sweden) share a strong tradition of internationalism on issues such as foreign aid, disarmament, human rights, and, more broadly, North-South relations. By choosing the term "internationalist," the pool of states available for analysis is significantly narrowed.

Classification on the basis of economic and political criteria is a beginning, but do shared characteristics lead to predictable, common behaviour? How large or small is the gap between internationalist rhetoric and practice in each case? To what extent do these states work together to promote objectives that are not commonly at the forefront of major-power interests? Finally, is there any evidence of a common identity and vision among these middle powers that could catalyse cooperation on international human rights?

The emphasis in this study is on policy output. The case material largely predates the collapse of the Berlin Wall and with it the demise of the Cold War, the Soviet Union, and the East European socialist economies. In order to discern whether these events substantially influenced the resolve of Western countries, the November 1991 massacre in East Timor, Indonesia, has also been included.

The Southern Cases: Dependency and Independence

There are about 120 developing countries, reflecting a range of human rights problems, together with a range of responses by Western states. Which of these to choose as case studies was a decision guided by three considerations. First, because this study focuses on the relationship between human rights and development aid, the subjects had to be countries in which the Western donors had a significant official development assistance (ODA) program, or where severe human rights abuses posed problems for the planning and delivery of development aid. Second, the study's main hypothesis could best be tested by choosing at least two cases for each donor: one in which economic, political, and strategic interests were high, and another in which the same interests were minimal or low. Third, because the focus is on Western diplomacy, the case studies had to tackle what the policy makers in each state thought was problematic or salient. "Salience" is a variable that requires explanation. It is partly a function of public concern. In Norway, debates in the Störting (parliament) have focused on Sri Lanka and Kenya, two major recipients of Norwegian aid that have growing human rights problems. In the Netherlands, colonial ties and economic links define the salient cases. Dutch policies in Indonesia and Suriname have been criticized in Parliament and by the media. In Canada, the geopolitical significance of a large aid program to China and small aid programs in Central America and Haiti have led to public debate. Table 1.1 outlines a case study matrix that incorporates most of the selection criteria discussed above.[54]

China is a constant for all three Western states. The Tiananmen Square massacre was a gross human rights violation calling for assertive international action. But each internationalist has significant economic and political interests in China that are likely to complicate human rights statecraft. Dutch and Norwegian ODA to China is modest, though Canada's aid program is large. Moreover, with China, relatively small Western states confronted perhaps the most powerful of all the less-developed countries. Sri Lanka raises different problems. Democratic breakdown and gross human rights violations in the context of a militarized ethnic conflict posed problems of policy adaptation, staff safety, and project viability for Norway and Canada; the

Table 1.1
Western Donors Discussed in Case Studies

Less-developed country	Western donor		
	Canada	Netherlands	Norway
China	*	*	*
Sri Lanka	*		*
Suriname		*	
Philippines	*	*	
Indonesia	*	*	

conflict shifted from a predominantly government-Tamil struggle to an island-wide, intragroup conflict. This raises the question of what role donors should play in a conflict zone. Suriname has important lessons for donors tempted to use aid as a stick to punish or coerce human rights violators. It is the clearest example of power asymmetry, aid dependence, and the suspension of ODA for human rights reasons. Did it work?

During the Aquino presidency, the Philippines posed donor dilemmas in adapting to a fluid political situation in a conflict zone. The Netherlands and Canada aided a new democratic regime, but a worsening human rights situation clouded their diplomacy. Should donors modify their aid programs to keep in step? Can they remain neutral in a polarized society? Should they speak up about rights violations and support human rights monitors? The Philippines case study is less preoccupied with a formal test of the realist paradigm than with the practical dilemmas of linking human rights to development aid. Finally, Dutch and Canadian reaction to the 1991 killings at the Santa Cruz cemetery in Dili, East Timor, is a litmus test of Western resolve to craft a principled human rights policy to defend fundamental human rights. As in the case of China, Western commercial interests complicated the prospects for projecting an assertive human rights statecraft towards Indonesia. The different way in which Canada and the Netherlands responded to the events in Dili is also an object lesson in the practical problems of crafting a sustainable and effective human rights policy.

The case study matrix ensures that each Western state confronts at least one case in which economic, political, or strategic interests are high and one case in which they are minimal. This tests the central hypothesis. The Canadian and Dutch case studies, in particular, add new knowledge about other countries to the already well-documented diplomacy towards Southern Africa and Central America.[55] The material on China and Indonesia is a deliberate "snapshot" of post-Tiananmen and post-Dili policies, not a comprehensive diplomatic history. Four of the case studies focus on events and diplomacy before the collapse of the Berlin Wall. One case study, on Indonesia, considers Western responses to human rights abuses after the demise of the Cold War, at a time of rapid acceleration of globalization and market-led development. These unprecedented changes in the world economy and in international relations have prompted an OECD consensus on the complementary role of good governance in market-led growth and on the linkage of human rights and development aid. Before moving to several frameworks for analysis, it remains to consider what human rights are, to examine the connections among rights, governance, aid, and democratic development, and to explain the onset of political conditionality among aid donors.

WHAT ARE HUMAN RIGHTS?

Edmund Burke said that "of all the loose concepts in the world, liberty is the most indefinite." Jeremy Bentham was more contemptuous. Rights, he said, were just "nonsense on stilts." For two reasons, rights can no longer be dismissed so easily. First, human rights are first and foremost individual and group entitlements.[56] Because rights address individuals everywhere, the language of rights is said to be universal. Human rights are possessions that each of us has simply by being human; they therefore logically take precedence over an individual's obligations to the state. They are moral entitlements that aim to challenge or change existing institutions. Finally, human rights are grounded in notions of equality and nondiscrimination. All human beings deserve to be treated with equal concern and respect.

Natural law arguments founder, however, against relativist claims that rights are not universal, because (a) they reflect Western traditions of individualism and rationality, and (b) some polities and cultures have no conception of individual rights, placing the group or nation before the individual.[57] The discourse of "cultural particularities" was taken up by several Asian and Arab states at the 1993 World Conference on Human Rights, held in Vienna. It is the clarion call for a growing North-South conflict. The concluding chapter of this study revisits this issue, but the point to make here is that individuals and communities increasingly call on human rights arguments to advance their social and political claims. That this occurs globally, irrespective of culture and polity, is a convincing expression of an emerging international civil society and undercuts the relativist claim that human rights have no universal appeal. As the Dalai Lama said in Vienna, "human rights and democracy are now a global agenda."[58]

CONCEPTS AND LINKAGES

Today, governments everywhere are challenged more than ever before by voices calling for democracy and fundamental freedoms. Democracy and the related issues of human rights, popular participation, and good governance are now widely seen as essential pillars of durable development. Human rights and democratic development have become coveted foreign policy values for most Western states.[59] Development aid is called on to promote both objectives. Canada, the Netherlands, and Norway are among the leaders of the contemporary initiatives to integrate these previously disconnected issues; there are sound conceptual, empirical, and practical reasons for doing so.

Conceptually, although human rights are not synonymous with democracy, they are closely related. Democracy is a political system grounded in conciliation and the tolerance of opposition. Democracies mediate political conflict without undue violence.[60] The heart of liberal democracy is the basic political right of all to equal concern and respect.[61] It is thus no accident that civil and political freedoms are better realized in democracies than in other political systems.[62] That is why "internationally recognized human rights [may] require a liberal regime."[63]

There are, at least, two practical reasons why Western states should support democratic development in the Third World. First, as Kant predicted, democracies are less prone to war among themselves.[64] Second, democratization has proceeded at an unprecedented pace in the 1980s and 1990s. Third, a remarkable feature of our times is the emergence of an international civil society. In 1968, at the first World Conference on Human Rights, in Tehran, just 76 non-governmental organizations (NGOs) attended the preparatory meeting. In 1993, at the second World Conference on Human Rights, in Vienna, 2,400 NGOs lobbied governments, protested abuses, and built durable networks.[65] Aid can play a modest role in reinforcing democratic aspirations, although democratization is neither a secular trend nor irreversible.[66] In the Third World, authoritarianism and cyclical regime change are still the modal political experiences.

Democracy, however, is still ideologically contested terrain. How states define it will influence how they use aid to help consolidate new Third World democracies. There are two polar positions along a continuum. Some official donors have tended to focus on procedural attributes in what can be described as electoral democracy. In this understanding, elections, political parties, legislatures, and power elites are the key ingredients of democracy.[67] Institutional changes such as judicial reforms, or innovations such as national human rights commissions, election commissions, and ombuds, are viewed as crucial for the development of a durable democratic culture. Critics of this approach counter that the focus is limited to political rights; it may also legitimize façade democracies in which real power resides with the military and human rights violations are rife. Critics have dubbed this approach "low intensity" democracy.

Many NGOs and popular movements in the South are sceptical of formal democratic processes and institutions. Supporters of "popular" or "developmental" democracy are more concerned that civil and political freedoms should be used as vehicles of empowerment to achieve equality of condition, not simply equality of opportunity. This approach embraces socio-economic rights and civil liberties as well as political rights.[68] The expansion of political space, popular participation, a just social order, a fair distribution of assets, and civilian control of the military are the preferred markers of democracy. In developmental democracy, political action is a means of empowering historically disadvantaged communities. Thus, ordinary people acquire the capacity to improve their material circumstances, strengthen their political voice, hold governments accountable, and develop their talents and interests relatively unrestrained by state control.

Neither electoral nor developmental democracy is sufficient in itself. Precisely because the meaning of "democracy" remains contested, the approach adopted here is to interpret democracy through the lens of international human rights. Seen this way, democracy is a political arrangement capable of achieving the complete range of human rights – social, economic, and cultural as well as civil and political. It is a political system in which the "will of the people shall be the basis of the authority of government." Article 21 of the Universal Declaration of Human Rights goes on to affirm that "everyone has the right to take part in government ... either directly or through freely chosen representatives." International human rights instruments thus envisage not only representative democracy in political institutions but participatory democracy in civil society as well.

HUMAN RIGHTS AND ECONOMIC DEVELOPMENT

Is there necessarily a trade-off between human rights and economic development?[69] The "cruel choice" school says that in modernizing societies, the first order of business is capital accumulation for rapid industrialization. Redistributive policies addressing social and economic rights shift resources and inhibit savings essential for investment and rapid economic growth. In the short run, rapid growth will widen inequalities, which will shrink over time as the benefits of growth "trickle down" to the poorest.[70] The political management of such transitional societies must be premised on order, not on participation or human rights.[71] A more nuanced argument, made on some empirical evidence, suggests a dialectic between economic and political development. In this view, modernization and the market are said to bring democracy in their train. In South Korea, Taiwan, Indonesia, and Thailand, authoritarian governments modernized by opening markets while suppressing wages and labour and muzzling dissent. As living standards and education improved, the Koreans, Thais, and Taiwanese pressed for rights and democracy to open up their political systems.[72] The Indonesians and Chinese have not been so lucky.

This conventional wisdom that growth must precede political development is now being questioned. First, regimes that suppress civil and political rights pay economic costs. Managing complex economies requires information, but this commodity is in short supply in authoritarian and especially totalitarian regimes. Freedom of speech, of assembly, and of association help keep a government informed. Participation and public scrutiny of state policy may avert planning disasters.[73] Second, rights-repressive regimes are unstable because they foster apathy and disaffection, which lead to economic inefficiency without securing the legitimacy needed to govern. Regimes without legitimacy require repression. And with coercion, additional resources are shifted to security and are lost to growth.[74] It remains unclear, for example, whether unionism helps or hinders economic development. Industrial unrest may abate only on the heels of state welfare provisions.[75] Third, property rights, which are fundamental to market-led development, are more secure under democratic than authoritarian auspices.[76] Finally, Robert Putnam, whose ideas have been influential within the Clinton administration, underlines the importance of "social capital" generated by citizens' initiatives and argues that the leverage of governments in promoting social priorities is much greater where the civic culture is free to play a dynamic role in social change.[77]

The empirical evidence, however, is largely equivocal.[78] There appears to be no "iron law" defining the relationship between political systems and economic growth. Some authoritarian regimes have been able modernizers, but most have not. In any case, the economic record of Third World democracies has been no worse than many nondemocratic regimes. Inequalities in these democracies have been less acute – or, at least, less stable – and debt loads have been lower than in nondemocratic Third World countries.[79] Contrary to the predictions of the "cruel choice" school, one empirical study found a positive correlation among three indices: "freedom," per capita product, and the physical quality-of-life index.[80] Another found that democratic stability and "civil and political rights cannot prevail if socio-economic rights are ignored."[81] Finally, the U.N. Development Programme (UNDP) has developed separate indices measuring human and political freedom. It found that countries with high levels of political freedom (civil and political rights) also produced high human development indices.[82]

This reassessment of the relationship between rights, repression, and growth has percolated into the rhetoric of aid donors.[83] The OECD's Development Assistance Committee now sees "a vital connection ... between open, democratic and accountable political systems, individual rights and the effective and equitable operation of economic systems."[84] Since the 1970s, theorists have recognized that ending poverty is more than a technical problem. "Meeting basic needs" became a new catch-phrase for aid planners. But poverty alleviation may be no more than a welfare program if it is disconnected from the political setting in which the poor find themselves. In the 1990s, the language of rights is being added to the development debate to bolster a renewed interest in the empowerment and participation of the oppressed.[85]

Aid was once thought to be the catalyst of growth, and prosperity the genesis of democracy; now, some theorists say that political openness and respect for human rights must accompany economic growth, not lag behind it.[86] According to this view, aid can activate political participation, safeguard human rights, and strengthen the transition to democracy. It suggests that donors must go beyond poverty alleviation – which is often equated with social and economic rights – to embrace issues of empowerment and self-determination, which are the essence of civil and political rights. In an expanded definition, "only development with participation is sustainable,"[87] because the real purpose of development is to enhance human capacity and choice by realizing human rights.[88]

The development agenda of the 1990s is being built on the concept of sustainable development. Durable development requires a political environment that sustains economic growth and empowers people. This means respecting human rights because, as the UNDP puts it, "people are the real wealth of a nation."[89] This enabling environment is now called "good governance," although international financial institutions such as the World Bank have formally adopted a narrow reading of the parameters of good governance.[90] There is a growing consensus that the real purpose of development is the enhancement of human capacity and choice. Returning the individual to the centre of the development stage is the thrust of the UNDP's *Human Development Report*. This emphasis is echoed by the U.N. Declaration on the Right to Development, which states, "The human person is the central subject of development and should be the active participant and beneficiary of the right to development." The Declaration on the Right to Development was vigorously promoted by the South, and it explicitly adds human rights to the objectives of development. NGO coalitions from the South also have made the empowerment of individuals and groups a centrepiece of their development visions.[91]

In contrast to international human rights law, which underlines the interdependence and indivisibility of all human rights, the primarily economic missions of international financial institutions such as the World Bank have separated rights into different generations. According to this view, civil and political rights can be postponed until basic human needs are met. This attitude, of course, is precisely that adopted by "development dictatorships" in many parts of the South.[92] In fact, attention to civil and political rights is an indispensable component of sound development strategies. Civil rights such as freedom of expression and association empower citizens in their material struggles and help civil society criticize unjust or inefficient state policies.

Moreover, as noted above, regimes that systematically suppress civil and political rights risk economic costs.[93] Such regimes may be economically inefficient because they foster apathy and corruption, and they may be politically unstable because they foster disaffection. Regimes without legitimacy require coercion, which may drain scarce resources towards security and away from sustainable development. States that restrict political space may force the opposition underground and drive it towards armed conflict, with potentially adverse effects on the nation's creditworthiness. An unequal distribution of national development resources is another area where politics and economics are intertwined. Discriminatory economic and public policies are a potent recipe for ethnic conflict and long-term economic decay.

Access to information and a free press can help uncover the developmental "inefficiencies" of corruption and malevolent governance. After all, newspaper publishers are also businesspeople. Should they not be protected from arbitrary arrest? A free press is essential as an early-warning device against impending famine, for instance, by ensuring that there is public debate and prompt state action. Several famines – notably, in China in 1958–61 and in Sudan and Ethiopia in 1984 – have occurred under authoritarian regimes that had little free expression or public debate of state policies.[94]

In sum, there is a growing appreciation that the fostering of democratic processes in government and society contributes to economic development by releasing creative energies, enhancing accountability, and deepening participation. Development agencies must therefore go beyond poverty alleviation to embrace issues of empowerment and participation. In an expanded definition, only development with participation is sustainable.

The emerging consensus among official donors on the importance of human rights and democratic pluralism in economic development has led to the growth of a new kind of official development assistance. The DAC donors have long supported projects to promote participatory development in economic assistance: providing services, strengthening the private sector or having local NGOs deliver services, and involving women in development. To these old-style participatory development issues are now added new ways of promoting good government and democratic pluralism. New-style participatory development includes projects to strengthen the rule of law, reform the civil service, curb corruption, and create an ombudsman, a national human rights commission, or an independent electoral commission. The promotion of formal democratic institutions or practices is mirrored by efforts to strengthen independent civil societies through support for advocacy NGOs, human rights monitors, media organizations, labour or peasant movements, and so on.

POLITICAL CONDITIONALITY

One controversial impact of the DAC policy consensus on the linkages between rights, democracy, and development has been a greater willingness to defend human rights by making aid conditional on improvements in the human rights performance of the recipient countries. The denial, postponement, or reconfiguration of development aid is sometimes described as political conditionality. I use the term to denote legitimate intervention by aid donors in the domestic affairs of borrowing countries in order to alter the political environment in ways that will sustain human as well as economic development. There are principally three forms this may take: support (through technical assistance to promote human rights and democratic development); persuasion (through policy dialogue); or political pressure.[95] Specific actions include imposing a timetable of reforms, rewarding countries that undertake political liberalization, and using (or threatening to use) economic sanctions by withholding aid to regimes that violate human rights. Persuasion and support are not generally controversial. Aid dialogue and human rights promotion are a significant part of the case studies on the Philippines and Sri Lanka. The controversial tactic of pressure is the central theme of this book and is a focus of the case studies on China, Suriname, and Indonesia.

A convergence of international and intellectual factors form the policy environment for linking human rights and development assistance. The constellation of influences includes:

- the normative global appeal of human rights and democracy, prompted in part by the collapse of authoritarian regimes in Eastern Europe and parts of the South;
- an erosion of the principle of state sovereignty;
- recasting the development agenda around the concepts of sustainability and participation, with civil and political rights as key ingredients of "good governance";
- new funding pressure (from Eastern and Central Europe) on scarce donor resources, and hence a preoccupation with questions of rate of returns and efficiency;
- the growth of policy-based structural adjustment lending and with it the discovery by the international financial institutions that "good governance" may be crucial to the success of economic reforms;
- the onset of multiple-donor conditionality in the economic, environmental, and military arenas;[96]
- the spillover effects from the policies of other bilateral donors to link human rights and foreign aid disbursements.

Of these influences, three are key factors in the argument that human rights should be considered in foreign aid policies: rethinking sovereignty, rethinking development, and the spillover effects of policies by other official development institutions. But before addressing these, it is worth considering the arguments against linking human rights and development assistance.

THE CASE AGAINST LINKAGE

At least four arguments can be mustered against linking human rights to development-funding decisions. Some of these are serious, while others are not compelling. Official donors sometimes say that withholding loans will doubly penalize the poorest. Why should they pay for the sins of their rulers? This tired argument is well off-base. In practice, Canada, the Netherlands, and Norway have some working principles to ensure that the most marginalized and powerless are not twice penalized. Current projects are rarely affected. Humanitarian assistance such as food aid is never cut off. Instead, balance-of-payments support is frozen or reduced by suspending new short-term and fast-disbursing structural adjustment loans or loans for major infrastructure projects. Only government-to-government aid is affected. People-to-people exchanges are preserved or even expanded. The aid program is thus effectively dictator-proofed as Western agencies bypass the recipient state and channel more aid through NGOs.

In the view of some intellectuals and many recipient governments, political conditionality is a form of neocolonialism that undermines national sovereignty. There is no question that imposing political reforms can be risky if there is a widespread public perception that they are externally imposed. Citizens and leaders rightly question how unilateral and fundamentally undemocratic actions by donor governments can foster democracy and human rights abroad. One answer to such complaints is that sovereignty is not sacrosanct; it is regularly undermined in a world of weaker and more powerful states. Another answer is that development aid is taxpayers' money; it is not a gift. When opinion polls show that citizens want to see their aid go to countries that respect human rights, it is entirely reasonable for the donors to seek value for money and ensure that funds are not diverted for nondevelopmental purposes.[97] Human rights and democratic principles are legitimate funding criteria. Conditionality is thus a vital part of good development work – an argument that I develop later.

The question of consistency is invoked as one more reason not to link human rights to development lending. According to this view, the moral force of conditionality is undermined by its selective application. This study will amply demonstrate that inconsistency bedevils the human rights diplomacy of all states, the small and principled as well as the powerful and self-serving. Activists complain of double standards when donors are tough with weak states (such as Kenya and Malawi) and pariah regimes (Suriname and Myanmar), yet soft-pedal with countries of greater commercial interest (China and Indonesia). While the activists rightly remind donors of the need for consistency, the politicians must wrestle with the trade-offs in aid withholding and consider whether conditionality will be effective in improving human rights.

Official donors sometimes defend their unwillingness to make development aid conditional on respect for human rights by arguing that such an approach has little impact. They may consider repressive regimes impervious to outside interference. Worse, powerful less-developed countries may punish those already victimized or retaliate against the donor, as the Indonesians did when the Dutch suspended government-to-government aid after the Dili "incident." There is, of course, no substitute for a case-by-case approach to applying conditions. And effectiveness must be a salient factor in determining action. But change is not the only criterion to take into account. There is usually a complex mix of other factors to consider. For instance, donors may want to avoid complicity with a repressive regime and to show solidarity with the victims of abuse, who may have called for international action. Moreover, aid sanctions may punish and deter even when the short-term impact is minimal. Setting international standards and deterring other would-be abusers is at least as important as prompting immediate change.

No government says that human rights must automatically determine aid allocations. But what Canada, the Netherlands, and Norway do say is that rights considerations should have an influence – along with other factors – on the level and type of aid spending. To draw an analogy from the criminal justice field, sentences are given to offenders for at least three reasons: as a punishment, as a deterrent, and to prompt change (rehabilitation). The obstacles to prompting change do not detract from the need to apply universal standards. So while the question of effectiveness must always be salient in policy making, reifying "impact" as the overriding criterion is a recipe for silence. If effectiveness were the single test for action, Canada, the Netherlands, and Norway would rarely if ever act to defend human rights. But, in fact, there are some qualified successes. Human rights conditions have worked best when applied by sustained donor coordination in aid-dependent economies, for instance, with Kenya and Malawi.

Joan Nelson has convincingly shown that conditionality works best with respect to "single shot" actions that are within the control of a few central government officials and are readily monitored.[98] This fact, coupled with the need for a case-by-case approach and cross-cutting commercial and economic pressures, will make for an inconsistent and episodic application of political pressure to defend human rights. However, consistent, pristine behaviour is as rare in international life as it is in personal behaviour. Half a loaf, even a quarter, is better than none. Inconsistency is endemic in all arenas of international human rights diplomacy. But while the issue of consistency is a problem to be confronted, it is not an excuse for silence.

THE CASE FOR LINKAGE

Several donor governments have begun to include human rights and democratic pluralism in the criteria influencing their aid-funding decisions. Others have begun programs for good government or grass-roots participation. In 1991, Prime Minister Brian Mulroney informed the Commonwealth Heads of Government Meeting in Harare and the leaders of La Francophonie at Chaillot that Canada intended to condition its bilateral aid on the human rights performance of the recipient nations, rewarding countries that were set on a more democratic path and reducing aid to those that abused human rights. Since then, Canada has reduced, suspended, reviewed, or redirected its aid to Peru, Zaire, Haiti, Indonesia, and Kenya.

Similar links between human rights, good governance, and aid disbursements have been made by the United Kingdom, the Netherlands, the Nordic countries, the United States, France, and Japan.[99] The year 1990 was a turning point. That was when the U.S. Agency for International Development began its "democracy initiative." It was also the year when in a much-publicized speech, the British foreign minister, Douglas Hurd, argued bluntly that "poverty does not justify torture, tyranny, or economic incompetence." Hurd called for a concerted approach to governance by the major donors, and he announced the establishment of the Westminster Foundation to assist fledgling political parties in much the same way as was being done by the German political foundations (*Stiftung*) and the American National Endowment for Democracy.[100] Hurd set out the British position by clearly linking funding decisions to trends in the quality of governance: "Countries which tend towards pluralism, public accountability, respect for the rule of law, human rights, and market principles should be encouraged. Governments which persist in repressive policies, corrupt management, wasteful and discredited economic systems should not expect us to support their folly with scarce aid resources which could be used better elsewhere."

In the same year, President Mitterrand announced that France would be less generous with its aid to "regimes which conduct themselves in an authoritarian manner without accepting evolution towards democracy." In 1991 Germany introduced a new set of aid policy guidelines with five funding criteria: respect for human rights, popular participation in the development process, the guarantee of a predictable legal framework, a market-friendly approach to economic development, and a commitment to poverty alleviation.[101] The European Union has added a human rights clause to its Lomé IV Convention, which formalizes trade and aid relations with the African, Caribbean, and Pacific countries.[102]

The emerging donor consensus on rights, governance, and democracy is nowhere better illustrated than in the Development Assistance Committee (DAC) of the OECD. In some remarkably tough-minded language, the DAC now accepts political conditionality as a legitimate instrument for defending human rights. While emphasizing a preference for "positive support," DAC member states "also wish to be clear about the potential for negative measures affecting the volume and form of their aid, in areas of serious and systematic violations of human rights and brutal reversals from democratization, or when a complete lack of good governance renders efficient and effective aid impossible."[103] In considering "areas for action," DAC members in "cases of grave and persistent violations of human rights ... will consider appropriate responses. In cases where such responses entail reducing or suspending aid, DAC Members endeavour to maintain their humanitarian assistance for the most vulnerable population groups."[104]

International financial institutions have also been drawn into the political conditionality debate. By design or default, some World Bank lending decisions have been affected by nonfinancial considerations. For instance, lending to China was temporarily frozen after the Tiananmen Square massacre, when the G7 lender countries insisted for almost a year that no new loans to China be considered. The World Bank's ability to put together a financial package for Kenya was affected by the decision of the consultative group in November 1991 to suspend new lending to Kenya for six months. Similarly, a new international financial institution, the European Bank for Reconstruction and Development, has explicitly acknowledged the intertwining of political and economic reform. It must "foster the transition towards open market oriented economies ... in the Central and Eastern European countries committed to and applying the principles of multiparty democracy, pluralism, and market economics," and its board of governors "may postpone, restrict or suspend operations" if a borrowing country is "implementing policies that are inconsistent with the Bank's purpose."[105] The bank is thus bound by its charter to pay attention to the human rights and governance dimensions of its lending policies and operations.

Another underpinning of the shift towards conditionality stems from a rethinking of sovereignty. State sovereignty has been eroding for some time. It is under challenge from within by ethnic groups seeking greater autonomy or complete secession, and it is challenged from without by growing economic and political interdependence. In countries where external aid makes up a significant proportion of total government budgets, sovereignty is almost a fiction. The globalization of trade and money markets involves both reciprocal gains and mutual vulnerability and hence the interdependence of all states. Finally, there are many transnational issues that call for collective resolution by the international community. In addition to global poverty and human rights, they include the environment, drug trafficking, and terrorism. And while powerful nations retain considerable autonomy, sovereign self-determination has diminished in all states. State sovereignty and the related principle of non-intervention in domestic affairs have long been two of the organizing principles of international relations. States, not persons, have traditionally been viewed as the main subjects of international law. Historically, what a state did to its own citizens was its own affair and beyond the reach of international action. Without falling hostage to any fiction about a new world order, there are signs, both rhetorical and substantive, that sovereignty is being rethought.

The issue of humanitarian intervention to protect groups during civil wars is germane to the debate on political conditionality. In one of his last speeches as U.N. secretary general, Pérez de Cuéllar stated, "We are clearly witnessing what is probably an irresistible shift in public attitudes towards the belief that the defence of the oppressed in the name of morality should prevail over frontiers and legal documents."[106] On what moorings should a new structure of international law and humanitarian practice rest, and what are the implications for bilateral and multilateral development agencies? There are at least four essential principles:

- State sovereignty is not sacrosanct. True sovereignty resides in the will of the people. As the Universal Declaration of Human Rights puts it, "The will of the people shall be the basis of the authority of government."
- State sovereignty is abused and loses its legitimacy when it seeks to shield gross violations of human rights or grievous and deliberate human suffering.
- The principle of non-intervention cannot be used to prohibit legitimate international action to protect human rights.
- The international community has a duty to act for the relief of human suffering and to end the gross violation of human rights.

Just as it is no longer acceptable for society, the police, or the courts to turn a blind eye to family violence, so it is unacceptable for international organizations that represent the family of nations to ignore violence and repression within national borders. In sum, sovereignty must not be used to excuse the "inept or malevolent practices of governments."[107] Human rights is one of the three pillars of the U.N. Charter, "one of the keystones in the arch of peace."[108] Not only must state sovereignty bow to these higher principles, but it is most secure when it respects them. The central development message in rethinking state sovereignty is that the concerns of citizens, not states, should be the primary focus of all development aid.

DEFENDING HUMAN RIGHTS: WHEN AND HOW TO CONDITION AID

If political pressure is an option, when and how should it be applied? The standard should be based on a pattern of systematic, persistent, and flagrant violations of fundamental human rights. The key abuses here are those that attack the physical integrity of the person: extrajudicial killings, systematic torture, and the deliberate withholding of food as a political weapon. Another marker might be widespread arbitrary arrests and prolonged detention without trial. Donors could consider withholding loans to countries where there is unequivocal evidence of state complicity in the perpetration of human rights abuses. Genocide as a systematic state policy should also prompt conditionality.

Human rights law has weak compliance mechanisms. Regimes can legitimately restrict many civil and political freedoms in times of bona fide emergency (so-called states of exception). Despite these qualifications, the legal and normative weight of several human rights are unassailable. Extrajudicial killing and torture are two "nonderogable" rights that must be respected even during a state of emergency. The illegality of abusing these fundamental rights, together with systematic arbitrary arrests and prolonged detention without trial, is now virtually beyond discussion. Respecting such rights is part of customary international law and is thus binding on all states, irrespective of their political character.[109] The World Bank freeze on new loans to China after the Tiananmen Square massacre is one example in which the severe violation of fundamental rights prompted political conditionality.

A more difficult judgment has to be made when other civil and political rights are restricted. While the contribution to economic growth of such rights as free association, free speech, and the rule of law is now being appreciated, many civil and political rights may not only be legitimately restricted by emergency regulations, but their democratic flavour may imply interference in the "political character" of the regime. Hence, action to defend these rights may be viewed as illegitimate. Conditionality prompted by reference to human rights norms is easier to justify than leverage to encourage or defend electoral democracy. Donors may legitimately cite human rights norms to which all U.N. members are nominally bound. By contrast, promoting democracy involves a much broader, complex, and diffuse policy agenda.[110] Moreover, the precise meaning and desirability of multiparty democracy is still a subject of intense debate, the collapse of socialism notwithstanding.[111]

Clearly, antidemocratic actions – a military coup, a violent or fraudulent election, or a crackdown on civil society and political parties – can be responded to by invoking human rights norms rather than with lofty pronouncements on making the world safe for democracy. Political pressure that insists on multiparty elections may be both naive and politically explosive. It is difficult to predict whether elections will lead to a durable democracy or whether they will unleash previously latent ethnic conflict or an antidemocratic backlash. An unscrupulous autocrat intent on staying in power may foment ethnic conflict to discredit the democratic process, thereby clearing the way for further repression in the name of law, order, and national unity. Moreover, what can be called "electoral conditionality" runs the risk of identifying with the narrow agenda of the political opposition rather than with the call for human rights and political openness by civil society at large. By contrast, human rights conditionality – to permit press freedom, to relax restrictions on NGOs, or to strengthen the rule of law – may be a slower but surer way to encourage the emergence of a durable democratic civil culture.[112]

There is in any case no substitute to a case-by-case judgment on political conditionality. A thorough appreciation of the historical, social, and cultural traditions of each country should underpin responses to such problems. As Joan Nelson cautions, some coups may occur "because civilian politics has reached a total impasse." In such circumstances, a military takeover (Algeria) or constitutional coup (Peru) may "at least permit improved governance and economic growth, while sacrificing an empty shell of democratic process."[113]

The withholding of aid is also a dubious instrument in countries experiencing civil war, partly because human rights violations are likely to be committed by all sides in the conflict, and partly because embattled governments may not be able to respond. In extreme cases, such as Somalia or Liberia, anarchy may prevail and there may be no rule of law or effective central government in control. Suspending projects or loans in such circumstances is a pragmatic recognition that serious development work is impossible in zones of conflict; it is not a commentary on human rights.[114]

How should political conditionality be applied? There are numerous options:

- placing ceilings on new funding;
- postponing fast-disbursing loans or projects that are in the pipeline;
- discouraging new multilateral development loans by threatening to vote against such applications;
- voting against new loan applications;[115]
- curtailing industrial loans and public-sector finance but continuing private-sector loans;
- curtailing projects directed by the central government, but continuing local public-sector loans and technical-assistance projects;
- reshaping donor activity towards participatory development projects and those in aid of the poor, where the "absorptive capacity" permits;
- adding human rights education programs to donor education-sector projects;

• including human rights training of the military and police forces, where possible.

A timetable of reforms could be agreed on as a precondition for the restoration of frozen loans and a return to business as usual. Depending on the circumstances of the individual country, international donors could insist on the release of political prisoners, the establishment of national and independent human rights commissions, access by international human rights monitors, action to stem corruption and improve government accountability and transparency, the relaxation or dismantling of legislation circumscribing the role of NGOs, and freedom of the press and of association. Building on the human rights principle of nondiscrimination, official donors might direct additional resources to ethnic minorities who have been disadvantaged in the allocation of the central government's resources.

Joan Nelson has argued that "semi-authoritarian" single-party regimes, in which the political elites include some progressive elements, may be especially ripe for the judicious application of political conditionality.[116] The degree to which civil society is organized and autonomous is also a key influence on the sustainability of donor-imposed human rights reforms. In sum, political conditionality may be an appropriate lever with which to defend human rights in a limited range of circumstances, but it is less useful as a means of promoting Western-style multiparty democracy. It is primarily an instrument of last resort in extreme cases of unequivocal state culpability in the perpetration of deliberate, systematic, or persistent human rights violations. Security Council actions that treat human rights as a threat to international peace and security may legally trigger mandatory sanctions by U.N. specialized agencies or their affiliates, such as the World Bank. An aid bonus should be made available to regimes that are taking visible steps to safeguard human rights. In the current climate of donor fiscal restraint, this seems unlikely, however. Political conditionality is most likely to be successful if applied through sustained donor coordination in aid-dependent economies. Because of this, as well as the need for a case-by-case approach, and because of the commercial and foreign policy interests of the most powerful countries, the application of political leverage to defend human rights is bound to be inconsistent and episodic.

2 Frameworks for Human Rights Analysis

In the last chapter, I explained why human rights should be linked to development aid. This chapter moves from theory to practice. Its focus is on method. Developed here are three analytic frameworks: for documenting human rights violations, for assessing national performance, and for choosing among a range of policy options to protect and promote human rights. These frameworks will be used to examine statecraft and to test, in case studies, the competing hypotheses. Method is thus a bridge from international relations theory to foreign policy practice.

The first framework organizes the documentation of human rights data. It focuses on several "core" rights – freedom from extrajudicial killing, freedom from torture, freedom from hunger, and freedom from discrimination. This will be called the "core rights" framework. While the gathering of data is the first step of policy analysis, the next is an assessment of overall national performance. Policy makers need a yardstick with which to measure this. The second framework provides one in the form of a human rights performance index, which measures whether conditions are improving, stable, deteriorating, or egregious. Fluctuations in national performance are monitored by concentrating on the status of core rights and the rule of law. These changes are then considered in the context of the social, political, and economic conditions that commonly arise in each of the index's four human rights patterns. This will be called the "performance index." Finally, policy makers must decide which instruments to use in order to promote or protect human rights abroad. The third framework helps guide this process by proposing a hierarchy of human rights options. Policy makers intuitively recognize a spectrum of policy levers ranging from the symbolic and unassertive to the coercive and punitive. These levers relate to the costs to other national interests, which rise as a state shifts from diplomatic and multilateral initiatives to unilateral, economic, or even military policy levers. Three broad groups of options in this framework signal unassertive, moderately assertive, and highly assertive statecraft. This framework will be called the "options hierarchy."

Common themes underpin each framework. First, each provides a basis for comparison in a variety of countries, at various times, and in various sociopolitical and economic settings. Second, each framework is premised on the problem of choice. Choosing among competing values is the essence of policy making. To choose is to fix priorities. Each framework is a ranking scheme – for deciding which human rights to monitor, for assessing national performance, or for considering policy options. Third, all three, as ranking schemes, could be subject to objections about the logic of ranking and about the particular priorities asserted. These problems are dealt with as they arise; but as a broad defence, I should point out that the performance index and the options hierarchy are simply heuristic devices to organize analysis. As ideal types, their categories will not be found anywhere in their pure form. The point is to use them to confront reality, not to escape it.

DOCUMENTING HUMAN RIGHTS PERFORMANCE

There has been a steady expansion of international human rights law since the adoption of the Universal Declaration in 1948. The addition of a covenant on civil and political rights and one on economic, social, and cultural rights completed the trinity comprising the International Bill of Rights. The bill is now *the* reference point in discussions of global human rights.[1] More specific conventions have grown alongside the Bill of Rights.[2] Few groups or social policy areas have remained untouched by this covenant diplomacy. The setting of standards has been the United Nations' greatest achievement in human rights. But while lawmaking continues, the international agenda is slowly shifting from standard setting to monitoring and implementation. This shift is welcome but difficult. A wide gulf separates declaratory support and effective action.

The accurate measurement and evaluation of human rights data are important factors in bridging this gulf. Good information supports all human rights statecraft, a point well made by Robert Johansen, who stated: "The central issue before scholars and officials is how to make *respect* for human rights as widespread and compelling as *belief* in them. This goal suggests three needs: (1) to develop concrete indicators for measuring the human rights performance of governments ...; (2) to apply these indicators to the behaviour of governments and international institutions; and (3) to identify and create incentives that will modify governmental behaviour and the structure of the international system."[3] Systems for reporting human rights have proliferated in the search for greater rigour in a notoriously unreliable field.[4] The U.S. *Country Reports* are relatively thorough if somewhat controversial annual public documents.[5] Virtually all Western states now have human rights units in their foreign ministries which report annually, usually in-house. Human rights institutes in Canada, the Netherlands, Sweden, and Norway collaborate to produce annual reports on the human rights performance of their development aid recipients.[6]

Emphasizing Core Rights

Because human rights performance varies through time, across states, and among different sets of rights, a summary of a country's performance will be impossible until policy makers construct an evaluation system. Holding to the concept of equality among rights can paralyse policy formulation. Thus, this study argues for an evaluation hierarchy focusing on the status of two nonderogable rights and two fundamental international norms. These four rights are freedom from arbitrary or extrajudicial killing, freedom from torture and other forms of cruel and inhuman treatment, freedom from hunger, and freedom from discrimination.[7] Core rights are emphasized for practical reasons and conceptual considerations. Nonderogable rights have a normative status that is less certain for other rights in the International Bill of Rights.[8] States that are party to the covenants are not permitted to violate nonderogable rights in any circumstances, even in a national emergency. Although human rights conventions are frequently derided as "soft law," nonderogable rights are non-negotiable. The illegality of torture and extrajudicial killing is now virtually beyond discussion.[9] These rights are now customary international law and thus are binding on all states.

As a report by the Dutch Human Rights and Foreign Policy Advisory Committee says, stressing the interrelatedness of human rights "does not solve all of the problems."[10] When policy makers shift their attention from documentation to evaluation and action, they cannot escape the problem of ranking rights. The Dutch report goes on to argue that "it is easier by and large to determine whether civil and political rights are being respected than whether economic, social and cultural rights are being realized."[11] It concludes "that the violation of certain fundamental rights – those classified as inviolable – can occur on such a scale and to an extent which encroaches on the human rights situation in its entirety. *A donor must regard this as the decisive factor when evaluating or making policy.*"[12] China's Tiananmen Square massacre emphasizes the Dutch report's premise that "the fundamental rights concern such essential human ... values and entail such weighty responsibilities on the part of the governments concerned that violation of them completely overshadows other rights, values and interests."[13] In the U.S. State Department's *Country Report*, a similar conclusion was drawn. Political killing and torture "came, in practice, to have priority. Other violations, particularly of civil or political rights, were seen as more ambiguous."[14]

Freedom from hunger and from discrimination are not nonderogable, but both rights are gaining normative status. The right to food and freedom from hunger (to be discussed later), are "generally considered to be the economic equivalent of the right to life,"[15] and the principle of nondiscrimination is embedded in the human rights covenants. Nondiscrimination is the glue that binds disparate human rights. No state may escape this right. Canada's and Australia's treatment of aboriginal peoples is as open to scrutiny as Indonesia's treatment of the Timorese or Bangladesh's treatment of Hill Tract tribes.[16] The principle of nondiscrimination appears throughout the covenants and is important to their implementation. Thus, article 2 of the Universal Declaration states that "everyone is entitled to all the rights and freedoms set forth in this Declaration, without distinction of any kind, such as race, colour, sex, language, religion, political or other opinion, national or social origin, property, birth or other status." This principle clearly signals that "the moral worth of human beings is not in any way connected with ... natural accidents" of birth or social status.[17] Widespread support for the U.S. civil rights movement and for the campaign to dismantle apartheid in South Africa prove that nondiscrimination is a "supra-positive" right with normative status.[18] It is no coincidence that the International Convention on the Elimination of All Forms of Racial Discrimination is one of the most widely ratified human rights instruments.

Evaluating national performance on nondiscrimination will be difficult for policy makers. The principle cuts across all facets of social and economic policy, affects many groups, and may become entangled in complex issues of cultural relativism and Western bias. Determining government culpability also will be extremely difficult. South Africa was exceptional as a clear case where racial discrimination was entrenched in the legal apparatus of the state. Despite these difficulties, focused evaluation is necessary because, in many developing societies, discrimination is behind ethnic conflict, political violence, severe abuse of nonderogable rights, and, *in extremis*, civil war or secession. Consider Bosnia, Rwanda, Bangladesh, Biafra, Sri Lanka, Eritrea, East Timor, and Irian Jaya. In the Third World, migrant workers, ethnic minorities and indigenous peoples are three groups that are particularly vulnerable to discrimination.[19] Human rights monitors often focus on nonderogable rights and on the right to food in states embroiled in ethnic conflicts. But a focus on discrimination could contribute to an early-warning system signalling more serious abuses. It could also spur diplomatic efforts to persuade a particular government to improve its performance or, more directly, it could lead to efforts to assist groups who are visibly discriminated against.

Freedom from extrajudicial killing, a central component to the right to life, is a cardinal concern for the international community. Protection from unauthorized killing is the most powerful proxy for the status of other groups of rights. Whether from deliberate starvation, prolonged torture, or the death squad, extrajudicial killing subsumes – indeed, assumes – the violation of other rights, such as freedom of expression, of association, and of the right to a fair trial. In short, the right to life is "a peremptory norm that enjoys a sacrosanct position in the hierarchy of international jurisprudence."[20]

There is less international consensus over other sets of rights. Most Western policy makers are highly equivocal about human rights reporting on a country's social and economic rights and its government's record on poverty alleviation. The problems of interpretation are compounded by the precarious juridical status of many social and economic rights. The obligations placed on participating states are even weaker than those entrenched in the civil and political covenant. Similarly, many countries of the South continue to object to the classic civil and political liberties associated with Western liberal democracy. Moreover, international forums such as the Inter-American Human Rights Commission accord the participating states considerable discretion to suspend other civil and political liberties in times of "public emergency which threatens the life of the nation." Human rights treaties also permit governments temporarily to suspend civil liberties, such as free speech, free association, and free movement, in order to maintain public order.[21]

There are also practical reasons why policy makers should focus on nonderogable rights. First, although all human rights reporting is imperfect, reported cases of torture or extrajudicial killing can at least be counted and compared with earlier levels in the same country. True, even one extrajudicial killing is serious, but few would deny that El

Table 2.1
A Framework for Evaluating National Human Rights Performance

	Covenants[1]
CORE RIGHTS	
Freedom from extrajudicial killing	UD, article 3
	CPR, article 6(1)
Freedom from torture	UD, article 5
	CPR, article 7
Freedom from hunger	UD, article 25
	ESC, articles 1(2), 11
Freedom from discrimination	UD, article 2
	CPR, article 2
	ESC, article 2
RULE OF LAW	
Habeas corpus	UD, articles 6,7,8
	CPR, article 9 (2, 3, 4)
Independence of the judiciary	CPR, articles 14, 16
PARTICIPATION RIGHTS	
Freedom of association	CPR, articles 21, 22
Freedom of opinion	CPR, article 19
Freedom of religion	CPR, article 18
Freedom of movement	CPR, article 12
Right to vote	CPR, article 25
Right to participation	CPR, article 25

[1]   UD denotes the Universal Declaration of Human Rights. CPR denotes the International Covenant on Civil and Political Rights. ESC denotes the International Covenant on Economic, Social, and Cultural Rights.

Salvador in the early 1970s differed greatly from El Salvador between 1979 and 1981, when the death squads killed many people. Numbers, unsavoury as they seem, powerfully sensitize domestic and international opinion to the severity of human rights violations. Violations of social and economic rights, however, are more difficult to attribute to deliberate government actions.

Freedom from extrajudicial killing, from torture, from discrimination, and from hunger should be given primary attention by Western policy makers for practical and legal reasons. This quartet of freedoms constitutes a minimal level of consensus in a highly politicized field. These considerations inform an alternative framework for assessing national human rights performance (see table 2.1). The two nonderogable core rights, together with freedom from hunger, which serves as a proxy for subsistence rights, protect the physical integrity of the person – Donnelly and Howard's "survival rights." The fourth core right, nondiscrimination, is a broader protection that obligates states to implement the human rights covenants impartially.

Human rights assessments should consider the following questions. Is there a "pattern of systematic and flagrant violations" of core rights? Is there evidence of state complicity in, or perpetration of, human rights violations? Are there executions or arbitrary killings without due legal process? Do individuals "disappear" by order or with the complicity of the state or opposition forces? In civil conflicts, are opposition groups also violating rights? What are the trends? Is the overall picture improving or deteriorating? Among legal rights, the questions are: Is the judiciary independent? Are abuses investigated by the courts? Is the judiciary able and willing to investigate alleged violations by the state's coercive apparatus? Are their decisions upheld? Have international human rights treaties been signed, and what reservations are in force? Does the state permit international investigation of alleged rights abuses?

Finally, a group of civil and political liberties are marked off as "participation rights" that Western states will wish to monitor, given their sociopolitical values. These rights address the familiar liberal democratic freedoms. A key issue here is whether civil interest groups and opposition parties operate in a relatively closed or open political arena. Is there freedom of assembly, association, and expression? Do historically disadvantaged groups enjoy adequate opportunities to make claims on the state and to share equitably in public resources? Such information may guide the promotion of human rights through civic education or through aid to trade unions, peasant organizations, churches, and the free press.

The normative status of these rights remains tenuous, however, because there are sharp ideological and cultural differences concerning their meaning and importance. This gives Western governments less leverage in criticizing their suppression and offers little basis for giving them first priority. While Western democracies are convinced of the importance of a multiparty system and of "free" and "genuine" elections, these do not necessarily guarantee that core rights will be safeguarded. There remain, unfortunately, all too many "façade democracies," where serious violations occur.

Social science discussions of human rights tend to ground their arguments in moral or political philosophy and to pay insufficient attention to the legal dimensions of rights. By scrutinizing the juridical bases of human rights reporting, this study argues that such systems must recognize the legal "softness" of many rights. Because human rights law provides Western states with limited leverage in responding to abuses, primary attention should be given to assessing a nation's record in safeguarding the four core rights. The legal status and moral force of these rights distinguish them as a group worthy of primary attention by governments and by international monitoring agencies.

THE HUMAN RIGHTS PERFORMANCE INDEX

After the priorities have been fixed on which rights to document, the next analytical step is to use the reporting system to evaluate national human rights performance. Are conditions improving, worsening, static, or negative? An index that refines a Canadian parliamentary committee's proposal is presented in table 2.2 below. A matrix linking regime type to sociopolitical and human rights conditions (table 2.3) complements the index.[22] The index assigns states to one of five categories of human rights performance: protected, improving, satisfactory, worsening, or negative. Nonderogable rights are central to this index because the covenants require their protection even in a national emergency; and systematic abuse of these rights constitutes gross human rights violations. Thus, deliberate starvation is a form of political killing. Nondiscrimination is also central to the index because it is central to the human rights conventions. Discriminatory state policies are often the precursors of protracted ethnic conflict and rights abuses. Autonomous civil organizations are key markers of pluralist democracy. A powerful and independent judiciary is basic to a democracy that reinforces pluralism and safeguards individuals and groups against arbitrary state policies. What is the relationship between human rights performance, sociopolitical conditions, and the type of regime?

Human Rights Protected

Rights, while not synonymous with democracy, are most likely to be realized in prosperous democratic regimes.[23] In such states, political struggles are tempered by agreement on the rules of the game in a "mutual security system."[24] Democracy is "a way of ruling in divided societies without undue violence."[25] In Adam Przeworski's felicitous phrase, democratic development is about "institutionalizing uncertainty."[26] The term polyarchy adds to this ingredient three others: competition for power, electoral participation for the selection of leaders, and the guarantee of key civil and political rights, such as freedom of expression, of the press, of religion, and of association.[27]

Table 2.2
An Index for Evaluating National Human Rights Performance

Human rights	Society/polity	Regime type
PROTECTED Core rights protected Formal equality Rule of law	Autonomous civil society Multipartism Regular elections Civilian control of army Relatively free press	Pluralistic democracy Social democracy
IMPROVING Core rights Civil/political rights restored Rule of law	Emerging civil society Multipartism Regular elections Civilian control of the army	Emerging democracy

SATISFACTORY
Core rights at risk
Growing discrimination
Civil/political rights
    suppressed
	Judiciary possibly not
	    independent
	Single party or regulated parties
	Controlled press and interest
	    groups
		Quasi democracy
		Military rule

WORSENING
Core rights at risk
Growing discrimination
Civil/political rights
    suppressed
	Rule of law eroding or
	    emergency rule
	Internal violence or ethnic
	    conflict
	Economic malaise?
	Army in politics?
	Press censorship
		Declining democracy
		One party dominant
		Military
		Façade democracy

NEGATIVE
Systematic abuse of core
    rights
Genocide
Ethnocide
Food withheld
Civil/political rights
    suppressed
	Civil society weak or controlled
	Routine state terror
	Army in politics
	Press censorship
		Military
		Quasi democracy

A political culture in which core rights are sacrosanct and civil and political freedoms are constitutionally guaranteed is the best foundation for nonviolent management of political conflict and competition. In most Western democracies, nonderogable rights are protected, the judiciary is independent, and civil and political freedoms are broadly realized. Discrimination may be present, but legal redress and, in some cases, a charter of rights provide some protection. Pluralist democracies

Table 2.3
A Third World Regime-Society Matrix

Regime type	Society/polity	Human rights
Pluralist democracy	Autonomous plural society Multipartism Regular elections Army under civilian control	Core, civil, and political rights protected Independent judiciary Relatively free press
Emerging democracy	Multipartism Emerging plural society Nonviolent social protest Elections Army in politics?	Rights legally entrenched Independent judiciary Free press Human rights commission

Declining democracy	Emergency rule
	Violence
	Internal war or state terror,
	   and weakening of
	   legislatures, judiciary
	Economic malaise
	Army in politics?
		Core rights abused
		Loss of civil/political rights
		Press restrictions

Façade democracy	Open dissent limited Civil-military oligarchy Vigilantism Insurgency Army in politics?	Security rights at risk Civil/political rights at risk Press self-censorship
Quasi democracy	One party dominates Restrictions on interest groups Personal rule Weak legislature	Civil/political rights restricted Security rights vulnerable No free press; self-censorship
Authoritarian regime	Military or personal rule Single party Civil groups weak and controlled State terror routine	Security rights abused Civil/political rights denied No free press

have a multiparty system, regular and fair elections, some executive accountability, a free press, and powerful interest groups. Some acknowledge welfare rights, particularly the northern European social democracies. Among the less-developed countries, perhaps only Botswana, Senegal, Costa Rica, Venezuela, India, Jamaica, and several Caribbean microstates have met the "procedural minimum" and broad protection of civil and political rights for any length of time.

Human Rights Improving

Emerging democracies have diverse roots. In Brazil, the military junta orchestrated a gradual *abertura*. In the Philippines, a fraudulent election prompted a popular uprising, the capitulation of the army, and the withdrawal of U.S. support, and led to the ouster of Ferdinand Marcos. In a rare African example, Léopold Senghor, Senegal's princely autocrat, experimented with a multiparty system. Thus, authoritarian rulers may permit and guide a partial political opening by expanding civil liberties without altering the structure of authority. The absence of executive accountability marks the limits of such liberalized authoritarian regimes (*dictablanda*) or quasi democracies.[28]

New democracies pledge to hold regular and fair elections. Civil liberties are restored and core rights are protected; as well, human rights commissions may be established to investigate past abuses. Human rights monitoring groups are supported or at least tolerated. Trade unions, churches, universities, and the media once more find their voices. All this occurs because the new regime pledges to respect the rule of law. Emotional loyalty to the new regime may be high at first, but the long-term improvement in human rights will depend on political factors and economic performance. Transitional regimes are marked by a great uncertainty among the political actors about non-violent mechanisms for conflict resolution and partisan competition. The re-emergence or creation of civil interest groups and political parties is vital for democratic stability. The role of the military also is crucial. There may be recalcitrant hardliners on both the left and the right of the political spectrum.[29] If a new political culture of compromise and tolerance of opposition views is not forged, the transitional regime may suffer a coup and, with it, the reimposition of authoritarian rule and the suppression of human rights. Six coup attempts in less than four years of democratic rule in the Philippines justify the "omnipresent fear" in all transitional regimes that a coup "will be attempted and succeed."[30]

Human Rights Satisfactory

Many of the less-developed countries fall into this category. Torture and political killings are rare, though there may be some arbitrary arrests and *incommunicado* detention. Violations of core rights will affect only a very few of the regime's political opponents – those directly involved in public affairs. While the rule of law may be present and the judiciary may be formally independent of the executive, legal safeguards against arbitrary arrest and detention may be weak. Preventive detention or special powers legislation may give the police wide powers of arrest and detention. Church and legal advocacy groups may still be able to monitor human rights violations, but investigations by foreign organizations may be discouraged.

Key civil and political rights will be circumscribed. These include restrictions on trade unions; strikes may be illegal and unions may be organized under a single state-managed association. The media are government-run or forced to practise self-censorship. Criticism of the president and government policy may lead to closure or detention. These human rights conditions have been common in many African single-party states, such as Zambia under Kenneth Kaunda and Tanzania under Julius Nyerere, and in benign African autocracies such as Houphouet-Boigny's Ivory Coast. Individual rights are circumscribed by a collectivist ideology that stresses national unity and economic growth. The legitimacy of such regimes may be conditional on economic performance.

Human Rights Worsening

A deteriorating human rights pattern develops against a backdrop of growing challenges to the state, widening suppression of all dissent, and declining respect for the rule of law. The independence of the judiciary may be compromised. Increasing intolerance of conventional political opposition is signalled by an extension of police powers of arrest and the suspension of habeas corpus. Unconventional dissent, such as civil disobedience, is vigorously suppressed. State actors will resort to unconventional politics, principally repression. This may include manipulation of the electoral process, censorship, surveillance, harassment, misuse of emergency powers, and the suspension of the constitution and civil liberties.[31] Opinion leaders from churches, universities, trade unions, the legal profession, and the media will be targets of vigilante groups and death squads. Human rights monitors will be less tolerated, and international fact-finding missions may not be welcome.

A worsening rights pattern may occur under a variety of regimes but is commonly associated with political decay during armed conflict. New or long-standing democracies may degenerate into façade regimes in which the military hold real power. Authoritarian regimes may use an ideology of national security to legitimize increased repression, as in Chile, Brazil, and Argentina. Consider four examples. In the Philippines, Ferdinand Marcos misused constitutional amendments and referenda to gain complete control of the government. Beginning with the imposition of martial law in 1972 to "save the nation" during a "state of rebellion," Marcos established a constitutional autocracy to centralize power and muzzle dissent. In Sri Lanka, the emergence of a one-party-dominant system after 1977 was accompanied by a centralization of power through the shift from a Westminster parliamentary system to a Gaullist presidential system. Discriminatory state polices against Tamils inflamed ethnic tensions and led to violence, civil war, and the virtual breakdown of democratic governance. The imposition of the Prevention of Terrorism Act led to serious abuses of core rights by the Sri Lankan army and the Indian Peacekeeping Force. In Kenya, an abortive coup attempt in 1982 marked the onset of a progressive worsening of human rights. Key signs included the creation of a *de jure* one-party state, the growing concentration of presidential power, use of voter "queues" instead of a secret ballot, removal of security of tenure for judges, and mounting deaths in police custody. Finally, in Suriname, the military strongman Desi Bouterse's political killing of fifteen opinion leaders is a notorious instance of the use of terror to instil fear and acquiescence to autocratic rule.

Human Rights Negative

States in this category are "extreme cases judged by the international community to be guilty of persistent, gross, and systemic violations."[32] Here, there is an egregious and systematic pattern of gross human rights violations. Rights abuses are no longer directed only at those involved in public affairs; they target more and more innocent civilians. The rule of law is either inoperative or inadequate to safeguard fundamental freedoms. Violence and terror are viewed by both state and nonstate actors as a legitimate way of waging conflict. Torture, assassinations, death squads, and disappearances become normal features of the political landscape.

Gross human rights violations often occur when protracted social conflicts become militarized. There are many scenarios. Sustained or intensified ethnic discrimination may provoke a violent backlash by oppressed groups, and possibly civil war (for example, the secessionist struggle in Sri Lanka and the Palestinian Intifada). States may also use gross human rights violations in a deliberate policy of ethnocide that involves systematic killings and forced resettlement of oppressed groups (for example, Indonesia's invasion of East Timor and its subsequent *transmigrasi* policy). In Ethiopia, the Mengistu regime used food as a political weapon in an unsuccessful struggle with rebel Tigre and Eritrea. In other instances, class or ideological struggles may be at the root of gross human rights violations, as with the Suharto regime's extermination of some 500,000 communists in Indonesia in 1965. There are, finally, those extreme examples of anarchy and genocide unleashed by psychotic dictators such as Pol Pot and Idi Amin.

Discussion

The performance index shows clearly that although human rights are best guaranteed in a democracy, in the Third World gross human rights violations may occur in transitional democracies such as the post-Marcos Philippines, in façade democracies such as El Salvador, and in declining democracies such as Sri Lanka. Elections and a multiparty system do not guarantee that nonderogable rights will be respected. In the South, the modal political regime is still some variant of authoritarian rule. While there are welcome signs of democratization in Latin America and parts of Asia, this trend may not be irreversible. Most Third World countries have cyclical regime changes. Democracies are capable of decay and are vulnerable to authoritarian solutions when their institutional roots remain shallow and their economic performance is weak.

The index could guide donor policy and help deepen democracy's roots. Each category contains a range of possible responses and a keyword to organize diplomatic orientation. For example, where human rights are improving, this should prompt proactive policies, including increases in aid allocations and institution building. Where human rights are stable, current policies and aid levels should be maintained. Most aid recipients will fall into this category. In states with a worsening record, Western governments should be vigilant. As the Winegard Report observes, "serious allegations have been made but there are many gray areas and development progress is still possible."[33] While maintaining aid levels, donors could legitimately voice their concern about growing reports of violations. Prudence counsels that this should be done by quiet rather than public diplomacy. It could include high-level discussions in which Western donors signal an intention to reduce or redirect bilateral aid in the medium term. Donors could consult with other Western states to monitor and exchange information on the extent of rights violations. Joint donor representations with the political elites of the recipient country might also be useful.

As well, donors could raise human rights issues with the international financial institutions (IFIS) when states with worsening human rights records apply for loans. Incentives could be tried, and initially

Western governments might prefer them, because this would allow them to maintain their presence and possible influence. For example, human rights training programs could be offered to prison officials, police, and military personnel. In states where violations remain severe but which nonetheless are undergoing a regime change, Western governments could seek the consent of the political elites to send fact-finding missions and to monitor elections. If all these avenues fail to influence the elites of the recipient country and if, after some years, the human rights record worsens with few signs of government efforts to improve the situation, Western states could then consider "going public" by redirecting more aid away from government agencies towards non-governmental agencies, and by abstaining in multilateral bank (IFI) "voting" for financial loans or pressing for IFI "conditions" when loans are being extended to countries with serious human rights violations.

There are, finally, those countries classified as "human rights negative." In these few cases, evidence of severe violations and state culpability is so unequivocal, extreme, and enduring that Western governments are justified in conducting a more open and possibly punitive diplomacy. In such pariah states, the government itself, willingly and efficiently, perpetrates human rights violations – as in Iraq, Pinochet's Chile, Amin's or Obote's Uganda, and South Africa in the days of apartheid. Because "human rights negative" states sponsor a pattern of gross and systematic violations and because their political elites are commonly immune from international censure or international law, Western states are justified in withdrawing ambassadors or otherwise reducing their diplomatic presence. They may also take more punitive action, such as economic sanctions, sporting and cultural bans, and the withdrawal or reduction of development aid.

Objections

Several objections to the index may be raised – practical, methodological, and epistemological. For practitioners, any index is quixotic and flawed. In their view, human rights violations arise, abate, and persist in unique situations which defy the application of general formulae. Thus, the responses also must be made case by case. An index has some pragmatic qualities which practitioners seldom admit to, for it provides a reference point from which to judge statecraft and criticize state complicity – by neglect or by design. Since the hallmark of foreign policy making is flexibility, a rigid, index-based human rights policy is likely to erode or undermine carefully nurtured economic, diplomatic, or geopolitical relations with rights-violating countries.

Methodological objections are equally worrisome. Human rights information is patchy at best. Culpable governments do not advertise their more heinous activities. The full scale of torture, arbitrary detention, and political killings in the numerous regimes closed to the Western media is unknown. If information is unreliable, what confidence can we place in the index? Moreover, will the index deal with those difficult cases that are on the boundaries of two categories? Kenya may be one example. When do stable or satisfactory human rights conditions deteriorate to the point of requiring vigilance and the reduction or redirection of development aid?

Epistemological complaints stem from a conviction that human rights are a Western, not a universal, concept. Thus, any "measure" of the "performance" of non-Western cultures is flawed because the indicators reflect an ethnocentric bias. Cultural relativism buttresses the practitioner's doubts and the methodological pitfalls.[34] Together, these are powerful objections to the performance index. On the other hand, although epistemological doubts may be relevant to some civil and political rights, they do not refute core rights such as freedom from extrajudicial killing and torture. Most cultures have moral or legal prohibitions on arbitrary and illegal killing or the infliction of pain.[35] Moreover, to dismiss human rights as a Western concept is to ignore the growing universalization of this language – whether raised in Tiananmen Square, Timisoara, or the developed West. The anti-statist content of human rights has an appeal that transcends culture and political ideology. The practitioner's doubts are disingenuous. Western states have already used human rights reasons to switch the aid current on or off. Unless such decisions were based solely on "feel," we must conclude that some form of measurement was in fact undertaken. The index simply makes public what until now have been ad hoc and secret evaluations.

The case-by-case argument is also a smokescreen. Policy makers face complex trade-offs in which moral duties must be tempered against national interests, the severity of the problem, and effectiveness. None of this, however, precludes general assessments that point to a range of policy options under conditions of varying severity. Finally, the methodological pitfalls are scarcely unique. Imperfect data are normal in the social sciences. Moreover, boundary problems are inherent in any ranking scheme; and any classification, in the end, involves an element of judgment. In sum, evaluating human rights performance is no more uncertain than, say, political risk analysis or explaining the behaviour of "rational" consumers. An index is a first step on the path to greater rigour in monitoring the human rights record of developing countries.

A HIERARCHY OF HUMAN RIGHTS
INSTRUMENTS

A method for comparing human rights diplomacy is vital if knowledge is to grow in this field. Table 2.4 outlines a "hierarchy of human rights policy options" to guide comparison by ranking policy options on the basis of their "assertiveness." It could also aid policy makers. Johan Galtung has argued that "the best service peace research could offer to the world today probably consists, not so much in understanding conflicts better, as in providing politicians with an enormous repertoire of actions short of violence that can be applied in conflict situations."[36] The hierarchy helps the decision maker weigh policy options, balancing the assertiveness of a particular option against the potential cost to other important national interests. There are various frameworks that attempt to help analysts describe human rights statecraft. Falk and Luard, for instance, provide simple checklists of the instruments available. Sajoo's matrix matches policies "in an ascending order of significance" with the "principal actors," such as interest groups, the legislature, and the executive. Matthews and Pratt provide a typology divided into bilateral, multilateral, and transnational channels and into economic, military, cultural, and diplomatic/political instruments.[37] Baldwin lists positive and negative forms of "economic statecraft," while Schmitz and Berry distinguish positive from negative human rights levers.[38]

None of these frameworks fully tackles the costs and benefits of particular options. They provide little guidance to the interpretation of statecraft. Despite these shortcomings, there is a common intuition among these scholars that policy levers range from mild to punitive. Baldwin argues that "economic sanctions lie somewhere between war and appeasement in terms of a continuum of toughness … They are stronger than diplomatic protests but weaker than military attack."[39] Weintraub recognizes that "trade sanctions may be more costly to the sending nation than to the target."[40] Pratt says that Canada has a one-track record on human rights: active at the United Nations, but weak at the bilateral level, particularly along economic channels.[41] By implication, a greater willingness to use bilateral channels and economic levers would signal a more assertive human rights policy. Nonetheless, these insights fall well short of a comprehensive ranking scheme.

If scholars shy away from ranking, states do not. The British Foreign Office has drawn up a list of fourteen policy instruments ranging from letters to politicians, through the cancellation of ministerial visits, to the curtailment of arms exports and trade sanctions.[42] Similarly, a Dutch report observed that "the possibilities open to the government

Table 2.4
A Hierarchy of Human Rights Policy Options

Policy Options	Assertiveness
Quiet diplomacy	Low
Declaratory diplomacy	
Roll-call diplomacy (U.N. Human Rights Commission)	
Standard setting (U.N. forums)	
Policy dialogue (ODA programs)[1]	
NEGATIVE SIGNALS	
Grant asylum	Moderate
Suspend cultural contacts	
Suspend high-level meetings	
Voluntary investment codes	
Voice criticism in IFIS[2]	
Legislate guidelines on military exports	
Redirect ODA to NGOS	
Recall ambassador (temporary)	
POSITIVE SIGNALS	
Increase ODA	
Reduce import tariffs	
Grant most-favoured-nation status	
Provide debt relief	
Increase refugee quotas	
Technical assistance (for human rights, good governance)	
Suspend IFI credits	High
Suspend or reduce ODA	
Suspend official export credits	
Impose arms sales embargo	
Recall ambassador (permanent)	
Withdraw most-favoured-nation status	
Impose mandatory trade sanctions	
Break diplomatic relations	
Consult with "liberation forces"	
Humanitarian aid to "liberation forces"	
Military and economic aid to "liberation forces"	
War	

[1] ODA is official development assistance and here denotes government-to-government aid.

[2] IFIS are international financial institutions such as the World Bank.

for influencing the conduct of other governments with regard to human rights constitute *a broad spectrum*, ranging from discreet pressure through submitting a formal complaint under a procedure of state complaint ... In exceptional circumstances, there may be reason to restrict diplomatic relations temporarily with the country concerned.

On the other hand, to break off diplomatic relations completely cannot as a rule be regarded as an appropriate reaction to violations of human rights."[43]

The options hierarchy extends other frameworks. First, it confronts the normative dimension of human rights. Second, it aids interpretation by asking the analyst to consider motives and policy trade-offs. Third, the concepts of "cost" and "assertiveness" (developed below) provide the logic for the hierarchy. These refinements make explicit the intuition that certain policies signal a resolve to defend human rights even at the cost of overriding other vital national interests. As an ideal type, the hierarchy confronts reality. Weber likened ideal types to a utopia arrived at by emphasizing certain elements of reality "which cannot be found empirically anywhere."[44] The hierarchy confronts the real world of statecraft by gauging policy "assertiveness" and policy "costs." Such concepts are realist fundamentals. In this view, states are self-interested, concerned essentially with the pursuit of power, wealth, and security. Politicians thus "think and act in terms of interest defined as power." Realists also assume that decision makers are rational actors employing a cost-benefit logic to weigh the likely consequences of policy options. Costly actions require or involve expenditure, loss, or sacrifice of some valued possession.

Cost-benefit analysis measures the perceived or actual losses (and benefits). Opportunity costs are the value of other opportunities lost in achieving some goal. In economics, opportunity costs can be measured using some common unit of account – usually money. In politics, there is no obvious common unit of account. Nevertheless, realism predicts that national interest will trump any contest with ethical principles, such as human rights.[45] This suggests that cost in the human rights hierarchy should be defined as follows: senior foreign policy makers will view as costly any action which, to a significant extent, will be likely to disrupt normal diplomatic relations, limit commercial opportunities, inflict domestic economic hardship, strain alliance structures, or provoke retaliation by a target state. Perceived high costs will inhibit assertive policies that are intended to signal resolve, inflict harm, or induce change. Assertiveness measures resolve and mirrors cost; a state is assertive in defending global human rights if it is prepared to transgress the norm of non-interference and sacrifice short-term gains to safeguard long-range values.

The hierarchy lists thirty-one options for human rights statecraft. The list is split into three broad policy categories: low, moderate, and high assertiveness. Although the categories ideally should be exclusive, this is impossible with human rights. The policy makers' assessment

Table 2.5
A Hierarchy of Human Rights Instruments: Channels, Objectives, Intended Impact

Assertiveness	Channel	Objectives	Intended impact
Low	Multilateral Diplomatic Solidarity	Publicity Promotion Influence	Symbolic
Moderate	Multilateral Bilateral Cultural Economic (aid)	Adjustment Promotion Influence	Symbolic/substantive
High	Unilateral Multilateral Diplomatic Economic Military	Punishment Coercion Disengagement Disruption	Substantive

of assertiveness will vary according to the country involved and their perceptions of what action(s) will be effective. Such contingencies, however, do not negate the heuristic value of the hierarchy. Four criteria help to distinguish between the three assertiveness levels. First, with what channel does a state principally respond to human rights violations? A shift from largely multilateral and diplomatic channels to bilateral channels signals growing policy assertiveness. The relationships beetween assertiveness, policy channels, and policy objectives is illustrated in table 2.5.

Second, what is the dominant objective in each category? This may shift from galvanizing public opinion, to engaging in a "critical dialogue," to a more openly punitive stance as states move from mild to assertive levers. Third, what is a Western state's position on sovereignty? This may be one of the strongest constraints on an assertive human rights policy. If non-interference is central to international relations, states should be unwilling to use intrusive bilateral economic or military levers. Table 2.6 shows that respect for these norms may be inversely proportional to a state's assertiveness on human rights. Where respect for sovereignty is strong, unassertive channels are likely to be preferred.[46] Other things being equal, a "rights-assertive" state will be willing to interfere in a target state's domestic affairs. Fourth, decision making becomes more complex with ascension from low, through moderate, to high levels of assertiveness (see table 2.7). Bureaucratic politics may complicate policy making because a decision to apply sanctions or reduce aid will affect the jurisdiction of departments

Table 2.6
A Hierarchy of Human Rights Instruments: Respect for International Law[1]

Assertiveness	Respect for international law
Low	Sovereignty (high respect)
High	Interference (low respect)

[1] The key legal expression of the territorial integrity and self-determination of sovereign states is article 2(7) of the U.N. Charter, which prohibits interference in matters "essentially within the domestic jurisdiction" of a member state.

Table 2.7
A Hierarchy of Human Rights Instruments: Bureaucratic Complexity

Assertiveness	Bureaucratic actors
Low	Foreign ministry
Moderate	Cabinet Foreign ministry Trade ministry Aid agency
High	Prime minister Cabinet Foreign ministry Trade ministry Export-credit agency Aid agency Immigration department Defence

beyond the foreign ministry. Large states with complex bureaucracies may be more prone to decisional complexity than smaller states.[47] This premise will be examined in the China case study.

In sum, a comparison of human rights diplomacy must be based on some yardstick that measures the assertiveness of states to defend global human rights. This "options hierarchy" provides an ideal-type reference point for analysis. Three broad categories of low, moderate, and high assertion are distinguished using four criteria, namely, principal policy channel(s), respect for sovereignty, decisional complexity, and dominant foreign policy style and objectives. The key markers signifying increasing policy assertiveness are (1) the transition from quiet to public diplomacy, (2) the transition from multilateral to bilateral levers, (3) a willingness to override the international norms of sovereignty and respect for domestic jurisdiction, and (4) a willingness to endure economic and political sacrifices in order to further human rights objectives.

CONCLUSION

This chapter has set out frameworks for assessing Third World human rights performance and Western policy responses. It is tempting to combine the index with the hierarchy to create a matrix in which, for example, improving human rights conditions would be met by additional aid for "democratic development," while worsening or negative conditions would meet with a reduction or removal of aid.

Besides the obvious objection that the "fit" will never be exact, practitioners will complain that rigid policy formulae are not credible. At most, as human rights conditions worsen, policy makers may consider a shift from quiet or multilateral diplomacy to more assertive policies. If, as our internationalists claim, human rights are integral to foreign policy, we should expect to see more assertive levers being used by Western states, *at some cost to other national interests*, in situations where human rights conditions are steadily worsening or where abuses are gross, systematic, and sustained. To test this hypothesis, this study will now turn to a series of case studies that examine the practice of Western states.

PART TWO
Practice

3 Dutch Aid to Suriname, 1975–1990: The Litmus Test for Political Conditionality

At 2 AM on 8 December 1982, fifteen people were taken from their beds in Paramaribo, Suriname's capital. Given no chance to dress, they were hauled into military vehicles and taken away.[1] The arrested were no ordinary group; they were journalists, lawyers, academics, army officers, businessmen, and a trade union leader. They were opinion leaders from major sectors of Surinamese society. Several were members of the Association for Democracy. All were suspected by military authorities, then ruling Suriname, to be conspirators in an impending coup attempt. The suspects were taken to Fort Zeelandia, an army barracks and prison. At 3:45 AM shots were heard in Paramaribo, and shortly thereafter three buildings were set alight: a radio station, a press office, and the office of the Moederbond, Suriname's largest trade union. By 7:00 AM on 9 December a rumour began to circulate that fleeing military men had been shot at Fort Zeelandia. At 11:00 AM a blue army pick-up truck arrived at the mortuary of the Academisch Ziekenhuis (University Hospital) to deliver ten body bags. That evening, Colonel Desi Bouterse, Suriname's military strongman, announced on television that the army had foiled an attempted coup and that "a number" of arrested people had been killed while fleeing the fort. Sources close to Bouterse had a different explanation: Bouterse is reputed to have initially said, "I killed them," but later to have declared that "this was not the intention, but things got out of hand."[2] The façade government resigned and Acting President Misier followed suit on 10 December.

Hundreds of people, including doctors, saw the fifteen corpses. Almost all the bodies had severe facial injuries and signs of mistreatment from punches and blows from a heavy object. Forensic experts later concluded that open wounds on the victims' faces may have been caused by a blunt object such as a rifle butt. Bullet wounds revealed that the victims had been shot from the front, a finding at odds with the official story that the fifteen had been shot while escaping the fort. Cyril Daal, the chairman of the Moederbond, is reported to have been castrated, and bullet wounds were found in his abdomen and face.[3] The injuries lead to the unmistakable conclusion that fourteen Surinamese and one Dutchman were intentionally tortured and arbitrarily killed.

Just two days after the killings were announced, the Dutch government suspended its massive aid program in Suriname. Other minor players, such as Canada, Venezuela, and Brazil, would later follow suit. More influential players, such as the United States and the World Bank, also severed their aid programs.

THE VICISSITUDES OF HUMAN RIGHTS CONDITIONALITY

Suriname is a textbook case of human rights conditionality. Donor countries used aid as both carrot and stick to improve human rights and hasten the restoration of democracy. It is a rare example of a situation in which a punitive and assertive lever – aid suspension – was used in direct response to human rights violations and in which the major aid donors worked in coordination to an unusual degree. Did suspension work? This chapter examines the special conditions that prompted a small Western state, the Netherlands, to override respect for sovereignty and domestic jurisdiction in response to the moral imperative of human rights.

Aid donors are more comfortable promoting human rights than using aid as a political lever when rights are abused. Donors normally leave a country only when an internal conflict undermines the viability of projects and the safety of aid personnel. This was the case in Uganda in the late 1970s, and in El Salvador and Guatemala when Canada suspended its aid there in the early 1980s.[4] Nevertheless, Canada, the Netherlands, Norway, and other OECD donors now agree that aid may be suspended when states systematically and persistently violate core rights (see chapter 9). Three motives may underpin such a decision: a desire to avoid complicity, to inflict punishment, or to induce change.

Practitioners commonly argue that a punitive approach to aid does more harm than good. It smacks of moral imperialism, undermines bilateral relations, severs all prospects of influence, and punishes the disadvantaged for the moral comfort of Western public opinion. Worse, suspension does not work as a lever to improve respect for human rights. Smaller donors have little impact on recipient economies and thus cannot coerce repressive regimes. Finally, suspension may prompt retaliation, either against the donor or against oppressed groups. Suriname provides a unique opportunity to weigh the arguments for and against "negative" conditionality.

The response of Dutch and other Western donors to the political killings in Suriname illustrates the issue of double standards in human rights statecraft. Why did the Dutch act so punitively to protest the death of fifteen opinion leaders in a small, isolated South American country when in its other former colony, Indonesia, the killing of between 150,000 and 500,000 communists in 1965 and the later atrocities against the Timorese prompted such a weak response? Why were the Americans and Canadians prepared to give their imprimatur to the Dutch suspension by terminating their small aid programs in Suriname, when Central American death squads have evoked far less assertive statecraft? The Dutch and Canadian responses to the 1989 Tiananmen Square massacre were much more muted than their actions on Suriname. What led them to take the moral high ground in Suriname? Was concern for human life the central issue? Or was the absence of significant competing interests the deciding factor? Why did a small, insignificant country evoke international interest – from respected human rights organizations and from multilateral forums such as the European Community, the United Nations, and the Organization of American States? Let us put these questions on hold while we consider the political context of the December killings and summarize Suriname's economic, political, and human rights history.

ECONOMY AND SOCIETY

Wedged between Guyana, Brazil, and French Guiana, Suriname is a sparsely populated country of some 411,000. A multi-ethnic society, its cultural diversity reflects its colonial past. Dutch is still the official language. Political and economic power is largely concentrated among Creoles and Hindustanis, though there are also small Chinese and Lebanese business enclaves. The Javanese, brought over by the Dutch, were slow to shed their role as farm and industrial labourers. Small numbers of Maroons, descendants of slaves, and Amerindians occupy the jungle hinterland of the country. Their impoverishment and marginal status has been the source of ethnic tension, which flared into a Maroon armed insurrection in 1986.

Suriname is a resource economy dominated by bauxite, which remains the principal source of foreign exchange. In the 1980s, despite a slump in the international price, bauxite accounted for about 70 per cent of export earnings. Other export products are rice, wood, and palm oil. Foreign multinational corporations dominate the economy. Subsidiaries of Royal Dutch–Shell and U.S.-based Alcoa are the largest bauxite concerns. A Dutch wood producer, Bruynzeel, the United Fruit Company, and the Colma Oil Company are also active in Suriname. These companies virtually monopolize their economic sectors. Suralco investments amounted to more than 50 per cent of all investments in Suriname between 1959 and 1974. The multinationals accentuate economic duality. The bauxite companies employ only 6 per cent of the country's workforce, but they pay their workers well above the national average. In the early 1980s, despite uneven development and the impoverishment of Amerindians and Maroons, Suriname was a relatively prosperous country. In 1981, per capita GNP was US$3,510, the second highest in South America. Key social indicators were also above Third World averages; life expectancy was 67 years for men and 72 for women, while 65 per cent of the adult population were literate.

Suriname's reliance on a single export makes it vulnerable to commodity market fluctuations. Bauxite prices declined in the 1980s, and Suriname now faces competition from new bauxite producers such as Brazil and Australia. Economic dependence on the multinationals, an inability to cushion a sudden fall in bauxite prices, and an overdependence on Dutch aid are the hallmarks of a dependent economy that is too weak to withstand external interference. This is an economic profile ripe for political manipulation.

POLITICS: THE CYCLE OF DEMOCRACY AND AUTHORITARIANISM

The Netherlands granted Suriname its independence on 25 November 1975. Its history since then has borne the mark, common to so many less-developed countries, of cyclical regime change between the poles of open democratic politics and closed military autocracy. At independence, Suriname adopted parliamentary democracy and a multiparty system drawn along ethnic lines. Individual rights were constitutionally guaranteed, the powers of the state were separated, and elections were to be secret and by universal suffrage.[5] But the early promise of democratic governance under Suriname's first post-independence regime quickly dissipated, and Henck Arron's government never acquired popular legitimacy. Two problems hastened his political demise. First, his popular support was undermined by corruption, nepotism, and the protection of vested interests. Second, conflicts over wages in the newly formed army led to disciplinary action by the Arron government. This harsh reaction fuelled grievances among a group of junior officers, and on 25 February 1980 Sergeant Desi Bouterse and sixteen Creole NCOs staged a successful *coup d'état*.[6]

At first, Bouterse cleverly maintained the rudiments of democratic governance while consolidating power. A new puppet government under Chin A Se was installed; the constitution remained in place. Real power, however, was in the hands of the National Military Council and in the person of Bouterse. This façade democracy gave Bouterse a veneer of legal legitimacy. The new government even promised elections for October 1982. But by August 1980, Bouterse had dispensed with the charade. After announcing that three members of the National Military Council were involved in an unsuccessful coup attempt, he declared a state of emergency, suspended the constitution, and dissolved Parliament. He then created a civil-military dyarchy with power shared between an appointed civilian cabinet and a military authority. By February 1982, the final semblance of civil accountability was shed by the centralization of power in a military-controlled "Policy Centre." The autocratic foundations for the violent abuse of human rights were now in place. From this point on, popular support for Bouterse evaporated. Resistance set in. Another coup attempt was mounted on 11 March 1982. It failed. A few months later, Moederbond called a series of strikes, demanding the army's return to the barracks and the restoration of democracy. Then came Bourterse's December 1982 pre-emption of a further coup by the arrest and murder of fifteen alleged conspirators.

The first steps towards the restoration of democracy in Suriname were taken as early as February 1984, when a military decree called on a new Council of Ministers to establish permanent democratic structures. A National Assembly, drawing on members of the military, trade unions, and business, was created as an interim structure to oversee the transition to democratic rule, which was envisaged to take twenty-seven months. In March 1987, the National Assembly drafted a new constitution, which was ratified by more than 90 per cent of the voters in September 1987. General elections for a new parliament were held on 25 November 1987, and on 12 January 1988 Ramsewak Shankar, a former minister in the Arron government, was elected president.

The only impediment to this orderly restoration of democracy was the eruption of an armed insurrection against the military by disaffected Maroons. Led by a former soldier, Ronnie Brunswijk, the Maroons formed a "Jungle Command," and in the spring of 1986 began to attack military posts and bauxite plants in eastern Suriname. This conflict escalated in the late 1980s, with allegations that the army was guilty of human rights atrocities. The destruction of Suriname's limited economic plant and the outflow of Maroon and Amerindian refugees to neighbouring French Guiana have complicated Dutch efforts to guide the transition to democracy and have caused them to question their decision to resume their aid program. I shall return to these matters later.

DOCUMENTING AND EVALUATING THE HUMAN RIGHTS RECORD

Four patterns of human rights performance in Suriname coincide with the principal phases in its political history. Set against the human rights performance index, Suriname drifted from "human rights protected" to "human rights worsening" in just seven years (1975–82) as key civil rights were suppressed and the rule of law was effectively abandoned. The events of December 1982 mark a brief "negative" phase. Between 1983 and 1989, despite the formal restoration of democracy, human rights abuses stemming from armed conflict undermined any clear "human rights improving" pattern.

Human Rights Protected: 1975–1980

Core rights, the rule of law, and civil liberties were protected during the early democratic phase in Suriname.[7] The Arron government became party to several international human rights instruments, including the optional protocol of the International Covenant on Civil and Political Rights, the Convention on the Elimination of all Forms of Racial Discrimination, the American Convention on Human Rights, and most of the International Labour Organization's human rights conventions. Consistent with Dutch experience, articles 106 and 107 of the 1977 constitution provided that self-executing international treaties would have precedence over national law.[8] Thus, suriname was fully bound to respect international human rights standards. Although Arron's government made little progress in realizing social and economic rights, Suriname's democratic structure "distinguished it favourably from many other Latin American countries ... [and] the negative aspects of the Arron government pale[d] beside the violations" after the 1980 military coup."[9]

Human Rights Worsening: 1980–1982

From February 1980, when Bouterse took power, to December 1982, when the killings occurred, core rights and many civil and political rights were violated. The suspension of the constitution in August 1980 hastened the deterioration of human rights. The International Commission of Jurists, after visiting Suriname in February 1981, spoke of widespread illegal arrests, the mistreatment of detainees, and restrictions on the freedom of the press. The commission noted an atmosphere of insecurity in the country and observed that citizens had little access to legal remedies against arbitrary arrests and other infringements of their liberties by the military authorities. It said that "a total disregard for the law permeated every rank of the military ... Lawyers refused to consider cases involving the military because they feared [for] their own safety."[10]

However, neither the International Commission of Jurists nor Amnesty International alleged torture, disappearances, or any pattern of "gross and systematic violations."[11] There was a single political killing during this period – of Sergeant-Major Wilfred Hawker, who was summarily executed by firing squad on 13 March 1982 after a failed coup attempt. This points to a "worsening" but not "negative" human rights pattern and suggests that "the December [1982] executions should thus not be seen as an isolated incident but as the climax to a series of events."[12]

A Mixed Record: December 1982–1986

The human rights pattern from December 1982 until the restoration of democracy in 1986 is difficult to judge. Systematic abuses of non-derogable rights, particularly freedom from torture and extrajudicial killings, constitute a "negative" pattern of gross human rights violations. In such a situation, the severe abuse of core rights is typically persistent and widespread, affecting large numbers of people, often innocent civilians outside the political process.[13]

The December killings were undoubtedly gross violations. They broke Suriname's nonviolent political tradition. The murder of key opinion leaders muzzled would-be dissidents with fear. State terror worked through intimidation and public insecurity instead of through direct political violence. In October 1983 the Inter-American Commission on Human Rights published a report on conditions in Suriname, which concluded that "the December massacre – reinforced by such measures as an expansion of the armed forces, inauguration of a popular militia, and the announcement of legislation threatening criminal penalties for the dissemination of literature deemed subversive – has utterly silenced those sectors of the population opposed to the continuation of a non-democratic government ... and has in general created a climate marked by extreme fear."[14] These tactics were not completely successful. On 30 January 1983, twenty people were arrested and accused of yet another attempted coup. They included two former government ministers and Major Horb, who had resigned from the government to protest the December killings. Major Horb was reported to have been found hanging in his cell in Fort Zeelandia.[15]

Despite this suspicious incident, in general, Bouterse had no need to use direct violence. Torture, assassinations, death squads, and disappearances – the normal features a "human rights negative" landscape – were not present. Other features of a "negative" human rights pattern were, however. Bouterse's regime no longer had any popular legitimacy. The appointment of judges by the military meant that the judiciary was no longer independent. Bouterse did not answer calls from international monitors for a full investigation of the December killings, even though "such an investigation would indicate a certain willingness on the part of the government to ensure that there will be no repetition to the tragic events of 8 December 1982."[16] A visit by the Kenyan lawyer Amos Wako on behalf of the United Nations Commission on Human Rights (UNCHR) was postponed indefinitely at the last minute. Monitors were unequivocal, nevertheless, in asserting that "high government officials were responsible for the deaths of these 15 people."[17]

Democratic Transition and Armed Insurrection: 1986–1990

The human rights pattern from 1986 to 1990 does not fall squarely into any of the five "performance" categories. Many features of an "improving" pattern were present as Suriname underwent a democratic transition. Interest groups and political parties were active once more. New human rights organizations pressed the government to stop violating fundamental rights. The November 1987 election was observed by a joint assembly of the European Community (EC) and the African-Caribbean-Pacific (ACP) countries, and by observer teams from the Netherlands, the United States, and the Organization of American States.[18] The State Department's 1987 Country Report found the election to have been "free and fair."[19] It led to a landslide victory for the Front for Democracy and Development. The new government invited delegations from international human rights organizations to visit Suriname and investigate human rights abuses. Among them was the International Committee of the Red Cross and Amos Wako, the UNCHR's rapporteur on summary executions. An EC/ACP delegation also visited the country to review the human rights situation in the context of possible economic aid.[20]

Yet core rights, which are normally protected in an "improving human rights" pattern, were violated more extensively during this period than they were in the worst years of the military dictatorship (1980–84). An armed Maroon insurrection led to the reimposition of a state of emergency in December 1986. Allegations of army death squads, torture during interrogation, and the killing of innocent civilians proliferated during 1986 and 1987.[21] The U.S. *Country Report* noted, "Innocent civilians are still being killed by an army intent on wiping out the insurgency and its perceived sympathizers."[22] Army "clean-up" actions used helicopter gunships to drive out civilians. The army also restricted food and medical supplies, causing serious food shortages and health problems in the interior.[23] Estimates suggest that 300 Maroons and Amerindians died in the internal conflict, with as many as 6,000–10,000 refugees fleeing to French Guiana.[24]

Other elements of an "improving human rights" picture were also missing or unclear. Both the media and the trade unions remained reluctant to express dissent. The Dutch granted two journalists from the independent *De Ware Tijd* political asylum in April 1987 when they claimed that threats against them made it too dangerous to return to Suriname.[25] Moreover, the government has done little to investigate past abuses and new violations. Resolving the armed conflict and the refugee problem are prerequisites for safeguarding human rights. The stumbling block is a constitutionally guaranteed role for the army in Suriname politics; and the military's revocation of that role is a Jungle Command precondition to end the insurrection. This uncertain political situation is the backdrop for the examination of Dutch policy in Suriname.

AID AND INFLUENCE

The Dutch have deep roots in Suriname. They seized the colony of "Surrinam" from the English in 1667. At the Treaty of Breda that same year, the two mercantile powers exchanged their New World colonies. The English acquired New Amsterdam, later renamed New York, and the Dutch gained legal control of Surrinam. During the following years, they imposed a plantation economy based on sugar, cocoa, coffee, and slavery. More than 300,000 West African slaves were imported to work the plantations. Slavery in Suriname is reputed to have been extremely harsh and was not abolished until half a century after the British colonies abolished it. Thousands of slaves escaped into the interior jungles and became *Bosnegers*, ancestors of the Maroons of today.[26] Much of their work on the plantations was taken over by indentured labourers from India – the Hindustanis.

By the 1970s, although Suriname's economic and administrative base was very weak, the Dutch wanted to shed their colonial mantle, which by now was out of date for a Western social democracy with a new-found role as an internationalist and a friend of the developing world. Many Surinamese were against independence. But the Dutch pushed on, using the threat of reduced aid to prod a reluctant politician, Lachmon, to accept early independence. Between 1973 and 1975, more than 150,000 (mostly Hindustani) Surinamese emigrated to the Netherlands.

Acknowledging long historical ties, a continuing sense of moral obligation, Suriname's weak economic base, and its very isolated international status, the Dutch were prepared to underwrite the newly independent democracy with a massive aid program. Two ingredients of this aid package make Suriname a case apart among those considered in this study. First, Dutch official development assistance (ODA) was set in a legally binding treaty between the two countries.[27] Second, the Netherlands was the largest aid donor to Suriname, with Dutch ODA accounting for 8 per cent of Suriname's GNP in 1982 and 20 per cent of the government's budget.[28] These were essential factors in the 1982 decision to suspend the ODA treaty. Under the ODA treaty, the Netherlands agreed to provide 3.5 billion guilders over fifteen years in technical and financial aid.[29] There was, however, one fateful omission: the treaty contained no clause obligating the government of Suriname to respect fundamental human rights. The Hindustani party had pressed for such a clause, but the Dutch thought it unnecessary and intrusive.[30] Respect for sovereignty and domestic jurisdiction, at this point, took precedence over international human rights.

Before December 1982, the Dutch had taken no assertive action to signal their concern about the 1980 military coup or the worsening human rights situation; their disapproval was, however, communicated through quiet diplomacy. Relations between the two countries suffered, culminating in the temporary recall of a senior Dutch official from Suriname in 1981.[31] This was a moderate lever, but no assertive decision to sever diplomatic relations was made, and aid continued to flow. However, the December killings forced the Dutch to rethink their relationship with Bouterse. On 10 December 1982, two days after the killings, the Netherlands government publicly voiced its "horror" at the executions and suspended all discussions on development cooperation, thus freezing any new aid commitments. It warned "that development cooperation may never serve to support repressive regimes nor may it involve complicity in grave violations of human rights."[32] Then, on 16 December, the Minister for Development Cooperation confirmed the immediate suspension of the 1975 ODA treaty.[33] The decision had all-party consensus. Additional agreements relating to the military and the police force were also suspended *sine die*.

In a rare departure, the Dutch persuaded other aid donors to suspend aid to Suriname. These donors included the United States, Canada, Brazil, Venezuela, and the World Bank (though the EC and the Inter-American Development Bank, continued to aid Suriname). While these donors had given little aid to Suriname, their action in cutting it off gave the Netherlands government an imprimatur and sealed Bouterse's economic and diplomatic isolation. That, at least, was the intention. Canada, for example, had disbursed CDN$221,000 to Suriname through its mission-administered funds in 1981–82. Suriname was classed as a category 3 country, eligible for small ad hoc development assistance. Canada had been considering raising its aid profile in Suriname to support Bouterse's ostensible guarantee of democratization,[34] but high-level contacts between the foreign ministries at Ottawa and The Hague prompted Canada to revise its thinking.[35] In Parliament, the secretary of state for external affairs, Allan MacEachen, announced Canada's decision to suspend its funding to Suriname as a direct response to the December killings. This was one of the very few instances when human rights were the explicit reason for Canada to suspend its government-to-government aid. Aid was resumed in 1987 in view of the democratic reforms then underway.

The Dutch also launched a diplomatic offensive at UNCHR, the U.N. General Assembly, and the Organization of American States. By drawing attention to the December killings, they ensured that monitors visited the country over the next several years. And by persistently criticizing Suriname's human rights record, they pressured the Bouterse regime towards democratic reform and reinforced their decision not to reopen the ODA treaty before human rights conditions had improved. At the 1983 UNCHR meeting in Geneva, the Dutch delegation circulated an eyewitness reconstruction of the December killings. But it did not press for a resolution condemning the killings or calling on Bouterse to respect international norms.[36] This may seem a surprising omission, given Suriname's weak international position; Suriname had no friends among the Western Group or the non-aligned bloc to counteract Dutch efforts. But the Dutch reasoned that a resolution might not pass or might be so watered down that it would lack moral force. Either result would have played into Bouterse's hand, allowing him to claim the failed vote as a victory and legitimizing his ongoing repression.[37]

Since moral imperatives underpinned its decision to suspend ODA, the Netherlands government was obliged to state the circumstances in which aid would be resumed. By early 1983, its position was that the resumption of aid "would be dependent upon clear and concrete steps towards a return to democracy and safeguarding human rights." This "condition" did not imply the full restoration of a parliamentary system and rule of law, or the retirement of Bouterse. "The requirement consisted only of *steps in the direction* of a state of affairs which would make such acts of terror as those of December 1982 unlikely."[38]

Democratic reforms in Suriname began as early as February 1984 with the creation of the Council of Ministers and gathered pace with the elections in 1987. This process allowed the Dutch to shift the diplomatic focus from punishment to support. The aid relationship was recommenced in May 1988 in the form of "transitional aid" of 60 million guilders. But resuming the aid program has brought with it several headaches for the Dutch, for they have to ensure that they will not be isolated if serious abuses occur in the future, perhaps in the context of another coup. This has meant spreading the risks by nudging Suriname to accept an International Monetary Fund/World Bank "proposal" for macroeconomic reform and by encouraging more aid donors to disburse funds. Japan, Belgium, and the European Community have started projects in the country, and Canada, the United States, Venezuela, and Brazil have agreed to provide nominal funding support. The "transitional aid" was dangled as a carrot to get Suriname to accept a World Bank adjustment and recovery program.[39] As the Dutch noted, "Once a [recovery] programme is available, it will serve as a basis for talks between the Netherlands and Suriname about the nature of their aid relations."[40] Eventually, the pressure worked, and the Dutch sought World Bank support to create a donor aid consortium as a forum for ODA pledges and for planning Suriname's long-term economic future.[41]

That meant greater "conditionality," something Suriname, like weak Third World states everywhere, has protested but is unable to resist. However, while the aid treaty has been "reactivated," the Netherlands has not sought an amendment that would condition future ODA on respect for human rights. This is a surprising omission, given the 1982 suspension and the ongoing debate about aid as a human rights lever. There are two probable reservations which the Dutch government may have. First, a human rights clause would further sour an already uneasy relationship with Suriname and would send a negative signal to the new democratic government. Second, it might be used as a precedent by domestic lobby groups who are pushing for similar action in other Dutch recipient countries where there are gross abuses. Whatever the reason, the absence of a human rights clause contradicts the central thrust of Dutch diplomacy in Suriname: the restoration of democracy, the improvement of human rights, and the assurance that ODA will not prop up an illegitimate and repressive regime.

The policy debate in the Netherlands centred on how best to deliver ODA – on a program basis with no strings on how the funds were spent, or on a case-by-case basis with strict control and approval of projects. Program aid could include commodity transfers and balance-of-payments support. This kind of lending allows a recipient government to spend (or misspend) the funds as it sees fit. Project aid, on the other hand, permits greater supervision of donor fund disbursement. Because program aid is fungible and could be used for nondevelopmental purposes, the Dutch will not provide balance-of-payments support. The new policy ensures that no money will go directly to the Suriname government. The Dutch were concerned that funds might be misappropriated or used by the military to fight counterinsurgency, thus possibly underwriting human rights violations.[42]

Not surprisingly, this degree of control has hurt bilateral relations. Conditionality and concern about the army's human rights abuses led to a tit-for-tat diplomatic impasse. The Dutch ambassador was expelled in January 1987. The Dutch retaliated by sending back the Surinamese *chargé d'affaires*.[43] In May 1989, aid negotiations temporarily broke down. Suriname wanted mainly food aid in order to boost its popular support. The Dutch preferred greater investment in production and infrastructure.[44] The Americans reported similar headaches in the resumption of their small ODA to Suriname. Beyond a US$500,000 seed grant to speed up parastatal privatization, the United States put an Extended Support Facility grant on hold because of "diplomatic problems" with the Surinamese.[45]

THE MOTIVES AND IMPACT OF CONDITIONALITY

This study uncovers the mixed motives behind Western human rights statecraft. Less attention is given to the effectiveness of human rights conditionality because smaller donors rarely make a significant impact on recipient economies and because isolating the impact of aid leverage from a host of intervening variables is problematic. But the large volume of Dutch aid to Suriname provides a rare opportunity to test the potential of development aid to catalyse political change and improve human rights.

While a moral desire to avoid complicity was the spark that initially caused the Netherlands to suspend aid, a political desire to induce change became the reason for its continuing the aid freeze for five years. Aid bureaucrats who object to the politicization of ODA single out Suriname as proof that aid is an ineffective lever for improving respect for human rights.[46] They hold that Dutch influence was overestimated. After all, it took nearly five years before elections were held. A more generous view argues that the aid freeze and international censure deterred Bouterse from committing further human rights abuses. But this generous view is weak. By freezing aid, the Dutch played their trump card and could no longer influence Bouterse. Moreover, the December killings created a climate of fear that made further atrocities unnecessary. According to this view, aid suspension had no effect either way. Another view has it that Bouterse began a process leading to the voluntary transfer of power as early as 1984, just two years after international aid was cut off. The suspension may thus have played a larger role than the detractors claim. The evidence is mixed, but there is certainly no unequivocal evidence that the aid freeze forced Bouterse to bend to Dutch pressure.

Aid accounted for about 20 per cent of the government budget in 1980. Much of the rest came through taxes from the bauxite multinationals and their well-paid employees. Cutting off aid made foreign exchange more scarce, and it contributed to economic atrophy, soaring unemployment, and a plunging per capita income; but it is unclear whether it was critical to Bouterse's agreement on a timetable for democratic reform. Other factors may have been as important or more so. Central, here, was the economic collapse of Suriname's staple export, bauxite, as international prices fell in the mid-1980s and as competition grew from new and aggressive producers such as Brazil and Australia.[47] But it should be noted that the real production slump came in 1987 and after, when the Jungle Command attacked several bauxite mines. So bauxite markets alone were not responsible for crippling Suriname's economy; it may have been a combination of lost bauxite revenues and lost ODA that helped put Bouterse on the democratic path. An underestimated but perhaps critical reason for Bouterse's change of heart was his pragmatic recognition that he had lost popular legitimacy after 1982 and that his army was an administratively weak institution, incapable of running the government and managing the economy.[48]

Sceptics say that the military elites were undeterred by the loss of economic aid: "After all, they continued to receive their salaries."[49] There was speculation that Bouterse was receiving help from Libya and Cuba, and that some of his senior command were involved in the drug trade. In fact, his second in command was jailed on drug charges in the United States in 1989.[50] But the sceptics miss a crucial point. The initial motive for suspending ODA was not to undermine Bouterse and hasten democratic reform; it was to find a principled response to an unequivocal human rights atrocity and to avoid indirectly sustaining an illegitimate and repressive regime.[51] Seen in this light, the suspension of aid was effective in sending an unmistakable signal that was consistent with the new Dutch aid policy.

In 1979 the Netherlands government had acknowledged that the suspension of ODA might be considered "where there is gross and persistent violation of fundamental rights." The government was also clear that "one should take care, at any rate, that aid does not contribute to the perpetuation of repression."[52] The 1982 abuses were certainly gross, though they were not persistent. The imperative for a principled response was, nevertheless, unusually intense in Suriname's case. There was strong evidence that Bouterse and other military leaders were directly involved in the killings and that the people executed had been tortured.[53] The killing of such high-profile leaders created a climate of fear and intimidation that initially strengthened Bouterse's grip on the country. Moreover, the abuses were of the inviolable core rights that should command primary attention by governments and multilateral forums. As the Dutch Human Rights and Foreign Policy Advisory Committee observed, abuses of these fundamental rights "can occur on such a scale and to an extent which encroaches on the human rights situation in its entirety. *A donor must regard this as the decisive factor when evaluating policy.*"[54]

After the initial decision to suspend ODA, Dutch policy quickly focused on a diplomatic offensive to isolate Bouterse through cooperation with other donors, particularly the United States, in order to hasten a return to democracy. Whether aid suspension was critical in prompting the military to allow a democratic transition remains unclear. Lower-rank Dutch officials were dubious about the importance and impact of suspension, but a senior official closely involved in the original decision stressed the Netherlands government's intention to push Bouterse towards democracy.

It is questionable whether total suspension *sine die* was needed. If leverage was the key issue, as it later became, a graduated "timetable approach" might have given the Dutch more influence on Bouterse. Why were the Dutch not prepared to redirect their aid through NGOs so that they would remain involved in the country, as Canada did in Haiti when it suspended government-to-government aid? Instead, the five-year aid famine, on top of a starved bauxite market, has set back the country's economic development by decades. And as the Dutch Human Rights Advisory Committee noted, the aid treaty's prime objective to reduce the differences in prosperity between the two countries and to promote economic growth and a fair distribution of welfare in Suriname may be "more remote than ever."[55]

DEVELOPMENT AID AND DEMOCRATIZATION

Hans van den Broek, who was then foreign affairs minister, signalled cautious optimism about Suriname's democratic transition by sending a Dutch ambassador to Paramaribo in early 1987. He acknowledged that the Dutch government had "reacted with a certain reserve" and that it remained to be seen whether the principles in the constitution would be put into practice.[56] By 1988, the Dutch ODA yearbook noted "clear and concrete steps in the process of democratic recovery ... and in the respect for other fundamental human rights."[57] But the timing of the decision to reactivate the ODA treaty may be open to criticism, given the fluid political situation in Suriname.

On 27 April 1988 the Tweede Kamer (the Netherlands' House of Commons) resolved to "normalize relations" between the Netherlands and Suriname.[58] An all-party Dutch parliamentary delegation visited Suriname that year to assess the human rights and political situation.[59] It identified five concerns. First, could the democratic government consolidate its power? The incumbents were the political old guard, and there was no new generation experienced in democratic politics. Second, despite two "peace protocols" between the protagonists, armed conflict continued. Third, Bouterse remained in command of the military and continued to exert political influence. He allegedly resisted efforts to integrate Maroons into the police and army, and may have been sabotaging efforts to conclude a peace accord with the rebels, stirring ethnic strife. As well, key media positions were occupied by Bouterse's cronies, casting doubt on press freedom. Fourth, bauxite prices remained low, and Suriname may have permanently lost some traditional markets. The economy was crippled[60] and per capita income had fallen from US$3,510 in 1981 to US$2,360 in 1987.[61] Finally, the military still retained control of investigations into abuses allegedly committed by the security forces. This put in question the rule of law. In sum, the democratic transition in Suriname looked extremely fragile, and the Dutch decision to reactivate the aid treaty may have been premature. In fact, renewed ODA to this fragile democracy came when there were more human rights abuses and refugee problems than in December 1982. If the armed conflict continues, one of the main premises of renewed aid – that it must benefit the entire population – will be impossible to meet. By 1988, Dutch ODA commitments were split between treaty commitments (60 million guilders) and nontreaty commitments (20 million guilders).[62]

CONCLUSION

The Dutch actions support the hypothesis central to this study, namely, that middle powers will sustain an assertive human rights policy only when the costs are believed to be low in terms of other foreign policy objectives. The Dutch used a punitive and assertive human rights lever because they knew that their actions would not affect the local regional powers – Brazil and Venezuela – or the United States. It was unlikely that they would be diplomatically isolated, and in fact just the reverse occurred; they won the support of virtually all the donors who were active in Suriname. A minor player such as Canada had virtually no interests in the country and thus had little difficulty taking a moral position.

The Dutch also had little to lose in Suriname, in contrast to the substantial trade, investment, and aid links they had with Indonesia – a former colony and a much more powerful country. Unlike Indonesia, Suriname could hardly have hurt the Dutch commercially or raised the costs of aid suspension. Neither Dutch trade with, nor investment in, Suriname appears to have suffered because of the suspension; both were negligible to begin with. The possibility that Bouterse might retaliate by nationalizing Dutch companies was never likely, given the fragile economy and the military's inability to administer the public sector.

The Dutch did have to consider some costs, however. By suspending ODA, they risked being criticized for abandoning the poor and contributing to the long-term economic devastation. The legality of suspending the ODA treaty was also questionable. At times, Bouterse threatened, without much conviction, to take the Netherlands to the International Court of Justice at The Hague for an illegal suspension of the aid treaty. Why did the Dutch suspend the treaty? Why were they punitive with Suriname when their reaction to the systematic genocide of West Papuans and Timorese in Indonesia was muted in the 1970s and 1980s? Policy makers argue that comparisons with Indonesia's 1965 anticommunist pogrom and 1975 East Timor invasion miss the point.[63] Aid leverage is applied when there is a reasonable expectation of influence. Consistency is utopian with human rights; each case is *sui generis*, and policy must be balanced by competing interests.

In Suriname, the Dutch had influence not only because they suspended aid but because few other countries had interests that Bouterse could use as a counterweight to the Netherlands. In contrast, Indonesia and China view the Netherlands as a minor diplomatic and trading partner, whereas these two countries are lucrative markets for Dutch exporters. The Netherlands may need Indonesia and China more than they need it. The case-by-case reasoning of Dutch policy makers and their focus on impact reinforce a realist interpretation of the decision to suspend the ODA treaty. On the other hand, effectiveness was a crucial though not exclusive concern. It will be recalled that the Netherlands' initial motive for the suspension was a commitment to finding a principled reaction to the December killings. This imperative may at first have overridden any assessment of the effectiveness of aid conditionality. Only later did the Dutch link aid restoration to political and human rights improvements.[64] This assessment refines a crude realist dismissal of Dutch motives for statecraft in Suriname.

Nonetheless, the Dutch actions broadly support the central hypothesis that nations will adopt assertive human rights policies only with weak states, only when they have few economic or diplomatic ties with these states, and only when their actions do not pose geostrategic complications for senior NATO allies. Suriname is certainly among the weakest and most isolated of states, and the Dutch actions posed few geostrategic complications for the United States or neighbouring countries. The costs to other important Dutch interests were thus low, as were the constraints against an assertive and principled intervention. As a weak, aid-dependent state, Suriname was in no position to retaliate, although Bouterse was allegedly able to develop links with Libya and Cuba, possibly offsetting the Western aid sanction.

Two subsidiary hypotheses – that junior alliance status may constrain human rights activism, and that the degree of policy assertiveness may be influenced by the strength of domestic lobbying – cannot, however, be supported. In the first place, there is no evidence that the United States tried to dissuade the Dutch. On the contrary, the Netherlands was able to persuade the United States and most other donors to join them in denying Bouterse aid. On the second point, domestic lobbying, it may at first appear that Dutch domestic considerations could have blocked the decision to suspend ODA. Although trade links between the Netherlands and Suriname are negligible, historical ties, a large Surinamese community in Holland, and the dilemma of penalizing an underdeveloped country complicated the policy calculus. As Minister van den Broek observed, "Suriname is no Nicaragua or El Salvador [for us]. Not only are there 200,000 Suriname people living on [Dutch] territory, but there is also an historically developed link between our two countries."[65] But Minister van den Broek's caveat aside, there is no evidence that immigrant lobby groups were active. Besides, most Surinamers supported tough action against Bouterse. The decision to freeze ODA was made with all-party consensus and within ten days of the December killings. Dutch ODA in the early 1980s was largely program aid, with few poverty-alleviation projects, and this fact no doubt eased any government misgivings about hurting the poorest groups.

The Dutch willingness to transgress the principle of non-intervention on human rights considerations suggests that the moral, or idealist, strain in Dutch statecraft may sometimes combine with, and even take precedence over, realist perspectives. But the two positions need not be mutually exclusive. Finally, the sudden clarity of the killings, the absence of significant military and commercial interests, and the consensus among political parties meant that the bureaucratic politics which theoretically would be anticipated in an assertive policy decision did not occur.

At the level of practice, the Dutch actions in Suriname pose complex questions and provide no easy answers. In a sense, the case is *sui generis*. Smaller aid donors rarely exercise such a degree of ODA leverage against an exceptionally weak and diplomatically isolated recipient. And seldom has a single event been so unequivocally branded by the international community as a flagrant abuse of human rights. Suriname is that rare case where human rights were paramount in the policy calculus. So the key question, "Did aid suspension work?" has wider implications. As a principled response and as a way of avoiding complicity, the Dutch aid freeze was effective. As a technique of leverage, there is no clear causal relationship between ODA suspension, redemocratization, and improved human rights. However, the withdrawal of the Netherlands and – very importantly – of the other aid donors may have had more impact than the detractors acknowledge. After all, Bouterse began a democratic process as early as February 1984. International bauxite prices and domestic production began to drop precipitously only after 1986. But whether the long-term damage to the economy was worth the short-term leverage and the moral comfort of principled intervention must rest, in the final analysis, with those who make policy and live with the consequences.

POSTSCRIPT

In a bloodless coup on Christmas Eve 1990, the democratic government of Ramsewak Shankar was replaced by military rulers. Colonel Bouterse, who had resigned his position as army chief earlier that day, was the real force behind the coup, which nominally was led by Lieutenant Graanoogst. The Dutch foreign ministry "sharply condemned" the coup and said that the Netherlands would indefinitely suspend its aid package to Suriname, worth about $115 million a year.[66] The aid freeze is about leverage, not human rights abuses per se. The military pledged to return Suriname to elected government in one hundred days. While the 1982 aid freeze may have helped tilt Bouterse towards democracy, renewing aid seems to have been less effective in consolidating the democratic transition. It remains to be seen what impact this latest Dutch aid freeze will have on the military.

4 The Philippines: Foreign Aid and Human Rights in an Uncertain Democracy

This case study examines Canadian and Dutch diplomacy during the Aquino administration in the Philippines and the problems that each donor faces in forging closer links between human rights, democratization, and development aid.[1] It considers several questions. First, how can an effective aid program be planned and implemented at a time of armed conflict and escalating human rights abuses? Second, can aid programs be adapted to keep up with rapidly changing political circumstances? Third, is a policy of strict neutrality possible in a deeply divided, militarized society? Fourth, who benefits from development aid? Can it redress social injustice and empower the disadvantaged? Finally, how can aid be effective in a setting where assistance may itself be part of the conflict?

FILIPINO DEMOCRACY: EMERGING, UNCERTAIN, OR FAÇADE?

Filipinos restored their democratic heritage with the ouster of Ferdinand Marcos in February 1986. The new incumbent, President Corazon Aquino, embodied the spirit of popular resistance to authoritarian rule. The challenges she faced were formidable: a debilitated economy, a debt burden of US$27 billion, rural and urban poverty, an Islamic secessionist movement, a communist insurgency, landlessness, and a politically powerful but deeply divided military. Despite these problems, the prospect of a democratic system reconstituted by "people's power" excited both domestic and international opinion.[2] Bilateral donors and multilateral development banks were quick to renew aid. But the transition to democracy has been neither smooth nor direct. The coalition of forces that brought Aquino to power proved ephemeral;[3] and the early promise of the February revolution has given way to deep political fissures and renewed armed conflict.

Ferdinand Marcos imposed martial law in 1972. Over the next decade he used the legal, coercive state apparatus to personalize power and silence dissent.[4] His "constitutional authoritarianism" legitimized human rights abuses. Critics say that the Aquino administration's human rights record was as bad as Marcos's. How well-grounded is their criticism?

Under Marcos, presidential decrees curtailed freedom of expression, of assembly, and of association; neither the press nor elections were free, nor were unions. The rule of law was abandoned with the suspension of habeas corpus. After martial law was lifted in 1981, arrests actually escalated under the new Preventive Detention Act. Extrajudicial killings, termed "salvaging," also increased.[5] Paramilitary groups such as the Civilian Home Defence Force, the police, and the military were responsible for these abuses. Anticommunist vigilante groups flourished with the encouragement of the president, and military authorities were given sweeping powers of incommunicado detention. Domestic and international human rights monitors who documented these abuses observed "a pattern of gross and systematic violations" and were unequivocal in their condemnation of the Marcos regime.[6]

AQUINO'S PROMISE: HUMAN RIGHTS AND DEMOCRATIC GOVERNANCE

With the election of a democratic government, Filipinos were optimistic that human rights would be restored. Human rights monitors such as the church-based Task Force for Detainees, and lawyers' groups such as the Free Legal Aid Group and the Philippine Alliance for Human Rights Advocates, had played a prominent role in documenting abuses under Marcos and were important among the many peoples' organizations that catalysed Marcos's downfall. Their credibility was renewed in the new regime.

The Aquino government's early performance on human rights was exemplary and raised expectations. The president released five hundred political detainees. Habeas corpus was fully restored. The government ratified the U.N. Convention against Torture and Protocol 2 of the Geneva Convention.[7] By March 1986, Aquino had established a presidential committee on human rights, citing a 1984 U.N. resolution that encouraged governments to establish "national institutions for the protection of human rights." The committee proposed the introduction of human rights education in the training of all police and military personnel, and the government agreed. Meanwhile, a new draft constitution sought a balance between authority and accountability, and attempted to embody the popular aspirations that underpinned the February revolution. Social justice was to be promoted "in all phases of national development." A bill of rights was proposed containing provisions to outlaw torture and all forms of incommunicado detention. The constitution also provided for a Permanent Commission on Human Rights and called for the dismantling of private armies and paramilitary units.

These formal mechanisms for the protection of human rights were important to the Philippines' political reconstruction. And their initial impact was positive. Amnesty International reported a marked decline in human rights abuses in 1986 and concluded that "the Aquino government's commitment to human rights and legal safeguards had led to major improvements."[8] With the adoption of the constitution by popular referendum in February 1987 and the convening of a new bicameral congress in July, the interim revolutionary administration ended, and it seemed that the transition to democracy would be smooth.

Unfortunately, the early promise of institutional reform was not sustained, and popular optimism quickly dissipated. The history of the Philippines during the Aquino administration was one of increasing political polarization, ineffectiveness of key democratic processes, shrinkage of political space (particularly for the legal left), and escalation of human rights abuses. Political gloom was offset only by an economy that grew by 5.5 per cent in 1987 and by 6.7 per cent in 1988.[9] Domestic investment picked up, and industries began to put unused capacity back to work. Still, the Aquino government scarcely began to tackle poverty or land and income distribution – the roots of conflict and the subsoil supporting the armed insurgency.[10] These issues remain unresolved today, and until they are adequately addressed, the Philippines will remain an "uncertain" democracy.[11]

The government's response to the communist insurgency and its relations with the military are central factors in the insecurity of Philippines democracy. The Armed Forces of the Philippines (AFP) consistently opposed President Aquino's attempts to begin a dialogue with the New People's Army (NPA). This fundamental opposition prompted six coup attempts by Marcos loyalists in the AFP. The most serious, in early December 1989, included elements of the Reformed Armed Forces Movement (RAM), who were disgruntled by Aquino's "soft line" on the insurgents and by her inability to tackle corruption. Juan Ponce Enrile and Salvador Laurel, former coalition allies but subsequently political opponents of Aquino, were implicated in the coup attempt – underlining the danger that a right-wing, civil-military alliance might overthrow the fragile democratic government.

Although the Aquino government survived all coup attempts, many believe that the army was strengthened as a result and that it exercises undue political influence. The military's ascendance also weakened the government's ability to safeguard even the most basic human rights. The breakdown of negotiations between the government and the NPA was the most important factor in the return of militarism. By February 1987, the ceasefire between the two sides had been abandoned. From this point on, the Aquino government favoured a military solution to the insurgency. Critics argue that in so doing the government gave responsibility for the counterinsurgency policy to the military.[12] The adoption of a "total war" strategy also legitimated a sharp increase in U.S. military aid and influence.[13]

In sum, the Philippines under Corazon Aquino was Janus-faced. Whether it can best be described as an "emerging," an "uncertain," or a "façade" democracy is hard to say. If one concentrates on the benign face, the Philippines was an emerging democracy; but a focus on the malign face reveals a façade democracy in which the military exercised real political power. If one recognizes both faces, the Philippines was an uncertain democracy. Each position along this continuum may imply very different aid policies and human rights statecraft.

DOCUMENTING AQUINO'S HUMAN RIGHTS RECORD

The military's rise and democracy's erosion began with the Mendiola Bridge incident. On 22 January 1987 in Manila, government anti-riot troops fired on supporters of a peasant organization during a violent demonstration for land reform, killing twelve and wounding thirty-nine.[14] Human rights monitors alleged that there were abuses by the AFP and paramilitary groups, and they documented a resurgence of extrajudicial killings, torture, disappearances, and arbitrary arrest and detention. Filipino groups reported 223 "missing victims" over the same period.[15] International monitors reported 135 cases of "salvaging" by August 1987, and 100 left-wing activists and trade union members arbitrarily killed in 1987 by security forces or vigilante groups.[16] Most of the victims were poor farmers, trade union activists, slum dwellers, church leaders, and human rights monitors – all with one thing in common. They were all labelled by the military and vigilante bands as communist sympathizers and members of the "legal-left" or "cause-oriented" organizations that act as fronts for the NPA. In the Philippines, "such accusations can be deadly."[17]

The military and the right-wing were not the only ones responsible for human rights abuses. In 1989 the NPA massacred thirty-nine tribal villagers – of whom only five were adult men – near Digos, Davao del Sur province, on the island of Mindanao. The massacre was "by far the worst rebel atrocity against civilians in the 20-year guerrilla war."[18] Moreover, a group of pro-NPA urban terrorists called "Sparrows" were responsible for a series of killings in Manila. The NPA's credibility as a viable alternative to President Aquino was undermined by such incidents. Nevertheless, whether committed by the extreme left or the extreme right, political killings under Aquino were increasing, and there were few means of redress. Indicative of the fragility of the rule of law was the growing persecution of human rights monitors and lawyers. Human Rights Watch singled out the Philippines for "the dubious distinction of accounting for the largest number of killings of human rights monitors [in 1988]."[19]

Finally, there were violations directly attributable to the counter-insurgency campaign conducted by the AFP. Most serious were strategic "hamletting, strafing, and food blockades.[20] Military "saturation drives" against the NPA created internal refugees, a new phenomenon in some parts of the Philippines. The problem was acute on Negros, and on 12 May 1989 the *Visayan Daily Star* reported 29,519 internal refugees.[21] Military operations were concentrated in the mountainous hinterland of the southern part of Negros, allegedly in response to a NPA raid which left seven soldiers dead in Caningay, Candoni. The military presence on the island in 1989 was astounding: 8 battalions, 10 companies of Special Forces, 35 vigilante groups, and 3,000 paramilitary Citizens' Armed Forces Geographical Units.[22] In some instances, refugees could no longer meet their basic human needs of food, health, and income. The camps were crowded, lacking facilities and food and water. Many children reportedly suffered from dysentery.[23]

A government's record in prosecuting those responsible for human rights abuses is a barometer of its commitment to the rule of law. By this measure, the Aquino administration was singularly ineffective. By 1990, the judicial system had made no successful prosecutions in cases of alleged abuses by vigilante groups. Until recently, the same could be said of alleged abuses by the military.[24] Critics cite two reasons for this poor record: first, the weakness of the Permanent Commission on Human Rights; second, the continuation of military jurisdiction over alleged abuses by the AFP and the police.

The Permanent Commission on Human Rights was an embattled government agency. Although it was empowered to "investigate on its own, or on complaint by any party, all forms of human rights violations involving civil and political rights" and to recommend prosecution where there was *prima facie* evidence of a violation, it had no independent power of prosecution. Its credibility was fragile. Critics charged that it was not aggressive in conducting investigations, and some domestic human rights groups stopped submitting reports to it. There was a series of well-publicized resignations from the commission and some dubious appointments; the chairwoman's credentials and her alleged partiality were an enduring irritant. In public statements, Mary Concepcion Bautista appeared to side with the government, defending state agents implicated in alleged abuses. She criticized domestic monitors who publicized abuses, and she referred to an Amnesty International report on political killings as "one-sided and therefore unacceptable."[25]

To her credit, President Aquino tried to remove Bautista and to improve the effectiveness of the commission by creating regional offices, providing a witness protection program, and considering a congressional bill to give the commission prosecutorial powers.[26] None of this, however, negates the dismal performance of the commission. Its ineffectiveness undermined the Aquino government's rhetoric on human rights.

EVALUATING THE HUMAN RIGHTS RECORD

The alarming growth in violations of nonderogable rights in the Philippines must be interpreted in the context of the AFP's counterinsurgency policy, the ineffectiveness of legal mechanisms to investigate and prosecute violators, the usefulness of vigilante groups in the total-war strategy, the endorsement of such groups by the government, and the deeply rooted culture of violence. Western policy makers should have asked themselves two difficult questions. First, was there "a pattern of gross and systematic violations of human rights?" Second, did the Aquino government bear any responsibility for the increasing violations? A "yes" on both counts might have prompted more assertive diplomacy.

U.N. human rights forums give primary attention to countries that exhibit "a pattern of gross and systematic violations of human rights." The full moral force of the language of rights is unleashed in this phrase. But its practical application and justiciability are weakened by at least two considerations. One, have state elites deliberately set in

motion a systematic pattern of abuses? Two, are there legal considerations exempting the offending state from the covenants? How do
these concerns apply to the Philippines? The second question is easy
to answer. International covenants contain a number of limitation
clauses permitting the signatory states to abrogate many rights. But
nonderogable rights are not to be circumscribed, even under conditions
of emergency "threatening the life of the nation." A counterinsurgency
policy notwithstanding, President Aquino did not declare martial law,
nor was there any legislation annulling key legal rights such as habeas
corpus. The government thus remained bound by the international
covenants to preserve, at a minimum, nonderogable rights under conditions of armed conflict.

Assessing the government's complicity in sponsoring "a pattern of
gross and systematic violations" is more complex. During much of
1987 and 1988, the great bulk of documented evidence pointed to
violations committed directly by the AFP, by the paramilitary Citizens'
Armed Forces Geographical Units (CAFGUS), and by vigilante anticommunist groups. NPA abuses mostly appeared to be confined to the Spar-
row death squads of metropolitan Manila. In 1989 the picture became
more cloudy. The NPA committed several well-documented atrocities,
though the communist leaders argued that these internal executions
reflected the pervasive infiltration of the NPA by AFP sympathizers.

The vigilantes and CAFGUS have been an essential ingredient of the
AFP's offensive against the NPA. The government's attitude to violations
committed by these groups was deeply worrying. President Aquino
appears to have endorsed the continued operation of some of the most
virulent vigilante organizations. In a speech to her military command-
ers on 23 March 1987, she argued that "the answer to the terrorism
of the left and the right ... is not social and economic reform, but
police and military action."[27] Similarly, her speech to the Philippine
Military Academy called for "a string of honourable victories" against
the insurgents.[28] In Davao City, home of the Alsa Masa vigilante group,
President Aquino sanctioned the vigilantes' role in the struggle against
communism: "We look to you as an example ... While other regions
are experiencing problems in fighting the insurgency, you here ... have
set the example."[29] These comments cast doubt on the government's
commitment to safeguard human rights. But a closer look at official
policy towards vigilantism and the government's record in laying down
a legal framework to investigate abuses and prosecute offenders must
precede any final assessment.

The Aquino administration's policy on vigilantism started with a call
to dismantle these groups but then shifted to equivocation and ultimately to qualified endorsement. The 1987 constitution required the

abolition of the Civilian Home Defence Force (CHDF) and the dismantling of private armies and other armed groups. In July 1987, President
Aquino issued an executive order (no. 275) calling for the gradual,
orderly dissolution of all paramilitary units, including the CHDF. This
never happened. Instead, the CHDF was restructured into the new
Citizens' Armed Forces Geographical Units (CAFGUS).[30] These reserv-
ists were to be deployed in the counterinsurgency campaign, but
"regulated" by the military.

Aquino's equivocation points to the fine line she trod between the
influential military officials who opposed the Senate report calling for
the abolition of vigilante groups and the human rights monitors who,
in mid-1987, were still a respected constituency. Eventually, official
policy tilted in favour of a qualified support of vigilantism, reasoning
that such groups should be unarmed.[31] Other guidelines designed to
ensure greater control of vigilantes included the stipulations that membership be entirely voluntary, that groups be geographically confined
to operate within specified *barangays*, and that they be organized
exclusively for defence purposes.[32] The government also called for the
joint supervision of these groups by the police, military, and local
civilian authorities.

Is the human rights picture in the Philippines under Aquino as ugly
as the worst excesses of the Marcos era? Although important features
of democratic governance were in place, democracy itself suffered.
Habeas corpus was in place as a basic legal protection. There was a
functioning opposition, and there had been democratic elections. There
was freedom of expression, an independent press, and, formally, freedom of association for trade unions and other "peoples' organizations."[33] Yet the status of nonderogable rights markedly deteriorated
after 1987. The exact numbers are contested, but as table 4.1 highlights, the number of arbitrary arrests and extrajudicial killings in 1988
approached that of the Marcos era. Other elements of the Marcos
years were also evident: vigilantes and other civilian volunteer defence
groups, counterinsurgency and strategic "hamletting," the surveillance
and attempted suffocation of the legal left, and the military's influential
role. Overall there was a pervasive climate of fear and intimidation
and "a growing cynicism in many quarters about the efficacy of redress
through legal channels."[34] When political violence is endemic, the
rights of association, expression, and peaceful political dissent, though
formally guaranteed, are in practice severely curtailed.

Does this mean that the Philippine government was responsible for
a systematic pattern of violations? A clear "yes" would require incontrovertible evidence of government intent and conscious planning.
Nothing here points unequivocally in that direction. Even President

Table 4.1
Human Rights Abuses under Presidents Marcos and Aquino (selected years)

Type of violation	1983 Marcos period	1988 Aquino period
Arbitrary arrest	3,038	2,282
Extrajudicial killing	368	249
Torture	644	784
Massacres	163	75

Source: For 1983, Richard Pierre Claude, "The Philippines," in J. Donnelly and R.E. Howard, eds., International Handbook of Human Rights (New York: Greenwood Press 1987), 283–4; for 1988, Philippine Human Rights Update, Manila, 15 March–15 April 1989.

Aquino's endorsement of the Alsa Masa is not conclusive, since other evidence points to government efforts to upgrade the Permanent Commission on Human Rights (charges of tokenism notwithstanding.) Moreover, the indictment of nine army personnel for the 1986 murder of trade union leader Rolando Olalia may "mark an important milestone in the strengthening of civilian institutions vis-à-vis the military."[35] Still, due process and the rule of law were weak in dealing with human rights cases. And it was worrying that Aquino kept a Marcos decree (no. 1850) insulating military and police personnel from the jurisdiction of the civil courts. The decree made clear the military's power and the limits of legal redress for human rights abuses.

The Philippines in 1989 fell into a "human rights worsening" category, or what the Winegard Report calls a "watch" category – one "where serious allegations have been made" but development is still possible.[36] The prognosis for human rights was bad. Divisions in Philippine society were widening; the stakes rose in the civil conflict as both left and right committed human rights abuses. Violence was linked to the deeper structural issues of land, poverty, and privilege. Radical land reform might have helped abate the civil conflict,[37] but this option was politically impossible for a fragile centrist government that was beholden to landowners and transnational agribusiness. The Comprehensive Agrarian Reform Program offered few immediate benefits for landless peasants while amply compensating landowners. The Aquino administration's inability to cut poverty was the principal reason for the resilience of the NPA and the National Democratic Front (NDF). While the NPA's internal purges and numerous "resignations" showed that the communist movement was tarnished and divided,[38] in the absence of any marked progress on land redistribution and other structural problems, communism retained a core support among parts of the impoverished rural sector.

PAVED WITH GOOD INTENTIONS:
CANADIAN DEVELOPMENT IN
THE PHILIPPINES

In the mid-1980s, Canada was a new and inexperienced player in the Philippines.[39] Its trade and investment was modest compared with that of its competitors.[40] Although the aid program is the centrepiece of Canadian-Filipino relations, here, too, Canada's contribution pales in comparison with that of other donors, accounting for only about 1 per cent of total donor finance. The big money in the Philippines is from Japan, the United States, the World Bank, and the Asian Development Bank. Measured by these indicators, Canada's interest and influence could be written off as negligible. But this assessment would be inaccurate for several reasons. Bare figures on aid, trade, and investment are not the whole story. Canada's interest in the Philippines has been evolving rapidly. First, there have been growing commercial interests. Two-way trade between the countries increased by $150 million between 1986 and 1988.[41] When President Aquino visited Canada on her North American tour, business was the first item on the agenda.[42] Second, strong political concerns underpin Canadian statecraft in the Philippines. Canada's policy objective was to support Aquino's fledgling democracy.[43] Although there were obvious strains in that democracy, Canadian policy is premised on a long-term view and adopts a generously broad conception of democratic rule. Strengthening democracy is in turn closely linked to the geopolitical objectives of the Western powers in Southeast Asia. Since the Philippines belong to the Association of Southeast Asian Nations (ASEAN), stimulating the country's economic growth and consolidating democratic rule are perceived as vital to Western security objectives in the region.

In many ways, Canada's aid program in the Philippines broke new ground. It was one of the first programs in which eligibility was linked to human rights and redemocratization, and in which decentralization and NGOs played a major role.[44] Although the Philippines ranks sixth among sources of immigrants to Canada and although there are some 100,000 Filipinos in the country, bilateral ties were negligible before 1986. The Canadian embassy in Manila had few contacts with Filipino "peoples' organizations" except for the links it cultivated with the Roman Catholic Church, a leader in the resistance to Marcos. The Philippines was listed under the old aid eligibility framework as a category 2, middle-income recipient, eligible for "selective" official development aid. Consequently, Canada's development aid was minimal, and it was wound down during the later stages of the Marcos era.

With the emergence of a democratic government in the Philippines in February 1986, conditions were ripe for a renewal and expansion of Canadian development aid. Interest was rekindled when Senator Alasdair Graham participated in an international group of observers monitoring the 1986 election. He presented evidence to the Canadian Parliament that the elections were fraudulent. Then, in April 1986, Progressive Conservative MP Jim Edwards visited the island of Negros, and on his return to Canada he addressed Parliament in glowing terms about the redemocratization process. In June 1986, External Affairs Minister Joe Clark was in Manila at a meeting of Western "dialogue partners" to the ASEAN group. He spent four days in the country, met President Aquino, visited Negros, where he met the provincial governor Daniel Lacson, and returned to Ottawa convinced that Canada should support the fledgling democracy. Development aid was to be the cornerstone of Canadian support, and Clark gave CIDA just ninety days to plan and start an aid program.[45]

Canada's aid strategy includes a country's human rights record and its "commitment to involving its population in the development process" among the criteria used to determine eligibility and establish confidential five-year planning figures.[46] The Philippines in 1986 scored high on both counts. Moreover, the Aquino administration's constitutional commitment to strengthen the "peoples' organizations" that emerged at the end of the Marcos era was promoted as a pillar of the new national development plan.[47] These tangible signs, along with the redemocratization underway, were necessary and sufficient to elevate the Philippines to a "core country" aid recipient.[48] In the language of the Winegard Report, the Philippines could now be placed in "the 'human rights positive category'... in which there has been a marked and sustained improvement in the human rights situation and the development orientation of the government." The report argued that aid in such cases "might be increased selectively in order to strengthen these positive directions."[49]

CIDA organized a planning mission to the Philippines in September 1986 and met with a spectrum of government agencies and peoples' organizations. Representatives of Canadian NGOs were also present. On 10 September 1986, President Aquino signed a Memorandum of Understanding for the Negros Rehabilitation and Development Fund and the Philippine Immunization Programme. On 20 October 1986, External Relations Minister Monique Landry pledged $100 million to the Philippines over the next five years. CIDA's interim strategy was released in November 1986. Canada subsequently joined a subcommittee of the World Bank's consultative group for aid donors to the Philippines, thereby opening the door to potential diplomatic influence.[50]

CIDA opted for an equal split between "immediate action" relief programs and longer-term bilateral support. The latter would include commodity assistance and other forms of balance-of-payments support, as well as a sectoral planning strategy to help overcome structural obstacles to economic growth. The agency also called for a country program review in 1988–89. While balance-of-payments support was initially part of the program, small-scale projects for community development, health, food, and fisheries were also important. NGOs received approximately one-third of CIDA funds between 1986 and 1989, and according to the 1989 country program review, in that year 65 per cent was government-to-government aid and 35 per cent was NGO aid.[51]

Because the Aquino government emphasized a decentralized, participatory approach to national development, CIDA was anxious from the outset to tap the Filipino NGO sector, recognizing the role these groups could play. The interim strategy conceded, however, that CIDA's knowledge of these groups "tend[ed] to be concentrated on the moderate or centrist NGOs. [It had] little direct experience in dealing with more leftist-oriented NGOs."[52] An NGO-driven aid program was a major departure for CIDA and posed two difficult hurdles. First, the usual tying constraints could not be applied to projects that were likely to be small scale, labour intensive, and administratively time-consuming. Second, personnel constraints meant that CIDA might have to delegate considerable responsibility to NGOs. One way around this potential loss of control was to develop direct links between CIDA and Filipino NGOs, effectively bypassing Canadian NGOs. This became an enduring irritant in CIDA's subsequent dealings with Canadian NGOs. The bypass strategy backfired badly. It strained relations between NGOs and CIDA and then isolated the agency when the media focused on what it described as another CIDA development disaster – this time on the island of Negros.

The island of Negros is a microcosm of the social and economic issues fuelling Filipino politics. Sugar is the traditional mainstay of the economy, with up to 90 per cent of the 2.3 million population in some way dependent on the crop. A quasi-feudal system of land tenure and production has entrenched a hacienda system, concentrating land and wealth among a small stratum of planters and dispossessing landless sugar workers. The Negros sugar economy was devastated when international sugar prices collapsed in the mid-1980s. The planters then began to diversify into non-labour-intensive agriculture, such as prawn farming, leaving the landless sugar workers to face mass unemployment and famine. The sugar workers, in turn, began to occupy the land abandoned by the planters.

A UNICEF relief operation attempted to combat malnutrition among women and children, and it was as part of this relief effort that CIDA began its involvement in Negros. But CIDA soon expanded its work there into a full-blown program designed to provide immediate poverty alleviation and longer-term self-reliant development. The agency wanted to respond, above all, to the needs of the poorest by helping sugar workers and peasants develop alternative forms of production and income generation. What emerged was the Negros Rehabilitation and Development Fund (NRDF). The fund was portrayed as an "innovative" and "transformational" strategy to reduce socio-economic disparities,[53] but CIDA's intervention in Negros was undermined by a number of unacknowledged constraints. These included (1) acute pressure to design a program within ninety days; (2) disbursement pressures and worries about the absorptive capacity of local NGOs; (3) a naive and flawed reading of local politics and socio-economic structures; and (4) a need to appear apolitical while (5) working with the provincial government.

Add to this bad timing. As Canada began its intervention, conditions on Negros suddenly changed. The planters had been prepared to accept Governor Lacson's "60-30-10" land reform program. Under this plan, 60 per cent of sugar-cane land was to be retained by the planters, 30 per cent was for crop diversification, and 10 per cent was to go to plantation workers and the unemployed.[54] But then sugar prices rose. Smelling new profits, the planters were no longer interested in giving out small portions of their haciendas to landless sugar workers. Island politics quickly polarized again. The private armies resurfaced, and Negros entered a new phase of confrontation between the landed elite and the insurgents. The Canadian fund's links with the landed elite could not have been made at a worse time.

Such rapid political change had not been factored into CIDA's thinking, and critics claim that its development model only deepened the feudal structures and entrenched dependency, instead of expanding participation, self-reliance, and empowerment.[55] There is substance to some of these criticisms. The NRDF targeted five types of projects: agricultural diversification and support services in non-sugar cash crops; agro-forestry; microenterprises to generate cottage-based income; agro-industries; and human resource development – organizing, training, and managing the NRDF projects. CIDA created a review committee to oversee the NRDF and quickly developed projects in cooperation with local NGOs and the provincial government. These projects included toy assembly, credit for sugar workers, and agricultural diversification. The target groups were displaced sugar workers, subsistence fisherfolk, and the urban poor.

Critics allege that CIDA was misguided in its choice of local NGOS – that these so-called "centrist" groups were led by planters and businessmen who were committed to maintaining the status quo. Eduardo Locsin, for example, acted as review committee chairman while also heading the Chito Foundation, which participated in the NRDF. In 1987 the Chito Foundation was reprimanded by the Ford Foundation for its paternalistic and authoritarian dealings with peasants.[56] CIDA appeared content to take on faith Governor Lacson's advice on which groups to include in the NRDF. This favoured some dubious groups on the right and excluded "peoples' organizations" on the left. Neither the review committee nor the NRDF could be considered "representative," since no legal-left organizations, not even the National Federation of Sugar Workers, part of the NRDF consultation process. The principal financial beneficiaries of the NRDF were planter organizations and state agencies.[57] Thus, by design or default, CIDA could be accused of taking sides in the reawakened conflict on Negros.

Bitter resentment was also generated by CIDA's toy-assembly project, which subjected employees to top-down management structures set by planters and business people and which offered no avenues for participation in decision making.[58] Moreover, the project's export focus continued the workers' dependence on foreign markets. CIDA projects that perpetuated the status quo were sharply contrasted with the initiatives of Filipino "peoples' organizations," which tried to promote local self-reliance in projects that encouraged participation by the target population, collective land ownership, and independence from foreign markets. There were, in effect, two diametrically opposed development models at work on Negros.

Caesar Espiritu and Clarence Dias have captured the essence of these two models in their study of a Philippine development project. The conservative model is a welfare system that tends "to see the 'poor' divorced from social reality ... as a target group whose poverty is a quantifiable deficiency ... Implementing agencies become institutions of the state, itself – a tendency which is attractive to consultants and donor agencies alike. Participation in decisions tends to be additional and optional." By contrast, the radical model attempts to tackle the structural causes of poverty by altering relations of production and property rights. Because the poor are in a contractually weak position, the radical strategy tries to reorganize production. This may require less emphasis on commodities and cash crops, and more attention to producing goods for local consumption. "The *vital* point is that the poor must participate in production decisions." Not surprisingly, the radical model "runs the risk of being ... unacceptable to the international aid agencies and national governments."[59] CIDA's preference for integrating the NRDF into Governor Lacson's "mini-Taiwan" export model translated into a conservative development strategy which, from a human rights perspective, added little to the participation rights of the poor islanders.

Sustained criticism of the NRDF by Canadian and Filipino groups, coupled with adverse media attention, prompted CIDA to reappraise its role in the Philippines.[60] First, the NRDF review committee was "opened up" in an effort to make it more representative. This strategy proved only partly effective. Three members representing planter foundations resigned and were replaced by church and "nonpopular" NGO representatives. Some thought was given to involving the NRDF in land reform activities on foreclosed and public lands – that is, going beyond Governor Lacson's 60–30–10 formula. CIDA partially reversed an October 1987 assessment by its Asia vice-president that the National Federation of Sugar Workers should be excluded from the steering committee to avoid "mass resignations." The union was invited, and it attended some committee meetings but subsequently left. Similarly, Bishop Fortich of the Negros Catholic Church, an outspoken defender of workers' rights, was invited to join the NRDF steering committee, but he too declined, saying that the "mechanism" needed improvement.[61]

Second, CIDA recognized the need for closer collaboration with Canadian and Filipino NGOs. It sponsored two annual "consultations" and encouraged a Canadian NGO umbrella group to act as a mediator.[62] Third, CIDA audited an NRDF project that was alleged to have misused funds, and it investigated allegations that money from the NRDF might have been indirectly supporting vigilante organizations. In public, CIDA denied both allegations.[63] This was disingenuous. In fact, the vigilante issue prompted a still-secret "in-house" review of the NRDF from a human rights perspective. One finding of that study was that members of a right-wing planter "foundation" on the NRDF planning committee had attended a Philippine military-sponsored "seminar" on counterinsurgency techniques.[64] CIDA's subsequent decision to remove the foundation from the NRDF was a tacit acknowledgment that the planter foundation was linked to – or at least that it endorsed – vigilantism.[65] Finally, the NRDF's problems prompted CIDA to speed up decentralization to the field, and the Philippines became the first country program to implement a major recommendation of the Winegard Report.[66] But most telling of all these changes was the fact that CIDA wound down its intervention in Negros and no new funds were allocated to the NRDF.

Notwithstanding its claim that "Canada deplores the continuing cycle of violence and attendant human rights abuses in the Philippines,"[67] the government resisted more assertive policies to signal its concern. While Canada, on one occasion, supported a resolution of the U.N. Commission on Human Rights that was critical of the Aquino government's performance, the foreign policy elite was not prepared to shift the diplomatic centre of gravity from multilateral to bilateral or from quiet to public diplomacy. In particular, the policy makers did not consider any form of aid conditionality that would have established "a specific punitive linkage" between aid and human rights performance.[68] The aid program, central to Canada's bilateral relations with the Philippines, cannot seriously be considered to "have made human rights an area of top priority."[69] Little imagination was used in developing "proactive" projects to strengthen human rights in the country.

Human rights factored into the aid program only in the context of eligibility, not in the specifics of planning and implementation. Rights issues were addressed more by default than by design in the poverty alleviation and human resource development projects, which are aid program priorities. There is little evidence that CIDA tried "to channel all existing and new aid projects through a policy filter to determine whether they contribute positively to the observance of human rights or whether, instead, they foster human rights violations."[70] Indeed, on Negros, CIDA may have retarded rather than advanced the social and economic rights of the poorest. The findings of the "in-house" study strengthen the view that elemental and dangerously compromising mistakes were made. That CIDA may have supported planter organizations connected to the counterinsurgency effort invites the suspicion, whether warranted or not, that on Negros, Canada's aid program was complementing the "hearts and minds" campaign of US AID, a policy that included using humanitarian relief to fight the communist insurgency.

Some lessons have been learned, and the NGO communities in Canada and the Philippines were crucial in nurturing a more sophisticated CIDA assessment of Filipino politics. CIDA is to be commended for forging a closer "partnership" with Canadian and Filipino NGOs, for reorienting the program towards greater NGO aid delivery, and for acknowledging at least some of the flaws in the Negros program. The agency continues to operate in difficult political circumstances and throughout the Aquino administration it was likely to be criticized whichever groups it supported. Political neutrality is a fiction in the polarized setting of the Philippines; and as a government agency, CIDA is severely limited in the extent to which it can support legal-left groups.

DUTCH AID: TAKING RISKS AND FACING CRITICISM

Democracy ... helps citizens to break out of the lethargy of a poverty-ridden destiny and to find a voice in our future. It helps in fighting terrorism and human rights violations. It helps people to come into their own, to live in dignity. Democracy also raises expectations which must be met ... [It] means more than just casting a vote.[71]

The Dutch, like the Canadians and other Western donors, responded to the global democratic tide by singling out the Philippines and five Central American states for aid aimed at "anchoring democracy through rapid improvements in the socio-economic conditions of their citizens."[72] Compared with Canada, the Netherlands was more circumspect on aid eligibility, more outspoken on human rights, and more willing to support human rights groups, but it was similar in its style of socio-economic projects and its choice of Philippine NGO partners. The eligibility framework for Dutch aid has three tiers: countries of concentration, "sector countries," and regional programs such as Central America. This hierarchy reflects different levels of intervention, planning, and financing. Countries of concentration thus receive a large amount of funding and comprehensive planning. In sector countries, Dutch aid is carefully targeted for specific purposes, such as infrastructure or rural development. In regional countries, funding is modest and planning is more ad hoc.

In contrast to the Canadian approach, the Dutch established a sector-country focus in the Philippines. This status reflects prudence, not lack of interest. Like Canada, the Netherlands had a limited knowledge of and presence in the Philippines during the Marcos era. Commercial links were modest, there was no government-to-government aid, and development work was left to missionaries and to NGOs such as the Netherlands Organization for International Development Cooperation (NOVIB) and ICCO (a church organization). These shallow roots were thought to be too precarious a foundation for a major aid concentration.[73] Aid commitments for 1988 amounted to over 57 million guilders, of which 17 million was disbursed through Dutch NGOs.[74] The sector focus has permitted the Dutch to single out specific but limited areas of concentration. These are rural development, population control, and community development. The Dutch have also played a role in the Philippine government's Comprehensive Agrarian Reform Program. Although not buying land or compensating landowners, the Dutch have developed "support service" projects for small farmers and landless peasants.

Dutch aid is guided by the principle of integration with the priorities of the Philippine National Economic Development Authority. The Aquino administration insisted that NGO initiatives be "woven around programs designated by the government, itself."[75] This amounted, in effect, to a system of "chartering" and monitoring NGOs, and it has had two worrisome consequences. First, the autonomy of Philippine NGOs is potentially eroded. Second, left-leaning organizations may be prevented from using Dutch funds; or, where the door remains open, the NGOs may themselves be ambivalent – attracted by the prospect of funding but repelled by the danger of government surveillance. Either way, a program aimed at altering entrenched inequality may be constrained if popular movements and the organizations of the poorest are excluded from Dutch aid projects.

The Dutch differ somewhat from most donors on human rights. While conditionality was not a serious option during the Aquino era, and while there was no structured mechanism to raise human rights abuses in the aid dialogue, the Dutch were a little more willing to question the Aquino government's record than Canada was, despite Canada's professed "critical collaboration." Bilateral relations suffered as a result. The strain can be examined along three fault lines: the presence of NPA and NDF elements in Holland; the Dutch government's occasional, mild but public criticism of the Aquino administration's human rights record; and the direct support of human rights groups in the Philippines.

During the Marcos era, the Netherlands became a sanctuary for some leading members of the Philippine communist movement. After Aquino came to power, several more sought political asylum, including Jose Maria Sison, a founder of the Philippine Communist Party.[76] These Filipino exiles have been at the heart of an "information service" called the Filipijnen groep, based in Utrecht.[77] The Philippines government, both during the Marcos period and under President Aquino, consistently viewed the *groep* as a communist front engaged in "subversive" activities prejudicial to national security. This led to diplomatic protests. The Dutch government stood its ground, arguing that under its domestic laws, the Filipijnen groep was a legitimate citizens' association. So long as Filipino political refugees abide by Dutch civil law, the Netherlands is not prepared to consider extradition.[78] The Dutch asked the Aquino administration to prove that the Utrecht group was subversive, but no proof was forthcoming.

The Dutch protested the human rights violations in the Philippines, but only among their donor partners in the aid consortium led by the World Bank. At the July 1989 aid consortium meeting in Tokyo, the Dutch representative stated that although the Philippines government faced "extraordinary circumstances," the Aquino administration should safeguard fundamental human rights. In the Dutch view, respect for human rights was imperative given the "extraordinary circumstances" – structural poverty and insurgency – facing the government.[79] This carefully worded criticism was a far cry from overt or even implicit threats of human rights conditionality. Nevertheless, it stood in contrast to the position of other donors at Tokyo, including Canada and the United States, and to the traditionally nonpolitical nature of such forums.

The most innovative and risky aspect of the Netherlands' intervention in the Philippines was its financial support of human rights organizations. For several years, a small pool of money, roughly 12 to 14 million guilders per year, has been available from the ODA program for human rights support. Called the Aarts Fund after the MP who pushed for its inception, it is officially designated for the support of victims of human rights violations and for emergency humanitarian assistance. However, its mandate is broadly interpreted, and in the Philippines the fund was used for more proactive human rights work. Aid to human rights monitors and advocates is a politically sensitive issue for any aid donor. Recipient governments fragmented by armed conflict will interpret such interventions as unwarranted interference and a breach of sovereignty. Channelling official development assistance through rich country NGOs who then link up with Third World rights groups is one way around this problem. In theory, indirect help allows the donor to promote human rights while avoiding criticism from a recipient government.

In practice, the Dutch have not escaped censure. Since 1986, Aarts Fund assistance has been channelled via two of the four main Dutch NGO groups: NOVIB, a secular group, and ICCO, a Protestant Church organization. Under the terms of a co-financing arrangement between the Dutch Ministry of Development Cooperation and the NGO community, Dutch NGOs are free to choose their Third World partners and design their own projects. About 15 million guilders a year in Dutch aid is sent to Philippines NGOs through the Dutch co-financing agencies. Official evaluations are normally post hoc. This hands-off approach allows funds to be disbursed quickly, an important consideration in helping the victims of violations. But there are exceptions. Should a Dutch NGO seek funds for a group which the Dutch government considers politically controversial, the government may try to block the initiative. Under the terms of the co-financing arrangement, the NGOs may then invoke a so-called doubt paragraph. This formalizes the divergence of opinion between government and NGO, but in theory it allows the NGO to go ahead with a proposed project. If the government is still opposed, it may ask the NGO for a detailed proposal. If all else fails, the matter can be referred to the Netherlands parliament, whose decision is final and binding. In practice, the Netherlands' consensus-building political culture makes such formal mechanisms unnecessary. Informal exchanges normally lead to a timely withdrawal of a controversial proposal.

In the Philippines, the Aarts Fund has been used to support four human rights organizations. Two of them, the Free Legal Aid Group (FLAG) and the Philippine Alliance of Human Rights Advocates (PAHRA), provide legal services for the victims of human rights violations. Two others, the Ecumenical Movement for Justice and Peace (EMJP) and the Task Force for Detainees of the Philippines (TFD), monitor human rights violations.[80] All four emerged during the Marcos era and played a valuable role in documenting abuses and seeking legal redress. At the outset of the Aquino era, the four groups enjoyed popular and official support, but the support soon evaporated. With the spread of counterinsurgency and vigilantism, human rights groups were increasingly labelled communist sympathizers and were themselves victims of political violence. The EMJP, the TFD, and FLAG had a number of their staff killed or tortured. Such circumstances might be considered grounds for redoubling Dutch support of these groups, but the issue was more complex than it seems.

The Dutch embassy in Manila received several protests from the Philippines government about its aid to the EMJP and TFD. The government criticized both groups for their alleged support of the insurgents. It accused them of being "infiltrated" by communists and no longer being impartial monitors. While officially the Dutch demanded incontrovertible proof, privately the allegations led to a reconsideration of future Aarts Fund support for the two groups. This in turn produced rifts between Dutch NGOs and the government and, within the government, between development aid officials and foreign affairs officials.[81] The Dutch equivocated on the TFD. The political wing of the foreign ministry argued that the group was overly concerned with "consciousness raising" and stressed that monitoring groups should be impartial and objective if they were to be credible. The TFD's refusal to investigate the alleged massacres on Mindanao by the New Peoples' Army compromised its credibility. Even so, Aarts Fund officials seemed even more prepared to continue funding the TFD, pointing to the courage of all such groups when their own personnel are the victims of political violence.

NOVIB, which had supported human rights work in the Philippines since 1976, wanted to support the TFD through private funds if Dutch ODA support ended. But it, too, had concerns about the TFD's credibility. It therefore asked an independent legal expert, Jose Zalaquett, to investigate the EMJP and the TFD. Zalaquett's report noted that the TFD applied restrictive reasoning for the noninvestigation of communist violations. The TFD maintained that the international human rights covenants regarded the protection of human rights as state business. Consequently, where rights were not protected, *strictu senso*, the state alone was responsible. As Zalaquett pointed out, while this claim was technically sound, in the Philippines' internal conflict such reasoning was unduly restrictive and compromised the TFD's claim to impartiality.[82] NOVIB then tried to persuade the TFD to agree on a more comprehensive and objective reporting system. It took until 1990, nearly four years into the Aquino administration, for the Dutch to evaluate their program and develop a future ODA strategy.

This tardiness is reflected in the mixed signals the aid program conveys. Striving for the closer integration of Philippines NGO partners with municipal and provincial governments is consistent with the objectives of the Philippine National Economic Development Authority. But this focus may inhibit the participation of most left-leaning groups and skew the development profile by creating projects managed by, or in the name of, landed and commercial interests. If this is the case, objectives such as "self-reliance," "empowerment," and "transformation" will have little place in Dutch aid projects. Moreover, support services and technical training for the government's discredited land-reform program are not in keeping with the aims of the main peasant organizations and agrarian trade unions representing the poorest, most disadvantaged communities.

But Dutch funding of some Filipino "peoples' organizations" may be unwise without close scrutiny of these organizations' attitudes to political violence. Two examples underline the need to assess this issue carefully. A "progressive" Dutch trade union, the Federatie Nederlandse Vakbeweging (FNV), had for several years extended financial aid to the Kilusang Mayo Uno (KMU),[83] a leading leftist Philippines peasant organization. Shortly after the Tiananmen Square massacre, the FNV was "shocked and deeply surprised" to learn that the KMU had tacitly condoned the Chinese government's brutal solution to dissent. The union's president, J. Stekelenburg, promptly severed contact with the KMU and suspended financial support. In a letter to the KMU chairman, Crispin Beltram, Stekelenberg wrote: "You gave us the strong impression that you justify all actions taken by the Chinese government and that you only condemn very clearly the negative and shocked reactions ... pleading for stopping the violence. It is clear that you consider those reactions as an unacceptable interference in internal affairs. This position ... is in direct conflict with the fundamental conception of the FNV concerning universal human and trade union rights and also with our opinion on the right to undertake actions for more democracy and our respect for human dignity."[84]

ICCO, one of the four Dutch co-financing agencies, also has supported legal-left groups such as the KMU. But like NOVIB, it has had
to reassess its support of groups that appeared to condone political
violence by the Communist Party and NPA while condemning state
abuses of human rights. However, ICCO and the Dutch Foreign Ministry's evaluation of Philippines "counterpart" organizations may have
inadequately examined the objectives of these groups and the way
Dutch aid funds were being used. A Dutch academic, Willem Wolters,
left the evaluation team because he felt that ICCO and the Netherlands
director general for development cooperation were colluding in a
cover-up. His own investigations pointed to strong political links
between "upperground" legal-left groups and the Communist Party
and NPA. He also suspected that aid funds were being funnelled to the
insurgents. In short, Wolters alleged that "mystification, not evaluation, was from the very beginning the purpose of this mission."[85]

The Dutch have been willing to speak out and face criticism on
rights abuses in the Philippines while closely supporting the Philippines
government's development plans that now include closer state supervision of local NGOs. The two limbs of Dutch policy – aid and human
rights – thus seem at odds with each other rather than being integrated
into a clear policy of strengthening democratization. Human rights
groups indirectly supported by ODA are now labelled as leftist –
precisely the sort of NGOs that Dutch socio-economic projects are
unlikely to embrace. In short, the Dutch are clear that as a "young
democracy" the Philippines must be supported. But they have yet to
develop a consistent and explicit statement about which sectors of
society and what kind of development they wish to support in the
Philippines.

CONCLUSION

Most societies are at some level divided societies. Democracy's virtue
is that it is "a way of ruling in divided societies without undue violence,
[and the] hallmark of free government everywhere ... is whether ...
opposition is tolerated."[86] On both measures, the post-Marcos Philippines has some distance to travel along the democratic path. The
consolidation of Philippines democracy will require an end to the cycle
of insurgency and counterinsurgency, vigilantism, and human rights
abuses. Civilian control must be reasserted over the military, and the
government must work to sever the structural roots of poverty and
landlessness.

Four years into the Aquino government, there was little basis for
optimism on many of these fronts. The democratic transition seemed

suspended between two opposed models of governance – an elite-based democracy and a people-power participatory democracy. Civil liberties, although constitutionally guaranteed, provided no protection for members of the legal left, who were routinely murdered, tortured, and arrested. Land hunger remained an explosive issue. But a thorough redistribution seemed no option for a centrist government. Landlessness and rights abuses thus continued to be potent sources of discontent. And on the right, lumpen elements were easily absorbed into the AFP's dirty war. The military, a divided institution and a threat to the future of democratic governance, played an ever-larger role in domestic politics.

Canada and the Netherlands stepped into this fluid setting to help stabilize the Aquino government and consolidate democratic processes. As small donors, they will have little impact on shaping the macro-environment with their aid programs. Their intervention may, nevertheless, help point the way to a more adequate donor role in conflict situations. A summary assessment is premature, but some initial insights are compelling.

First, aid is rarely neutral during protracted armed conflict. Eventually, governments must deal with governments. Shifting the aid focus in an NGO direction does not solve this problem; it merely transfers it to another setting. CIDA, to its credit, has tried with mixed success to cover the middle ground by supporting groups across the political spectrum. It took stock of its development debacle on Negros and relaxed control on the NGO delivery channels, which subsequently accounted for 35 per cent of bilateral ODA. Mutual suspicion and hostility have given way to greater transparency and cooperation.[87] The Dutch seem set to follow the Canadian lead in developing "partnerships" with the NGOs. However, their readiness also to work closely with provincial governments may diminish the effectiveness of their grass-roots projects by compromising the autonomy of many Philippines NGOs.

Finding a middle way in a politically polarized country is an unenviable challenge. Broadening the spectrum of the civil society that a donor works with might help build a more equitable presence, but it is a process fraught with danger. The key factor here is an organization's attitude to political violence. This case study underlines the danger of blindly supporting groups – at either political pole – which condone violence. The TFD's unwillingness to investigate NPA abuses is a tacit tolerance of violence. The Dutch trade union's "shock" at discovering the KMU's position on the Tiananmen Square massacre led to the suspension of all financial support. ICCO belatedly suspended aid to the KMU, although both NOVIB and ICCO were reluctant to concede that legal-left groups might have political links with the NPA. And there was concern that the Netherlands government and Dutch NGOs had possibly colluded to deny that Dutch-aided legal-left groups had in fact been infiltrated. CIDA's discovery that a planter foundation connected to the NRDF was also sending personnel to counterinsurgency seminars compromised the agency's credibility and led to the foundation's removal from the NRDF.

The second point to be noted is that both donors appear to have been wedded to a technical conception of poverty alleviation instead of a more openly transformational development strategy. Is it reasonable to expect more? If they had funded organizations such as BAYAN and the National Federation of Sugar Workers, which are closely linked to the NDF, this would likely have strained bilateral relations with the Aquino government, for both unions actively support economic destabilization tactics that come perilously close to condoning political violence.[88] Third, each donor may have been too eager to support the fledgling democracy and too easily swayed by Aquino's personality and popularity. Canada's rush to develop a program on Negros was a costly error. The pressure to disburse funds left CIDA open to manipulation by sophisticated, politically suspect planter groups, who were skilled at exploiting the sudden influx of Western aid funds. Fourth, democratization and human rights are supposed to be two sides of a single coin, each reinforcing the other. In the Philippines, democracy remains fragile and human rights have deteriorated. This poses a problem for aid donors – how to adapt to a worsening human rights picture while keeping one's sights fixed on long-term support for the Philippine government and for democratic development.

Fifth, although the Dutch have spoken out and taken risks in support of human rights groups, neither the Netherlands nor Canada is prepared to condition future aid on an improved human rights record, and neither has consciously integrated human rights into the planning and implementation of poverty-alleviation projects. Empowerment should be the basis for any grass-roots project. The lessons of the NRDF may help this principle take root in other Canadian projects. Sixth, despite efforts to hear no evil and see no evil, human rights questions have intruded into the technical problems of planning aid projects. CIDA claims that it "does not program human rights; it is an eligibility question."[89] This is naive, perhaps even irresponsible. Donors know full well that in an armed conflict, local project workers are at risk from political violence. By 1989, the security of NOVIB aid workers had become so precarious that the Dutch NGO had abandoned its projects in the Cordillera region of Luzon and was thinking of doing the same on Mindanao.[90]

Canada's unwillingness to support human rights groups or to protest violations threatens to undo the modest achievement of embracing legal-left groups. In the Philippines, such cause-oriented groups are the main targets of vigilante death squads. If Canada intends to work with these groups, it must be willing to protest when their staff are in danger. Meanwhile, the NGOs have taken action. A steering committee of the CIDA-funded Philippine-Canada Human Resources Development program has set up a "crisis response" system to deal with safety questions and potential human rights abuses. There has already been occasion to use the system.[91]

Dutch and Canadian diplomacy broadly support my argument that states will only pursue an assertive human rights policy when the costs to other national interests are low. Set in the light of the "instruments hierarchy," Canadian diplomacy has been unassertive. Canada refused steadfastly to undermine bilateral relations or to jeopardize commercial opportunities in the Philippines by speaking out on human rights. The only exception was the co-sponsorship at the U.N. Commission on Human Rights, in 1987, of a resolution critical of the Aquino government's human rights, but this was an unassertive lever. Although Canada is committed to sustaining the Philippines' fragile democracy, it is some distance from building a proactive human rights support program. In the early 1990s, in an effort to stimulate Canadian investment in the Philippines, Prime Minister Mulroney publicly praised President Aquino's achievements and defended her human rights record.

In contrast, Dutch statecraft has been moderately assertive. The Dutch have raised human rights questions with the international financial institutions, have refused to bow to Philippines protests about alleged "subversive elements" among Filipino exiles in Holland, and have given indirect support to human rights groups, despite growing misgivings about the links such groups have with the communist insurgents. These actions have cost the Netherlands by souring bilateral relations, but there is no evidence of retaliation by the Philippine government.

The differences between Holland and Canada should not be overdrawn. Indeed, by the late 1980s they appeared to be converging in their approaches – the Dutch by rethinking how to support human rights groups, and the Canadians by building closer links with the legal left (through dialogue if not through outright support). In the long run, each donor could profit from the best elements of the other's aid program – the Canadians by building a framework for direct human rights support while avoiding the pitfalls of the Dutch experience, and the Dutch by building a partnership or consultation mechanism without the problems of Canada's early experience with NGO-based aid delivery.

5 Principled Intervention: Norway, Canada, and the Sri Lankan Conflict

Once a focus of international interest for its stable polity and progressive welfare system, Sri Lanka today is a grim example of the resurgence of communal violence in many parts of the world. Closer now to Bosnia than to Costa Rica, Sri Lanka's democratic stability has been shaken by a cycle of ethnic violence that will shape its political course for several generations.

This case study poses several questions about Norwegian and Canadian diplomacy in Sri Lanka.[1] Is a consistent human rights policy possible? How should donors adapt their aid programs to rapid social and political change in recipient countries? Does criticism of a government's human rights record amount to taking sides in a complex ethnic conflict? Will an assertive human rights policy unduly damage bilateral relations? How effective was Canadian and Norwegian human rights statecraft? The study underlines the conundrums that policy makers face when human rights confront the norms of non-intervention and state sovereignty. It also helps answer theoretical questions, such as the relationship between assertive human rights diplomacy and competing national interests, the impact of alliance membership, and the influence of domestic interests.

PARADISE LOST: FROM MODEL DEMOCRACY TO POLITICAL DECAY

The intractability of Sri Lanka's ethnic conflict is politically focused on the substance and scope of power devolution and on the failure to find a formula for devolution that is acceptable to all parties. Democratic governance has given way to political decay, ethnic violence, and civil war. Some welfare programs were cut back as defence spending increased – by 60 per cent in 1986 and by another 50 per cent in 1987. The World Bank estimated the costs of the conflict at US$1.8 billion by 1987. Sri Lanka has joined the list of Third World protracted social conflicts that are resistant to durable solution and susceptible to periodic phases of violent confrontation. What went wrong?

Alleged discrimination against the Tamil minority by Sinhalese-dominated governments is a key element in the conflict. The impetus for state-sponsored discrimination was a combustible mix of Sinhalese chauvinism, competition for jobs, and population pressures. It took six main forms: discrimination in jobs, language, education, economic development, land, and, for some Tamils, citizenship rights.[2]

DOCUMENTING THE HUMAN RIGHTS RECORD

Human rights abuses are the most visible manifestation of conflict.[3] All the armed actors – state, non-state, and external (India) – have committed atrocities in a spiral of terror perhaps unequalled anywhere. The toll of political violence may have reached 12,500 deaths between 1983 and 1988. The barbarity became, if anything, more acute at the end of the 1980s, leading one observer to speak of Sri Lanka's descent into "political cannibalism." Human rights lawyers have been victimized, and since at least 1987 local aid projects and development workers have been sporadically targeted. These developments add to the climate of insecurity surrounding donor aid projects in Sri Lanka. Dozens of human rights missions and the weight of the principal human rights bodies point, at a minimum, to government complicity or toleration of rights abuses by the security forces. This assessment must, however, be tempered by the recognition that Sri Lanka faces a national emergency threatening the survival of a democratic state and that radical Tamil and Sinhalese groups have used terror and violence with impunity. A closer examination of core rights and the rule of law in Sri Lanka during the 1980s is given below.

Core Rights

Abuses of core rights, notably freedom from extrajudicial killing, from arbitrary arrest, and from torture, intensified as the conflict spread over much of the island after the arrival of the Indian Peacekeeping Force in 1987 and the onset of violence by the Tamil militants in the south. Political violence during this period was characterized by indiscriminate "revenge killings" by both militants and security forces. Consistent with a drift from a "worsening" to a "negative" human rights pattern, the killings increasingly affected civilians as well as combatants, politicians, and administrators. A favoured technique of the Tamil militants was the so-called lamp-post murder, whereby victims were strung up on the roadside as graphic reminders of the price of collaboration. For their part, the security forces favoured beatings. Men's buttocks, soles, and spines were beaten, and the victims were then hung by their feet over a chilli fire. Women were raped, some having had police batons forced into their vaginas.

Rule of Law

A decade of political violence would in most countries be ample proof that the rule of law was defunct. While the president guardian's misuse of the emergency regulations eroded the legal system's ability to protect fundamental liberties, as late as 1987 the Nordic human rights yearbook could still claim that "the independence of the judiciary is not seriously affected by the concentration of executive powers." Even though many high court judges were political appointments, several Supreme Court decisions went against the government. Nevertheless, several provisions of the Prevention of Terrorism Act (PTA) went well beyond common emergency regulations. These included retroactive culpability and denial of due process, such as access to lawyers, contact with family, and presentation before a court within twenty-four hours of arrest. The security forces could hold the accused incommunicado for up to eighteen months, transport him or her to "any place" for interrogation, permit "confessions" given to high-ranking police officers as admissible evidence, and place on the accused the burden of proving that a confession was made under duress.

The extensive powers given to the security forces by the PTA – among the widest anywhere – left them room to commit torture with impunity. These sweeping powers were subsequently enlarged to permit the security forces to dispose of dead bodies without an inquest. The security forces' immunity was strengthened in 1988 when the government passed an indemnity bill prohibiting the trial of security personnel for violent acts committed in "good faith" under the PTA. The bill was made retroactive to 1979, the year in which the PTA came into force.

EVALUATING THE HUMAN RIGHTS RECORD

There are three broad phases in Sri Lanka's human rights record. Phase one, from 1977 to 1983, is a "human rights worsening" pattern. It coincides with the 1977 anti-Tamil riots, the onset of sporadic but carefully orchestrated violence by Tamil militants, the 1979 PTA, and the 1981 anti-Tamil riots. Political legitimacy gradually declined, with many Tamils no longer willing to participate in democratic politics, and unconventional and violent politics emerging to distort the political process. Phase two, from July 1983 to October 1987, is a "human rights negative" pattern. It coincides with a shift from sporadic violence to virtual civil war. While much of the action remained confined to the north and east, it was punctuated by spells of violence in Colombo, the central tea districts, and elsewhere in the south. A clear pattern of gross and systematic human rights abuses emerged during this phase, and the principal conflict was between government security forces and Tamil militants. Phase three, from 1987 to 1989, was also a negative pattern, marked by escalating violence (which was now spread throughout the island), by the onset of two geographically separate military campaigns, and by extreme intra-ethnic conflict between the Liberation Tigers of Tamil Eelam and Indian-backed groups such as the Eelam People's Revolutionary Front, and between the government security forces and the Janatha Vimukthi Peramuna (JVP) in the south. Emergency regulations were further extended, paramilitary groups were more active, human rights lawyers and NGOs were no longer immune from violence, and a third (Muslim) ethnic front emerged in the eastern province. Violence in the electoral process and rejection of democratic politics by groups from both major ethnic communities underlined the collapse of political legitimacy. A pattern of egregious abuses and "political cannibalism" characterized this phase of the conflict.

Demarcating human rights abuses is only the first step in evaluation. The more difficult task is assessing the government's role in those abuses. There are at least five possible assessments. (1) guilt: the government deliberately used state terrorism against both Tamil militants and elements of the civilian population; (2) complicity: the government was indirectly culpable by tolerating abuses committed by its security forces; (3) innocence: the government cannot be criticized for rights abuses, given the long-standing state of emergency, the Tamil and JVP terror tactics, and the civil war conditions prevailing since 1983; (4) change: the government may share some responsibility for excesses committed between 1983 and 1987 but should be defended for its actions after 1987; (5) agnostic: all actors committed human rights abuses, and the complexity of the conflict precludes any decisive judgment. Each of these positions implies potentially different Western statecraft.

A close examination of the government's use of emergency legislation is the best way to frame the evaluation, because critics argue that misuse of these powers facilitated abuses by the security forces. The

PTA was made permanent in 1983. Article 4 of the U.N. Covenant on Civil and Political Rights, of which Sri Lanka is a signatory, permits the participating states to suspend many civil liberties "in time of public emergency which threatens the life of the nation." But this is immediately qualified by a provision stating that such actions should be proportional to the severity of the danger, that the international community must be notified, that certain inalienable rights must be safeguarded, and that the regulations must be applied without discrimination.[4] These qualifications are a safeguard against the misuse of emergency regulations.

In Sri Lanka, however, the PTA was kept on the books for long periods and created a climate in which nonderogable rights could be abused, and it weakened protection against arbitrary killings and disappearances by proscribing judicial supervision over the actions of the security forces. As Joan Hartman argues, "No derogation is legitimate unless it is clearly aimed in good faith at the preservation of democratic institutions and a return to their full operation at their earliest convenience." The indemnity bill and such added PTA provisions as the ability to burn bodies without an inquest appear to be cynical denials of judicial process and democratic traditions. Hartman's generic analysis of emergency regulations is telling when applied to Sri Lanka's drift towards authoritarian rule: "Experience has shown that the most widespread patterns of abuse develop in nations under a 'state of siege.' While realism demands concessions to imperilled nations to take extraordinary measures to preserve their democratic institutions against challenges, suspensions of fundamental rights all too often serve to strengthen autocratic rule rather than to forestall it."[5]

The corroboration of numerous human rights missions to Sri Lanka and the weight of the principal U.N. human rights bodies point, at a minimum, to the government's complicity or toleration of abuses committed in the early phases of the conflict. Equally, the state's misuse of emergency and indemnity laws shows a cynical disregard for due process that could imply complicity in a systematic pattern of gross human rights violations committed by security forces. Since 1989, most aid donors have grown more convinced of the state's direct role in human rights abuses.

PRINCIPLED INTERVENTION: THE ADAPTATION OF NORWEGIAN DEVELOPMENT AID TO SRI LANKA

Norway's reaction to the Sri Lankan conflict is a test case of donor adaptation to deepening human rights abuses. It was the first, and arguably the only, clear Norwegian example where human rights concerns directly influenced aid policy. Several conclusions emerge from this study. First, the premises underpinning Norway's aid to Sri Lanka began to alter almost from the outset, and Norway, like other donors, was caught unprepared to deal with the July 1983 riots and their aftermath. Second, domestic pressure from Tamil lobby groups and intense media attention prompted Norway to take a critical line, which the Sri Lankan government perceived as a biased, pro-Tamil policy. Third, shifting official development assistance (ODA) priorities towards human rights soured bilateral relations, but aid continued to flow. Fourth, as the communal discord deepened, Norway's central concern partly shifted from human rights conditionality to project viability and personnel security. Finally, individuals played a key role in crafting an assertive Norwegian policy, and the experience prompted a white paper on the relationship between human rights and development aid.

A BASIS FOR POLICY COHERENCE

Norway's statecraft in Sri Lanka is a rare instance of a small, affluent Western democracy forging a relatively coherent and ethically principled human rights policy. Special circumstances made this possible. Foreign aid is Norway's *raison d'être* in Sri Lanka. Prior to 1983, Norway enjoyed an excellent reputation for the quality and poverty orientation of its aid. Moreover, there were few of the conflicts of interest that routinely undermine a coherent and principled human rights statecraft. There was no legacy of colonial exploitation; economic and security interests were negligible; and there were no diplomatic complications such as membership in the Commonwealth. Norway could thus afford to privilege ethical concerns in its policies towards Sri Lanka. The only complication was a small but politically sophisticated Tamil community in Norway, which was important in galvanizing, and perhaps compromising, Norwegian diplomacy.

Norway had no significant diplomatic links with Sri Lanka until the mid-1970s. Sri Lanka asked Norway for development aid when much of the donor community was turning its back on Prime Minister Sirimavo Bandaranaike's socialist policies. By 1977 Sri Lanka was designated a "main partner country" of Norway. Sri Lanka's solid welfare tradition was a prime motive for getting involved. The focus on welfare resonated with Norway's social democracy and with the funding criterion that recipient governments must tackle poverty and social injustice. Bandaranaike's policies were judged to be "development-oriented and socially just for all parts of the population."[6]

Ironically, Norway's aid commitment in 1977 was swiftly followed by a change in government and different development priorities in Sri

Lanka. The incoming United National Party (UNP) government, backed by foreign aid donors, spearheaded economic reforms, a retreat from welfare, and the loss of workers' rights in free trade zones. It also made political changes that quickened the onset of state repression and ethnic conflict. The initial premises guiding Norway's decision were thus already compromised almost at the point of entry. But it was six years before these shifts were acknowledged publicly. The July 1983 riots finally compelled the Norwegian government to reassess the premises of its aid program in Sri Lanka. And it took another two years before the program began to register the impact of the changes.

Lacking expert knowledge of the country, the Storting (Norwegian parliament) and cabinet had been persuaded by uninformed but well-meaning NGOs that civil and political rights were still intact in Sri Lanka and that social welfare was a priority. In fact, public spending on welfare had decreased in 1974, and it continued to do so after the UNP government came to power. Once engaged, the Norwegians were reluctant to reconsider or to concede that their decision had been based on an embarrassingly inadequate knowledge of the country. Thus it was not until 1983 that the Norwegian Agency for Development Cooperation (NORAD) admitted that the UNP's policies were no longer in line with Norwegian criteria for selecting partner countries.[7]

At first, Norway took little notice of the signs of discrimination and ethnic conflict. The bulk of its aid consisted of balance-of-payments financing to the government and of integrated rural development projects in the south, with the Sinhalese as the principal beneficiaries. Before 1984, Norway was thus unwittingly lending its support to a discriminatory and increasingly autocratic government and was appearing to favour the dominant ethnic community. Its subsequent policy falls into two distinct phases, which correspond to shifts in the island's politics.

PHASE ONE: CRITICAL COLLABORATION, 1983–1987

The July 1983 riots galvanized Norway's Tamil community and prompted a public debate on aid to Sri Lanka. As late as November 1982, Svenn Stray, minister of foreign affairs, told the Storting that there was no reason for any multilateral or aid-related response to the treatment of Tamils. But the July riots introduced three new elements which no Western government could ignore. First, the gravity of the violence exceeded earlier outbreaks. Second, there were charges by international human rights groups and eyewitnesses that the government either was wilfully supporting the excesses committed by the security forces or was woefully negligent in preventing them. Third, Amnesty International alleged that Sri Lanka now showed a pattern of serious and consistent violations of human rights.

The Tamil community in Norway began a lobbying campaign to sensitize the public and pressure the government into punitive action against Sri Lanka. Several MPs then demanded that the Storting and the cabinet "consider whether aid to Sri Lanka was in accordance with the criteria for selecting development partners."[8] The parliament debated an appropriate response to the July riots and how to refashion Norway's aid program in Sri Lanka. Some Tamil groups demanded a complete suspension of ODA. So did the Socialist Left Party, which wanted to transfer the Sri Lanka funds to Nicaragua, where they would be put to better use in fighting poverty by an allegedly socially just government. But the governing Christian Peoples Party said "no" to an aid cut-off. Prime Minister Kare Willoch, applying well-worn logic, stated a fortnight after the riots: "Norwegian aid to Sri Lanka will continue. Any kind of abrupt cessation now will make problems even worse for the people we attempt to help."[9] Willoch neglected to mention that "the people" Norway was then helping were largely Sinhalese, not the Tamils who had borne the brunt of human rights abuses during the riots, and that the bulk of Norwegian aid was commodity assistance which directly benefited the government, not necessarily "the people."

In the end, a consensus emerged to maintain but gradually modify the aid program to reflect human rights considerations. Norway then embarked on a multi-track policy. Human rights were raised in high-level bilateral meetings between the two governments and in the aid dialogue. A diplomatic offensive was launched in U.N. human rights forums. Norway played a significant role in tilting the international community to a critical view of the Sri Lankan government's human rights record. Aid was retargeted to avoid complicity with a suspect Sri Lankan government. Finally, Norway consistently raised human rights concerns at the annual Sri Lanka Consultative Group meetings of aid donors.

Bilateral Diplomacy

Norway's development minister, Mr Brusletten, met Sri Lanka's minister of foreign affairs, Mr Hameed, in Geneva in August 1983 and again in Oslo in June 1984. Hameed promised publicly that Norwegian aid would contribute to national reconciliation through socioeconomic development in both communities.

A key player in Norway's early human rights statecraft was Odd Jostein Saeter. As state secretary for international development[10] at the Ministry of Foreign Affairs, Saeter used his experience as a former rights activist to prod a recalcitrant bureaucracy into a more assertive and critical position on human rights abuses.[11] Saeter's experience with Sri Lanka prompted a white paper that laid down guidelines to integrate human rights in Norwegian development aid.[12] In November 1983 Saeter led an ad hoc delegation to Sri Lanka. The mission was to examine the implications of the ethnic conflict for the aid program. The delegation met Foreign Minister Hameed and high-ranking officials in the Ministry of Finance. Saeter then met President Jayawardene. Such high-level contact on aid issues was unusual and marked the seriousness with which the Sri Lankan government was now taking Norwegian concerns.

Saeter conveyed a two-track message about the emerging conflict. On the one hand, he felt that the Sri Lankan government must take "substantial responsibility" for the July riots and the abuses accompanying and succeeding them. At the same time, he noted that although the events preceding the riots were the result of discriminatory state policies, only a small influential element within the UNP government – and not the whole administration – was culpable. He made it known that Norway supported the moderate elements of the UNP government, which "actively [sought] to promote reconciliation between the ethnic groups."

Saeter recalled that his meeting with President Jayawardene had a "special atmosphere" – a euphemism for a tense, hostile encounter. He raised the issue of human rights and the need for "active steps" towards reconciliation, but he made no overt linkage to ODA. Jayawardene responded with a brief, noncommittal statement that his government was "concerned" about reported abuses and was looking for a peaceful solution to the conflict. The president refused to go into specifics on human rights and was annoyed that a small distant country should raise (and even pass judgment on) "domestic" matters.

Shifting Aid Priorities

On his return to Norway, Saeter told the press, "We have achieved what we wanted. In the negotiations about future Norwegian development aid we made it a precondition that aid should reach the Tamils. This was accepted by the authorities in Sri Lanka. It proves that development aid can be used in the work of human rights."[13] Saeter then told NORAD to retarget ODA towards the Tamils. NORAD was sceptical of a complete tilt towards the Tamils, pointing out that it might have adverse effect on the aid relationship. A compromise was therefore achieved. NORAD suggested that a subtle human rights message could be conveyed by joining a World Bank/Dutch project to supply basic human needs to the Estate Tamils. This would help balance a heavily Sinhalese-focused program. NORAD also began to upgrade direct relief and rehabilitation to Tamil refugees. Neither initiative was likely to sour relations with the Sri Lanka government. By these actions, Saeter hoped to plant the seeds of a more balanced Norwegian policy, to reorient the program as a Norwegian "commentary" on the reasons for the conflict, and to reassure the Norwegian public. Saeter was not, however, willing to consider the more extreme demands of the Tamils in Norway to suspend ODA immediately or to develop projects exclusively in Tamil Tiger strongholds in the north of the island.

Four new components marked the adaptation of Norwegian aid after 1984. First, increased resources were given for the rehabilitation of the victims of ethnic disturbances. Second, NORAD joined poverty-alleviation projects for Estate Tamils, the island's most disadvantaged group. Third, NORAD began to channel more aid directly to Sri Lankan NGOs or via their Norwegian NGO counterparts. Fourth, direct government-to-government assistance by commodity aid and import support, which had accounted for 70–80 per cent of all Norwegian aid in 1982 and 1983, was reduced. This meant that total aid from Norway would drop over time. The decision on the modified aid program was approved by the cabinet and signed by Prime Minister Kare Willoch on 3 April 1985.

The Aid Dialogue

One result of Saeter's visit to Sri Lanka was the addition of human rights to the annual aid negotiations, to the country program review, and to Norway's interventions at the consultative group meetings. Managing this new-style dialogue was problematic for both sides at first. For NORAD, human rights conditionality was at odds with the principle of "recipient orientation" – a hands-off approach – as the ideal aid relationship. For the Sri Lankans, sustained Tamil lobbying, adverse media coverage, and critical reports from independent Norwegian researchers soured relations between the two countries.

There were also marked differences of opinion between the Ministry of Foreign Affairs and the Ministry of Development Cooperation on policy and on the institutional jurisdiction for human rights.[14] Foreign Minister Stray's decision to single out the Sri Lankan government as being partly responsible for abuses was made against the advice of senior foreign ministry officials, who were calling for a more even-handed policy. Two Norwegian actions further strained relations with the Sri Lankan government. In 1985 NORAD sponsored an independent report on the human rights performance of Norway's main aid-partner countries; and in 1986 the Ministry of Development Cooperation commissioned an independent five-year country-program review of NORAD aid programs in Sri Lanka. The Sri Lankans did not like the negative conclusions of either study.

In theory, the human rights yearbook (which published the former report) was an independent publication and was in no way representative of the Norwegian government's views. But the Sri Lankan government interpreted NORAD's funding of the yearbook as official endorsement of its contents. The Sri Lankan ambassador in Stockholm complained that the neutrality line "doesn't cut water with anyone."[15] The 1985 yearbook was very critical of the Sri Lankan government's human rights record. It was presented to the Storting and played an important role in sustaining parliamentary pressure on the government to condition aid on human rights performance. Inevitably, the report prompted a hostile backlash from the Sri Lankans. In a letter to the Storting, Ambassador Kurukulasuriya claimed that the yearbook was full of "demonstrable inaccuracies, subtle half-truths, and perhaps even more significant, an inexplicable selectivity and partiality."[16] He argued that "a report which fails to conform to norms [of impartiality and objectivity] not only affects the credibility of the human rights activists who author them, *but also raises awkward questions of motive.*"[17]

The University of Bergen's country study of Sri Lanka also took a punitive line, but it saw a paradox. On the one hand, it noted, "the Government of Sri Lanka bears ... considerable responsibility both for the escalation [of the ethnic conflict] and for the counter-productive brutality with which the conflict is being pursued by the armed forces."[18] But at the same time, "it is unlikely that Norway has a better and more focused programme in any other recipient country." How then could one reconcile "one of the success stories of NORAD" with "serious doubts [about] whether the Government of Sri Lanka can presently be considered eligible" for aid?

The Bergen team recommended that Norway discontinue all aid by 1988 if the human rights situation did not improve over the coming months. The team used four arguments to back its case: first, that "in relation to human rights, non-intervention cannot be maintained as an acceptable principle" of state behaviour; second, that a Norwegian white paper (no. 36) underlined the role of "local authorities" in tolerating or carrying out abuses as a criterion for suspending ODA;

third, that although Norwegian aid had been successful, "we are now repairing the damage which the Sri Lankan government has itself caused"; and fourth, that Tamil rights abuses did not neutralize the government of Sri Lanka's culpability and that "Norwegian authorities have to relate first and foremost to undertakings of the Government of Sri Lanka." The Norwegian cabinet did not accept the Bergen study's proposal to suspend the aid program, but it did support its conclusion on the role of Sri Lankan authorities. In a strongly worded statement, Deputy Development Cooperation Minister Hans Bugge argued that "particular responsibility lies with the Government of Sri Lanka, *as a government*, to do its utmost to assure the security and human rights for the citizens of the country."[19]

The Sri Lankans, not surprisingly, took exception to these criticisms and "postponed" the aid dialogue meeting. Aid continued to flow, however. Contact was maintained at a lower level by annual consultations that focused on technical issues. Norway thus implemented further shifts in its policy unilaterally without high-level approval or dialogue. It had to wait until December 1987 before Sri Lanka officially approved the five-year ODA policy. By then key elements of the policy had changed in response to the signing of the Indo–Sri Lanka peace accord.

The Annual ODA Consultations

The low-level aid "consultations" provide some insight into the strained atmosphere in which Norway maintained an aid presence in Sri Lanka before the signing of the peace accord. For example, at the 1986 consultation the Sri Lankans wanted quick-disbursing balance-of-payments aid to be restored. The Norwegians declined for human rights reasons and served notice that the future levels of ODA might be influenced by the human rights record. But a carrot came with the stick. Norway stressed that "moves towards a negotiated settlement, together with a thrust towards a reconstruction process, will be followed by a *close and supportive interest* by the Norwegian government."[20] However, while softening the Sri Lankans with bilateral incentives, Norway pursued a critical line at the multilateral level.

Multilateral Diplomacy

Strategically placed individuals can sometimes play a key role in the foreign policy of small states.[21] A prominent Norwegian scholar, Asbjorn Eide, who had close links to key policy makers such as State

Secretary Saeter, was also active in the U.N. Subcommission on the Prevention of Discrimination and the Protection of Minorities. This expert body meets before the sessions of the U.N. Commission on Human Rights (UNCHR) in Geneva and proposes to UNCHR "country cases" for closer scrutiny. Eide was active in ensuring that UNCHR took up a watching brief on Sri Lanka in 1984. His presence in Geneva was also influential in prompting the active interest of the Norwegian governmental delegation.

However, Norway had to wait until 1987 before it could sponsor (along with like-minded Canada and newly democratic Argentina) a UNCHR resolution condemning human rights abuses in Sri Lanka. Argentina, as a prominent member of the non-aligned group, was crucial in ensuring that the resolution passed.[22] The resolution called on *all* parties to the conflict to respect the humanitarian laws of armed conflict, and it called on the government of Sri Lanka to cooperate with international monitoring by giving the International Committee for the Red Cross access to victims of the conflict, by cooperating with the U.N. Working Group on Disappearances, and by informing UNCHR in 1988 of its progress in implementing the resolution.

The lowest common denominator usually prevails at the U.N. Commission on Human Rights. Still, the Sri Lanka resolution amounted to a strong condemnation of the government's human rights record.[23] It added to already critical assessments made by the special rapporteur on torture, the Working Group on Disappearances, and the special rapporteur on summary executions. With these three reports being released alongside the U.N. resolution, Sri Lanka graduated into a special league (in the company of Guatemala, El Salvador, and Iraq) of some of the world's worst human rights violators.

PHASE TWO: AMBIGUITY AND CHANGE, 1987–1990

A turning point in Sri Lanka's history came in 1987. Western donors pressed President Jayawardene to sign, with Prime Minister Rajiv Gandhi, the Indo–Sri Lanka Agreement to Establish Peace and Normalcy in Sri Lanka. There was widespread optimism that the accord would bring peace and would improve human rights. However, the accord failed. By mid-October 1987, the Indian Peacekeeping Force was embroiled in a war with the Tamil Tigers in the north. Soon afterwards, Sri Lankan security forces were coping with Sinhalese extremist violence in the south. Despite this setback, Norway signalled appreciation of the positive steps taken by the government over the accord. Those initiatives were interpreted as revealing good faith and a genuine commitment to resolve the protracted social conflict. As a result, aid was increased and balance-of-payments support was restored. There were two major provisos, however. The first, relating to human rights, was that "under no circumstances could military use of NORAD-funded project equipment be accepted by the Norwegian government." The second proviso was that Norway would closely supervise the design of aid projects and the spending of its funds. Although this was at odds with the principle of recipient orientation, the Norwegians required this guarantee to ensure that funds were not used for military purposes, particularly in the Batticaloa district – a scene of heavy fighting between Tamils, Muslims, and Sinhalese.[24]

The country program consultations signalled improved relations between the two countries even as the ethnic conflict escalated and even though human rights monitors continued to document abuses by Sri Lankan security forces.[25] Since 1987, Norway has tried to be more even-handed in its relations with the Sri Lankan government. For example, in the 1988 ODA consultation, Norway praised the government's "recent legislation granting citizenship to stateless plantation workers," while expressing concern about the slowdown in the reconstruction and rehabilitation program in the north and about the slow progress in relief work in war-torn Batticaloa. There was, however, no direct mention of human rights in the 1988 bilateral consultation, a fact that perhaps reflected the growing complexity of the conflict and the increasing ambiguity regarding oppressor and oppressed.

A similar mix of criticism and praise was evident in the Norwegian statement at the 1989 Sri Lanka Aid Group meeting. The Norwegian delegate praised the "commendable progress in bringing the militant groups in the North and East into the political process" and said that "like others, we welcome the [government's] decision to invite the ICRC." But the delegate added, "My country is deeply concerned about … the violations by the parties involved and the loss of innocent lives." The delegate also noted that project implementation was "increasingly hampered by the deteriorating human rights situation" and that Norway expected "substantial" funds to be undisbursed in 1989 and 1990. The Norwegian statement ended with an element of human rights conditionality: "The future of our assistance will depend on further developments towards peace and reconciliation."[26] The aid program mirrored these political uncertainties. What emerged from the latter half of 1988 onwards was an increasing Norwegian preoccupation with issues of personnel security and crisis management. Aid projects were no longer immune from the ethnic conflict in Sri Lanka.

Policy Options: Preparing for the Worst

As the conflict escalated into an island-wide intra-ethnic affair, NORAD prepared for the worst. In a policy options paper, any dramatic shifts in ODA would require at least one of four conditions: that aid personnel become targets of violence or terrorism; that the security situation worsens, making it impossible to carry out development work; that a military coup is followed by martial law and the total dismantling of democratic institutions; that total war leads to an emergency war cabinet and the "setting-aside" of the legally elected government. These scenarios could prompt some mix of the following policy options: more NGO and multilateral ODA; a shift from project and program aid to more emergency aid; the suspension of commodity and import support; and/or a rapid reduction of the ODA budget.[27]

An Effective Human Rights Policy?

How effective was Norway's human rights diplomacy in Sri Lanka? If effectiveness means reducing conflict and human rights abuses, then Norway (and all other donors) were singularly ineffective. Violence was more widespread at the end of the 1980s than at the beginning of the decade. But the blame for the demise of democratic governance and the persistence of violent conflict lies with the warring parties, not with the Western aid group. On the other hand, if effectiveness is measured by policy coherence and the maintenance of dialogue and influence, then Norway was relatively successful. Norway's goals and expectations were modest, but much was achieved by a country with a small aid program and thus limited leverage. This case study has identified two distinct phases of Norwegian statecraft.

Between 1983 and 1987, Norway was able to craft a morally principled and integrated policy along several channels: bilateral aid and diplomacy, and multilateral statecraft through UNCHR and the Sri Lanka Consultative Group. Norway's stand at meetings of the consultative group may have helped convince the donor community to pressure Jayawardene to sign the peace accord and to ensure that Tamils were given limited autonomy. According to the late Martin Ennals (who at the time was president of International Alert, an international monitoring group), "because Norway took action, other donors had to follow."[28] The Norwegians used a creative mix of incentives, threats, and ODA shifts to "comment" on the Sri Lankan government's human rights record and to foster initiatives to end the conflict. Their two-track aid policy combined shifting funds away from government and moving them towards NGOs and Tamil areas. Reduced balance-of-payments support was a morally principled action. All aid is somewhat fungible, and Norway took steps to ensure that commodity and import support did not indirectly help the government by releasing funds for military purposes.

However, Norwegian policy became less coherent after the breakdown of the peace accord in October 1987. The salience of human rights in the aid relationship partly gave way to a preoccupation with project viability and the safety of aid workers. Three factors help explain this second phase of Norwegian statecraft. First, the changing nature of the conflict – from a principally Tamil-versus-government contest to one that was island-wide and involved both intra-ethnic and inter-ethnic violence – blurred the human rights picture and made assessment difficult. Second, domestic interest in Sri Lanka waned; the media coverage was toned down, and the Tamil community became virtually silent. Third, the Ministry of Foreign Affairs, understaffed and overstretched during much of 1989, was preoccupied with China and the Tibetan Dalai Lama's visit to Norway.

There is, finally, a measure of effectiveness that supersedes influence. It concerns institutional learning. Sri Lanka was a test case for Norway in which the aid donor learned firsthand the vicissitudes of integrating human rights in development aid. In doing so, NORAD had to abandon its "hands-off" ideal and closely supervise the disbursement of funds. Human rights and recipient orientation are difficult to reconcile. Human rights imply interference in domestic affairs. The experience gained in Sri Lanka prompted a white paper to guide Norwegian policy on the relationship between human rights and development aid.

Norwegian diplomacy thus combined relatively unassertive public and private verbal criticism with a redirection of ODA, an indicator of greater policy resolve. High assertion levers were never credible options. Aid suspension was held to be untenable for four reasons: it would foreclose Norwegian influence, adversely affect target groups, have little impact because Norway would be acting alone, and potentially be exploited by Tamil groups as an endorsement of their political position – a "very unfortunate" unintended consequence.[29]

Contrary to some practitioners' reservations, adding human rights to Norway's interests in Sri Lanka did not irrevocably undermine bilateral relations. Granted, circumstances allowing for a coherent policy were unusually favourable – a weak aid-dependent recipient and a donor with few competing interests. Nevertheless, the aid relationship survived a brief separation, and Norway persuaded Sri Lanka that human rights were a legitimate and routine point of discussion. This breakthrough had not, by 1990, spilled over to other "main partner" countries such as Kenya. But the ability to "stay the course" in Sri Lanka may yet inspire other examples of principled and effective Norwegian human rights diplomacy.

PRINCIPLES AND PRAGMATISM: CANADA AND THE SRI LANKAN CONFLICT

Canada's response to the Sri Lankan conflict in many ways mirrors Norway's human rights statecraft. There are some important differences, however. While Norway initially took a moderately assertive and interventionist stance, attempting to adjust its entire aid program, Canada at first was more agnostic, carefully avoiding any punitive signals such as suspending or adjusting the aid program on human rights considerations. Unlike Norway, Canada faced a complex political and human rights issue at the project level. The issue demanded and produced a clear, principled response.

Since 1987, however, Canada has grown more critical of the Sri Lankan government's human rights record and has been less willing to maintain a large aid program. This reflects a trend among all the major donors in Sri Lanka. But the recent reduction is premised as much on a pragmatic assessment of the deepening conflict and fear for the project workers' safety as on sending an overt signal about the government's human rights performance. One interesting outcome of the deepening violence and growing donor frustration is that several donors have tried to coordinate their efforts to apply pressure on the Sri Lankan government. Separate initiatives along these lines by Norway and Canada some years earlier did not succeed.

This case study centres on Canada's Maduru Oya dam-building project because it raises issues that reverberate well beyond the confines of the project. The politics of ethnic resettlement risked reproducing the national conflict within the project itself, something that Canada wanted to avoid at all costs. Additional material is drawn from Canadian actions at the United Nations and the Sri Lanka aid consortium. The non-aid issues help test the degree of integration and consistency in the various facets of Canada's human rights statecraft.

Several conclusions emerge. First, human rights issues, such as access to land, are embedded in the design and implementation of ODA projects. Donors ignore them at their peril. Conditionality is usually seen as a macro-policy issue with implications for a donor's total activity in a recipient country. Canada's experience with the Maduru Oya project suggests that donors who fail to consider the political dimensions of individual projects may become unwitting accomplices in human rights abuses. Canada's experience reinforces calls to put aid projects, particularly megaprojects, through a "human rights filter" *before* implementation.[30]

Second, Canada, like Norway and the rest of the donor community, was caught unprepared by the 1983 riots and the ensuing conflict. Canada appeared to have no human rights policy at that time but was compelled by circumstances to develop one. Third, contrary to the concerns of practitioners, human rights considerations need not irrevocably damage an aid relationship. Although human rights made Canada's aid dialogue with Sri Lanka more turbulent, Canada seems to have avoided the level of policy discord that developed between Norway and Sri Lanka. Fourth, a more interventionist and punitive form of aid leverage was briefly considered but was found to be impractical without active donor coordination. Fifth, a mild form of bureaucratic politics accompanied the policy process. However, these centrifugal pressures were contained by a culture of consensus building. CIDA held strong reservations about the intrusion of politics in aid planning and showed discomfort over the loss of program continuity and commercial opportunities. It successfully resisted a proposal to withdraw commodity aid and balance-of-payments support as a punitive human rights lever. Finally, the resettlement issue was a principled Canadian human rights intervention, worked out *before* the policy debate on human rights and development aid. So far, however, the Madura Oya experience has not led to any CIDA policy to put proposed megaprojects through a "human rights filter."

A BASIS FOR POLICY COHERENCE

Canada's involvement in international development began with its participation in the Commonwealth-sponsored Colombo Plan in 1950. Initially, Canada endorsed the Cold War policy of the Colombo Plan to stave off communism in South Asia by a timely injection of Western aid. But these geostrategic concerns were superseded by more benign thinking. Sri Lanka's image as a model Third World democracy with a commitment to social justice, the imprimatur of the World Bank–led aid consortium, and the potential for commercial advantage were the main reasons for subsequently building a large aid program. In the early 1980s, Sri Lanka was the largest Asian recipient of Canadian aid on a per capita basis.

Canada had few competing interests to muddy a consistent and principled human rights policy towards Sri Lanka. A possible exception was the Commonwealth link, which may have raised the stakes against a punitive or assertive statecraft.[31] This "club" dimension was absent in Norway's relations with Sri Lanka, lowering the stakes against assertive statecraft. Canada also had a relatively large Sri Lankan immigrant and refugee population.[32] These "new Canadians" sparked an angry debate on Canada's refugee determination process, but Tamil and Sinhalese lobby groups seem to have been less salient as a domestic variable influencing policy than the Tamil lobby was in Norway.

Economic interests did not block Canada's rethinking of its aid relationship with Sri Lanka. Canadian bilateral ODA of $27.99 million in 1985–86 almost matched Canadian exports of $28.89 million that year. Sri Lankan imports to Canada in 1985–86 stood at $35.81 million, giving Canada a small bilateral trade deficit. The ratio of ODA to total trade in 1985–86 was 0.43. Canada's minimal trade interests did not clash with human rights imperatives. Instead, ODA was central to the bilateral economic relationship and was thus a natural though not exclusive focus of Canadian diplomacy towards Sri Lanka.

Taken as a whole, Canadian domestic politics had the potential to be helpful in resolving the ethnic conflict in Sri Lanka. Canada's federal experience, its multicultural image, and the periodic crises of culture, language, and power sharing between the two "founding nations" amount to a "political self-interest in the survival of binational states."[33] This potential was underdeveloped in the early stages of the Sri Lankan conflict and is only now, in the 1990s, being built into Canadian policy towards Sri Lanka.

THE POLITICS OF AID PROJECTS: ETHNICITY, LAND, AND DISCRIMINATION

A key element of the UNP government's economic restructuring was a plan to dam, divert, and harness the waters of the Mahaweli Ganga, Sri Lanka's major river system. The river had been exploited for irrigation and agriculture nearly two thousand years before by a sophisticated hydraulic civilization. The new master plan was to build fifteen reservoirs, four on the Mahaweli, ten on its tributaries, and one, to be built by Canadians, on the Maduru Oya. These dams would then generate up to 550 megawatts of hydroelectric energy and would feed a complex and extensive system of canals and dikes to irrigate 360,000 hectares of scrubland.

Several sound development goals came together in the Mahaweli Scheme. Building the dam and irrigation systems would create local employment and transfer technology. The harnessed energy and water would irrigate scrubland in the infertile dry zone of the north and east of the island. Irrigation would in turn make possible the resettlement of up to 750,000 landless peasants to small-scale farms on once-barren land. The UNP government saw the scheme as a safety valve to relieve population pressures in the overcrowded, Sinhalese-dominated south and southwest of the island. This megaproject had something for everyone: a capital-intensive infrastructure offering rich pickings for Western engineering and construction firms; a poverty-alleviation component consistent with a Sri Lankan commitment to equity; and increased agricultural productivity. Inspired by the engineering feats of an ancient kingdom and hailed as the world's largest foreign aid project, the Mahaweli Scheme was to be a symbol of progress and national identity. None of these hopes materialized. Instead, the scheme became another irritant, adding to the already explosive communal tensions. The Tamils complained that Mahaweli continued the historical agenda of Sinhalese-dominated governments to use resettlement to alter the island's demographic mix and to undercut Tamil claims on the eastern province.

Whatever the motives, events conspired against the government. Armed conflict and a dispute over resettlement ratios killed the project. By the late 1980s, the Mahaweli Scheme had become a white elephant. Reservoirs lay dormant with the irrigation systems not built and the surrounding land still barren and unused.[34] By March 1990, the World Bank had pulled out, sounding the death knell for the scheme.

The Maduru Oya Project: An Aid Planner's Nightmare

The Sri Lankan government established the Ministry for Mahaweli Development to oversee the project and commissioned aid donors to construct the dams and irrigation systems. The main donors were West Germany, Sweden, Britain, the United States, Saudi Arabia, Canada, and the World Bank. Canada has been associated with the scheme since 1980. A consortium of Canadian firms, including Acres Ltd of Ontario, built a large rock-fill dam and tunnel system to divert the waters of the Maduru Oya. This was the first phase in a plan to irrigate over 39,400 hectares of land.[35] CIDA provided $100 million in funding. Canada's problems began when work was to start on the next phase – an irrigation and canal system to convert the scrubland into productive smallholder farms. Canada had allocated $60 million to phase four of the Mahaweli project in the form of equipment, training, and technical assistance. But politics soon intruded, and by 1992 only $12 million had been disbursed on engineering studies, none on construction.

The World Bank allocated US$42 million for the Maduru Oya complex. The other key player, Saudi Arabia, was slated to build the canal system. But the Saudis pulled out in 1984, before starting work, in retaliation for Sri Lanka's growing links with Israel. The European Community was eventually persuaded to take over from the Saudis, but it too never started. This was because security concerns made work impossible in the Maduru Oya catchment area. Interviews with CIDA and External Affairs officials confirm that at the planning stage virtually no attention had been given to the project's impact on the fragile ethnic balance of Batticaloa district, in which resettlement would occur.[36] In the memorandum of understanding that was signed between the two governments, there is no evidence of sensitivity to such human rights as participation and nondiscrimination by, for example, canvassing the opinions of local Tamil politicians or ensuring that an equitable ethnic balance was guaranteed. CIDA seems to have uncritically accepted the government's proposed resettlement formula. Canada's unwillingness to examine the political implications of the aid project proved costly.[37]

The outbreak of armed conflict in the eastern province in 1983, and its escalation in 1984, compelled Canada to consider whether the project could fuel communal tensions between Tamils and Sinhalese. Ottawa concluded that the UNP government's resettlement ratios for the right bank of the Oya River compromised Canada's relatively passive position on human rights and threatened to plunge Canada into a political controversy at home and abroad. The Canadian government wanted to avoid any perception that it was taking sides in the conflict or that it was complicitous in actions that discriminated against Tamils. The heart of the matter was whether resettlement should proceed on the basis of national ethnic ratios or district ethnic ratios. The UNP government had devised a resettlement formula that mirrored the national ethnic balance – 74 per cent Sinhalese, 12 per cent Sri Lankan Tamil, 6 per cent Estate Tamil, 6 per cent Muslim, and 2 per cent other. By this formula, Sri Lankan Tamils would make up just 12 per cent of the 750,000 people settled in the Mahaweli Scheme.

This seemingly fair provision was politically explosive because a number of the irrigation projects were in districts where the Tamils were in the majority, and the resettlement formula would weaken this majority. From a Tamil perspective, the national formula masked a hidden UNP agenda. Resettlement on the right bank of the Maduru Oya meant that there would be a rapid influx of Sinhalese to the Batticaloa district, where the Tamils comprised more than two-thirds of the population.[38] Following the national formula would have altered the district's demographic balance and undermined the precarious Tamil claim on the eastern province as a whole. Their slim majority in the province was the basis of the Tamils' demand for district development councils and substantial provincial autonomy.

A second formula – favoured by the Tamils and eventually by Canada – had resettlement proceeding according to the district ethnic ratio. In effect, this meant that the right bank of the Oya River would be settled predominantly by Tamil farmers; it would preserve the Tamil majority in the Batticaloa district. The Sri Lankan government had always contested the concept of a Tamil "traditional homeland" in the eastern province. It reasoned that the fruits of the Mahaweli project should be available to all ethnic groups and denied that its formula was a deliberate attempt to alter the ethnic balance.

Canada became concerned about Maduru Oya in 1984 because President Jayawardene's "national ethnic formula" was announced just before an all-party conference seeking a consensus on the resolution of the Tamil question. The government and the Tamil United Liberation Front had proposed district development councils which, in 1984, were seen as a viable way of devolving power and enhancing Tamil autonomy without fracturing the Sri Lankan state. Jayawardene's timing of the resettlement formula could not have been more ill-considered, and it put in question the government's commitment to grant meaningful local autonomy to the Tamils of the eastern province. A senior Canadian official in Sri Lanka later described the national ethnic formula as "a type of gerrymandering" and said that it "heightened the sensitivity of the Oya project well beyond the local impact." The official explained that Jayawardene's formula "put us in a difficult position because as an aid donor you can't go around telling a recipient how it's going to conduct its internal affairs, particularly over sensitive issues, such as land resettlement. A principle of domestic jurisdiction [over internal affairs] has been our tradition. On the other hand, we weren't very happy about our money going into something that was going to cause more dissension, and, in fact, to a scheme you could argue simply wasn't fair."[39]

Canada was careful not to adopt an overtly punitive approach. It tried, instead, to set its concerns in the context of the all-party conference and as an opportunity for ethnic reconciliation. In a carefully modulated dialogue, Canada made clear its preference for a district ethnic formula favouring the Tamils, though "formally we resisted dictating our own formulas and ratios," as the senior official recalled: "The line I took was not 'You will settle this or this percentage of a particular ethnic group or we will not pay the money' but 'This aid program ... is a gesture of Canada's good will. We don't want to get caught in a political issue so why don't you sort out a solution with all the communities to ensure that it does not become an issue' ... 'Surely if you're looking for reconciliation a [district formula] is a golden opportunity to prove that the government is concerned with their future.'"[40]

Canada's implied message, however, was clear enough – that it might have to reconsider its funding of the Oya project if the Sri Lankan government did not change its formula. Canada's overture led to a lengthy and ultimately unsuccessful dialogue between the two governments. "This little minuet," as one official described it, continued for two years, from 1984 to 1986, and the Canadians never obtained a clear answer. The Sri Lankans' implicit attitude was, "You sign the cheques fella, let us deliver the goods."[41] Yet Canada recognized its potential leverage as an important player in the Mahaweli Scheme. Aid was vital to an economy unsettled by the conflict and as a substitute for risk capital that had virtually dried up. Aid could be used as a signal. As the official explained, the Sri Lankans "didn't want a major donor like Canada to be seen as lagging behind in delivering aid, because it might worry other donors."[42] Even so, the two-year diplomatic tussle ended in a stand-off. The Sri Lankans never said "yes – we accept the district formula," and the Canadians never said "no – we are pulling out."

Policy Options: The Big Stick or Business as Usual?

Canada did, however, examine a number of policy options, including aid suspension. The policy process is revealing. The story, recounted by some of the key participants, displays the institutional differences between External Affairs and CIDA, the role of individual policy makers, and the government's shrewd assessments of the opportunities and limitations of Canadian influence. With the conflict's escalation in 1985, and with Tamil groups in Canada increasingly protesting human rights abuses, External Affairs reviewed its relationship with Sri Lanka. There were two broad concerns. First and foremost was the aid program's status. By this time, the conflict was so bad that clearly the entire program and not just Maduru Oya had to be rethought and adapted to the new reality.

A second, more muted, discussion turned on a potential Canadian bridge-building role, moving the warring parties towards reconciliation. In 1986, then Secretary of State for External Affairs Joe Clark, took a personal interest in this option and in exploring greater U.N. involvement. Meanwhile, Sir Shridath Ramphal, the Commonwealth secretary general, wrote to Clark to gauge support for a South Africa-style eminent persons group. This idea was dropped when the Indian foreign ministry in Delhi sent Ramphal a clear message to "back off."[43]

Clark was also informed by the Indian foreign minister that resolving the conflict was India's responsibility. Told clearly, "That is the way it is," Clark finally believed it, and he dropped the idea. In 1986, it made sense to regard India, the regional power, as the only country able to wield the big stick. But in view of the violent and ineffectual record of the Indian Peacekeeping Force in Sri Lanka, it is unfortunate that Canada and the Commonwealth did not promote a bridge-building role more aggressively.

The aid program's adaptation revealed a distinctively Canadian form of bureaucratic politics: the partial reduction of initially wide institutional differences by a genuine effort at consensus building.[44] There were at least three competing constituencies, each with its own diagnosis and preferred remedy. One was External Affairs' Asia-Pacific branch, which was pessimistic about Sri Lanka's future. It preferred a policy of gradually withdrawing aid and retargeting unused funds to less-troubled recipients – in Southeast Asia, for example.[45] External Affairs argued that the basis for Canada's presence in Sri Lanka had radically altered. The large aid program had "emerged historically but had never been matched by any objective assessment of the nature of Canadian interests in the country." The rationale – aiding a model developing nation – was now "obviously undercut." Moreover, although the conflict was still confined to the north and east of the island, External Affairs saw that it was likely to worsen: "The trend line was down and it was going to stay down."[46] There were rumours about closing down the high commission in Colombo, but they were never serious. Basically, "our inclination was to scale down our presence and hunker down for the long haul."[47] This constituency saw "no purpose in clinging to the assumption that the next round of talks would produce a solution so that we could all get back to business as usual."[48]

CIDA was a second constituency. The agency combined a "peculiar mix" of idealism, organizational imperatives, and hard-nosed pragmatism in arguing that Canada should maintain its current aid volume and proceed with the next phase of Maduru Oya. The idealism was a natural expression of CIDA's mandate to help the poorest groups and countries. CIDA saw no reason to undermine its developmental objectives in order to make a political point, and it argued strongly that Mahaweli combined sound development goals – notably, alleviating poverty, relieving population pressures, and enhancing the carrying capacity of the most infertile parts of the island.

CIDA's organizational imperatives centred on worries about continuity and on disbursement pressures. Unused funds would not be renewed, which meant that the program would simply wither away.

According to one External Affairs official, CIDA had a "desperate concern about the lack of continuity" if the program was allowed to phase down or particular projects were abandoned. CIDA officials also resented the intrusion of political issues into the technical problems of aid delivery. CIDA's pragmatic antipathy to using aid as a political lever had less to do with defending a development profile in Sri Lanka and more to do with its relationship with some high-profile Canadian companies that had been contracted to work on Mahaweli. CIDA officials "spoke with disarming frankness" of the commercial contracts already negotiated with three of Canada's largest engineering firms. CIDA had, in any case, already sunk $100 million into building the Maduru dam. It saw no way for Canada "to quietly phase down" after it had spent $100 million. With $60 million still allocated to the project, and with prestigious companies "with bags of political influence" hinting at litigation if the project stalled, CIDA wanted to proceed "without being reckless, in order to realize the developmental potential and commercial benefits."[49]

As one diplomat read CIDA's position, the agency "was more concerned about the direct access of these companies to their own minister ... and was quite unmoved by the fuss going on about human rights violations." For CIDA, human rights were "a political problem for the Sri Lankans to sort out. For some time CIDA did not want to read the telexes the way we [at External Affairs] did," noted the diplomat. Once CIDA agreed that the situation in Sri Lanka was "disturbed," it fell back on the position that pulling out was unnecessary because a political dialogue was underway.[50]

A third constituency advocated using aid as a political lever. This position was projected by one influential individual, Marcel Massé, the then undersecretary of external affairs, a Canadian representative at the World Bank, and a former president of CIDA. Having been president of CIDA, Massé was interested in aid conditionality. It was his "fascination" with aid as a foreign policy lever, not "any particular affinity" for Sri Lanka, that prompted him to direct his bureaucrats to "tell him whether he could or could not exercise leverage."[51] He knew that conditionality in Sri Lanka was not something Canada could use unilaterally. It would only work in concert with other donors.

After other donors had been canvassed, it became clear that conditionality was not an option. The United States opposed it, and the Europeans were uninterested because of commercial or diplomatic ties. Of all the donors, only Canada faced a human rights issue at the project level. Acting alone, Canada "would not have much clout when weighed against the total emotional involvement of national survival. [The Sri Lankan] government was never going to trade off even a valuable aid project against the issue of national sovereignty. So the scenario simply played itself out."[52]

The upshot of this debate was a memorandum to the secretary of state for external affairs. Minister Clark was presented with two choices: option A, to cancel the project, as External Affairs favoured; and option B, to keep the project alive at a slow disbursement rate, as CIDA preferred. The minister chose the latter, which kept the project alive and enabled the Canadian firms to continue the engineering studies at a cost of just $5 million over eighteen months. In effect, the decision was "a matter of buying time politically. [The project] wasn't frozen in an explicit sense; it simply wasn't going anywhere."[53] After protracted discussions, CIDA managed to persuade the Sri Lankans to sign a new memorandum of understanding that formalized the snail's-pace disbursement rate.

Canada's principled action may have had a modest impact. One of the first breakthroughs leading to the Indo–Sri Lankan peace accord was an agreement that the right bank of the Maduru Oya would be settled mostly by Tamils. As a senior official put it, "I like to think our initiative had some influence. Had we agreed with the [national ethnic formula] this breakthrough may never have been possible."[54] The policy review also led to three new operating principles for the entire aid program, not simply Maduru Oya. First, Canada would not take any action likely to worsen the communal conflict. Second, Canada would take into account the communal dimension of any work it did. Third, where feasible, Canada would promote projects that fostered ethnic harmony and understanding. In practice, the second and third principles were difficult to realize. Some modest mission-administered funds were directed to women's groups and Tamil groups in the north, and NGOs were used more, but the escalating conflict made it hard to identify projects that would "foster ethnic harmony."[55] Thus, with few projects in Tamil areas, Canadian aid to Sri Lanka was declining by 1985–86. And as one official noted, "the aid program became even more commodity-centred and formula-driven."[56]

In 1984, Canada confronted a project-level human rights problem and worked gradually towards a pragmatic solution that minimized the disruption of its aid relationship with Sri Lanka. The central factors here were self-determination and collective rights, but nondiscrimination and equality were among the other rights at risk. More punitive options, such as project suspension and joint-aid conditionality, were considered but rejected. A desire to avoid complicity was behind Canadian actions. Canada also recognized the potentially adverse impact of the government's resettlement formula on the peace process in Sri Lanka. Its principled refusal to go ahead with Maduru

Oya may have made a modest contribution to the initial peace accord negotiations.

Interestingly, External Affairs appeared to be more concerned about human rights than CIDA, which seemed more worried about organizational imperatives and loss of contracts. Canada did not alter its entire aid program as a commentary on the Sri Lankan government's human rights record; conditionality was project-specific. However, care was taken to ensure that Canadian activity in Sri Lanka did not worsen the communal tensions. A diplomatic trial balloon on a possible Canadian peacemaking role burst when India made it clear that it would be responsible for overseeing an end to hostilities. The government's pragmatic recognition of Canada's inability to act alone and its unwillingness to be assertive in bridge building in the face of Indian resistance mark the limits of Canadian influence and the realism of its policy makers.

Multilateral Diplomacy

Between 1984 and 1986, Canada was preoccupied with the Maduru Oya project. Less attention was given to Sri Lanka in the United Nations, a traditional focus of Canadian human rights activism, though Canada did support a 1984 watching brief recommended by the Subcommission on the Prevention of Discrimination and the Protection of Minorities. By 1987, however, Canada was prepared to co-sponsor (with Norway and Argentina) the first resolution adopted by UNCHR on the human rights situation in Sri Lanka. Although moderate in tone, the resolution was unequivocal in stating that the Sri Lankan government shared responsibility for the worsening human rights situation. By calling on "all parties" to renounce violence, the resolution also undermined the "terrorism versus law and order" argument of the Sri Lankan government.

In 1988 Canada, with the rest of the Western Group, still saw the Indo–Sri Lanka accord as "the best hope for restoring peace in Sri Lanka [because it] provides for a measure of regional autonomy and appears to meet most of the demands of the Tamil people."[57] With the accord's failure and the soaring "kill ratio," Canada has grown more critical of the Sri Lankan government's human rights record. While it has not tried to sponsor another resolution at the UNCHR or to denounce publicly the abuses committed by the Indian Peacekeeping Force, Canada's item 12 speech at Geneva in March 1990 denounced the Sri Lankan government: "Canada deplores the continued and deepening cycle of violence in Sri Lanka and the appalling human rights situation there. We are concerned that few specific policies or actions have been adopted by the government of Sri Lanka to contribute to controlling the violence and bringing it to an end."[58]

By 1989, Sri Lanka had descended into an fury of blood-letting that was unparalleled anywhere else in the 1980s. Figures quoted by Western diplomats suggest that as many as 30,000 people may have been killed, most during the first six months.[59] As donors began to murmur about reducing aid, the Western European and Others Group of the UNCHR met in Geneva to consider the situation. The idea of a strongly worded resolution was suggested but was finally dropped.[60] The key issue was impact. As one delegate observed, "Whereas with China, one may simply want to register concern – just getting the issue aired was enough, even if you lost the vote it would have been a moral victory – with Sri Lanka, you would want to win" the vote. A failed resolution would aid the Sri Lankan government.

Some Western delegations felt that Sri Lanka was experienced at getting support from the Middle Eastern states and from large portions of the non-aligned bloc, and that a resolution would therefore fail. Moreover, the Sri Lankan government had for several years played a politically astute game, announcing modest reforms just before the Geneva meetings. Clause 55FF of the Prevention of Terrorism Act is a case in point. It had long been seen as easing the use of torture by making it less visible, and its removal was thus a step forward. But since this occurred just two months before the Geneva meeting, several delegations, including Canada, were sceptical of the Sri Lankan government's sincerity. A consensus emerged not to push for a resolution, but to attempt, instead, a private *démarche*. The head of the Sri Lankan delegation, J.H. Jayawardene, invited this "informal discussion" in which the Western states called for the emergency regulations to be dismantled as a prerequisite for the restoration of human rights.

Canada also took a more critical position at the annual Sri Lanka Aid Group meetings. This broke with the tradition against raising political issues, such as human rights, in forums that focus on economic issues, such as development aid.[61] At the 1988 consultative group meeting in Paris, the Canadian delegate's comments were obliquely critical, noting, for example, that "defence continues to demand a high level of expenditures, one of the many direct links between the economy and the civil conflict."[62] The delegate also voiced Canada's concern "as a long-standing partner with Sri Lanka, about the severity of [its] problems and ... the need for early policy decisions and action to end the downward spiral in which Sri Lanka has been now caught for many years."

At the 1989 aid group meeting, Canada took a tougher line. The Canadian delegate "stress[ed] that it is not purely economic considerations which concern us ... [Canada] would be remiss not to bring to the group's attention our concerns about the difficulties *now* being faced in implementing development programs ... [including] increasing risks to development personnel as well as threats to innocent civilians."[63] The Canadian representative made a further point: "A number of delegates have raised the issue of human rights in Sri Lanka. Canada has not traditionally raised this issue in consultative forums such as this. We do, however, share many of the concerns mentioned by [other] delegates and have raised these bilaterally with the government of Sri Lanka."[64]

By 1989, Canada had arrived where Norway had been between 1984 and 1986. Like Norwegian State Secretary Saeter, a Canadian official argued that "a special responsibility lies with the [Sri Lankan] government for human rights because it is responsible for the administration of law." The official noted the growing presence of private militias, some responsible to senior government ministers, and death-squad activity linked both to the militias and to the security forces.[65] To demonstrate its resolve on human rights, Canada, with several other donors, was now prepared to raise the issue at the aid group meeting.

Ironically, Canada had been relatively agnostic in the early stages of the conflict when fighting was geographically confined to the north and portions of the east, and when the principal cleavage pitted government forces against Tamil guerrillas. By 1989, human rights abuses were being committed by at least five armed groups, and the conflict was now as much within as between the two main communities. Despite this complexity, which clouded any assessment of governmental responsibility, Canada and other Western governments became increasingly convinced that the Sri Lankan government was substantially culpable for the excesses committed during 1989. The sheer number of killings may, for once, have helped tilt some Western countries to a more critical position on Sri Lanka. As we shall see, security concerns also played a part.

PREPARING FOR THE FUTURE

The decision to put the Maduru Oya scheme on hold and the inability to find enough small-scale projects in Tamil areas meant that Canadian aid to Sri Lanka became largely commodity based and that overall bilateral ODA began to fall off. The extent of this decline in ODA disbursement is shown in table 5.1, which records a drop from $46.02 million in fiscal year 1982–83 to $24.5 million in fiscal year 1987–88. Especially revealing is the rising disbursement trend line before 1983, when armed conflict emerged in earnest, and its rapid decline thereafter.

Table 5.1
Canadian Bilateral ODA to Sri Lanka, 1980–1988

Year	$ millions
1980–81	37.69
1981–82	42.24
1982–83	46.02
1983–84	35.41
1984–85	24.43
1985–86	18.72
1986–87	17.87
1987–88	24.50

Source: Canadian International Development Agency, *Annual Report* (various years), and *Country Profile: Sri Lanka* (Hull: CIDA 1989).

Prior to 1983–84, Canada was thus fully committed to the Sri Lankan government and to national development. Growing evidence of discrimination and ethnic tension was not reflected in Canadian ODA. As table 5.1 shows, ODA disbursements actually rose during the early 1980s.

In 1990, Canada recast its relationship with Sri Lanka through a country program review, a five-year exercise setting the aid programs' funding levels and parameters. The review took account of the worst year of violence in the last decade, a growing "aid fatigue" among the donor community, fears for the security of aid personnel, and a new "get-tough" attitude that has led some donors to threaten aid suspension if the Sri Lankan government does not improve its human rights record. It was premised on a recognition that economic growth and development cannot proceed without political and communal stability. Hence, "Canada's long-term policy in Sri Lanka is to promote political stability and economic growth." The country program review recommended that Canada try:

(a) to seek a resolution [of the conflict] based on compromise and devolution of power to the provinces;
(b) [to premise aid] on equitability of the fruits of development to all Sri Lankans regardless of ethnic background;
(c) to acquaint Sri Lankan leaders with the Canadian experience in bilingualism and multiculturalism;
(d) to raise more intensively our concerns with Sri Lankan authorities on human rights;
(e) to cancel projects which cannot be implemented under present circumstances;

(f) to refocus development assistance programs on the root causes of the current conflict, such as ethnic animosity, by job creation and youth education;

(g) to support key institutions which can play a role in economic reform and in promoting human rights and democratic development;

(h) to promote community level economic activity especially among disaffected youth ... those whose unfulfilled aspirations have fuelled the conflict;

(i) to assist multi-cultural organizations in the delivery of basic social services and, when conditions are ripe, to assist in reconstruction and rehabilitation.[66]

The policy options are a curious mix of pessimism and optimism. They underline a deep uncertainty about Sri Lanka's future. Pessimism is evident in the decision to close down the Maduru Oya scheme and twenty smaller projects. They could not be continued because project personnel were endangered and because the Sri Lankans could not meet the local financing costs.[67] The security dimension is all too real. So far, CIDA has not lost any personnel, but it has recalled some local staff from the field. In 1990, South Asia Partnership, CIDA's main conduit for grass-roots work, had two local staff killed by the Janatha Vimukthi Peramuna.[68] An External Affairs official has since seen the security issue as more pressing than human rights conditionality: "The linkage of human rights and aid is not being drawn extensively by Canada."[69]

Optimism is evident in the attempt to promote human rights and ethnic reconciliation. Human rights and legal aid groups could be funded, although in view of the British experience (considered below), care will have to be taken not to alienate the Sri Lankan government or to endanger funding recipients. The proposal to acquaint Sri Lankan leaders with the Canadian experience of bilingualism and multiculturalism is creative but could be too little too late. Moreover, Canada's constitutional impasse and such incidents as the 1990 stand-off between Mohawks and the army at Oka, as well as the 1989 report of the Human Rights Commission criticizing state treatment of native peoples in Canada,[70] put in doubt Canada's ability to teach others. Nevertheless, Canada is searching for a role in building peace in Sri Lanka and is considering human rights by ensuring that future projects pay attention to equity issues.

The policy review calls for a tougher stance on the Sri Lankan government's human rights performance. Although Canada's views will be communicated in private and in concert with other donors, Canada has grown impatient with the Sri Lankan government's intransigence on human rights. As one official complained, "We do not see any evidence that [the government] will rescind the emergency measures which we feel legitimize human rights abuses ... What we haven't seen is a stated recognition by the government that they have a human rights problem ... [or] that they have a human rights policy that they intend to push through ... We would like to see an acknowledgment that the government has been as culpable as the other [armed] groups. Their insistence that there is no government involvement is pure nonsense."[71]

Still, Canada's "get-tough" attitude does not mean the suspension of government-to-government aid. Officials say that cutting aid would "damage" the groups Canada is trying to help. More revealing, however, was their acknowledgment that suspending aid runs the "risk of establishing precedents [and strengthens] the voice of the more aggressive NGOs" demanding an automatic aid penalty against repressive regimes.[72]

THE LEVERAGE OF AID

As the ethnic conflict has deepened, evidence has mounted, among the donor community, of "aid fatigue" and of a new willingness to use aid as a political lever. The most visible sign of fatigue was the World Bank's decision to pull out of the Mahaweli Scheme. On 31 March 1990, the date on which the scheme had originally been scheduled for completion, the World Bank informed the Sri Lankans that it would abandon Mahaweli. As a bank official explained, "We were no longer able to justify to our management funds that had been unused for the better part of a decade." The project "was just not going to fly" and had become "an embarrassment" to the donors and to the Sri Lankans. The bank's timing – coinciding with the departure of the Indian Peacekeeping Force – could not have been worse. It sent an ambiguous signal. Acknowledging that the pull-out effectively killed the project, the bank official stressed that the World Bank had not "abandoned" Sri Lanka but was shifting from project aid to a greater emphasis on macroeconomic planning and fast-disbursing program aid.[73] That the bank, as chair of the aid group and guarantor of Sri Lanka's external funding, pulled out of Mahaweli underlined the growing frustration among the donor community. The impact of the decision was felt deeply by the UNP government, since the bank had been a prime architect of the original scheme.

Aid fatigue is not confined to the World Bank. In a striking departure from earlier thinking, the Dutch, in mid-January 1990, warned Sri Lanka that unless its human rights record improved by June, the

Netherlands would reduce its aid program.[74] Even the United Kingdom, linked to Sri Lanka by history and the Commonwealth, lost patience with the Sri Lankan government when the latter cited Britain's funding of a Tamil Law Society as support for a terrorist organization.[75] In an interesting example of donor coordination, the Dutch led the search for support from Norway, Canada, West Germany, and Sweden, and they plan to use a joint political *démarche* to focus the concerns and strengthen the leverage of like-minded donors.[76] As late as October 1989 the Dutch, though critizing Sri Lanka in the aid group and having put several projects on hold, saw no immediate need to threaten aid suspension. Since then, however, they have concluded that development work is impossible until the security and human rights situations improve.

Several aid donors are now prepared to use aid as a lever to press for improved human rights, and several, including the countries examined in this study, are working together. This is indicative of the donor community's perception that human rights abuses have been severe. But this development is ironic, given Norway's lonely protest of government abuses in the mid-1980s and Canada's punctured trial balloon on "concertation." Evidently, sheer numbers – an estimated 30,000 killings in 1989 – and an inability to deliver aid in dangerous conditions eventually galvanized the donor community into action.

By the early 1990s, the donors were in a commanding position to pressure the Sri Lankans. Foreign aid had become an integral prop for an economy sagging under the weight of a debt which in 1988 stood at us$5.189 million, or 75 per cent of GNP – much of it spent on internal security.[77] The World Bank estimated that Sri Lanka would require us$2.4 billion between 1990 and 1992. Despite growing misgivings, the aid group pledged us$785 million to Sri Lanka for 1990.[78] The Sri Lankan government, no longer able to afford the rupee expenditures for aid projects, asked for more donor local-cost financing.[79]

Despite this room for leverage, the assertiveness of donors such as Canada, the Netherlands, and Norway had limits. They shared information and coordinated joint *démarches*, but they were not a heavy-handed donor cartel. Nor were they pressing for an assertive sanction, such as the conditioning of new World Bank loans on human rights criteria. The timing of donor concertation and aid leverage seems to have been calculated to ensure that the Sri Lankan government would act immediately to seek a permanent end to hostilities, to lift emergency regulations, and to improve human rights rapidly. But considering the carnage that had happened since 1987 and the abysmal record of the Indian Peacekeeping Force, it seems likely that a more assertive and principled use of leverage before 1987 might have helped speed an end to the conflict. Aid had as much potential leverage between 1984 and 1987 as it does today. Why did the donor community take so long to act?

CONCLUSION

The human rights diplomacy of Norway and Canada substantially support the central hypothesis of this study. Each state was able to pursue a coherent, moderately assertive human rights policy because the costs to other vital national interests were perceived to be low. As a weak, aid-dependent state, Sri Lanka was in no position to retaliate. Commercial and security interests were negligible, and this gave each actor a relatively free hand to craft a principled response. The Commonwealth connection may have contributed to a more moderate Canadian stance. Norway had no such complication, a fact that may have permitted it to follow a more assertive policy.

Both countries did, however, take decisive actions to protest abuses (Norway) and prevent abuses (Canada) in a way that broke with tradition. Significantly, each donor was prepared to work alone when others were unprepared to voice their concern. Norway's action was the first time human rights considerations had been applied to a main Norwegian aid partner.[80] And Canada's action on Maduru Oya is the first example of human rights criteria being considered at the project level. Principled intervention was based on a moral imperative to respond to the plight of individuals beyond national boundaries. Adapting the aid program was a central though not exclusive focus for each country. It is a measure of Norway's and Canada's resolve, that they co-sponsored the first UNCHR resolution critical of the Sri Lankan government's human rights record.

One subsidiary hypothesis, that junior NATO alliance members may be constrained in their human rights activism, is only partly supported. Canada canvassed the views of other donors and dropped the idea of conditionality when it discovered U.S. opposition and European disinterest. The Norwegians, however, pushed ahead unilaterally with aid conditionality despite their junior status in the alliance. There is no evidence that the United States or any other donor actively sought to dissuade the Norwegians. Geopolitical and security interests were not salient to the Sri Lankan equation.[81] Another subsidiary hypothesis – that the level of policy assertiveness will correspond with the degree of domestic interest – finds some support. Sophisticated Tamil lobbies prompted media and parliamentary attention in Norway. Sustained public debate and critical assessments by independent research institutes helped tilt the Norwegian government towards a relatively hard line on Sri Lanka. In Canada, by contrast, the Tamil and Sinhalese lobby groups do not appear to have broken the government's "attention barrier." Nor did they reach Parliament, which was virtually silent on Canada's aid program in Sri Lanka. With little public interest, Canada may have felt less obliged to engage in public criticism or such a bold stroke as aid suspension.

The Norwegian and Canadian foreign policies are also consistent with two other premises underpinning the hierarchy of human rights instruments. The first is that there is a connection between the level of policy assertiveness and respect for the fundamental international norms of non-intervention and domestic jurisdiction. States face an inescapable tension when the moral norm of human rights confronts the international tradition of non-intervention. When states confine their diplomacy to unassertive instruments, respect for sovereignty may have constrained more assertive statecraft. When states implement assertive instruments, such as economic sanctions, *ceteris paribus*, human rights may have trumped respect for sovereignty. How did this work out in the context of Norwegian and Canadian statecraft towards Sri Lanka?

Both states focused mostly on low and moderately assertive levers. Norway did push through one assertive instrument, a reduction of some forms of government-to-government ODA, but it fell well short of policies that would have seriously compromised Sri Lankan sovereignty. These levers could have included consultations with Tamil "liberation forces," mandatory trade sanctions, and voting against loans for Sri Lanka in the international financial institutions. Canada undertook a single assertive policy at a project level rather than at a program level. The Maduru Oya project was first frozen for human rights reasons, but it was only taken off the books because management could no longer justify unallocated funds. Respect for sovereignty and non-intervention may partly explain Canada's reticence. In a telling comment, a senior Canadian official observed, "We do not take the more aggressive policy formulations that the Nordics seem to do. We find [the Scandinavians] more interventionist than we want to be."[82]

Table 5.2 shows each actor's emphasis on low and moderate assertiveness policies and the remarkable similarity in the instruments chosen and the timing of their application. Two exceptions are that Norway attempted to redirect its program in 1985 for human rights reasons, while Canada waited until 1990 to begin doing so; and that Norway was more openly critical at the aid consortium from 1983 onwards, while Canada waited until the late 1980s to voice its criticism in public.

Table 5.2
Canadian and Norwegian Human Rights Statecraft: Policy Options, Levels of
Assertiveness, and Timing

Policy options (assertiveness)	Canada	Norway
LOW		
Quiet diplomacy (bilateral and multilateral)	1983–90, intermittently	1983–90, intermittently
Roll-call diplomacy (UNCHR)	1987 (co-sponsor)	1987 (co-sponsor)
Declaratory diplomacy (item 12)	1987, 1990	1987, 1990
MODERATE		
Aid consortium (criticism)	1988, 1989	1983–89
Increase refugee quotas	1983–89	1983–89
Redirect ODA	1990	1985
Institution building	1990	1989
HIGH		
Reduce ODA	1985–86 (project)	1985 (program)

The instruments hierarchy predicts that as states begin to consider more assertive levers, the policy process will involve more players, higher stakes, and a degree of bureaucratic politics not associated with less assertive levers. Two reasons may explain this prediction. First, the more assertive levers generally implicate other vital national interests, calling for policy concessions by powerful bureaucratic actors such as trade or finance departments. Second, the more assertive levers are highly interventionist and contradict the norms of respect for sovereignty and non-intervention. This second concern was more salient for Norwegian and Canadian policy makers, given the absence of significant commercial or military interests. The result was a mild form of bureaucratic politics. It will be recalled that the Norwegian Ministry of Foreign Affairs had misgivings about NORAD's self-imposed human rights advocacy and its encroachment into the ministry's domain; the ministry complained that passages of its "even-handed" human rights appraisal were "worded out" in favour of a more critical stance. Arguably, the institutional differences were more divisive in Canada, with External Affairs prepared to scrap Maduru Oya and phase down the program, with Marcel Massé interested in aid leverage, and with CIDA defending its development mandate, program continuity, and commercial interests. If Canadian and Norwegian diplomacy had been confined to the United Nations, this degree of bureaucratic infighting would likely have been less evident.

In the realm of practice, there are many commonalities and some significant differences in the way each donor country handled the conflict and human rights. The premise is that Western policy makers evaluating the Sri Lankan human rights record will likely choose among five alternative assessments, each of which has statecraft implications. The evaluations were guilt, complicity, agnosticism, innocence, and change. In a broad sweep, Norway between 1983 and 1987 appears to have taken the stance that the Sri Lankan government was complicitous, with some elements of a guilt stance. From 1987 to 1989 there were elements of an agnostic and change position in a setting of optimism, stemming from the Indo–Sri Lanka accord. Canada, by contrast, appears to have been more consistently agnostic between 1983 and 1987, but by 1989 it began more visibly to view the Sri Lankan government as complicitous in the escalation of human rights abuses. What impact did these shifting evaluations have on policy?

Norway, from the outset, was more interventionist and somewhat more punitive than Canada. Moral considerations were important and led to an early, politically driven modification of the ODA program. A deliberate though only partially successful effort was made to target the Tamil community. The program was consciously modified to ensure that Norwegian ODA did not indirectly support a repressive regime. This meant reducing commodity aid and balance-of-payments support for principled, not pragmatic, reasons. There is no evidence of resistance from Norwegian commercial interests.

Canada, in contrast, was initially agnostic, and between 1983 and 1987 it showed little inclination to criticize the Sri Lankan government's human rights record publicly by raising the matter at the aid consortium meetings, the UNCHR, or the U.N. General Assembly. One senior policy maker was interested in using aid as a human-rights lever, but there was no support for this option among the government officials with direct knowledge of Sri Lanka. The option was nullified when it became clear that other donors would not work with Canada to apply leverage on the Sri Lankans. Realism on the issue of policy effectiveness trumped any moral imperative calling for a more assertive or punitive response. But CIDA was forced by circumstances to put on hold its lead project because questions of equity intruded into the project's implementation. CIDA had not wanted to do so initially, arguing that aid beneficiaries would be needlessly penalized, that program continuity would be lost, and that there were commercial costs to consider.

Individuals in Norway were more important in developing an active Norwegian policy than they were in Canada. State Secretary Saeter and Deputy Minister Bugge were determined to modify the aid program and accept the souring of bilateral relations. Moreover, until the 1985 diplomatic rupture, there had been active discussion between high-level

Norwegian and Sri Lankan policy makers. In Canada, although Secretary of State Clark insisted on a careful appraisal of the Maduru Oya resettlement plan, there is no evidence that senior policy makers were interested in directing policy according to their individual dictates. Undersecretary Massé accepted that a more assertive form of aid leverage was unworkable; and Clark, in the end, opted for CIDA's preference to keep the project alive rather than killing it in order to send a curt message to the Sri Lankan government about its human rights record.

What accounts for these differences in diplomatic style and policy? Foreign policy often reflects domestic pressures. Issue visibility and domestic lobby group strength can sometimes push foreign policy elites to action which may not be taken otherwise. In the case of South Africa, domestic and international NGOs nudged countries such as Canada and the Nordic states towards sanctions. Granted, in Sri Lanka both donors could take a moral position, because they were not significantly compromised by conflicting security or commercial considerations – though Canada may have felt more constrained in pursuing an assertive human rights policy because of the Commonwealth connection and the commercial interests of domestic engineering firms. But that is not the whole story.

In Norway, a sophisticated and vocal Tamil community made Sri Lanka a media issue. The Norwegian parliament, too, took an active interest in Sri Lanka. Finally, the institutional framework for human rights and ODA in Norway allowed independent research centres that took a critical view of the Sri Lankan government's human rights record to be actively involved in policy making. These three domestic influences, combined with the influence of key senior policy makers, help explain why a reticent aid and foreign affairs bureaucracy was compelled to change the aid program.

In Canada, Sri Lanka has never captured media attention or popular imagination in the way Central America or South African apartheid has. True, stirrings of a principled resolution of the resettlement question were partly prompted by media exposure; and there are some 11,000 Sri Lankan refugees in Canada, with both Sinhalese and Tamil lobby groups. Nevertheless, my interviews with policy makers at CIDA and External Affairs consistently revealed a perception that domestic lobbies were not important in policy formulation. Unlike Norway's Storting, the Canadian parliament played virtually no role in the affair. Parliament's interest was confined to refugee issues. Canadian policy makers were thus relatively free of domestic pressures. The aggressive lobbying and media exposure in Norway may account for the unusually high-level involvement in the aid relationship with Sri Lanka. In contrast, Canada never embarked on high-level consultations, an indication of Sri Lanka's low position in Canada's foreign policy priorities.

There were also limits to the lengths each country was prepared to go on behalf of human rights. First, neither country seriously considered a highly assertive lever such as suspending the entire aid program. In Canada, pragmatism – the fear of setting precedents – seems to have been as strong a motive in avoiding aid suspension as was concern about losing influence and penalizing the poorest groups. Second, neither country criticized the human rights abuses committed by the Indian Peacekeeping Force or questioned its poor performance as peacekeeper. On the contrary, Canada quickly dropped the idea of playing "the helpful fixer" when India made it clear that Sri Lanka was in its sphere of influence and that conflict resolution was India's responsibility.

Questions of policy effectiveness and appropriateness are more difficult to answer. The Norwegians, by their actions at the aid consortium, may have helped galvanize the donor community to press Sri Lanka for an accord with India. Bilaterally, after surviving strained relations, Norway persuaded Sri Lanka that human rights were a legitimate issue in the aid dialogue. However, the Norwegian policy makers' commitment to project this concern seems to have been weak since 1987. Canada never received a clear answer from the Sri Lankans on resettlement ratios, but its carefully modulated actions on Maduru Oya did not unduly disrupt bilateral relations. Canada's principled action may have contributed, in a modest way, to the peace accord negotiations. But Canada was singularly ineffective in persuading the rest of the donor community to consider joint action.

The donor community was slow to recognize the potential leverage of aid. Policy coordination was driven as much by pragmatism – the recognition that conflict stalls development – as by an overriding concern for human rights. Safety is vitally important, of course, but to consider withdrawal only when development work is impracticable makes a donor's commitment to human rights seem insincere and self-interested. Safety, and not human rights per se, seem to have been the most important motivation to Canada's "downsizing" in Sri Lanka. Canada's willingness to continue commodity support also needs to be scrutinized. Commercial considerations may have underpinned CIDA's reluctance to acknowledge that commodity and import support help support a repressive regime.

Would the situation have improved if the donors had acted together earlier? While conditionality may not have improved human rights in the short run, it might have pressured the government to "get serious" about seeking a settlement. After years of violence, Western donors finally seemed prepared to act on the principle that peace is the best guarantor of human rights and democracy in Sri Lanka.

6 Riding the Tiger: Western Responses to Tiananmen Square

Last June, there occurred in Beijing, a rebellion which was supported by hostile forces abroad and [which] constituted an attempt to overthrow the legitimate system set forth in the Constitution through violent means. The Chinese government took resolute measures to quell the rebellion in the interests of the overwhelming majority of the Chinese people. *This is entirely China's internal affair and is a matter different in nature from the question of human rights.*

> Speech by the permanent representative of the People's Republic of China at the United Nations, 1 December 1989 (emphasis added)

This case study is a "snapshot" of Canadian, Dutch, and Norwegian responses to the Tiananmen Square events of 1989. It sets out to answer two questions: What happened in Tiananmen Square? And how did the West respond?[1] The People's Republic of China is the litmus test of each state's commitment to promote and protect human rights. China is the most powerful of the less-developed countries, altering the usual North-South power dynamic; China to Norway is like Gulliver to the Lilliputians. All three countries have significant commercial interests in the People's Republic, and each country's diplomacy was influenced by international coordination. All these factors were potential constraints on policy autonomy and an assertive human rights statecraft. What impact did they have in practice? But government-to-government aid is only part of this narrative. By also looking at the three countries' actions at the World Bank and the United Nations, one can assess the coherence or trade-offs in the Dutch, Canadian, and Norwegian reactions to Tiananmen Square. The comparative method here is thematic and looks at low, moderate, and highly assertive policies.

WHAT HAPPENED AT TIANANMEN SQUARE?

The death of Hu Yao Bang, the former secretary general of the Chinese Communist Party, on 15 April 1989 sparked a demonstration by about three thousand students in Beijing's Tiananmen Square.[2] The students subsequently articulated their grievances in a seven-point petition, which was presented to the National People's Congress, China's parliament. They demanded:

- a reappraisal of Hu Yao Bang's historical role;
- a reassessment of the campaigns against "spiritual pollution" (1983);
- rehabiliation of the victims of the 1983 and 1987 campaigns;
- the disclosure of the private bank accounts of the top leaders and their families;
- guarantees of freedom of speech and freedom of the press;
- an increase to education spending and better treatment of intellectuals; and
- a restoration of the right to demonstrate.[3]

On 24 April students at approximately thirty of Beijing's seventy colleges began a strike to press for further political reform. On 4 May, the seventieth anniversary of China's first modern political campaign, about one million people peacefully occupied the square. The students were joined by many sectors of Chinese society – civil servants, journalists, lawyers, doctors, miners, and even some members of the security forces. On 13 May about one thousand students began a hunger strike to dramatize their call for a "genuine dialogue" with the Chinese government. The hunger strike sparked unprecedented international media attention and coincided with the Sino-Soviet summit, 15–18 May. On 18 May Premier Li Peng held talks with the hunger strikers, who rejected his calls to end their fast.

Between 18 and 20 May the hardliners won the struggle between the more moderate and authoritarian factions within the leadership. Party Secretary General Zhao Ziyang was removed and publicly disgraced, and Premier Li Peng announced martial law in Beijing on 20 May. Troops appeared in the city in large numbers, and by the end of May at least 150,000 soldiers from thirteen of China's twenty-four armies were reported to have surrounded Beijing.[4] By early June, however, the number of protestors in the square began to decrease, and on the afternoon of 2 June only a few thousand students remained there.

It is not necessary to recount the horrifying denouement of that Chinese spring. The broad outlines are indelibly imprinted on the collective consciousness. Some features of the "incident" are, however, worth recalling. First, the demonstrations were almost entirely peaceful. Second, conventional methods of crowd control were not used. The troops opened fired at random or shot deliberately at the crowds without warning. These actions against unarmed civilians were extrajudicial killings. They violated the international standards that lethal force should be used only when absolutely necessary and in direct proportion to the legitimate objective it is intended to achieve. Instead, the troops deliberately killed people who were no immediate threat to them.[5] Third, intense media coverage prompted global calls for principled action by the global community. Fourth, in the aftermath of Tiananmen, the Beijing leadership embarked on a systematic campaign of repression, reprisal, and propaganda. They purged all union and student associations, used Orwellian methods to rewrite history, began hollow campaigns to create revolutionary heroes and restore public confidence in the People's Liberation Army, incited citizens to expose alleged conspirators, held show trials with public confessions, imposed compulsory "re-education" in remote labour camps, publicly executed "ruffians" for deterrent effect, and denounced Western "interference" in China's internal affairs.

The mismatch between official and unofficial figures is standard fare in human rights monitoring. Disagreements about the exact number of dead and wounded cannot, however, obscure the central fact that the army's actions at Tiananmen Square were unequivocal "gross and systematic" human rights violations. The clarity of the abuses and the culpability of the Chinese leaders contrasts with the more muddied picture of state culpability in the Philippines, Kenya, and Sri Lanka. Only Bouterse's actions in Suriname were as clear. In sum, the events of 3 and 4 June 1989 and their aftermath point to a "human rights negative" pattern, one of those "extreme cases of a state judged by the international community to be guilty of persistent, gross and systematic violations."[6] These features helped shape a surprisingly assertive Western reaction to Tiananmen.

HISTORICAL INFLUENCES ON HUMAN RIGHTS DIPLOMACY

When the communists defeated the Guomindang in 1949, most Western states, Canada among them, refused to recognize the People's

Republic. China's U.N. seat was occupied by Formosa. Whether there was one China or two would preoccupy international diplomacy for the next two decades. In 1950 the United Kingdom, Norway, the Netherlands, Denmark, Sweden, Switzerland, and Austria recognized the People's Republic of China. Norway and the Netherlands were thus among those who settled on a "one China" policy. But during the 1980s, the Netherlands and Norway were both embroiled in incidents that soured bilateral relations with China – the Dutch in a commercial impasse with political consequences; the Norwegians in a political impasse which threatened commercial interests. The Sino-Dutch conflict centred on the sale of submarines to Taiwan in 1983. Norway's impasse centred on an October 1988 visit by the Tibetan Dalai Lama. In both cases, the discipline of power prevailed, and Norway and the Netherlands pragmatically bowed to Chinese wishes.

Commerce and Conflict: Dutch Arms Exports to Taiwan

In the early 1980s, the Dutch merchant shipbuilding industry was collapsing in the face of an international recession.[7] Seeing an opportunity to shift the industry into naval construction, the Ministry of Economic Affairs tried to help an ailing Rotterdam shipyard by selling four submarines to Taiwan. The proposed arms sale required cabinet approval and led to an intense domestic political and bureaucratic conflict and to a serious deterioration in Sino-Dutch relations. The economic affairs minister predicted shipyard closures and job losses if the sale fell through. But the foreign affairs minister, Van der Klaaw, opposed the sale because it would overturn Holland's "one China" policy, because "Chinese pragmatism would not easily overcome hurt diplomatic pride," and because several European Community partners and the United States also opposed the proposed sale. The Chinese, meanwhile, reacted with a strongly worded diplomatic note describing the proposed sale as "provocative" and "aggressive."[8]

Immediate commercial imperatives prevailed over diplomatic risks, and the contract between RSV, the Dutch shipbuilder, and Taiwan was signed in September 1981. The Chinese reacted not through economic means, as had been feared, but by downgrading diplomatic relations to the pre-1972 level of chargé d'affaires. However, a second proposed sale of Dutch submarines to Taiwan, in 1983, fell through. After the Reagan administration bowed to Chinese pressure against the proposed sale of Northrop F5G fighter bombers to Taiwan, the Dutch cabinet was persuaded that the Chinese might retaliate, and it therefore refused to grant the export licence. The decision enabled the two countries to "normalize" relations and restore their diplomatic presence to embassy level.

Norway's Tibet Conundrum

In the 1980s, Norway broke into sectors of the Chinese market in which Norwegian firms held a competitive advantage, including oil and hydrocarbon technology, hydro-electric power, chemicals, and shipping and ancillary services. By 1987, China had become Norway's third-largest export market in Asia with sales valued at 600 million kroner.[9] The prospect of tapping China's huge market, however, was threatened by the Dalai Lama's visit to Norway in October 1988.

China has long regarded Tibet as part of its territory. Under a Russo-British agreement of 1907, China's legal sovereignty over Tibet was formally recognized, but it was deferred in practice, leaving Tibet essentially independent until Mao Zedong invaded and annexed the country in the 1950s. Virtually all Western nations now recognize China's legal sovereignty over the territory, which is formally described as an "autonomous region" within the People's Republic. In 1987 and 1988, Tibetan resistance to the harsh policies of assimilation and discrimination arose when Buddhist monks led demonstrations. The Chinese authorities' suppression of these protests led to allegations of torture and other human rights abuses.[10]

The exiled Dalai Lama visited several Western countries to muster international support against the human rights abuses in Tibet.[11] His proposed visit to Norway posed a problem for the Norwegian government because, from a Chinese perspective, the Dalai Lama was not only the spiritual leader but the political voice of a people who were unwilling to accept Chinese rule and were pressing for greater self-determination.[12] If the Norwegian government officially received the Dalai Lama, it would be tantamount to acknowledging Tibetan political demands and Chinese human rights abuses. Yet Norway's official recognition of the People's Republic implied, ipso facto, legal recognition of China's jurisdiction over Tibet. Moreover, receiving the Dalai Lama could be construed as indirect interference in China's internal affairs, the nonviolation of which has been a basic principle of China's diplomatic relations with all Western countries.

Fortunately, the government had only to look at history – and at the way its Nordic neighbours were dealing with the Dalai Lama – to resolve the problem. The Dalai Lama had made one previous visit to Norway in 1973. He had come as a private individual and had not been received by the Korvald administration. In Finland, Denmark, and Sweden, private organizations invited the Tibetan leader in 1988. None of the governments in these countries was prepared to receive the Dalai Lama officially, for the Chinese had given clear signals of their displeasure to all countries.

In Norway, however, there appears to have been disagreement among senior cabinet members and even within the Ministry of Foreign Affairs, which might have been expected to be unanimous in counselling caution. On one side were those who recognized China's acute sensitivity regarding Tibet and the danger that retaliation might lead to the loss of contracts and jobs. On the other side were those who took issue with kowtowing to Chinese pressure and giving commercial interests precedence over human rights principles. This latter group, which included the smaller radical parties such as the Socialist Left Party, also pointed to the hypocrisy of Western countries pressuring the Soviet Union and Eastern European states on human rights but doing nothing about China's equally poor record.

Prime Minister Gro Harlem Brundtland and the former prime minister, Kare Willoch, who was chairman of the Storting's foreign affairs committee, were opposed to receiving the Dalai Lama. The foreign minister, Thorvald Stoltenberg, sought a compromise by permitting the Dalai Lama to be received officially by Mari Kvidal, the minister of clerical affairs and education. This tactic had the advantage of stressing the Dalai Lama's credentials as a spiritual rather than political leader. But it was not enough to assuage the Chinese, Stoltenberg's colleagues in the cabinet, or the advisers at the foreign ministry. News that the Norwegian government was planning to receive the Dalai Lama brought a swift Chinese reaction. Li Baoching, China's ambassador in Norway, told foreign ministry officials that bilateral relations would be seriously damaged if the Dalai Lama was received.[13] The Chinese issued blunt but vague threats that commercial contracts could be affected by an inappropriate Norwegian decision.[14]

Brundtland's government eventually bowed to Chinese pressure and to Norway's commercial interests. The Dalai Lama would be received not by the clerical affairs minister but by a civilian representative, the chairman of the Norwegian Council of Bishops. Stoltenberg told the Storting that the decision had been made "following a strong Chinese reaction"[15] and explained "the embarrassingly impolite treatment" of the Dalai Lama by saying that Norway considered Tibet to be a part of China.[16] The parliament and the media had a field day. An editorial in *Dagbladet*, for example, suggested that "Mr. Carefulness is employed in the Norwegian Ministry of Foreign Affairs and walks daily on rubber soles."[17]

Canada and China: The Search for Mutual Advantage

Unlike the Netherlands and Norway, Canada has excellent political and economic relations with China. This is a legacy of Prime Minister

Trudeau's 1970 initiative to establish full diplomatic relations with the People's Republic, making Canada the first of a large group of ambivalent Western states to do so.[18] Canada also helped break the U.N. impasse and pave the way to grant the People's Republic the China seat in the General Assembly.[19] Prime Minister Trudeau's visit to Beijing in October 1973 set the tone for future Sino-Canadian relations. His special assistant, Ivan Head, noted that "one priority in the discussion was to impress upon the Chinese the need for easier access to China for Canadian businessmen."[20] Trudeau told the Chinese, "We are incapable of forcing our relations with you." He explained: "We have invested our faith in the avoidance of conflict and in the easing of tensions. We seek friendly relations with those countries who sympathise with our goals. We seek the mutual advantages which are offered by increased diplomatic, commercial and cultural exchanges. That search has brought me to China."[21] Trudeau's comments thus acknowledged China's power and signalled Canada's intention to develop trade links but not to interfere in China's internal affairs. Trudeau signed a long-term agreement on wheat sales that has since become the staple in Canada's export trade with China. By 1988, China was Canada's fourth-largest export market and Canada was China's eighth-largest trade partner.

In sum, the early postwar history reveals a strong foundation for cordial Sino-Dutch and Sino-Norwegian relations, though strains emerged in the 1980s when both the Netherlands and Norway were obliged to accommodate Chinese wishes. Canada, on the other hand, had had good relations with China since Trudeau's visit helped persuade the West to recognize the People's Republic and restore its U.N. seat. What implications does each actor's history have for its post-Tiananmen statecraft? A realist would say that each state had reason to downplay human rights. In China's earlier joint communiqués with Norway and the Netherlands, it had insisted that all three states agree to the principle of non-interference in each other's internal affairs. A 1972 Sino-Dutch joint communiqué noted that "the Netherlands holds that the principle of peaceful co-existence should imply non-interference in each other's internal affairs ... The government of the People's Republic of China appreciates this stand.[22] Before Tiananmen, this principle was respected. None of our self-styled moralists actively protested human rights abuses during the Cultural Revolution or in Tibet.[23] Before Tiananmen, Canada had little reason to disrupt its cordial and increasingly profitable relations with the People's Republic by public human rights criticism.[24] After Tiananmen, Canada pursued a subtle course that combined rhetorical condemnation with minimizing economic costs.

Realist thinking predicts that as small, relatively weak states, Norway and the Netherlands should have heeded the lessons of history and opted for unassertive policies after Tiananmen. The impulse to "soft pedal" should have been even greater for the Norwegians, because the lesson of the Dalai Lama's visit would have been fresh in their minds, just seven months before Tiananmen. In fact, these crude realist premises were substantially unrealized in both cases. The evidence indicates that both states were largely undeterred by the prospect of Chinese retaliation; and both imposed relatively assertive policies to express deeply held moral convictions. There were, however, special circumstances driving Dutch and Norwegian statecraft.

TIANANMEN SQUARE: INITIAL RESPONSES

Canada was one of the first Western states to develop a coherent response to Tiananmen. The government went to unusual lengths to consult experts and tap public opinion. It arranged for a national round table of officials, business leaders, representatives from Canada's large Chinese community, NGOs, and academics. Parliament, meanwhile, held a special debate, and opposition MPs urged the government to consider action in the Security Council and to reconsider aid and export credits to China. Earl Drake, Canada's ambassador to China, was recalled for consultations, and the trade mission in Beijing was reduced from nine officials to six. Both actions were intended to convey Canada's disquiet about the actions of the hardline leaders.

The national round table helped frame the parameters of Canada's response. External Affairs Minister Joe Clark afterwards released a comprehensive policy statement on 30 June 1989.[25] He outlined the following policy premises: "First, Tiananmen Square and the subsequent campaign of repression have changed the relationship between Canada and China. The Chinese authorities have called for 'business as usual'; this cannot be accepted. Second, we value the friendship between our two peoples – we have not become, and will not become, 'anti-China.' Third, we must try to avoid measures that will push China towards isolation; and Fourth, we should try to maximize the impact of whatever measures we adopt via a relatively co-ordinated approach of 'like-minded' countries." These premises led to three criteria that were to guide action: first, existing links "should be preserved to the extent possible"; second, new initiatives should focus on people-to-people exchanges; third, "programs which benefit or lend prestige to the current hardline policies of the Chinese government, most particularly the military or state propaganda apparatus, should be avoided."[26]

In Holland, Foreign Minister Hans van den Broek served notice that Dutch responses would be driven by EC political cooperation. He used the *Statement of the Twelve on China* as his brief to the second chamber of the Dutch parliament. The EC statement warned, "Continuing repressive actions, in violation of universally recognised human rights principles, will greatly prejudice China's international standing and compromise the reform and open-door policies which the European Community and its member states have actively supported." EC policy subsequently crystallized in the Madrid Declaration of 27 June 1989, the chief elements of which were that EC states would:

(a) raise human rights issues in U.N. forums;
(b) impose an embargo on arms trade with China;
(c) suspend bilateral ministerial and high level contacts;
(d) postpone new aid and credit "cooperation" projects;
(e) reduce cultural, technical and scientific cooperation;
(f) extend Chinese student visas; and
(g) recommend postponement of new World Bank credits.[27]

In Norway, the Brundtland government abruptly shifted its policy towards China and took measures that substantially paralleled EC policy. It suspended high-level meetings and cultural contacts, and froze credits and aid. However, the government's reaction was complicated by the decision of the Oslo Nobel Institution – an independent body – to award the 1989 Nobel Peace Prize to the Dalai Lama.[28] By custom, the winner has a private meeting with the king, the prime minister, and the foreign minister after the ceremony. Moreover, the Nobel Prize had more than a symbolic significance – the message of the Dalai Lama's award was not likely to be lost on the Chinese government or on the Tibetan people. From the Chinese perspective, any official contact between the Dalai Lama and the Norwegian government would appear to legitimize the Tibetan struggle and to undermine Chinese sovereignty.

China's reaction was predictable if unrealistic and ultimately ineffective. The Chinese could not accept that the Nobel Institution was a private organization. To the Chinese, the award was a betrayal by the Norwegian government. Norway's ambassador in Beijing was summoned to the Chinese foreign ministry, and "strong views" were communicated, advising the Norwegian government that the best policy would be not to invite the Tibetan leader and that, at all costs, he should not be received by the king or by members of the government. In addition, subtle threats were communicated, once again hinting at the possible loss of commercial contracts.

On this occasion, the government was on firmer ground and did not bow to Chinese pressure. Both the newly elected Prime Minister Syse and Foreign Minister Bondevik attended the prize-giving ceremony and officially received the Dalai Lama. The government explained to the disbelieving Chinese that custom required an official meeting, but it emphasized that the Dalai Lama was being received merely as an individual. The government had no other choice. To have snubbed the Tibetan leader again would have undermined domestic credibility of a new, fragile minority government and would have provided another embarrassing example of Norwegian timidity in the face of Chinese bullying. It would also have made nonsense of Norway's hard-line policy on Tiananmen Square. But while Norway rode the tiger at home, its foreign ministry was quiet at the United Nations.

CHINA AT THE UNITED NATIONS: POWER POLITICS AND NORTH-SOUTH CONFLICT

At the United Nations, human rights are considered in four main forums. The cycle begins each summer in Geneva at the Subcommission on the Prevention of Discrimination and the Protection of Minorities. It then moves to the General Assembly in New York, where it is dealt with in the third committee on social, economic, and cultural affairs and in the human rights committee. The real action, however, is in mid-winter in Geneva at the U.N. Commission on Human Rights (UNCHR).[29] The Dutch were active in the General Assembly; Canada tried to use its influence in the Security Council; and Norway, perhaps conscious of the repercussions of an activist approach, kept a low profile. All three states, however, supported Western Group initiatives to raise the subject of the Beijing leadership's human rights abuses in a public world forum. But beyond airing the issue, nothing tangible was achieved by the West at the United Nations.

The intensity of the Chinese lobbying underlines the politicization of U.N. human rights forums and the deep rifts between North and South on country-specific human rights abuses. And China is no ordinary actor. Faced with the People's Republic's strident defence of the principle of non-intervention in domestic affairs and its use of intimidation and persuasion at every turn, the Western Group was forced to consider carefully the most appropriate tactics to ensure maximum visibility of the issue with minimum risk of retaliation.

The subcommission's deliberations on China set a useful foundation for subsequent Western actions at the United Nations. Its independent experts – including a prominent Norwegian and Dutchman[30] – produced a mild resolution calling on the secretary general "to transmit to the Human Rights Commission information provided by the government of China and by other reliable sources." It also appealed for clemency for "persons deprived of their liberty as a result" of Tiananmen Square.[31] The resolution was adopted by fifteen votes to five with two abstentions. But several experts complained of deliberate efforts by Chinese observers to bribe them into voting against it – a tactic that revealed Chinese machinations elsewhere in the United Nations. African experts reportedly were threatened, some with the withdrawal of Chinese aid to their countries. Others were reportedly offered all-expenses-paid "research trips" to China in return for blocking the resolution.[32] So intense was the Chinese lobbying that the subcommission was persuaded by its African experts to take the very unusual step of a secret ballot. Norwegian, Dutch, and Canadian observer delegations at the subcommission supported the resolution.

At the forty-fourth session of the U.N. General Assembly, the Dutch played a prominent and unusually assertive role in criticizing the Beijing leadership's human rights record. They did so by introducing a draft resolution on "freedom of expression and the right of peaceful assembly."[33] The resolution was ostensibly thematic, not country-specific, and was intended to strengthen the status of two rights enshrined in the International Bill of Human Rights but still subject to "blatant violations."[34] The Netherlands' timing, however, left no doubt that it was using the resolution to comment on China's suppression of these rights. The Dutch hoped the text would be adopted without a vote. But they were outmanoeuvered by the Chinese, and the draft text was never voted on.

The Chinese defended themselves by taking the offensive. They introduced a proposal to restrict the United Nations' right to criticize a country's human rights record. This was prompted by the fear that China's human rights record would be on the item 12 agenda at the UNCHR meeting, which was only two months away. With other Third World countries, the People's Republic proposed an amendment to the Dutch draft resolution reiterating a U.N. basic principle on the "inadmissibility of intervention in the domestic affairs of states." The proposed amendment cited the U.N. Charter's creed of non-intervention and U.N. provisions that "no state shall organize, assist, foment, finance, incite or tolerate subversive terrorist or armed activities directed towards the violent overthrow of another state, or interfere in civil strife in another state."[35] The Chinese representative, Li Luye, said that "the principle of non-interference in the internal affairs of other countries should also apply to the issue of human rights."[36] The publication Xinhua,[37] commenting on the draft resolution "meticulously cooked up by the Netherlands," noted that freedom of assembly and expression could be exercised only in conformity with domestic law "concerning national security, people's safety and public order."[38]

The Netherlands and other Western "human rights guardians" parried by describing the Chinese initiative as a new motion, not an amendment, and they demanded an immediate vote, hoping that a victory would allow the reintroduction of their own resolution. The Dutch motion was defeated, however, with thirty votes for, eighty-five against, and nine abstentions.[39] With the Chinese amendment intact, the Dutch were obliged to withdraw the original draft resolution on behalf of their Western Group co-sponsors. Savouring victory, *Xinhua* claimed that "the latest event at the U.N. made it clear that it is always unpopular and unsuccessful for anyone who deliberately disconnects the exercise of human rights with a state's sovereignty and plays power politics to meddle in the internal affairs of other nations under the pretext of human rights."[40]

The interpretation of Dutch, Canadian, and Norwegian action at UNCHR must be premised on three facts. First, as observer delegations, Norway and the Netherlands were more constrained in their response to China, because although they were able to participate in debates and could even draft and introduce resolutions, they were unable to vote. Canada, on the other hand, was a full member of the commission in 1990 and could vote.[41] Second, all three states are part of the larger Western Group, which meets regularly to share information and coordinate strategy. The group is a mix of relatively conservative major powers, such as Japan and West Germany, and more outspoken human rights entrepreneurs, such as the Nordic states and the Netherlands. Third, the Dutch experience at the General Assembly had a salutary effect on the Western states and made for a more cautious approach on China.[42] Nevertheless, considerable attention was paid to China at the commission. Tiananmen was raised under item 10 on "Human Rights of All Persons Subjected to any Form of Detention or Imprisonment" and under item 12 on "Human Rights Violations in All Parts of the World." Oral interventions were made by Austria, Canada, Sweden, the EC, and several NGOs.[43]

The Western Group agreed that it would attempt a resolution on China, reasoning that even if it failed, the adverse publicity and the weight of international opinion might influence the Beijing leadership.[44] Group members differed on strategy and tactics. The signal effect of "the politics of shame" was undeniable. A resolution on China would be the first time any permanent member of the Security Council had been publicly criticized at the commission for its human rights record. A successful resolution might also bring into question China's domestic stability, with reverberations on trade, investment, IFI loans, and tourism. But the Western Group had to avoid any perception that it was merely "an imperialist coalition," because the Chinese could exploit this; and consistent with the general international position not to isolate China, the resolution would have to be relatively mild, emphasizing whatever progress had been made by the Beijing leadership and avoiding overly punitive language.

Australia introduced a draft resolution and coordinated a campaign to persuade non-aligned states to vote for it. A similar draft was later introduced by Japan, and the final text merged the two drafts. The resolution, in part, read:

1 **Recalling** Sub-Commission resolution 1989/5 of 31 August 1989;
2 **Concerned** at allegations of violations of human rights in China; ...
3 **Endorses** the appeal of the Sub-Commission for clemency towards persons deprived of their liberty as a result of the events in June 1989;
4 **Welcomes,** as steps in the right direction, the decisions of the government of China in January 1990 to lift martial law in Beijing and to release 583 persons who had been detained;
5 **Urges** the government of China to continue to take measures along the same lines to ensure full observance of human rights, as affirmed in the Universal Declaration of Human Rights;

Requests the Secretary General to transmit to the 47th session of the Commission on Human Rights additional information, including that provided by the government of China.

The Western Group considered several options regarding the signing and introduction of the text. Australia and one other Western state could co-sponsor it with a representative from the non-aligned group, but this had the disadvantage of isolating three states for possible retaliation by the People's Republic of China. A second option was to co-sponsor with representatives from all the principal regional groupings, but this might have been difficult to achieve, given that non-Western countries tend to be sceptical of country-specific resolutions, and that China was lobbying to dissuade non-aligned states from voting in favour of the resolution. A third option was to leave the text unsigned and unintroduced. This option had the merit of avoiding retaliation, but at the cost of weakening the resolution's moral force.[45] It was the option chosen, an indication of the Western states' nervousness about possible Chinese retaliation. However, China, with the help of its allies, was able to pre-empt a vote on the resolution. Pakistan, still a geopolitical ally of China, introduced a procedural resolution that no action be taken on the draft resolution.[46] Two Marxist states, Somalia and Cuba, supported the Pakistani initiative. The procedural resolution narrowly passed in a roll-call vote, with seventeen for, fifteen against, and eleven abstentions. Thus, the Chinese delegation avoided any official record of even a defeated motion of criticism regarding the human rights situation in China.

Although Norway supported the final Western Group resolution, its delegation kept a low profile during the discussions on China. The delegation made no attempt to push for a strongly worded text. Norway agreed with the concept of shared responsibility for the text but apparently not with the option of public signature. For a country with a tradition of U.N. activism, this inactivity seems puzzling. One explanations is that Norway usually does not introduce resolutions when it is an observer delegation. But Norway's strained relations with China is a more compelling reason. As one official explained, China perceives Norway as "an almost unfriendly nation. And the Chinese do not forget their enemies ... Our outstanding problems [with China] means that we cannot be the flagbearer [at the United Nations]. We have already taken a lot of blows from the Chinese."[47] An assertive role at the human rights commission would have added insult to injury.

Unlike the Canadian and Norwegian delegations, the Dutch delegation was involved in two sets of discussions on the China resolution – with the Western Group and with the EC states. The Netherlands supported the draft resolution, but it also pressed for a common signature of another resolution by the twelve EC countries, arguing that this was consistent with the already public position of the European Community as laid out in the Madrid Declaration.[48] The Dutch could not, however, persuade their EC partners.[49] Beyond this single initiative, observer status gave the Dutch delegation "an easy way out" on China – a legitimate reason not to initiate a resolution.[50] Their General Assembly experience had blunted any Dutch appetite for further activism on China.

Canada's item 12 speech at Geneva contained some strong language on China. Ambassador Andreychuk observed:

The military crackdown in June 1989, and the subsequent campaign of repression has provided the world with dramatic evidence of human rights abuses in the People's Republic of China. Use of the death penalty without effective appeal, torture, ill treatment of prisoners and procedural rights of the accused persons, have characterized the Chinese criminal justice system since last June. Although these practices marred the Chinese human rights record before June, progress had been made in bringing greater predictability to the justice system. While China is far from returning to the anarchy and level of human rights violations of the Cultural Revolution period, the present situation represents a real setback for the respect of human rights. Further changes are needed.

These include: the release of persons arrested since Tiananmen; the ending of further arrests and the lifting of martial law in Tibet, where human rights violations are of particular concern.[51]

Although the speech avoided blaming state leaders directly for the Tiananmen abuses, it did refer to Tibet and it outlined several "needed" human rights improvements. China does not respond well to a "shopping list" approach, and the Canadian list doubtless irritated the Chinese delegation.[52] Canada also supported the draft resolution on China, although, like others, the delegation knew that the resolution would probably fail. But the effort was still judged worthwhile because it would "unequivocally" reflect the West's legitimate concern about human rights in China.[53] Nevertheless, the Canadians thought it inappropriate for the resolution to refer specifically to Tibet, their stated reason being China's acute defensiveness on questions of sovereignty and the poor quality of information regarding abuses in Tibet. But a more telling reason for the silence on Tibet is that Canada recognizes China's claim on Tibet (a Canadian delegate described Tibet as "yesterday's news").[54]

In theory, Canada's place as a nonpermanent member of the Security Council provided an influential forum in which to raise China's human rights record. The Chinese-Canadian National Council met External Affairs Minister Clark on 8 June and urged Canada to introduce a motion in the Security Council condemning the People's Republic. In Parliament, André Ouellet, the Liberal foreign affairs spokesman, "saw potential to use discreet Canadian influence" in the Security Council. Yves Fortier, Canada's ambassador at the United Nations, confirmed that he had "contacted all members of the Security Council" and had communicated Parliament's views on Tiananmen Square to the U.N. Secretary General. But Fortier played down the scope for Canadian influence, noting that the U.N. Charter, which determines the jurisdiction of the Security Council, forbids involvement in a state's internal affairs unless international peace and security are at risk.[55] Fortier denied that China's veto power in the Security Council was the main stumbling block to greater Canadian activism in that arena, though this must have undermined any role for the council.[56] In any case, Canada's status at that time as one of ten nonpermanent members of the Security Council offered no real opportunity to persuade other council members to get tough on China. As the assistant deputy minister Jean McCloskey told a parliamentary committee, "So far, there has been no way we could have sparked a debate in the Security Council. It is not for lack of trying, believe me."[57]

U.N. diplomacy was not the only setting for Dutch, Canadian, and Norwegian statecraft. The three countries also pressed several moderately assertive bilateral levers. These included easing refugee guidelines, tightening arms sale restrictions, freezing new aid projects, and suspending high-level meetings. All three countries suspended ministerial and other high-level contacts with the Chinese government *sine die*. The Dutch were obliged to do so by the European Community's Madrid Declaration. Norway appears to have followed the EC position on this issue. In the spring of 1990, for example, the Norwegian environment minister had been planning to visit his Chinese counterpart to discuss environmental cooperation; but despite the central role that China will likely play in global environmental diplomacy, the proposed visit was blocked by Foreign Minister Bondevik as being inconsistent with the freeze on high-level contacts with the People's Republic.

Canada, although intending to "defer" high-level contacts "for the time being,"[58] found it impossible to implement the policy. Within a year and a half of Tiananmen Square, there were at least four examples of high-level Sino-Canadian contacts. The secretary of state for external affairs, Joe Clark, met the Chinese foreign minister, Quian Qichen, several times in Paris during the July 1989 peace conference on Cambodia. Jean McCloskey, assistant deputy minister for external affairs, visited China in February 1990 to discuss Hong Kong and Cambodia. In May 1990, Monique Landry, minister of state for external relations, was visited by the president of the Bank of China at a meeting of the Asian Development Bank in Delhi. The Chinese were canvassing support for a return to normal lending by the Asian Development Bank. Reportedly, Landry took the opportunity to raise Canada's concerns about human rights and the importance of enhanced political stability as the necessary prerequisite for the resumption of normal diplomatic relations.[59] Finally, the Canadian deputy foreign minister, De Montigny Marchand, visited Beijing on 20 July 1990. His visit was only ten days after the Houston Summit had revealed a formal split among the G7, with the six bowing to Japan's plan to resume its US$5.6 billion loan program to the People's Republic. Marchand claimed that his presence in China "by no means constitutes a return to a normal state of affairs." He told his Chinese counterparts of the "deep concern in many Canadian circles that on the political front the pace and direction of reform were not keeping in step."[60] His disclaimers notwithstanding, Marchand's visit was a signal of Canada's interest in yet another "relationship adjustment." At the very least, Canada had now formally abandoned its June 1989 policy of suspending high-level contacts with the People's Republic of China.

THE INTERNATIONAL
FINANCIAL INSTITUTIONS

International financial institutions (IFIS) are officially politically neutral; they do not mix politics with the economics of loan decisions. Yet after Tiananmen Square, the World Bank and the Asian Development ment Bank decided to postpone, or "put on hold," several loans that were already in the pipeline and to freeze the consideration of new loans to China. This study will focus on World Bank lending because its policy and that of the Asian Development Bank are similar.

Since the onset of its open-door policy in the late 1970s, China has become increasingly involved in the international economic system. Central to this process was its decision to join the International Monetary Fund and the World Bank Group in 1980. China has since become a significant player in several IFIS.[61] Before June 1989, the World Bank had approved loans and credits to China totalling US$8.6 billion,[62] and as of 4 June 1989 there were seven loans and credits, totalling US$786 million, which were scheduled for consideration by the bank's board of governors.[63] The World Bank, despite its articles of agreement dictating that loans be given on developmental and economic criteria alone,[64] is in fact deeply politicized. As a critic has observed, "If it is a political act to withhold [loans], it is also a political act to grant them. At the very least, the effects of such an act have important political implications and consequences."[65] This statement was particularly applicable to China as pressure built to unfreeze "postponed" loans and begin new lending initiatives.

The United States has frequently abstained or voted against IFI loans to repressive regimes, though critics point to deep inconsistencies in the U.S. record.[66] Similarly, even though Canada, the Netherlands, and Norway all officially adhere to the IFI neutrality doctrine, each applied human rights conditionality to proposed World Bank loans to Chile. The Chile precedent was less important in guiding Dutch, Canadian, and Norwegian thinking, however, than the emergence of a coordinated Western position on IFI lending to China. As with U.N. diplomacy, a united front on IFI lending policy was a key factor in maintaining leverage on the Chinese leadership. (For example, a Canadian official mentioned the importance of "keeping good company" – consulting with like-minded countries and with G7 partners.)[67] Furthermore, an informal commitment not to subject any loan considerations on China to a formal vote was indicative of Western pragmatism within the IFIS.[68] This policy avoided humiliating China if a loan proposal failed, and it also ensured against possible Chinese reprisals.[69]

A coordinated Western position on IFI lending to China began to emerge after June 1989 when an ad hoc OECD group started to meet regularly to coordinate IFI policy towards China. It appears, however, that the G7 led the policy making. The G7 countries made a key statement at the 1989 Paris Summit, where they agreed that "in view of current economic uncertainties, the examination of new loans by the World Bank be postponed." But they also stated, "We look to the Chinese authorities to create conditions which will avoid their isolation and provide for a return to cooperation based upon a resumption of movement towards political and economic reform, and openness."[70] Add to this the desire for an early return to normal lending on the part of World Bank's staff and its president, Barbara Conable, as well (needless to say) as China.[71] Leadership from the G7 conveniently allowed minor OECD players to remain invisible while they quietly supported the major players' positions.[72] Canada, the Netherlands, and Norway each has only a small voting share in the IFIs,[73] but that does not mean they lack influence. The Nordic Group, of which Norway is a member, is relatively homogeneous and may thus wield more influence than its voting share suggests. Similarly, Canada has been important to World Bank lending to China because it is a G7 player and because its representative, Frank Potter, is the longest-serving executive director and thus has considerable authority. Moreover, Canada is the third-largest non-Asian contributor to the Asian Development Bank (after Japan and the United States). The OECD position on IFI lending evolved through several stages. Canada, Norway, and the Netherlands each initially supported the IFI policy on China. The Dutch were bound by the EC Madrid Declaration's recommendation to freeze new World Bank lending; and Norway supported the general Nordic position, though it kept a low profile within the Nordic Group and in the wider OECD discussions on China.

By early spring 1990, sharp rifts had emerged between, on the one hand, the U.S. State Department and World Bank staff, who wanted to normalize IFI lending, and, on the other hand, several other OECD players, including Canada, the Netherlands, and Norway, who remained sceptical of China's economic and political progress and were more reluctant to normalize IFI lending.[74] The initial decision to postpone loans had been taken by World Bank staff but had been supported by virtually all the OECD countries. The bank's staff had argued in favour of postponing the loans on purely economic criteria – that the loans had been approved on the basis of circumstances that no longer existed after 4 June 1989.[75] China's unstable economic climate made it impossible to implement planned projects or to approve new ones. Officials in Canada, Norway, and the Netherlands recognized the artificiality of separating economic and political criteria in the case of China, but felt it was safer to phrase any arguments against the early resumption of normal lending in purely economic terms. To do otherwise would be to invite legitimate Chinese complaints of an abrogation of the bank's articles of agreement.[76]

A shift in the bank's policy on China was first visible in early February 1990, when its staff consulted the executive directors for a fresh US$30 million loan to China for earthquake relief.[77] Canada, the Netherlands, and Norway agreed, but they resisted what they saw as U.S. State Department and World Bank collusion to slip through another credit for an agricultural loan to Jiangxi Province. The bank staff argued, *ex post facto*, that the loan could be considered humanitarian because it addressed the needs of the poorest of the poor, but most OECD countries were sceptical and considered the proposal a routine credit. Canada and the Netherlands protested this alleged White House–World Bank sleight of hand. Reportedly, Canada's executive director led the successful delay of the agricultural loan's consideration.[78] However, none of our three internationalists saw the "humanitarian" loan as undermining the West's IFI policy.[79] The executive directors' request that the World Bank undertake a comprehensive assessment of economic conditions in China signalled the growing pressure to return to normal lending. The subsequent Country Economic Memorandum was debated on 29 May 1990. But the expected thaw in IFI lending did not happen for at least two reasons. First, many OECD countries remained sceptical about conditions in China. The Dutch "didn't find the [bank's] memorandum very convincing," and a Canadian official described it as "a crowd pleaser." Second, the timing of the meeting, less than one week before the anniversary of Tiananmen Square, was, as a Dutch official put it, "extremely unfortunate."[80] Canada's executive director succeeded once more in postponing the consideration of several non-humanitarian loans.

This resolve could not last indefinitely. The U.S. decision to renew China's most-favoured-nation status and the G7's Houston Summit in July 1990 added pressure to normalize lending. Japan and several European G7 members were reportedly eager to do so. Some saw Canada as siding with the U.S. Congress in opposing the resumption of new loans.[81] Even though the G7 countries agreed to maintain the freeze on new IFI lending, Japan reactivated its US$5.6 billion loan package to China, thereby undermining whatever slim agreement remained. But the decisive event was China's agreement to support the U.N. Security Council's embargo against Iraq, a quid pro quo that paved the way for a return to normal World Bank and export-credit lending.[82] Ironically, the thaw in Western policy towards China coincided with an Amnesty International report claiming that more than five hundred people had been executed in 1990.[83]

AID AND TRADE: COMMERCE OVER CONSCIENCE?

Trade with less-developed countries is not important in the export trade of the Netherlands, Norway, or Canada. This, theoretically, enables them to frame more assertive policies towards any repressive regimes in such countries, the trade-off between commerce and conscience being less acute. But each of the three states has made a special effort to stimulate trade with China. Thus, the trade-offs between commerce and conscience are in fact acute where China is concerned. Two-way trade with China has increased in each case. Norwegian exports to China grew slightly, from 643 million kroner in 1984 to 717 million in 1989, though the balance of trade shifted from a 393-million-kroner surplus in Norway's favour to a 440-million-kroner trade deficit.[84]

Canadian exports to China took off in the late 1970s, rising from 196 million dollars in 1976 to 2.593 billion by 1988.[85] Similarly, Dutch exports to China rose quickly after the mid-1970s. In 1975, exports stood at 336 million guilders, and in 1985 they peaked at 811 million.[86] By 1988, the Netherlands was China's eleventh-largest trading partner.[87] The trade growth for both countries coincided with the onset of China's open-door policy in the mid-1970s.

Canada is China's eighth-largest trading partner, and China is Canada's fourth-largest export market in the developing world and the largest market for its grains (mostly wheat). In 1988 total two-way trade between the countries stood at US$3.54 billion, with a US$1.63 billion trade balance in Canada's favour.[88] Cereals accounted for more than half of all Canadian exports to China in 1988. After 1985, the Mulroney government made China a priority market under its National Trade Strategy, with a focus on expanding hydropower, wheat, petrochemicals, and transport-sector sales.[89] Future trade expansion is promising because China's import and infrastructure needs correspond well with traditional Canadian exporting strengths.

The Canadian, Dutch, and Norwegian states have all helped their respective business communities break into the Chinese market through granting export credits and development aid – another indicator of the intense commercial interest in China.

Development Aid

Three common threads in Dutch, Canadian, and Norwegian aid to China point to a strong commercial emphasis. First, their aid programs all began in the 1980s. Norway's began in 1983 with a bilateral agreement to build an ocean-research vessel valued at 71 million kroner.[90] The Dutch program began in 1985. Canada's first aid to China was a four-million-dollar food-aid package in 1981, but its aid program did not really take off until 1984. China is not a "main partner country" for the Netherlands, or for Norway. Instead, these donors have sectoral interests in China, emphasizing industrial development. For Canada's aid program, however, China is a "country of concentration," emphasizing human resource development, agriculture, forestry, energy, transportation, telecommunications, and management.

Second, aid volumes have risen quickly since the programs were established. The Netherlands, for example, committed only 4.8 million guilders to China in 1985. In 1986 its ODA commitments climbed to 26.25 million, and by 1988 they had soared to 170 million guilders, the lion's share (168 million) being for export promotion using concessional aid funds.[91] Similarly, Canadian aid to China has grown rapidly. In the fiscal year 1988–89, Canadian aid to China from all channels stood at 129 million dollars.

Third, all three programs have a large mixed-credit and/or parallel-financing component. These instruments are called "associated financing" by the Development Assistance Committee (DAC) of OECD, and they have been used by DAC members to give prime exports global protectionism and a competitive position in the Third World capital-goods market. Virtually all DAC members now blend aid funds into more commercial loan packages to subsidize their national firms so that they can undercut competitors. ODA is, in effect, a "sweetener" to soften the terms of essentially commercial loans by delaying or lengthening repayment times and reducing interest rates. Mixed credits typically add concessional ODA funds, in the form of grants, to the regular credits at or near market terms, which are offered by the donor's export-credit agency. Parallel financing is a variation on this theme; in this case, the donor adds ODA to a larger multilateral aid package supervised by a regional development bank or the World Bank Group.[92] Parallel financing has the advantage of introducing a national firm to the multilateral development banks and thus to the much larger pools of funding which those banks command. Although aid-blended loan packages must demonstrate a clear development component (for example, the project should be in a sector emphasized in a national development plan), critics complain that commercial, not developmental, objectives drive these mechanisms.[93] Moreover, the packages are, in effect, completely tied to donor procurement. Such associated financing is compelling evidence of the commercialization of donor aid programs in China.

In sum, the newness of the aid programs, their rapid expansion, their emphasis on industrial development, and their reliance on associated financing and on capital-goods and consulting services indicate that Dutch, Canadian, and Norwegian aid to China is strongly driven by commercial interests. These economic interests are premised on (a) using aid to help domestic firms gain a foothold in an enormous market; and (b) the recognition by OECD countries that China is a "spoiled" market in which concessional financing is essential if one is to compete successfully.[94]

Dutch policy on aid and export credits to China follows the EC's Madrid Declaration. Accordingly, the Dutch were obliged to accept the EC stricture that no new credits be approved after 4 June 1989 and that development cooperation be curtailed except for humanitarian assistance. As already noted, the bulk of Dutch ODA to China was in the form of "soft loan" financing. The Dutch call their mixed-credit projects less concessional loans (LCLs). Potentially, the Madrid Declaration could have played havoc with the Dutch firms that held LCL contracts. In 1988, LCL commitments stood at 168 million guilders. But in fact the economic costs were less painful than might have been expected. In concert with common OECD practice, the Dutch permitted those LCLs for which final government-to-government agreements had been struck *before* 4 June to proceed; but pending loans that were in less complete stages of the approval process were blocked. Moreover, disbursement problems with the mixed-credit/LCL program had led, effectively, to a funding freeze at the end of 1988.

All this meant that relatively few Dutch firms were directly affected by the EC credit freeze directive. Dutch officials experienced much less intense lobbying from domestic firms than their Norwegian counterparts did. The single exception was a large Dutch company, which in May 1990 presented a case to Development Cooperation Minister Jan Pronk asking for "special treatment," that is, for reconsideration of a mixed-credit deal allegedly struck before 4 June 1989. The company claimed exemption from the EC policy on the grounds that the proposed project contained a training component, which allegedly qualified as humanitarian assistance. The firm was reputedly supported by the Dutch embassy in Beijing. Somewhat surprisingly, the Dutch also cancelled their student scholarships and technical training fellowships funded through the ODA budget. The Chinese had benefited from Dutch technical expertise and training in hydrogeology, aerial mapping, fruit growing, environmental technology, construction technology, rural and urban planning, and management.

Various commercial Dutch export-credit schemes to China were also affected by the EC's Madrid Declaration policy. Two government agencies, the Directorate General for Foreign Economic Relations of the Ministry of Economic Affairs and the Nederlandsche Credietverzkering Maatschappij (the Dutch equivalent of the U.S. Exim Bank), are the principal vehicles that assist domestic firms to promote exports to the developing world. Of the four vehicles used to stimulate Dutch exports in this area, the Program for Economic Cooperation was the one most commonly used to help Dutch firms in the China market. This program is not strictly a subsidy, but it can help Dutch firms by offsetting the cost of project identification, training placements, trade missions, and feasibility studies.[95]

Finally, EC policy affected Sino-Dutch trade negotiations. A Sino-Dutch "mixed commission" had been created in 1988 as a forum to discuss all aspects of aid and trade relations between the two countries. It proved a useful forum for Dutch business to get acquainted with the Chinese market, and officials report that at least one LCL deal was struck as a direct consequence of a Dutch business delegation's presence at the first mixed commission meeting.[96] Because the meetings are held at a fairly high level (the two trade ministers presided over the first meeting), the 1989 mixed commission meeting was cancelled in keeping with the general Western position to curtail high-level or ministerial contacts with the Beijing leadership. In 1990, however, the Sino-Dutch mixed commission met again, thus signalling a return to business as usual.

The impact of Canada's statecraft on aid and export credits was modest in comparison with that of Norway and the Netherlands. Consistent with a policy not to isolate China, Canada essentially maintained its aid and export-credit profile, making only the changes necessary to register some degree of disengagement from the Beijing leadership and from the repressive apparatus of the state. External Affairs Minister Clark's "three criteria" – to preserve existing links, to shift new initiatives to a people-to-people focus, and to avoid programs "which benefit or lend prestige" to the repressive leadership, the military, or the state propaganda machine – guided the decisions on which projects to freeze and which to withdraw.

The CIDA policy makers "burned a lot of midnight oil" before withdrawing three projects that failed to meet Clark's three criteria.[97] These projects involved a lube oil centre, urban traffic management, and the training of state auditors. In addition, CIDA put on hold four of the five project agreements for which the government-to-government signing was postponed immediately after Tiananmen. At the same time, Canada, in sharp contrast to Norway and the Netherlands, planned to increase the number of Chinese students entering the country. In addition, the government claimed that a decision to suspend indefinitely "all activity associated with the Three Gorges Project" was a direct response to Tiananmen Square. This seems to have been a principled decision taken at some economic cost, because CIDA disbursements had already produced almost $14 million in contracts to Canadian firms and consulting services, with the prospect of more to follow. But the ODA suspensions smack of tokenism. How, for example, does withdrawing a lube oil centre avoid complicity with a repressive state apparatus? The state auditor scheme may at first sight seem a more appropriate candidate. But here, too, the logic is less than watertight. The project was intended to strengthen China's economic reforms – a stated Canadian development goal – by raising financial and managerial competence throughout the Chinese government. And the project had almost run its course, with $3.4 million of a planned Canadian contribution of $3.92 million already disbursed.[98]

Canada could have more clearly demonstrated a principled use of ODA conditionality by freezing or cancelling more lucrative projects that were vital to the Beijing leadership's prestige and legitimacy. There were several possibilities: an oil and gas technology transfer program with a planned CIDA contribution of $29 million; the Guangzhou air-traffic-control project with a planned CIDA budget of $6.4 million; the South China Power Studies project with a planned budget of $8.1 million; and a domestic satellite system with a planned Canadian contribution of $4.2 million.[99] Moreover, the oil and gas program and the Guangzhou project had disbursed only $1.9 million between them, unlike the state auditor program.

Of course, freezing these more lucrative projects would have been more costly and might have created some acrimony between CIDA and its Canadian contractors. One only has to remember the difficulties that CIDA encountered with the Maduru Oya project in Sri Lanka. As it was, the chosen projects were easy tokens to throw, giving the appearance that Canada had taken the moral high road on China. In fact, it might be more accurate to say that CIDA's "midnight oil" was burned to minimize the immediate costs to Canadian contractors. It is not sufficient to argue that the projects were chosen because they had a particularly large government-to-government component.[100] Virtually all ODA to a largely state-run economy, such as China's, is government-to-government aid.

There were at least two other markers of insincerity from Ottawa. Contrary to official claims, the "withdrawal" from the Three Gorges project had little to do with Tiananmen Square. Funding problems at the Chinese end were the real reason for the delay, and they had already led the Chinese government to put the project on hold before Tiananmen.[101] Canada's decision also to put its contribution to the project on hold simply confirmed the bottleneck in Chinese funding. The second example of government insincerity concerns export credits. The Export Development Corporation (EDC), a self-financing crown corporation, is Canada's principal export-credit institution. Its mandate is to promote Canadian exports by providing insurance guarantees and direct loans. Developing countries are a major focus of EDC activity.

Canada's credit sanctions differed markedly from those of both Norway and the Netherlands. In contrast to the Madrid Declaration's policy to suspend all new state-supported credit arrangements with the People's Republic, Canada insisted only that any new credits comply with Clark's three criteria. The EDC was thus empowered to continue actively seeking contracts in China, and Canadian firms were still able to draw on a $2 billion line of credit to China. This line of credit, which was established between the EDC and the Bank of China in 1986, contains a $350 million concessional *tranche* to strengthen the competitiveness of Canadian loan packages.

After Tiananmen, the government cancelled one project – a television transmission facility – "which [was] clearly supportive of China's state propaganda apparatus."[102] The Shanghai television tower was to have been funded under section 31 of the Export Development Corporation Act. It could be legitimately withdrawn because the act specifies that section 31 loan approvals must meet "national interest" criteria. Clark had thus made a political decision that the television tower was a project "not in Canada's national interest."[103] However, sectors of the Canadian public were upset by media reports that just one month after Tiananmen, the federal cabinet approved $100 million in EDC loans to help sell telephone and switching equipment to China. The loans were to help finance exports by Canada Wire and Cable Ltd and by Northern Telecom, a global leader in telecommunications.[104] At about the same time, the federal government gave final approval to a $130 million loan for a hydroelectric project, the funds being drawn from the EDC's $2 billion line of credit.[105]

As Dutch and Norwegian experience confirms, export-credit financing has a complicated series of approval phases – approval in principle, a contract stage between Western and developing companies, and finally a formal agreement between the two governments. The hydro and telecom projects were in their final approval stages just before Tiananmen, needing only the government-to-government signing before being activated. Cabinet actually had authorized the hydro deal in April 1989. Both projects were thus in the pipeline, and Canada, like other OECD countries, had pushed through loans signed before 4 June.[106] A third EDC project loan was pushed through in December 1989.

Neither loan approval need be interpreted as evidence of government perfidy. But what is questionable is the way the Canadian government tried to slip each deal through quietly. In no case did it follow the normal practice of releasing a public statement announcing the deal. A federal government source claimed, "There has been a conscious decision by the government to keep it quiet."[107] Clark's spokesman offered the dubious reasoning that an announcement in July was not necessary because the deal was already in the "public domain."[108] More likely, the timing of the final loan agreements just one month after Tiananmen would have opened the government to criticism had the deals been announced. The Prime Minister's Office – which, according to the media reports, had insisted on there being no press release – denied any involvement.[109]

Norway, although it was not a member of the European Community and was thus able to go its own way on sanctions against China, chose to follow the EC's Madrid Declaration and impose selective credit (and virtually comprehensive) aid sanctions. As with the Dutch, this meant no new loans to China. This decision came with some trade-offs, because mixed credit, parallel financing, and more commercial credits had given Norwegian firms lucrative contracts in China, amounting to commitments of 877 million kronor in 1988. China accounted for a large share of Norway's worldwide parallel-financing and mixed-credit commitments. Surprisingly, Norway also froze humanitarian projects, such as aid to handicapped children, and human resource initiatives, such as the Norwegian Agency for Development Cooperation's (NORAD's) scholarship program for Chinese students. Why did Norway follow EC policy? Given the already strained relations with the People's Republic, it was in Norway's national interest not to be out of step with the rest of the international community – either in applying sanctions or in withdrawing them. As a small nation, Norway gained strength and sought cover by following the crowd rather than striking out on its own.

The Madrid Declaration strictures affected two ministries, Development Cooperation/NORAD and Trade, and two instruments of Norwegian foreign economic policy, export credit and aid-blended concessional loans (mixed credit). Both instruments were used heavily in the "spoiled" Chinese market. The principal sectors of the Norwegian economy targeted for export-subsidy help in China were hydropower (dams and generators), telecommunications, fisheries, paper

production, and distilleries. The firms aided by export credits included
Norskdata, Norskhydro, and Statoil. Credit guarantees to China
exceeded those to Eastern Europe, North America, Latin America,
Africa, and Oceania. China accounted for the most Norwegian credits
to a single country in 1989.[110]

Norway followed the Dutch practice of freezing the consideration
of new credits. A complex formula was put in place to deal with mixed-
credit packages in various stages of finalization.[111] Where an agreement
for a credit or aid-blended loan had been signed between the two
governments before 4 June 1989, the deal went ahead. But if a contract
between a Norwegian firm and its Chinese counterpart had been signed
and NORAD had agreed only in principle to a concessional "aid sweetener," or if NORAD had yet to approve the concessional component,
the pending contract was frozen. This formula meant that mixed
credits valued at 172.5 million kroner, with an aid "gift" component
of 61.4 million kroner, were immediately frozen. Four Norwegian firms
were affected by the mixed-credit freeze. The government, however,
was prepared to make an exception for one Norwegian company,
which argued that if the mixed-credit package was frozen and project
implementation delayed, the company would fold.[112]

The new government made important shifts in the policy on mixed
credits to China. It introduced a loophole allowing project approvals
to be made without formal government-to-government agreements[113]
(purportedly, nothing in the OECD Consensus Arrangement prevented
Norway from doing this) and in March 1990 it decided to review
mixed-credit projects on a case-by-case basis. Shortly afterwards,
Elkem was notified that the Chengdu project could go ahead because
NORAD now was permitted to unfreeze the concessional ODA component. Renewed pressure from firms affected by the suspension led to
the unfreezing of a second mixed-credit package for 45 million kroner
in the telecommunications sector in May 1990.[114]

Norway complied faithfully with the Madrid Declaration's policy
curbing new export credits, despite concern about the loss of markets
and reports that the Italians, French, and Spanish were not complying
with the declaration.[115] Norwegian officials asserted that the newly
elected minister of trade, Kolle Feive, opposed any relaxation of the
policy on non-aid-blended credits and would not move until the EC
relaxed its policy.[116] Despite this commendable resolve, Norway began
chipping away at its China policy and edging towards business as usual
wherever possible: by renewing the NORAD scholarship program, by
permitting aid to flow again to poverty-alleviation projects, and by
bowing to commercial pressure to unfreeze the mixed-credit program.

CONCLUSION

Tiananmen helps test the premise that states considering assertive human rights statecraft will face bureaucratic infighting as institutions struggle to defend or advance organizational interests. In fact, the policy makers in all three countries reported relative consensus in policy formulation. Even on World Bank policy, where there is sometimes institutional rivalry or jurisdictional ambiguity between finance and foreign affairs ministries, there appears to have been no real policy conflicts.[117]

What accounts for this finding? In the Netherlands and Norway, the absence of institutional conflict was partly the function of policies set elsewhere: Holland was obliged to follow the EC's Madrid Declaration; Norway was not, but did so anyway. To some degree, institutional consensus was a function of salience. In contrast to the Maduru Oya project in Sri Lanka and the bureaucratic dispute it caused between Canada's CIDA and External Affairs, Tiananmen was highly visible and policy was set by domestic and international political imperatives. There was thus little scope for the bureaucratic infighting that can accompany more routine problems or less sensitive cases. An adequate response to Tiananmen required intra- and intergovernmental consultation. Despite this complexity, all three actors were remarkably consistent across disparate policy arenas, such as aid, trade, and immigration. The crisis atmosphere created by Tiananmen produced ad hoc consultative groups drawn from several ministries. These forums helped create and maintain policy coherence. These groups appear to have met frequently during the early stages of policy development, but were less active once they decided on an initial set of actions.[118]

China is the best test of Canadian, Dutch, and Norwegian resolve to protest human rights abuses beyond their borders. First, the clarity of the abuses and the culpability of state elites are unequivocal. Second, all three Western countries have significant and growing commercial interests in China. Third, China is the most powerful developing country, a fact that alters the usual North-South power dynamic in human rights statecraft. Nowhere was this more evident than in the vicissitudes of Norwegian statecraft towards China.[119] But all three countries were conscious, at various points, of the risk of reprisal. Fourth, China is a regional power in the Asia-Pacific arena. It is a vital player geopolitically in the resolution of regional conflicts, such as Cambodia, and commercially as the largest market in Asia, which perhaps may soon be the fulcrum of the international economy. With

China, it is not just commerce versus conscience; human rights must also be weighed against the imperatives of world order and regional stability.

Finally, Tiananmen was an international issue that provoked a degree of Western information sharing and policy coordination rarely seen in major cases of gross human rights violations. Some argue that the foreign policy of small and medium powers is constrained by their external environments.[120] With China, external alliances were more salient than in the other cases considered in this study. European political cooperation dictated Dutch responses to Tiananmen. Norway, although not an EC member, followed the EC's Madrid Declaration almost to the letter. Canada had to consider G7 policy coordination. All three states were part of OECD coordination at the World Bank and Western Group coordination at UNCHR.

The challenge facing Western policy makers was to find some middle ground by choosing actions that would convey moral conviction but would not isolate China, damage carefully nurtured relations, or risk reprisal. On one hand, a morally principled response demanded assertive actions. Western aid and credits had been given to China as rewards and privileges for its open-door policies and its importance in maintaining regional stability and resolving geostrategic issues. After Tiananmen, the rationale for these privileges was no longer clear.[121] On the other hand, such punitive logic was at odds with one lesson of history – that an isolated China is a dangerous China, bellicose abroad and brutally repressive at home. The Cultural Revolution's excesses had occurred when China was virtually closed to the West in the 1960s. By contrast, in the years just before Tiananmen the Chinese government had orchestrated phases of political relaxation as the People's Republic opened its doors to the West.[122] Besides, an overly punitive approach using comprehensive and indefinite sanctions, *qua* the South African experience, would have been counterproductive when China had normalized relations with the Soviet Union, disavowed support for communist movements in Southeast Asia,[123] reopened a dialogue with Indonesia, was poised to resume control of the capitalist strongholds of Hong Kong and Macao, and would in future have to play a central role in global environmental diplomacy.[124] These verities seem to have weighed particularly heavily in Canada's policy deliberations, which from the outset emphasized that China should not be isolated.

Commercial interests, geopolitics, international coordination, and reprisal anxieties add up, in a realist lexicon, to competing national interests and external constraints that are likely to override the domestic pressure for an assertive human rights statecraft. How were these

Table 6.1
A Hierarchy of Human Rights Instruments: Policy Responses to Tiananmen Square[1]

Policy options	Canada	Netherlands	Norway
LOW ASSERTIVENESS			
Quiet diplomacy	Yes	Yes	Yes
Public statements	Yes	Yes	Yes
U.N. roll-calls	Attempted	Attempted	Attempted
Standard setting	No	Attempted	No
MODERATE ASSERTIVENESS			
Increase refugee quotas	No	No	No
Extend visas	Yes	Yes	Yes
Suspend cultural contacts	No	Yes	Yes
Voluntary investment codes	No	No	No
Criticism in IFIS	Yes	Yes	Yes
Redirect ODA	NA[2]	NA[2]	NA[2]
Recall ambassador (for consultation)	Yes	No	No
Downgrade trade mission	Yes	No	No
Suspend high-level meetings	Yes	Yes	Yes
HIGH ASSERTIVENESS			
Suspend trade commission	No	Yes	Yes
Suspend IFI credits	Yes	Yes	Yes
Lower or suspend ODA	Token	Yes	Yes
Freeze export credits	Partial	Yes	Yes
Embargo on arms sales	No	Yes	Yes
Recall ambassador (permanently)	No	No	No
Close trade mission	No	No	No
Impose trade sanctions (mandatory)	No	No	No
Aid opposition	No	No	No
Break diplomatic relations	No	No	No

[1] Not all instruments in the hierarchy are set our here. See table 2.4 for the complete list.
[2] Not applicable.

competing pressures resolved? At first blush, the three countries' policy responses to Tiananmen seem to have been remarkably similar, but a closer reading brings out some significant differences, most notably on aid and credits. Canada also differed from Norway and the Netherlands by recalling its ambassador temporarily and by enhancing rather than suspending cultural ties with China.

The three countries' actions in the context of the human rights hierarchy are summarized in table 6.1. Several trends emerge. Note, first, the wide range of actions through a variety of channels, such as aid, trade, immigration, the international financial institutions (IFIS), and the United Nations. This range of responses differs from Norwegian and Canadian actions towards Sri Lanka, where bilateral aid, quiet diplomacy, and U.N. resolutions were the principal modalities. It differs from Dutch actions in Suriname, where aid suspension was the main policy lever. And it differs from Dutch and Canadian policy towards the Philippines, where there was little public criticism of the Aquino government's human rights record. Second, there is an almost uniform spread across the levers of low, moderate, and high assertiveness. This finding seems at odds with realist predictions that these internationalists would have focused on unassertive U.N. levers. However, these seemingly assertive and morally principled policies are, in all three cases, full of qualifications and loopholes, which confirms a refined realist reasoning.

Moreover, the untried instruments mark the limits of each actor's policy assertiveness. None attempted to circumscribe the private sector by laying down investment codes or by imposing mandatory and comprehensive trade sanctions. There was no question, for example, that Canada would disrupt its profitable wheat exports to China. Doing so would have unfairly punished the Chinese people and needlessly hurt Canadian prairie farmers. Nor was there any impulse to disengage diplomatically by closing down a trade mission, withdrawing an ambassador, or breaking diplomatic relations. Nor was there any attempt to aid any opposition to the Beijing regime.[125] The main motive underpinning Norwegian, Dutch, and Canadian credit and aid sanctions was a desire to avoid complicity with a repressive regime. The small sums involved cannot have been expected to damage the Chinese economy. The punitive motive was more evident in the resolve to maintain the freeze on current and future IFI loans, where much larger sums were involved. Almost all the other levers, from U.N. initiatives to recalling the Canadian ambassador, were primarily symbolic attempts to signal solidarity with the Chinese people.

All three states have an activist tradition at the United Nations and therefore should have emphasized this relatively unassertive channel to protest the Beijing massacre. The Netherlands and Canada tested every avenue open to them at the United Nations, but the limits of their influence were soon exposed in the Security Council and the General Assembly. Norway, on the other hand, was inactive at the United Nations and seems to have chosen the path of least resistance. Observer status may partly explain Norwegian passivity, but more likely Norway did not want to sour further its already damaged bilateral relationship with China. On balance, Dutch activism in the third committee suggests that the Netherlands exhibited a greater willingness to risk reprisal than either Canada or Norway did. However, the Western Group's unwillingness to sign the UNCHR resolution and China's ability to parry Western initiatives at every turn underscore the unassertive-ness and minimal pay-off of this form of human rights statecraft.

All three states also used a number of high-assertiveness levers, such as suspending new IFI loans or suspending or circumscribing bilateral aid and credit. This contradicts the realist predictions underpinning the hierarchy – that smaller Western states would focus most readily on low or, possibly, moderately assertive levers that do not threaten other national interests, such as trade and security, and which essen-tially do not challenge the principle of non-intervention. Realist pre-mises would suggest that, *ceteris paribus*, Western states would be unwilling to suffer the commercial or political costs implicit in highly assertive levers. In a policy trade-off among competing national inter-ests, moral imperatives such as human rights would be trumped by instrumental interests.

However, it is argued here that while Norway and the Netherlands were willing to pay a higher price for their policy resolve than Canada, the economic sacrifices by all three states were less acute than might be expected. All three actors stood to lose some economic benefits by deciding to freeze or circumscribe export credits and ODA, since their aid programs are driven by commercial interest. Moreover, export-credit officials in each country were nervous about the loss of market niches, citing rumours of other competitors willing to circumvent or break the international consensus on new credits.[126] Yet the Dutch mixed-credit freeze was a small sacrifice because the program was inactive in June 1989. Canada was even more pragmatic on credit and ODA. Clark's criteria enabled Canada to set what seemed like morally principled restrictions on aid and credits, but which actually imposed few real costs on Canadian exporters. The Export Development Cor-poration was free to continue helping Canadian firms seeking contracts in China, in contrast to its Dutch and Norwegians counterparts. Thus, this study argues that Canada's aid and trade restrictions were more token than substantive (see table 6.1). If Canadian policy makers had been resolved to avoid complicity with the Beijing regime, they surely would have considered freezing *all* new aid and credit activity. The projects CIDA actually froze are emblematic of this tendency to mini-mize real costs and maintain as near-normal commercial relations as domestic sentiment would tolerate.

Unusually intense international coordination may have been behind the apparent resolve of one small state and two middle powers to pro-test the human rights abuses of the world's most powerful developing nation. This argument brings us back to realist perspectives. Probably, Canada, the Netherlands, and Norway would not have taken such a range of actions against China without the security of knowing they were in good company. But before dismissing our three internationalists as fair-weather human rights activists, let us consider their actions in the context of U.S. policy towards China. Despite spirited congressional pressure, the business lobby and geopolitical interests won out in the struggle to reshape U.S. policy after Tiananmen. The following are some markers of official duplicity and commercial interest:

June 1989	President Bush announces the suspension of high-level contact and export credits, and bans the sale of military technology.
July	Bush sends National Security Advisor Brent Scowcroft on a secret mission to Beijing; Bush grants a waiver to Boeing to sell three 757 aircraft (which use military-style navigation systems).
November	Bush vetoes an act of Congress to guarantee that Chinese students in the United States would not be forced to return to China while they were still in danger.
December	Bush approves the sale of three U.S.-made satellites, saying they are not for defence purposes; he waives the ban on U.S. Exim Bank credit support for U.S. exports to China.
January 1990	Bush extends China's "most-favoured nation" status for another year.
Spring	The State Department presses for the reactivation of World Bank loans.[127]

Canada's disingenuous, quiet approval of several Export Development Corporation loans pales in comparison with the secret U.S. missions, the dubious satellite sales, and the veto of a congressional act to guarantee the safe residence of Chinese students in the United States. It will be recalled that at the World Bank, Canada, Norway, and the Netherlands long resisted American and bank pressure to normalize relations.

The argument here compels some refinement of a crude realist assessment of Norwegian, Dutch, and Canadian diplomacy towards China. On the one hand, these states' actions were tougher than might have been predicted, particularly in the case of Norway – the weakest of the three and the one with the most strained relations with China. On the other hand, none of these states would have been likely to consider such actions on its own. Tiananmen Square brought a remarkable degree of international coordination among the Western states. Granted, there were many examples of countries circumventing the consensus on freezing new aid and credits;[128] and granted, thirteen months after Tiananmen – a respectable mourning period – the Houston Summit marked the official demise of a coordinated Western position. Nevertheless, that such concerted international action happened at all is surprising. Although OECD coordination is a testament to China's power, and although the breathtaking political *abertura* in Eastern Europe might have strengthened Western resolve, the West's actions cannot be dismissed as empty symbolism. However, it would be naive to conclude that Tiananmen marks a sea-change in the West's commitment to global human rights. Other high-profile human rights "events" produced no similar Western response. Consider, for example, the Tibetan uprising of 1987 and 1988. The Canadian government in 1990, like the Norwegian government in 1988, refused to meet the Dalai Lama.[129] The silence of Western states on Tibet, including that of our self-styled moralists, has been deafening.

What impact Western policies have had on the Chinese leadership is difficult to tell. Canadian, Dutch, and Norwegian policy makers are sceptical, with good reason, of Chinese overtures such as the lifting of martial law in Beijing and Tibet, and the release of some eight hundred political prisoners in 1990. These are necessary but insufficient signs of political relaxation. As a Norwegian official observed of Fang Lizhi's release, "One swallow does not make a summer."[130] In the longer term, it is doubtful that the 1989 protestors will resurface in any organized way. Nor have democratic values become deeply rooted among the masses. For the past century, the Chinese understanding of democracy has been a strong state for national development, not individual liberties and limited government *qua* the Western liberal ideal.[131]

Before Tiananmen, much of the West was dazzled by China's economic reforms and blinded to the many indications of political repression. If nothing more, Tiananmen has dispelled any lingering illusion that "China is different." Politics and economics are everywhere intertwined. The need for political reform remains acute even if the political culture is antithetical to Western models of governance. The Chinese leadership faces a central contradiction – that a half-reformed economy is inherently unstable, but a stable environment is a prerequisite of further reform. Opening the Chinese economy may not succeed in the long run without transforming the polity. The tension between these opposing forces will mark China's development into the next century.

7 Defending Rights in East Timor: Canadian and Dutch Relations with Indonesia

On 12 November 1991, Indonesian troops opened fire on a procession of mourners as they walked towards the cemetery in Dili, East Timor, where a youth who had been shot dead two weeks before was buried. No one knows how many died that day. The initial official verdict was nineteen dead. A commission of inquiry established by President Suharto later put the death toll at "about fifty." Human rights organizations have estimated that three hundred is nearer the mark. Claims and counterclaims about political killings have been common since the Indonesian invasion of East Timor in 1975, but this time there was incontrovertible proof. The massacre took place while a U.N. human rights team was visiting Dili, and it was graphically filmed by a British television crew. Over the years, Jakarta had blocked out almost any hard news from East Timor, a key weapon to silence critics of its human rights record. The Dili footage was a public relations nightmare which, like the media glare on Tiananmen Square, prompted public protest in Canada and the Netherlands. And as with Tiananmen, the public outcry partly explains why the Netherlands and Canada used the moderately assertive policy lever of political conditionality.

East Timor is a former Portuguese colony that was annexed by Indonesia in 1976 following a unilateral declaration of independence by the leftist liberation group Fretilin. Indonesia's attempts to gain international acceptance of its annexation of East Timor have been only partially successful. The United Nations continues to recognize Portugal as the territory's "administering power." In 1991, in a further effort to legitimize its role in East Timor, Jakarta agreed to permit a

U.N.-sponsored fact-finding mission – a group of Portuguese parliamentarians – to visit the territory. Jakarta expected to persuade Lisbon that East Timor had made economic progress under Indonesian rule, and it thus hoped to convince Portugal to recognize Indonesian sovereignty over East Timor. Unfortunately, procedural wrangles led to postponements, and the visit was cancelled on 26 October 1991, less than a week before it was scheduled to begin.

The proposed mission had prompted both excitement and anxiety in East Timor. To coincide with the visit, many Timorese had planned public protests against Jakarta, which the authorities wanted to prevent. Despite the cancellation, violent clashes between anti-Indonesian activists and the security forces were almost inevitable. The first occurred on 28 October at the Montael Church in Dili. Two youths were killed in the clash. It was the funeral of one of these youths, Sebastio Gomez, that sparked the 12 November killings. The funeral attracted about two thousand mourners, who gathered for a memorial mass at the church and then made their way to the Santa Cruz cemetery, many of them carrying nationalist banners and posters. Their initial plan, to pass the governor's office and the hotel, where a visiting U.N. official was staying, was thwarted by the security forces who lined the three-kilometre route between the church and the cemetery. At the cemetery, the mourners began an impromptu protest rally. This was observed by a number of foreigners, including the twenty-year-old Malaysian-born New Zealand journalist and aid worker, Kamla Bamadhaj, two American journalists – Amy Goodman of the Pacific Radio Network and Alan Nairn of the *New Yorker* magazine – and Max Stahl, a cameraman for Yorkshire Television. Stahl's secret film recorded the killings.

No one disputes that the Indonesian army fired on the protesters, but the number of those killed, wounded, and arrested is disputed. Journalist Bamadhaj was shot dead. Goodman and Nairn were badly beaten up by the troops as they attempted to stop the killings. The brazenness of the military action and the rare presence of foreigners who got the news out made for a powerful and angry international response. The situation was inflamed by the defiant statements of President Suharto in mid-December 1991 that the East Timor issue was "a small matter" that had been exaggerated by Western countries and their press. At the United Nations, the Indonesian permanent mission, though expressing concern for the loss of life, described the incident as a "riot ... instigated by remnants of a group of security disturbance perpetrators," and it blamed "certain elements" in the crowd who rejected the "persuasive approach" of the security forces.[1] Even more damaging was the statement of the commander in chief of the armed forces, General Try Sutrisno, who argued publicly that "in the end" the Timorese demonstrators "had to be blasted." He added, "Delinquents like these agitators have to be shot and we will shoot them ... We will wipe out all separatist elements who have tainted the government's dignity."

The Indonesian authorities were surprised by the international reaction to the killings and fumbled their first attempts to justify the military's actions. The initial accounts presented by the military and security agencies described the Timorese mourners' march and rally as a well-planned demonstration against the territory's integration into Indonesia. The spokesmen claimed that as the crowd approached the Santa Cruz cemetery it grew more riotous and unruly, attacking the troops lining the procession route with stones and "hundreds of long knives." The security forces "unsuccessfully tried to disperse the wild mob through persuasive means," but when a grenade was thrown at them, they panicked; they misunderstood their commanding officer's order not to fire and began shooting "in fear of their lives." This narrative was refuted by both foreign and local eyewitnesses. While the procession had indeed been planned in advance, there was broad agreement that it was peaceful and disciplined and that the marchers were unarmed. The eyewitnesses unanimously described the actions of the soldiers who opened fire as deliberate, premeditated, and unprovoked.

JAKARTA RESPONDS: THE NATIONAL INVESTIGATION COMMISSION

The official story was so lacking in credibility that the international community called for an independent international inquiry. Jakarta rejected this out of hand as an unacceptable infringement of the country's sovereignty, but the outcry did prompt the president to launch a judicial inquiry of his own. A presidential decree established the National Investigation Commission headed by Judge M. Jaelani of the Supreme Court of Indonesia. An advance report of its findings, which was later declared to be final, was published on 26 December 1991. This report raised the number of fatalities to "about fifty," though Judge Jaelani noted later that the incident might even have claimed sixty or a hundred lives – "We cannot provide the exact number, although three hundred is impossible." While agreeing that the security forces had been provoked by the "belligerent and aggressive" demonstrators, the report did stress that "the actions of a number of security personnel exceeded acceptable norms" and that "action must be taken against all who were involved in the 12 November 1991 incident in Dili and suspected of having violated the law." It also stated that the killings were a "tragedy that should be deeply regretted" and emphasized that this was "clearly not an act ordered by or reflecting the policy of the government or the armed forces."

These findings represented the most favourable of three possible outcomes for the Indonesian government. If the commission had fully endorsed the military view in the immediate aftermath of the killings, this would have been regarded as a whitewash that could affect aid and investment flows. If the commission had closely echoed eyewitness accounts, the military-dominated government would have lost credibility. By choosing the middle path, the commission soothed foreign sensibilities and limited the embarrassment suffered by the armed forces and other official spokesmen. Outside Indonesia, most foreign governments were willing to accept the commission's basic tenet that the massacre was the work of a few uncontrolled soldiers, and they were satisfied by its recommendation that the soldiers be punished according to Indonesian law. This, in part, rehabilitated Indonesia's standing in the world community and ensured that aid continued to flow.

President Suharto instructed an "honorary council" to examine the performance of the security apparatus in East Timor and identify those responsible for the killings. The council's findings, announced on 27 February 1992, placed prime responsibility on fourteen members of the armed forces. Six senior officers were alleged to have been guilty of "mistake and negligence," and eight lower-ranking officers were alleged to have "violated the ethics of military discipline." The senior officers' punishment was not disclosed, though they were discharged, and the lower-ranking officers were recommended for court martial.

Jakarta responded swiftly to the commission findings in order to repair its international image. Foreign Minister Ali Alatas was dispatched abroad in February and March 1992. His job was to reassure Indonesia's major trade and aid partners that any transgression of the law, irrespective of whether it was committed by separatist demonstrators or by the military, would be subject to the due process of the law. With none of his host governments relishing a serious rupture of economic relations with a country as politically and economically important as Indonesia, his assurances were, for the most part, accepted. Although he was reminded of the need to uphold human rights, Alatas generally received a warm welcome in Europe, Canada, the United States, and Japan, all of which expressed their satisfaction with Jakarta's handling of the Dili affair.

SOFTLY, SOFTLY AT THE UNITED NATIONS

By 1992, Jakarta's efforts to assuage the international indignation over the Dili massacre had been successful. In March, at the forty-eighth annual session of the U.N. Commission on Human Rights (UNCHR), Portugal, on behalf of the European Community, drafted a resolution condemning Indonesia's role in East Timor. The resolution failed, despite strong supporting evidence of widespread torture, which was presented by the head of the Dutch delegation, P.H. Kooijmans, who had been in Dili as a special U.N. rapporteur on human rights during the incident. Portugal was forced to compromise by drafting a weaker chairman's statement as a consensus position that Indonesia also agreed to sign.

A year later the situation was remarkably different. Having neglected the East Timor issue for more than a decade, the UNCHR, on 12 March 1993, passed a resolution by twenty-two votes to twelve, expressing "deep concern" over persistent charges of human rights violations in Indonesia, especially in East Timor. The resolution called on the Indonesian government to permit human rights experts from the U.N. and other organizations to visit East Timor to investigate these allegations. Particularly worrysome for Indonesia was the U.S. support for the resolution. Under Presidents Reagan and Bush the United States had blocked similar resolutions against Indonesia's role in East Timor.

At the 1994 meeting of the UNCHR, the OECD democracies took a different tack. Rather than pressing for a resolution that condemned Indonesia but guaranteed Jakarta noncooperation on East Timor, they opted for a chairman's consensus statement which would be signed by Jakarta and would commit it to measurable progress on human rights. The statement, which was duly signed by Indonesia, welcomed Indonesian actions to open East Timor to United Nations and international observation. It also encouraged the U.N. secretary general to prompt dialogue between Indonesia and Portugal to "achieve a just, comprehensive and internationally acceptable, settlement to the question of East Timor." However, Amnesty International subsequently emphasized that Indonesia had failed to live up to its obligations to comply with the 1993 UNCHR resolution.[2]

ECONOMY AND SOCIETY

An archipelago of 13,000 islands and 185 million people – the world's fourth most populous country – Indonesia is one of the giants of the South. It is modernizing at a feverish pace. Its economy has grown at about 7 per cent a year since the 1960s. Assiduous investment in education and infrastructure has helped raise per capita income from US$70 in the 1960s to US$650 in the 1990s. Indonesia's chairmanship of the Non-Aligned Movement, its leadership in the Association of Southeast Asian Nations, and its commercial potential have made it a rising economic star. It is also a bell-wether of Asian relations with the industrial democracies.

Unquestionably, President Suharto's greatest achievement has been to lift the country out of poverty. The World Bank estimates that while 60 per cent of Indonesians lived in abject poverty in 1967, today just 15 per cent do. The absolute poor, about 27 million, almost matches Canada's population, but on virtually every measure of development – infant mortality, adult literacy, number of doctors – there have been marked improvements in the nation's quality of life. By the turn of the century, the national income is expected to rise to US$1,000 per person, lifting Indonesia to middle-income status. But Indonesia's progress in meeting social and economic needs has not been matched by equal attention to civil and political liberties. Economic success has come at a high social cost. The political stability that has attracted foreign investment has been bought at the expense of human rights. In 1992, Indonesia was in the first rank of developing countries in the United Nations Development Programme's "Human Development" index, but it ranked near the bottom (77th out of 88 countries) on the "Human Freedom" index, which puts it on a par with such unenlightened regimes as Syria and North Korea.

There are shoots of democracy, though they have yet to take root. The middle class – usually at the forefront of pressures for reform in Asia – is very small, about 12 million in a country of 185 million, and is highly dependent on government largesse. Criticizing the president is still akin to lèse-majesté; political parties must be licensed according to restrictive criteria, NGOs are watched, and dissidents are silenced. In its rush to build factories and to exploit mineral and forestry resources, the government has been confiscating land, sometimes without compensation. Peasant protests then lead to violence.[3] Added to this are fissiparous tendencies in Aceh, Irian Jaya, and East Timor, whose communities refuse to submit to Jakarta's rule. The government's response to these separatist tendencies has invariably been brutal and uncompromising.

Foreign money has fuelled much of Indonesia's prosperity. It receives about US$4.5 billion a year in official development assistance. Its external debt is high, and its debt service ratio is about 30 per cent, though the debt burden is manageable at current growth rates. Foreign aid is crucial in this phase of development, and Jakarta cannot do without aid for at least another six or seven years. At the 1993 meeting of the Consultative Group for Indonesia, the donor governments urged Indonesia to cut its dependence on foreign aid, but they still pledged us$5.1 billion – an increase of 3.4 per cent on the previous year.

CANADA AND EAST TIMOR: HISTORICAL INFLUENCES ON HUMAN RIGHTS DIPLOMACY

Canada applied political aid conditions to Indonesia long before human rights, good governance, and democratic pluralism became official criteria influencing aid funding. In 1964, Canadian food aid to Indonesia was terminated for two years, and no new capital projects or commodity shipments were undertaken in fiscal year 1965–66. This action was prompted by President Sukarno's unprovoked military assault on Malaysia in violation of international norms of territorial sovereignty and self-determination.

Under President Suharto, Indonesia began to put its economic house in order, and Canada increased its aid and trade links. In 1979, Canada decided to concentrate more funds for development programs in Indonesia. By 1987, Indonesia was the fourth-largest Canadian aid recipient. Aid grew despite evidence of persistent human rights abuses, including arbitrary arrests, protracted detention without trial, and extrajudicial killings. But the most internationally visible human rights issue was Indonesia's treatment of the former Portuguese colony of East Timor, which it had invaded and occupied in 1975. As one observer put it, "There is no evidence to 1987 that Indonesia's gross and persistent violations of basic security and subsistence rights affected the amount or character of Canadian aid to its regime."[4] Canada's decision not to link aid volume or modalities to the 1975 invasion of East Timor was in striking contrast to the mid-1960s aid suspension prompted by Sukarno's bellicose but much less destructive invasion of Malaysia. Canada's silence on Timor made absurd the Trudeau government's 1981 assertion that it would withdraw "aid programs from those countries whose scarce resources are diverted to war and conquest."

THE DILI KILLINGS: PRELUDE TO POLITICAL STRINGS

Why would Canada risk souring so significant a diplomatic, aid, and commercial relationship with one of the most powerful developing countries? Canada has a large economic interest in Indonesia. Two-way trade is about $800 million per year; and with about $3 billion in foreign direct investment, Canada is the fifth-largest investor in Indonesia. It sells five times as much to Indonesia as it imports. There are more than three hundred Canadian companies operating in manufacturing, importing, and consulting. Major Canadian firms include the shoemaker Bata, the engineering consultants Lavalin, and the Inco nickel-mining company. Canada has also sold ammunition, transport planes, and military vehicles.

Development aid has been a pillar of bilateral relations. By 1994, Indonesia had become the second-biggest recipient of Canadian aid. Disbursements since 1985 have ranged from $40 to $75 million per year. Although Canada accounts for less than one per cent of the total assistance Indonesia receives each year from international donors, the quality of Canada's aid program is sound. Much of the program focuses on Indonesia's less-developed eastern region, on human resource development, and on people-to-people exchanges, particularly through universities. For example, CIDA has helped set up Indonesian women's networks in science and technology; it has supported institutional strengthening and skills development of state ministries concerned with women's development, it has promoted decentralized, rural development planning on the island of Sulawesi, and has trained environmental specialists to develop a regulatory framework for the environment.

The Dili killings put Canada's high-quality program at risk. The intense media glare and the unequivocal nature of the killings were part of the reason why Canada eventually put conditions on some of its aid projects. But arguably the most important reason was the emphatic position on rights which Prime Minister Brian Mulroney had taken just one week earlier at the Chaillot meeting of La Francophonie and one month earlier at the Heads of Government Meeting of the Commonwealth in Harare. Mulroney had told his sceptical Commonwealth peers: "In Canada's judgement it is indispensable to the integrity of the Commonwealth that its Harare Declaration make clear that nothing is more important than respect for individual freedoms and human rights." In future, Canada would link aid funding to trends in human rights and democratic pluralism. Mulroney's statements were grand theatre, but they failed to say how the policy would be implemented.

The Dili killings, which occurred so soon after the prime minister's brave words, posed the worst of all possible tests for the Canadian resolve to defend human rights abroad. In fact, a clear policy did not emerge until 9 December 1991 – three weeks after the Dili killings. At CIDA, the discussion on an appropriate response went all the way to Monique Landry, the junior minister for development aid. Since the response would likely implicate the full range of Canada's bilateral relations with Indonesia, the cabinet was also involved, and officials acknowledge that ODA suspension was not the only option considered. Group of Seven coordination was another option that would ensure that Canada need not act alone.[5]

On 18 November the external affairs minister, Barbara McDougall, told the House of Commons that Ottawa had not made up its mind, though she hinted broadly that nothing draconian was planned. Ottawa's policy contained three elements.[6] First, three new projects "that directly benefited the Indonesian government" were to be put on hold.[7] This sanction was a symbolic expression of Canadian concern and would distance Ottawa from Jakarta's alleged culpability. Second, the rest of the aid program would continue unhindered. This signalled that Canada still wanted to do business with Indonesia and that by continuing aid, Ottawa still had a credible voice in Jakarta. Finally, Canada would take into account the findings of President Suharto's commission of inquiry during upcoming cabinet reviews of country aid allocations. This emphasized that new aid was contingent on Jakarta's visible action to right wrongs.

Ottawa would later add further conditions before restoring normal relations. It waited for the report of U.N. special rapporteur, Amos Wako; and, in a symbolic gesture, Canada chose to sit as an observer rather than as a full participant at the 1992 Paris meeting of the Consultative Group for Indonesia. Although Canada had discussed plans for new aid disbursements with Indonesian officials, no new pledge was made at Paris.

In Parliament it fell to Minister McDougall to fend off opposition attacks on the government's failure to "practice what it preaches" (Svend Robinson, New Democrat) or "live up to its own rhetoric" (Beryl Gaffney, Liberal). Acknowledging that the government had called for a review of Canada's aid to Indonesia, McDougall informed Parliament that she had called in the Canadian ambassador for talks and that on the day after the killings she had spoken to the Indonesian foreign minister, Ali Alatas, during a meeting they were both attending in Seoul. In that discussion she had urged Indonesia to accept the U.N.-sponsored Portuguese delegation to East Timor.[8] McDougall noted, however, that most of Canada's aid to Indonesia was "grass-roots aid" channelled through NGOs rather than government. She bluntly refused to support a Canadian all-party parliamentary delegation in a fact-finding visit to East Timor.

Like their Dutch counterparts, Canadian MPs were not satisfied with the results of the Indonesian government's commission of inquiry. Christine Stewart (Liberal) called for an independent investigation of the Dili killings.[9] On 4 February 1993, the New Democrat MP Dan Heap introduced Bill C-401, a private member's bill, to terminate Canadian assistance to Indonesia "until Indonesia ceases illegal occupation and human rights violations in East Timor." The bill, which did not pass first reading, would have shut down all Canadian financial support to Indonesia except humanitarian, food, medical, refugee, and disaster relief. It would also have directed the Canadian executive directors of the International Monetary Fund and the International Development Association (the World Bank's soft-loan window) to "oppose any use of funds of those institutions for the benefit of Indonesia." It also called for Indonesia's nonentitlement as a beneficiary of the most-favoured-nation tariff or any other preferential customs tariff. Another New Democrat MP, Lynn Hunter, blasted Minister McDougall's acceptance of de facto Indonesian sovereignty over East Timor as a display of "monumental ignorance." Hunter urged the government "not to repeat the sorry history of empty rhetoric but to put real substance behind the Prime Minister's statement and turn around Canada's record on international investment and human rights."[10] The Canadian government ignored much of this parliamentary carping on East Timor. NGOs were treated with the same disregard. In the words of Lawrence T. Dickenson, who is currently Canada's ambassador in Jakarta, Canadian NGOs had a "dated, stereotyped image of Indonesia," one that was fixated on East Timor; unlike them, the government ought to look at "trend lines, not individual events."[11] In the government's view, there was more cause for optimism, particularly given Jakarta's impressive capacity to lift much of the population out of grinding poverty. Moreover, Canada accepts the de facto administration of East Timor by Jakarta, though it does not recognize Indonesia's de jure annexation and sovereignty over the territory.[12] By contrast, Australia, which has mineral resource interests in the lucrative Timor Gap, has long recognized Jakarta as having de jure sovereignty over Timor. Canada's diplomatic splitting of hairs is a convenient way of salvaging some "brownie points" while abandoning any practical pretension to challenge the status quo on East Timor. Instead of doing so, Canada, with other OECD democracies, has encouraged Portugal and Indonesia to meet with the U.N. secretary general to resolve the issue.

In sum, prime ministerial rhetoric, intense media interest, and public moral outrage pushed Canada into invoking sanctions. In contrast to Ottawa's modulated response to Tiananmen Square, Canada's reaction to the Dili killings was more complicated and less disposed to clear-cut solutions. Indonesia was by then the second-largest recipient of Canadian bilateral aid. Moreover, the Dili killings were not an isolated incident but were part of a broader pattern of state repression against aggrieved ethnic and regional minorities. State-sponsored political killings and torture had been going on in East Timor for years. Less known but equally savage action by Indonesian authorities was also occurring in Irian Jaya (West Papua); and more recently, developments in Aceh, Northern Sumatra – a new separatist flashpoint – have prompted Indonesian repression of unparalleled ferocity.

The nature of the violence and the issue of state culpability was much more equivocal than in Tiananmen Square. The Beijing killings were premeditated; they were sanctioned by political leaders and carried out by the military. In Dili, the question of state sponsorship was more murky. The Indonesian government denied premeditation, insisting that this was simply a case of a few soldiers running amok in a remote province. While the commission of inquiry exposed a degree of malintent by local army officers, we may never know for certain if more senior government of military figures were implicated. Finally, Jakarta in general and President Suharto in particular were, as a Canadian diplomat put it, "extraordinarily prickly" about foreign meddling in East Timor.[13]

These uncertainties may be part of the explanation for Ottawa's decision (in contrast to its China policy after Tiananmen) to continue high-level meetings with Indonesian officials. As noted above, Canada's external affairs minister, Barbara McDougall, spoke with the Indonesian foreign minister, Ali Alatas, at an international meeting in Seoul "hours after news of the killings" to "express the outrage of the Canadian people." Indonesia's industry minister, Radius Prawiro, met Canada's international trade minister, Michael Wilson, in May 1992. And during the ASEAN post-ministerial conference in July 1993, the new Canadian secretary of state for external affairs, Perrin Beatty, at a meeting with Ali Alatas, signalled that Canada was ready to turn a new page in bilateral relations. He indicated that a substantive aid program with Indonesia would continue. Finally, the new Liberal prime minister, Jean Chrétien, raised the rights issue privately with President Suharto during the 1994 Seattle meeting of the Asia-Pacific Economic Cooperation forum. But some interactions with Jakarta were undoubtedly tense. Although BAPPENAS, the Indonesian national planning agency, never brought up the three projects during annual aid consultations with CIDA, and although there was no public rebuke of Canadian officials to suggest that Jakarta might retaliate, senior Indonesian officials did make a last-minute cancellation of a November 1992 visit of provincial governors to Canada, and one Canadian diplomat conceded that Jakarta thought that Canada might cut off all aid.[14]

By 1995, Canada was using development aid as a key element in what is now described as "constructive engagement" with Indonesia on human rights. Human rights promotion projects have included support for a computerized information network for the Legal Aid Foundation of Indonesia; for a documentation system for YAPUSHAM, a human rights think-tank; for small projects related to governance and decentralization; and for community development projects in East Timor. Aid to East Timor has been provided through NGOs such as CARE, the Roman Catholic Church, and UNICEF. A directed Canada Fund of $500,000 per year had by 1995 funded more than 120 small community projects in East Timor. Between 1979 and 1995, Canada invested a modest $900,000 in community development for East Timor. More active downstream programming in human rights and good governance is being considered and may include strengthening Indonesia's National Human Rights Commission following a visit by Max Yalden, head of the Canadian Human Rights Commission, to Indonesia in April 1995.

SANCTIONS AND RETALIATION: DILI AND THE CRISIS OF INDO-DUTCH RELATIONS

On 16 November 1991, four days after the Dili killings, the Dutch government suspended new ODA to Indonesia. A planned consultation between the two governments to set new aid levels and modalities was cancelled, but current programs were unaffected. Jakarta had always insisted that East Timor was an internal matter, and it had resisted international interference. The Indonesian government took a tough stance against the Netherlands' aid suspension. Many Indonesians saw the Dutch decision as an unwarranted meddling in domestic politics, rekindling memories of an unhappy colonial past. In March 1992, Jakarta blunty informed The Hague that Indonesia would accept no further aid, and it told the Netherlands to relinquish its chairmanship of the Inter-Governmental Group for Indonesia (IGGI) the principal aid-pledging forum. The IGGI was summarily dissolved.[15] This was the culmination of Indonesia's anger at Dutch human rights diplomacy on East Timor and the high-handed sermonizing of Jan Pronk, the Dutch development cooperation minister.

The formal request to terminate Dutch aid in Indonesia was outlined in a letter signed by Radius Prawiro, coordinating minister for economy, finance, industry, and development supervision. It was submitted to the Government of the Netherlands on 25 March 1992 by the

Indonesian ambassador, Tjoeroaminoto Bintoro. The communiqué called on the Dutch government:

1 To terminate the disbursement of all on-going development assistance (both loans and grants) from the Netherlands to Indonesia;
2 Not to prepare new development assistance to Indonesia; and
3 Not to convene a meeting of the IGGI and to terminate its chairmanship of the IGGI.

It continued:

The Government of Indonesia greatly appreciates the role of the Government of the Netherlands in convening and chairing IGGI meetings as well as the assistance received from the Netherlands during the last twenty-four years.

However, relations between the two nations have recently deteriorated sharply as a consequence of the reckless use of development assistance as an instrument of intimidation or as a tool of threatening Indonesia.

The Indonesian Government does not wish to be a party to letting relations between the two nations degenerate towards a complete breakdown. Nor has the Government of Indonesia any desire to watch the Netherlands Government be put repeatedly in an awkward predicament as a consequence of not being able to put an effective brake on an exaggerated eagerness to continue utilizing development assistance as an instrument of threat to Indonesia.

Since this exaggerated eagerness to resort to the use of development assistance as an instrument of intimidation seems to continue unabated, the only remaining option is to terminate development assistance from the Netherlands to Indonesia.

PRELUDE TO DISASTER

Strains in Indo-Dutch relations had been visible before the Dutch suspended new ODA. Jakarta's quarrel with The Hague went beyond interstate relations or the clash of cultures. Personalities also played a part. The decision to ask the Dutch to leave was made by President Suharto himself. On the Dutch side, Jan Pronk, the development cooperation minister, had played a key role in tilting Holland towards sanctions. There was a history of bad blood between the two men. Suharto knew Pronk from the 1970s when, as development cooperation minister, Pronk had first linked Dutch ODA to Indonesia's human rights performance. Dutch foreign ministry officials describe Pronk as "undiplomatic," "very stubborn," and inclined not to consult with staff or political peers. Almost from the outset of his second tenure as minister of development cooperation, Pronk was judged by one senior official to be on a "collision course" with Indonesia.[16]

Returning as the ODA minister in 1990, Pronk was quick to integrate human rights criteria into project approval procedures, and he pushed his aid officials to focus more on human rights, much to the annoyance of Hans van den Broek, who was foreign minister at the time. Pronk used the 1990 IGGI meeting to criticize Indonesia. The Indonesians found him hypocritical and sarcastically referred to him as "the inspector." Pronk's Calvinist background and church activism, coupled with a lack of social graces and a tendency to bypass protocol, led to small unilateral adventures that irritated his Indonesian counterparts. In his 1991 trip to the Moluccas, Pronk managed to stir up anti-Dutch sentiment in the Indonesian press by openly criticizing Jakarta's exploitation of fragile rain forest for profit. Even after Dili, in February 1992, Pronk continued to defy diplomatic sanity. He used his chairmanship of the IGGI to announce unilaterally that he was going to visit Aceh, the region with separatist sentiments where the Indonesian military had allegedly been involved in human rights violations. When Pronk's provocative act aroused no official Indonesian rebuke, Dutch officials knew something was wrong, though they were still unaware that a diplomatic time bomb was ticking. On one reading, Pronk in the 1990s was still acting on 1970s assumptions. In the social democratic era of the 1970s, he had flourished, for at that time Dutch foreign policy had been outspoken in condemning the rights-repressive regimes of Greece and Portugal. But by the 1980s, van den Broek's Christian Democrats had shifted to quiet diplomacy. The foreign ministry considered this approach to be more in line with the new international realities of a more heterogenous developing world and with the emergence of the Asia-Pacific Rim as the pivot of the global economy.

The Dutch parliament was another key player.[17] After the Dili killings, the right-wing Dutch parties in the Netherlands immediately called for a partial suspension of ODA, and even the ruling Christian Democrats pressed for a token suspension of government-to-government aid. Dutch parliamentary outrage was prompted by having a high-profile Dutchman at the scene of the killings. The Dutch foreign minister, P.H.P. Kooijmans, had formerly been the U.N. rapporteur on torture, and he had been in Dili in this capacity at the time of the incident.

There were other factors too that helped shape reaction to Dili. Dutch pleas to spare several aging *tapols* (political prisoners incarcerated after the 1965 purge of communists) who were facing execution, Pronk's use of the rights card in the IGGI, his unwelcome criticism of

a population program that allegedly coerced women into family planning – these and other irritants were early fissures building to the rift
over Dili. But the trigger that provoked Jakarta's retaliation was Pronk
and van den Broek's suggestion to the Dutch parliament that a European Union communiqué, which was issued after the report of the
Indonesian commission of inquiry, should nevertheless entertain the
possibility of further international investigation into the killings.[18]
After Dili, persistent Dutch statements on Indonesia's human rights
record continued to rankle Jakarta, and already there were warnings
that Indonesia might reject Dutch aid that was tied to political
demands. The depth of Jakarta's anger was revealed in mid-February
1992 when President Suharto publicly castigated Dutch policy while
receiving the credentials of the new Dutch ambassador to Indonesia,
J.H.R.D. van Roijen. Suharto said that the Netherlands' attempt to
impose its values on Indonesia was a "violation of human rights and
the rights of a sovereign nation." Astonishingly, the Dutch seemed not
to read the writing on the wall.

PRESIDENT SUHARTO'S GAMBIT

Although it was politically motivated, Suharto's decision to reject
Dutch aid and dissolve the IGGI was taken only after a careful assessment of the likely economic consequences. In this sense it differed markedly from President Sukarno's invitation to the United States some
thirty years ago to "go to hell with your aid," with which the 1992
rejection has frequently been compared. Suharto planned his gambit
carefully. He quietly asked Japan, the United States, and the World
Bank whether they would be likely to side with The Hague if the Dutch
were asked to relinquish their chairmanship. Japan's assurance that it
was satisfied with Jakarta's handling of the Dili killings and would not
impose political conditionality was particularly welcome. Japan is Indonesia's largest donor, and in 1991–92 it accounted for almost 28 per
cent of the total IGGI financial pledges. The Dutch seem to have been
unaware of these manœuvres, nor did they go on the offensive to try
and win over powerful friends to their cause. That said, the Dutch and
the Danes (another country that imposed token aid suspensions) had
few friends in the European Union and soon recognized that there was
little prospect for a coordinated approach to aid sanctions.

Losing the IGGI chair was, without question, a terrible shock for
the Dutch. Minister Pronk tried to put the best face on it, casting the
decision as a measure of a growing Indonesian self-confidence and
maturity, so that they were now truly equal partners in development.
But the brutal fact is that Holland will never assume any prominent

role in the Consultative Group for Indonesia. Suharto turned the tables on the Dutch. The IGGI was replaced in short order by the Consultative Group for Indonesia, which is now under the chairmanship of the World Bank. The Netherlands continues to be excluded from it. Seemingly oblivious to the diplomatic fallout over Dili, the consultative group, at its first meeting in Paris in July 1992, committed a record US$4.9 billion in aid, of which US$4.1 billion was from Japan, the World Bank, and the Asian Development Bank. This happened despite an attempt by Portugal, via the European Union, to link the flow of aid to human rights issues and a resolution of the East Timor question. By 1994, the donors had mustered a record US$5.2 billion, of which US$1.6 billion came from Japan.

Moreover, the dissolution of the IGGI and the exclusion of the Netherlands from the Consultative Group for Indonesia did not prompt any former IGGI donors, such as Canada, to withdraw voluntarily from the consultative group. In fact, the group attracted new members that had not previously belonged to the IGGI: South Korea, Denmark, the Nordic Investment Bank, the Kuwait Fund for Arab Economic Development, and the Saudi Fund for Development. Not surprisingly, the Indonesian government saw this as a vindication of its decision to disband the IGGI, and President Suharto described the growing membership as proof of continuing international confidence in his country's stability and growth path.

Suharto's timing was impeccable. He may have made up his mind to liquidate the Dutch program as early as December 1991;[19] but in order to score points, he waited until March 1992 before going public. Indonesia had taken over the chairmanship of the Non-Aligned Movement, which was set to meet at Jakarta in May 1992. Suharto's actions, though calculated for success, were – in tone, at least – reminiscent of the brinkmanship of his predecessor Sukarno. His dismissal of the Dutch was sure to resound well among his non-aligned peers and to bolster Indonesia's intellectual and political stewardship of the Non-Aligned Movement. Suharto used the May meeting to attack the trend in OECD countries to tie political strings to aid. The West had been put on notice. Suharto may also have seen the Dutch ouster as a way of mollifying those in the military who resented the punishment of army staff in the wake of the commission of inquiry. In Indonesia, the human rights issues involved in the Dili killings were submerged by the wave of national feeling that Suharto evoked by his ouster of the former colonial power. It was also an expression of Indonesia's growing economic power and self-confidence.

The report of the Indonesian commission of inquiry was tabled on 21 December 1991, but The Hague did not respond until 20 January

1992 – a measure of the intense debate within the Dutch government. The lull was interpreted by the Indonesians as a sign of bad faith. By New Year's Eve 1991, Minister Pronk had conceded that he had been wrong. In an interview on Dutch television he said, "Minister van den Broek's judgement on Indonesian problems was better than mine."[20] In acknowledging that the report to Parliament included the fateful "statement of which he was the author," calling for European Union aid sanctions unless there was an independent inquiry into the Dili killings, he noted that Jakarta would not have cut development cooperation without a genuine perception of serious provocation. As Pronk explained, "At the time I did not realize how seriously Indonesia would judge such a statement."[21]

THE FALLOUT ON NON-GOVERNMENTAL ORGANIZATIONS

The loss of the official Dutch development assistance, which amounted to a modest US$91.3 million in the fiscal year 1991–92, was felt mainly by local NGOs, including human rights and environmental groups.[22] Jakarta imposed a blanket ban on the acceptance of any Dutch funds by domestic NGOs, backing this up with warnings from the minister for home affairs that there would be stern action against any organizations that disregarded the ban. One of Indonesia's leading NGOs, the Legal Aid Foundation, was prepared to test the ban legally. The foundation depends on Dutch funding for a significant portion of its budget. Arguing that a mere statement by a minister does not carry the force of law, it went on record saying that it intended to continue to accept Dutch aid.

Ironically, most Indonesian NGOs were not supportive of Pronk's action, and the prevailing atmosphere in Indonesia – both among the NGO community and the public – was overwhelmingly anti-Dutch. The rupture in bilateral relations has worked to the advantage of Indonesian NGOs. They have become more confident with their Dutch counterparts and are now looking at self-financing arrangements. But there was some negative fallout. Suharto purged the Christian members of some regional cabinets, notably in the Moluccas, as a signal that he was unhappy with their close relations with Dutch society. In Bali, the governor instructed all local NGOs not to receive any funds from Dutch counterpart organizations. The outer islands probably suffered more. The Mollucas and Irian Jaya, which have pressed for greater autonomy from Indonesia, received few funds after the Dutch left. And after the rift with Holland, the Indonesian government screened and registered every single domestic NGO. There is, however, no evidence of serious intimidation, harassment, or physical violence by state authorities towards the NGO sector.

The liquidation of the Dutch aid program complicated but did not end the delivery of Dutch NGO funds. Where possible, Dutch NGOs that had anticipated a freeze on their ability to fund quickly approved projects that were still pending and thus beat the 25 April 1992 deadline, when the funding of Indonesian partners with Dutch government funds was to stop. The Netherlands Organization for International Development Cooperation (NOVIB) kept working in Indonesia by drawing on its own private funds. HIVOS, another Dutch co-financing agency, was able to continue operating in Indonesia by swapping country programs with NOVIB. In this arrangement, NOVIB used 1.5 million guilders of its private funds to support what had been HIVOS projects, while HIVOS used its Dutch co-financing government funds originally earmarked for Indonesia to support NOVIB projects in Malaysia and Sri Lanka. HIVOS thus did not lose Dutch ODA co-financing funds. In much the same way, CEBEMO, another Dutch NGO, transferred its government funds to other European Catholic organizations that were still able to work in Indonesia. Thus Miserior, a German NGO, took over CEBEMO's Indonesia program, while CEBEMO took financial responsibility for Miserior's Zambia program. But there has been a long-term cost for at least two of the four major co-financing agencies. By 1993, CEBEMO and ICCO, another Dutch NGO, were winding down their activities in Indonesia partly because of their inability to use Dutch government ODA directly to fund Indonesian partners. Moreover, Home Affairs Minister Rudini's edict is still technically in place. Although his views were never actually law, the chilling effect on Dutch and Indonesian NGOs was unequivocal.

MENDING FENCES

After Dili, and in response to international pressure, Indonesia established the National Human Rights Commission and allowed access by prominent human rights organizations such as Asia Watch and Amnesty International. A Swedish parliamentary delegation visited Indonesia on 13–16 September 1993, and a high-profile delegation of Dutch MPs did so in December 1993. The latter was led by the speaker of the Tweede Kamer and the leaders of three major Dutch political parties: Labour (VVD), Christian Democrats, and D66 (Liberals). The delegation met President Suharto and Foreign Minister Ali Alatas. Hans van Mirlo, the D66 leader, met Ponge Princen, a human rights activist.

Although the Dutch aid program of 300 million guilders per year had gone, probably for good (one official has suggested that formal government-to-government ODA will not be restored "as long as Suharto lives")²³, nevertheless, Dutch society in 1994 still managed to contribute 6 million guilders from private sources to support Indonesian development projects. In March 1994, Prime Minister Ruud Lubbers and Foreign Minister P.H.P. Koiijmans (the former U.N. torture rapporteur) went to Indonesia to try to normalize relations. For his part, Suharto was vainly hoping that the Dutch queen would visit in 1995 to mark, from the Indonesian perspective, fifty years of independence. The Dutch, however, may prefer to mark this symbolically in 1999, the anniversary of the year in which the Netherlands formally relinquished sovereign control.

WHAT PRICE PRINCIPLES?

Why did The Hague react so harshly to Dili? Part of the answer is irrational. The Dutch are often quite outspoken on human rights, but when former colonies are involved there is an extra dimension: emotion. The three countries that generate intense Dutch debate are South Africa, Suriname, and Indonesia. The Dutch have never been able to let go of Indonesia, and many stubbornly perpetuate a negative view of Indonesian political life.²⁴

Parliament is another part of the answer. Parliament ensured that Foreign Minister van den Broek did not opt for private *démarches* or rely on the results of Jakarta's commission of inquiry. Dutch MPs wanted an international investigation. Parliament was clearly frustrated by van den Broek's earlier quiet diplomacy by which he had failed to prevent the execution of long-standing political prisoners. Despite the best Dutch efforts, the Suharto regime had regularly been executing incarcerated *tapols* since at least the mid-1980s. With Dili, Parliament was in no mood for another round of fruitless quiet diplomacy. In any case, the two issues were markedly different. With the *tapols*, lives were at stake and were retrievable. In Dili, lives had been lost and it was punishment and accountability that were at stake.

By mid-December 1992, the Dutch government was ready to lift aid sanctions after the preliminary report of the Indonesian commission of inquiry had been privately made available. The Dutch also assumed that Amos Wako, the U.N. envoy, would be able to visit East Timor. Bureaucrats who privately "deplored" the decisions taken by their ministers nonetheless set about drafting a text to be presented in Parliament saying that the Netherlands government would contact the European Union through the European Political Cooperation mechanism if Amos Wako was hampered in his work in East Timor. Van den Broek may have seen this concession as a "trick" or ploy simply to assuage Parliament, and he had no intention of following through. Jan

Pronk, on the other hand, saw the European Union dimension as critical and had every intention of following through. But Ambassador Bintoro, Jakarta's man at The Hague and a political appointee directly nominated by Suharto, was reportedly shocked by potential Dutch calls for action by the European Union before the Indonesian commission of inquiry had officially reported. He contacted Suharto directly with the news. In the words of one Dutch diplomat, "From that point on, everything went wrong."[25]

In the meantime, contrary to the belief of the Indonesian ambassador that there was a Dutch lobby to win over the European Union, the Dutch were in fact trying to put the brake on the more radical disposition of the Portuguese and were pressing for a softer line on East Timor. The Dutch evidently succeeded in getting Britain and Germany to push for a more even-handed European Union text which, while criticizing the bloodshed in Dili, broadly agreed with the findings of the commission of inquiry. This proved to be the last moderate statement of the "twelve" on the Dili affair. The matter then went into a period the Dutch call the windstilte – the calm before the storm.

Dutch diplomacy failed badly on East Timor. Relations between the Netherlands and Indonesia had been far more complicated and tense in the mid-1970s after the annexation of East Timor and when the Dutch were concerned about the fate of Christian minorities in the Moluccas. Yet by using quiet diplomacy, the Netherlands had managed to engineer, with the help of the United States, Britain, and Canada, the release of some ten thousand political prisoners who had been held since the 1965 blood-letting against the Indonesian communists. The release was achieved without a rupture in diplomatic or aid relations.

By late February 1992, the Dutch were ready to abandon aid sanctions; and Foreign Minister van den Broek persuaded the cabinet and Parliament that the language confirming new relations between the two countries should not contain explicit human rights considerations. Beneath their need for a combined and unified face before Parliament, van den Broek and Pronk were in fact miles apart. The difference in the diplomatic approach of these two men – the preacher and the pragmatist – underlines the abiding tension between idealism and realism in Dutch foreign policy. Meanwhile, Canada, Denmark, and the Netherlands – the donors who had invoked aid sanctions – had kept one another informed about their perceptions and actions but had not coordinated their actions. The Dutch evidently saw coordination as fruitless because the European Community was indifferent to an assertive response to Dili.

Were aid sanctions counterproductive? Would quiet diplomacy have been more effective in moving Jakarta? The aid sanctions were unquestionably a disaster for the Dutch. But this has more to do with the manner in which they were introduced – by a sermonizing minister and as a comprehensive freeze on all new aid; it is not a blanket condemnation of the use of political measures to defend human rights. Indonesian feathers are easily ruffled. While the Dutch have a reputation for bluntly speaking their minds, "it was not the Dutch who killed the demonstrators at Dili."[26] In the final analysis, the Dili killings were an atrocity that required plain speaking from the international community. And although most Indonesian NGOs were critical of the Dutch aid suspension, some dissented. One NGO saw through Suharto's "attempts at engineering public opinion" to equate the rejection of Dutch aid as an act of "patriotism" and "national-ism.". The NGO observed that the government's "act of dishonesty" manipulated emotion as a way of covering "certain practices in the exercise of power."

The question of linking foreign aid to demands for ... human rights and democratization is an epiphenomenon of another [fundamental] fact, namely the weak bargaining position of [civil society] vis-à-vis the New Order state. It is for this reason that linking basic human rights and democratization to foreign credits is not merely the idea of foreign states. Behind the question of a rejection of Dutch credits a serious question is hidden: the ways, the room for manœuvre and the future of (Indonesian) democratization is confronted with a serious obstruction ... Nationalism as an argument to legitimize the rejection of foreign credits, is a farce intended to divert the attention of people away from this serious question.[27]

For the Dutch, the principal lesson from Dili is "Be sure of your allies before you act." This applies particularly to the Europeans. The second lesson is that brinkmanship will likely fail if there is no credible threat. Indonesia could do without Dutch money, which made up just 4 per cent of total IGGI financing in 1990. Jakarta was thus in a strong position to retaliate. The third lesson is "Safeguard NGO initiatives before you act or be prepared to live with the fallout on NGOs." Some Dutch human rights and governance initiatives, particularly in the legal cooperation sector, suffered as a result of the rupture in diplomatic and aid relations; and two Dutch co-financing agencies had to wind down their operations in Indonesia.

LESSONS LEARNED: THE LIMITS OF POLITICAL CONDITIONALITY

Ottawa and The Hague faced the same dilemma: how to craft a principled response to an extreme human rights abuse, how to prompt change in the Indonesian authorities, and how to signal solidarity with the Timorese, all without rupturing important diplomatic and commercial interests. Canada sought the golden mean of distancing itself from state violence by freezing three planned projects, but without sacrificing its bilateral relations or an aid program that was trying to advance women's development, encourage sustainable development, promote regional development, and foster commercial links. The challenge of mixing money and morals was to make a point and perhaps even prompt change without losing influence or markets. Did the Dutch and Canadians succeed?

Canada's response underlines some painful lessons about crafting a morally credible foreign policy. First, one must consistently register concern about human rights before a crisis erupts. It is disingenuous to address a crisis in isolation, pretending that there is no history of precedents.[28] Second, rhetoric will haunt a government unless it is backed by a workable policy of implementation to meet every human rights contingency. Public statements will pressure a government to deliver for fear of looking foolish both at home and abroad. When a crisis does occur, there may be little room for manouevre. Cutting aid, against the better judgment of diplomats, may then be the only way to prove that a government is capable of putting its money where its mouth is.

What impact did symbolic political conditions have? The sceptical view would be that Canada's "protest was cosmetic. We unburdened ourselves. The Indonesians nodded, made promises and returned to business as usual. Earnest and outraged, we objected, equivocated, and then began to regret and retreat. A lone voice in the wilderness is simply unlikely to be heard in Indonesia. The country is too big and its sources of support too broad."[29] Foreign Minister Ali Alatas told *Financial Post* journalist Andrew Cohen that he would rather see Canada suspend its aid than listen to advice from a well-meaning, misguided friend.[30] The Dutch tied money to morals and were thrown out. The Danes tried to follow suit but capitulated to Indonesian pressure. Canada found a middle way to protest without damaging its commercial interests. Canada's modulated approach allowed it to maintain a policy dialogue with the Indonesians, albeit under strained circumstances. Ministerial contact was maintained with Canada waiting for certain "benchmarks" before the limited suspension was lifted and relations were normalized.

Acting alone, Canada, the Netherlands, and Denmark had no clear effect in convincing Jakarta to respond to international criticism. But their gestures should not be dismissed as empty. On one view, aid conditionality helped concentrate the minds of the Indonesian authorities and may have tilted them towards establishing the independent commission of inquiry into the events at Dili. As Andrew Dickenson, Canada's ambassador in Jakarta, observed, Dili "brought home to the Indonesian elites the need to pay attention to international opinion." President Suharto's commission of inquiry was unprecedented. Putting its findings on public record was, "in the context of Indonesian history and politics, surprising and dramatic." Christopher Dagg has suggested that "in a culture where office holders are sometimes seen to be insulated from accountability, the disciplinary action taken against senior military officers was ... a dramatic expression of the Indonesian Government's sensitivity to human rights."[31]

A more weary view is that Suharto's actions amounted to damage control and public relations rather than "sensitivity" to human rights. Contrary to the breezy optimism of Ambassador Dickenson, Jakarta is still unable to tolerate a negative international press. While Indonesia has joined the U.N. Commission on Human Rights, its stance at the 1993 World Human Rights Conference was to insist that human rights conditionality was inappropriate and to emphasize "cultural particularities" in the face of the claims of universal human rights. Both these positions were reflected in the final Vienna Declaration. In 1993, when Belgium tried to negotiate human rights language in a memorandum of understanding that would underpin its aid relationship with Indonesia, President Suharto is reported to have intervened personally to prevent any such reference. The memorandum of understanding was left unsigned. In 1994, Jakarta successfully pressured the Philippines and Malaysia into disallowing planned international conferences on East Timor. Indonesia also pressed the Thai government to close down a meeting organized by Southeast Asian NGOs to parallel the ASEAN intergovernmental meeting in Bangkok in July 1994. Reportedly, Indonesian Foreign Minister Ali Alatas threatened not to participate if the NGO meeting went ahead; the NGOs had unpardonably invited several Timorese groups to attend.[32]

Canada has also felt the sting of Indonesian displeasure. In May 1994, Jakarta cancelled a $38 million CIDA-funded development project in Sulawesi, which was managed by the University of Guelph. The university, responding to growing campus criticism of its role in Indonesia, had released an independent report on the project which also criticized the country's human rights record. The project, which was aimed at community participation in local development, was a pilot for a new form of regional development planning. Jack Macdonald, Guelph's academic vice-president, was clear that the Indonesians' decision was political. He noted, "We have been given no notice in writing."[33] The Canadian government defended the principle of academic freedom, reiterating that the university was free to undertake an independent asessment. Ottawa considered that Indonesian citizens were the ultimate losers, since the Sulawesi project was a potential national blueprint for regional development that would have been endorsed by President Suharto. When Canada tried to raise the Guleph project at the 1994 bilateral aid consultations, the Indonesians bluntly replied that the purpose of the consultation was to review the entire aid package, not to discuss a single project.[34]

In sum, there is no direct cause and effect relationship between international pressure and Jakarta's response to the Dili killings. A principled and effective diplomacy, whether public or private, coercive or persuasive, will always be problematic with a country as ill disposed as Indonesia to foreign meddling and the so-called export of Western values. Aid conditions may not have had much impact, but neither did quiet diplomacy. Despite Dutch and other OECD *démarches*, Jakarta went ahead and regularly executed several of the "class of 1965" – political prisoners who had languished for years in Indonesia's prisons.

The Canadian and Dutch action, though principled, underlines the limits of small and middle-power diplomacy. Only the United States and Japan have the raw power to influence Jakarta unilaterally. While the U.S. Congress did cut military assistance to Indonesia after the East Timor killings, the Bush administration did not condition economic aid on human rights improvements in Timor. Under Clinton, the United States has been more prepared to push its weight around, but, interestingly, the rights issue has turned not on East Timor but on labour standards and workers' rights. The 1993 rape and political murder of Marsinah, a young woman labour activist who had organized a strike at her factory in East Java, is emblematic of the growing struggle between the state and organized labour over the minimum wage and freedom of association. It is no accident that much of the labour unrest has taken place in the shoe and garment industries, sectors that employ mostly women, because wages there are often lower than in other industries. The Indonesian military intervened in the strike, and Indonesia's Legal Aid Foundation pointed to military involvement in Marsinah's death. The case was placed before Indonesia's new National Commission on Human Rights.

In February 1994 the U.S. trade representative Mickey Kantor said that the United States would give Indonesia a six-months reprieve from its threat to impose economic penalties unless Jakarta improved its workers' rights record.[35] Under the provisions of the U.S. generalized system of preferences, preferential trade treatment is given to Indonesian goods. In 1993, Indonesia took US$1.5 billion in exports from the United States, making it the seventh-largest beneficiary of the preferences system. But American law allows such concessions to be withdrawn if the countries benefiting from them do not treat their workers in accordance with internationally recognized standards. It seems unlikely that Canada would follow the U.S. lead in defending workers' rights. Ambassador Dickenson said in Montreal that he had not met and had no imminent plans to meet labour leaders in Indonesia.

The size of Indonesia's debt, with a debt service ratio of about 30 per cent, its appetite for new investment, and the centrality of large ODA flows in national development planning point in theory to multilateral coordination through the donor aid consortium as the best place for Canada to integrate human rights and governance considerations into its lending policies. Indonesia has not reached the stage where it can dismiss the international community or stop borrowing from the World Bank, from which it received US$1.4 billion in 1993 alone. But nothing in the history of the Indonesian aid consortium suggests any prospect of collective action in this crucial arena.[36] At the 1994 meeting of the Consultative Group for Indonesia, the donors pledged US$5.2 billion in development aid, with US$1.6 billion coming from Japan alone.

PART THREE
Policies

8 Between Discretion and Participation: Institutional Frameworks for Human Rights Policy

The comfortable tradition that external affairs is the prerogative of the Crown is now being rudely disturbed by the pressures of participatory democracy. Canadians are knocking at the door of this country's foreign policy with more than messages: they want in.

Independence and Internationalism, 1986[1]

I want now to turn from the specific to the general, from practice to policies. What governments do must be matched against what they say. Policy blueprints and institutional innovations are among the unassertive levers of statecraft. They signal the emergence of an issue but may not explain activism in the field. That is why I shall briefly consider the influence of domestic political culture before turning to institutional innovations in order to examine the tension between democratic participation and executive discretion in foreign policy.

Canada and the Netherlands are the main focus here. Moreover, since many of the structures are new, my observations are provisional, pointing to tendencies rather than to immutable fact. I want to argue (1) that while bureaucratic innovations can help foster more awareness of human rights among state officials, they do not, ipso facto, institutionalize interests; and (2) that although parliaments and activists have influenced the policy process, the limits of participation may already have been reached.

PRAGMATISTS AND PURITANS:
THE DETERMINANTS OF HUMAN RIGHTS
ACTIVISM

Canada claims that human rights are a "fundamental and integral" part of its foreign policy; the Netherlands says they are a "cornerstone" and "main pillar"; and Norway says they "occupy an important position" in foreign policy.[2] What accounts for the activism of these self-styled moralists? One assessment of Canadian, Dutch, and Scandinavian Third World policies uncovered a common "concern with moral principles," a "disposition towards responsible activism," and a commitment to "humane internationalism." It found that the three states all held a deep obligation to alleviate global poverty, were convinced that tackling global poverty was in the national interest, and saw international responsibilities as consistent with social welfare at home.[3]

Strong domestic welfare traditions inform the humane internationalism of these "like-minded" states. Cranford Pratt has noted a correlation between ODA as a percentage of GNP and a commitment to high levels of domestic employment and social welfare. In all three states, the ODA/GNP ratio exceeds the OECD average. Social democratic traditions may explain why Norway and the Netherlands regularly compete for the highest ODA/GNP contributions among OECD states and why these countries undertook, for a short period, a more reformist new international economic order policy. Canada, where a liberal capitalist ideology is dominant, has been more muted in its new international economic order policy and less generous in its proportion of ODA as a percentage of GNP.[4]

In Canada, several steps were taken both nationally and internationally after 1975, which marks a watershed in the development of a more active human rights culture in both government and society. Before 1975, a major constraint to a more active international voice on human rights was the unwillingness of federal governments to offend the provinces by speaking out on issues that could have an impact on provincial jursidiction.[5] Following the 1975 federal-provincial ministerial conference on human rights and Canada's election to the U.N. Commission on Human Rights, human rights gradually emerged as a more significant component of Canadian foreign policy. The decision at the ministerial conference that Canada should ratify the international covenants and the Optional Protocol served notice that Canada was prepared to subject its domestic human rights performance to international scrutiny.

Domestic political values influence foreign policy traditions.[6] Observers have commented on a Calvinist streak in Dutch foreign policy, on a juxtaposition of contradictory impulses – the merchant and the preacher – and on the simultaneous pursuit of "peace, profits and principles."[7] The Dutch also have a tradition of domestic interest in human rights. Daalder notes "the co-existence of [a] strong degree of conservatism" with "an insistence on individual freedoms, not to speak of outright libertarianism."[8] An interest in global human rights is an expression of post-material values, and the Netherlands is an exemplar of the "new politics" in Western Europe. A passion for liberty, law, and pluralism is thus deeply embedded in Dutch society. The Dutch are perhaps unique in having a constitution that makes the promotion of an international legal order a state obligation.

Hveem describes Norway as an "over-achiever" in seeking stability, peace, and security from international society.[9] But he notes "a certain inferiority complex" stemming from its position as a peripheral state.[10] Norway may "compensate" for its humble rank by emphasizing international cooperation in order to achieve national goals and international status. The late J.J. Holst spoke of a "tacit bargain" in Norwegian foreign policy: "The discipline of [NATO] alignment is accepted as long as the state can demonstrate independence and project idealist visions in contexts that do not directly involve matters of national security."[11] Development aid and human rights are such contexts. They are "the moral bank of the nation ... whose symbolic purpose is to reinforce the dominant value system within Norwegian society."[12]

Canada differs from the North Europeans in several ways. First, social democracy has not dominated federal politics,[13] though some social policies have. Second, the church has been less influential. Third, aboriginal rights to land and to self-government are an Achilles' heel that hurts Canada's credibility in international human rights forums.[14] Nevertheless, Canadian foreign policy has a "voluntarist tradition," which is expressed as the "search for moral opportunity."[15] Canada is often seen as the "helpful fixer" and "committed internationalist, distinguished by its diligent pursuit ... of steadily constructing a more durable international order."[16] A more sober assessment characterizes the Canadian foreign policy culture as "distrust of dogma and the doctrinaire, fear of extremes, suspicion of the rhetoric of grand design, respect for diversity ... anticipation of conflict, belief in compromise, preoccupation with the limits of the possible, and dedication, ultimately, to the pragmatic."[17]

In Canada, Norway, and the Netherlands, the domestic foundations of internationalism combine with systemic or structural features, such

Table 8.1
Evolution of Norwegian Human Rights Policy

1976	White paper, Storting report no. 93 (1976–77), *Norway and the International Protection of Human Rights* (draft version by scholar Asbjorn Eide).
1979	Scholars establish Norwegian Human Rights Project.
1984	Experience in Sri Lanka prompts a white paper on the linkage of human rights to ODA, Storting report no. 36 (1984–85).
	Storting Foreign Affairs Committee reiterates call for a government-funded Norwegian Institute of Human Rights.
	Ministry of Development Cooperation funds a human rights research and information project, which leads to
1985	Publication of the Nordic yearbook on human rights in developing countries.
1986	Storting report no. 34 (1986–87), on human rights and ODA.
	Recommendation Storting no. 186, *Relating to Key Issues on Norwegian Development Cooperation* (Standing Committee on Foreign Affairs and the Constitution).
1987	Establishment of the Norwegian Institute of Human Rights.
1988	Four NGOs establish the Norwegian Human Rights Fund. The government agrees to provide financial support.
1989	Ministry of Foreign Affairs establishes a Norwegian human rights committee. Budget announced creation of a "democracy fund."

as military weakness, junior alliance status, and trade-driven economies, to produce "a remarkably wide consensus in each country that it should play a conciliatory role ... and support international institutions and regimes."[18] This commitment is evident in practice. Each state bears a disproportionate financial burden in the U.N. system. Each is also a significant supplier of peacekeeping troops. A study of "national support for world order" ranked Norway fourth, Canada seventh, and the Netherlands fifteenth.[19]

Indicative of their commitment to international law, all three states have signed the principal human rights conventions, including the Optional Protocol of the civil and political covenant, which permits international scrutiny of a state's domestic human rights performance. By contrast, the United States has still not ratified either the International Covenant on Civil and Political Rights or the International Covenant on Economic, Social, and Cultural Rights. Norway and the Netherlands are, in addition, among a handful of states that have submitted themselves unconditionally to the jurisdiction of the International Court of Justice.

Political culture and national role conceptions are the foundations for an interest in global human rights. They do not, however, explain why the policy framework in each state was so late in emerging, particularly on bilateral initiatives such as development aid. The relative recency of such frameworks is underlined in tables 8.1, 8.2, and 8.3,

Table 8.2
Evolution of Dutch Human Rights Policy

1976	NOVIB[1] begins funding human rights projects.
1979	Government memorandum on *Human Rights and Foreign Policy*.
	The Netherlands lobbies for a human rights clause in the EC-ACP[2] Lomé Convention on development aid and trade.
1981	The position of human rights coordinator is created in the Ministry of Foreign Affairs.
	NOVIB sponsors a major conference on human rights and development.
	Government proposes a bill to establish the Human Rights and Foreign Policy Advisory Committee.
1984	The advisory committee publishes *On an Equal Footing: Foreign Affairs and Human Rights*; recommends expanded in-service human rights training.
	Government expands human rights training for public servants.
1985	Government establishes Aarts Fund for human rights and humanitarian aid.

[1] Netherlands Organization for International Development.

[2] European Community and the African-Caribbean-Pacific countries.

Table 8.3
Evolution of Canadian Human Rights Policy

1977	Two private members' bills are introduced in Parliament to legislate termination of Canadian aid to rights-repressive recipient regimes.
1978	Government acknowledges human rights as legitimate factor in determining bilateral relations with developing countries.
1982	House of Commons subcommittee on Canada's relations with Latin America and the Caribbean recommends the reduction or cessation of aid to rights-repressive regimes.
1986	Publication of *Independence and Internationalism*, the report of the Special Joint Committee on Canada's International Relations; it recommends creation of a human rights centre and closer linkage of human rights and ODA.
1987	*For Whose Benefit?* ODA report of a House Standing Committee on External Affairs and International Trade; it recommends a human rights "grid," a CIDA human rights unit, and an annual public ODA–human rights review.
	The government's response, *To Benefit a Better World*, rejects the grid and the public ODA-rights review.
	Rapporteurs publish *International Cooperation for the Development of Human Rights and Democratic Institutions*.
1988	*Sharing Our Future*, CIDA aid strategy, includes human rights among criteria for aid eligibility.
	The International Centre for Human Rights and Democratic Development is established (of which Ed Broadbent is appointed president in January 1989).
1989	A House of Commons Subcommittee on International Human Rights is established.
1993	CIDA establishes a Human Rights and Governance Unit, which develops new policy on rights, democracy, and governance.
1994–95	There is a government and parliamentary review of Canadian foreign policy.

which trace some key steps in the evolution of Canadian, Dutch, and Norwegian human rights foreign policy frameowrks. Why, for example, were human rights not a salient feature during the Pearson era, Canada's "golden age" of internationalism? Other factors must be examined for any sufficient explanation.

Several events reinforced the domestic awareness of international human rights. At Helsinki in 1975, the NATO and Warsaw Pact states agreed that human rights were legitimate items for discussion at the Conference on Security and Cooperation in Europe. In 1976, both the International Covenant on Civil and Political Rights and the International Covenant on Economic, Social, and Cultural Rights came into force. In the mid-1970s, the U.S. Congress introduced legislation to condition aid on human rights performance. And in 1977, Jimmy Carter, in his inaugural presidential address, called human rights "the soul" of U.S. foreign policy. These events predate the principal Dutch and Canadian policy statements and took the same position as Norway's 1975–76 white paper on human rights and foreign policy. Although Carter's policies probably sparked the policy debates on human rights and development aid, Norway and the Netherlands had been active well before then, albeit largely in Europe. In the late 1960s, they had jointly denounced the Greek "colonels' regime" and had successfully pressed for the departure of Greece from the European Council. And in the early 1970s, they had publicly tried to isolate the Salazar regime in Portugal.

Finally, the personal interest of key individuals fostered a government constituency for human rights. This neglected variable was especially influential in the Netherlands. For example, former foreign minister Max van der Stoel was personally active on country-specific human rights statecraft. Similarly, the position of human rights coordinator was created by the single-mindedness of its first incumbent, Toigne van Dongen. Several Dutchmen have alternated between academe, pressure group activism, government, and international organizations, and this tradition lends credibility to Dutch statecraft in the field. The best example is Theo van Boven, a former director of the U.N. Human Rights Centre. Another is Jan Pronk, minister of development cooperation, a former church activist and chairman of the U.N. Conference on Trade and Development, who has an interest in human rights.[20] There are fewer examples in Norway and Canada, though Odd Saeter's commitment to human rights shaped Norway's principled policy towards Sri Lanka. It was Saeter's insistence that led to the 1984–85 white paper on human rights and development aid. In Canada, former external affairs minister Joe Clark has taken a personal interest in human rights, particularly in Eastern Europe, Palestine, and

South Africa, and in the genesis of the International Centre for Human Rights and Democratic Development.

Deeply rooted democratic principles, egalitarian traditions (particularly in the Netherlands and Norway), an active welfare state, and a vocation of internationalism are the foundations of Dutch, Canadian, and Norwegian human rights activism. Systemic influences and key individuals, although not decisive, have reinforced a disposition already evident in political culture and foreign policy traditions. Together, these determinants have helped make each state a leading advocate of international human rights.

INCOMPATIBLE OR ESSENTIAL? DEMOCRATIC PARTICIPATION IN FOREIGN POLICY MAKING

The tension between executive discretion and public participation in foreign policy springs from contending visions of international relations. The Wilsonian ideal posits openness as a road to peace, but realists see openness as inefficient, dangerous, and irrational.[21] According to this view, *raison d'état* is the bedrock of foreign policy. In a world preoccupied with security, there is little scope for the democratic participation of the domestic public in it. External forces are fundamental, and foreign policy is the preserve of the mandarins and political executive. The uncertainties of an anarchical international system, the limited policy autonomy of smaller powers, alliance commitments, and the imperative of having flexibility to respond to crises are compelling reasons for minimizing public input and retaining executive discretion.

This line of reasoning has a long pedigree. John Locke, the defender of civil society, nevertheless argued that "the power of war and peace, leagues and alliances and all transactions with all persons and communities without the Commonwealth [must] ... be left in great part to the Prudence of those who have this Power committed to them, to be managed by the best of their Skill, for the advantage of the Commonwealth."[22] While Locke was opposed normatively to participation, de Tocqueville was opposed empirically. He argued that democratic governments were less efficient in crafting foreign policy because they were "unable to regulate the details of an important undertaking, to persevere in a design, and to work out its execution in the presence of serious obstacles."[23] Walter Lippmann was more blunt: "Democratic officials ... have been compelled to make the big mistakes that public opinion has insisted upon."[24] And in the same vein, Rosenau once described the masses as "impulsive, unstable, unreasoning, capable of

suddenly shifting direction or of going in several contradictory directions at the same time. [Hence] instability and irrationality enter the
policy-making process."[25] If the circumstances of foreign policy
making militate against democratic participation, so also, we are led
to believe, does the low level of public comprehension[26] and interest.[27]
In sum, three principles explain why foreign policy should not be open
to democratic participation: the principle of supreme interest (*raison
d'état*), the principle of remoteness (public apathy), and the principle
of bargaining (systemic constraints).[28]

The language of human rights, on the other hand, is at odds with
the realist conception of foreign policy making. It is all about political
participation. Human rights conventions permit Western states to criticize or otherwise "interfere" in the domestic affairs of developing
countries. Canada, Norway, and the Netherlands have pledged to
strengthen democracies abroad. Yet this would be hollow rhetoric if
each state disallowed greater participation in the foreign policy process. How far "policy transparency" can or should extend in foreign
policy is not clear, however. Realists overlook the possibility that
rational policies may emerge from more open debate, but idealists are
convinced of it. There are three aspects to democratic foreign policy
making: (1) access to information; (2) structured opportunities for
participation; and (3) responsiveness – the extent to which the executive and foreign policy bureaucracy represent and/or implement popular interests.[29]

Although foreign policy remains an elite preserve in most Western
countries, diplomacy has changed profoundly since the 1960s. Global
interdependence has been accompanied by the emergence of "informed
publics" and skilled special interest groups.[30] The upsurge of post-
material issues in Western society has found its international expression
in the explosion of groups addressing global issues of poverty, the
environment, human rights, social justice, apartheid, peace, and the
rights of indigenous peoples and ethnic minorities.[31] This has brought
more pressure on the tradition of executive discretion.

While the general public may know little about the specifics of aid
or human rights policies, people do have opinions. And opinions
influence both policy and practice. A poll conducted for CIDA found
that two-thirds of the respondents would prefer Canada's aid to be
spent on governments that respect human rights.[32] Similarly, a North-
South Institute poll found that 68 per cent of the respondents believed
that Canada should protest strongly against violations, while only 29
per cent believed that other countries' human rights records were not
Canada's business.[33] There is no reason to assume a different public
disposition in Norway or the Netherlands.

Pressure groups and parliaments have pushed states to develop human rights policies. Because rights are subversive of the status quo, the state is less likely to promote the issue actively. In the mid-1980s, for example, an External Affairs green paper on Canada's international relations was replete with realist assumptions and trade and security agendas but was mostly silent on human rights.[34] Progress in pushing governments in Canada, the Netherlands, and Norway beyond a traditional U.N. focus is largely attributable to activists and parliamentarians.[35] The discussion below illustrates the public's ability to add new issues to the policy agenda and press for new institutions. Efforts to constrain executive discretion in the conduct of foreign policy have been less successful, however.

INSTITUTIONAL INNOVATION: COSMETIC OR SUBSTANTIVE PARTICIPATION?

Political science once emphasized how political behaviour is shaped by the institutional structure of rules, norms, traditions, and expectations. The behavioural revolution, with a more society-centred approach, eroded this perspective, reducing the state's importance. But there is a renewed interest in the role of institutions.[36] This "new institutionalism" challenges mainstream analyses, which make political outcomes a function of interests or power. It seeks to show that "processes internal to political institutions affect the flow of history."[37] Institutional innovations inside the bureaucracy or between the state and society are "intervening variables" potentially influencing the trade-offs between ethically driven and self-interested motives. This relationship is sketched in table 8.4, which shows how national interests, such as commerce, security, and world order, are filtered by state, society, and international institutions before emerging as human rights policy. These policies then become part of the stock of knowledge and tradition influencing the relative weight of different national interests, and the assertiveness with which human rights principles are promoted and defended.

Do new structures and institutions prompt an activist human rights policy? Or are they simply cosmetic – a way of defusing an impatient public and maintaining the status quo?[38] Bureaucratic attitudes are the key. The annual U.S. *Country Report* may have fostered an expertise on human rights in the State Department.[39] American diplomats have been called "able implementors of whatever policy high-ranking officials decide to pursue. Their premier characteristic appears to be their responsiveness, their willingness to adapt to changing policy orientations."[40] But the conventional wisdom is that diplomats "focus

Table 8.4
The Impact of Institutional Variables on Human Rights Policy

Interests	Institutions/practices	Output
Commerce	STATE Executive Bureaucracy	
Security	SOCIETY Legislatures Media Civic associations (NGOs,[1] academe, etc.)	HUMAN RIGHTS POLICY
World order (Human rights) (Development) (Environment)	INTERNATIONAL Multilateral organizations Legal norms and conventions	
	Knowledge and Tradition	

Source: Adapted from Egeland, *Impotent Superpower – Potent Small State,* 24.

[1]   Non-governmental organization.

on the demands of the [external] environment and avoid being dis-
tracted by other considerations."[41] The "free masonry of diplomacy"
encourages career diplomats to overlook, downplay, or make excuses
for the human rights failings of client states.[42] In this view, then,
bureaucratic inertia, not political activism, marks the area of human
rights issues.

DEMOCRATIC PARTICIPATION: THE DUTCH HUMAN RIGHTS ADVISORY COMMITTEE

Canada, the Netherlands, and Norway have all made institutional
innovations to enhance the place of human rights in foreign policy and
to maximize democratic participation. The Dutch have a consensus-
building political tradition. This consociational political culture has
affected foreign policy in two ways: by spawning strong interest
groups[43] and by moderating the tendency for policy to be made only
by political and bureaucratic elites. Advisory councils express Dutch
democratic participation. They are potential safeguards against
executuve fiat. For example, the Council on Peace and Security is an
independent body of experts empowered to advise the government on
request or on its own initiative (though the imperative of secrecy
normally reduces public information on, and participation in, defence

policy). Similarly, the National Advisory Council on Development Cooperation informs and advises the minister for Development Cooperation on aid and other Third World issues.

Expert bodies may complement the parliament as a channel for the articulation of domestic opinion. In several ways, they may be more effective. Parliamentary expertise, even in a well-functioning committee system, is constrained by four factors: (1) time pressures, since MPs must attend to disparate policy issues and to caucus and constituency affairs; (2) rapid electoral turnover, with the result that MPs may not have time to become experts; (3) limited research capability, particularly in small parliaments such as those of the Netherlands and Norway; and (4) the danger of partisan conflicts leading to policy paralysis. By contrast, an advisory committee is composed of academics and activists with proven expertise. Moreover, because a committee also includes government officials, it may be useful in mediating between civil society and the state.

In April 1983 the Netherlands established the Human Rights and Foreign Policy Advisory Committee.[44] This committee is not a "partner" in some tripartite foreign policy structure; quite the contrary. Its formal role, like that of other advisory committees, is not to advocate or to make decisions but to advise the minister of foreign affairs "on issues of human rights ... upon request *or on its own initiative.*"[45] At the committee's inauguration, Foreign Minister Hans van den Broek recognized the potential for conflict between the committee and the government when he observed:

The Committee is intended to give all sections of society that deal with human rights direct access to influence policy-making. Seen from the point of view of the Government, this is a dangerous operation. After all, no Government minister will be keen to facilitate direct criticism of its policies, especially on a subject like this. At the same time, the Committee should be seen as a necessary step in making our democratic system more perfect and in promoting the openness of our governmental structure. That presupposes *faith*. *Faith* on the part of the Minister that the Committee will contribute in a positive and constructive way to the thinking of policy-makers. *Faith* on the part of the Committee that something is done with the recommendations.[46]

The minister recognized that he might have sponsored a Trojan horse, and the committee's subsequent history has confirmed that in subject choice and, occasionally, in advice content the foreign ministry and the committee "have not always seen eye to eye."[47] When the ministry has invited reports on procedural or technical issues (such as enhancing the bureaucratic framework for human rights, for freedom of information, for women, for refugees, and for mobility rights), the ministry and the committee have largely agreed, but unsolicited reports have led to friction. A good example was the committee's uninvited study of human rights in Suriname.

The committee's terms of reference anticipate state opposition to the discussion of country situations. They confine recommendations "on a particular human rights situation ... [to] a general approach to the subject."[48] As expected, the minister announced that he "did not need" any advice on Suriname. But as a former chairman of the committee remarked, "when [the minister] said he did not need advice ... he really meant that he did not *want* such an advice."[49] The committee was unanimous that Suriname specifically raised broader issues about the link between human rights and development aid that needed investigation. Similarly, when Amnesty International asked the committee to examine how foreign ministry reports were used in judging asylum applications, the minister was opposed, partly because the admission of refugees is seen as a domestic matter and thus outside the committee's jurisdiction, and partly because the minister was concerned that the committee might evolve from an advisory to a supervisory body.[50]

In sum, the Human Rights and Foreign Policy Advisory Committee embodies all three aspects of democratic foreign policy making. It enhances participation and monitors state policy. It informs government, Parliament, and the public. It is an index of the state's democratic credentials because, as Minister van den Broek observed, "no government will be keen to facilitate criticism of its policies," yet the committee can and does do just that. While its relations with the government have hardly been conflict-free, the committee remains autonomous and has not faced the depth of state opposition directed towards the Peace and Security Council.[51] The human rights committee may do little to alter government policy towards specific countries, but by examining broad policy issues such as the linkage of human rights and development aid or the relationship between human rights and trade policy, it may play a constructive role in the gradual evolution of Dutch policy on international human rights.[52]

ACCOUNTABILITY AND PARTICIPATION IN CANADA'S HUMAN RIGHTS POLICY FRAMEWORK

Permanent advisory bodies are not part of Canada's foreign policy tradition. Parliamentary committees are the traditional mechanism for public scrutiny of foreign policy. However, after lobbying from NGOs, parliamentary committees have proposed the creation of advisory bodies for development aid and human rights, which suggests that MPs are aware of Parliament's limited resources to study such complex issues effectively. For example, the Winegard Committee reviewing Canada's aid program called for an ODA advisory council similar to the Dutch body.[53] The government rejected the proposal because "it is not considered essential to ensure consultation with Canadians ... The primary responsibility for advising the government rests with Parliament." Instead, the government agreed only to a cosmetic "dialogue" with the private sector on a designated "development day."[54]

In 1986 the Hockin-Simard Report urged that "the government immediately investigate the most effective means of creating a Human Rights Advisory Commission."[55] In its response to this report, the government did not rule out the possibility of creating such a commission, but it clearly preferred a strengthened committee system to a body of experts: "[The government] will consider the recommendation on a Human Rights Advisory Commission when there is greater clarity concerning the interests and activities of the Standing Committee [on Human Rights] and their means of liaison with the Canadian groups concerned."[56]

Given the Winegard Committee's focus on aid and its call for a development advisory council, its report did not recommend a similar body in the human rights field. The idea of a human rights advisory commission was eventually overtaken by the creation of a parliamentary subcommittee on international human rights. The Task Force on the Churches and Corporate Responsibility first proposed the idea that Parliament should annually and publicly review the human rights record of Canada's main aid and trade partners. The recommendation came in its 1982 brief to the parliamentary subcommittee on Latin America and the Caribbean, which was also presented to the Standing Committee on Finance, Trade, and Economic Affairs and to the Special Committee on the Reform of the House of Commons.[57] The task force based its recommendations on the assumption that (1) a regular review of human rights issues in Canadian foreign policy is desirable; (2) Parliament and the public ought to have an opportunity to participate in such a review; and (3) Parliament should have access to government information for an effective review.[58]

The task force's idea was taken up obliquely by the Hockin-Simard Report on Canada's international relations.[59] In the context of a new standing committee on human rights, Hockin-Simard recommended that the committee "examine cases of gross and systematic violations of human rights, especially where they involve countries where Canada has large [ODA] programs or significant trade relations." The suggestion falls short of an annual review, but the report recognized that the committee's recommendations "could form an important element in cabinet considerations of eligibility for [ODA] if the Committee requested a comprehensive response to their reports from the government."[60] The government's reply was evasive. It agreed to "take into account" the committee's human rights reports[61] but gave no indication whether it welcomed or objected to an annual review, or whether Parliament would have access to confidential information.

The Winegard Committee examining Canada's aid program did call for an annual human rights report.[62] However, in contrast to the approach of Hockin-Simard, the Winegard Committee felt that an annual ODA-human rights report should be produced jointly by CIDA and External Affairs and then reviewed publicly by Parliament. The state's true position on public review finally emerged: "The Government does not believe that annual reports to Parliament, in which concrete cases ... are evaluated and judgments drawn, would serve the foreign policy interests of Canada. The experience of other countries, as well as Canada's experience in limited cases, indicate that such reporting procedures become in themselves an object of criticism and contention which compromise our ability for effective action by way of normal diplomatic channels."[63] Although the government agreed to "provide information," it counselled that "given the subject matter, the committees may wish to hold such meetings *in camera*."[64] Unable to dictate how the committees called witnesses, the inference was clear: public cross-examination of state officials would yield little cooperation and less insight.

Parliament established a subcommittee on international human rights in September 1989. This improves on the previous division of labour between the Standing Committee on External Affairs and the Standing Committee on Human Rights. The former could devote little time to human rights, given the breadth of its mandate, while the latter concentrated largely on domestic human rights. The subcommittee may (or may not) emerge as the fulcrum of public input on Canada's human rights policy. It was briefly suspended with the change of government in 1993 but was reinstated after the Liberal government's 1995 foreign policy review. The subcommittee could perform many of the tasks of an advisory council, sponsoring thematic studies or investigating Canada's relations with specific countries. Access to information will be crucial. One subcommittee member has complained of being "locked out" from government knowledge.[65] And in a 1990 subcommittee report, members were "troubled by the degree that the process of applying human rights considerations in policy is carried on behind closed doors, insulated from review either by Parliament or the public."[66]

Although the Liberal government of Prime Minister Jean Chrétien has made much of the need to open up and "democratize" the foreign policy process and has institutionalized an annual National Forum on International Relations, little of this commitment to particpation has filtered into the human rights or development aid arena. As I will show in chapter 10, the Liberals unlinked aid and trade with scarcely a murmur of public debate or consultation. In view of the government's reluctance to share information, the subcommittee was looking (during the Mulroney era) for a closer partnership with Canada's quasi-independent International Centre for Human Rights and Democratic Development. However, as will be discussed in chapter 9, the centre's willingness to criticize policy or produce an independent annual human rights review of Canada's aid partners is by no means clear.

One other Canadian innovation is worth noting. In response to persistent complaints by NGOs, External Affairs holds an annual two-day "consultation" with human rights groups before the U.N. Commission on Human Rights meets. To the government's credit, this consultation is unique among Western countries attending the commission. The consultation allows for democratic participation, though access is not synonymous with influence. Which "side" gains more from the forum is a moot point.[67] On the one hand, it does grant activists an opportunity to press for country-specific resolutions and to confront official readings of the human rights record in less-developed countries. Moreover, the consultation has prompted activists to organize. They have formed the Human Rights Network to share information, and they now meet prior to the consultation to prepare strategy. But, on the other hand, some activists complain of manipulation; Canada's delegation uses NGOs to bolster its resolution diplomacy while ignoring the lobby groups when they disagree with official positions, most commonly on Central America.

NORWAY'S HUMAN RIGHTS YEARBOOK

Norway's human rights framework is less developed than that of either the Netherlands or Canada. Nor is it immune from bureaucratic resistance. Initially, MPs relied on Question Time to raise human rights issues, for they had no specialized parliamentary committee to focus their concerns until a Dutch-style advisory Human Rights Committee was established in 1989; and it took ten years of administrative foot dragging before the Ministry of Development Cooperation agreed to provide funds for the creation of a Norwegian Institute for Human Rights.[68]

But the government has taken a participatory approach to monitoring by its commitment "to ensure that the Storting and the administration and [NGOs] have *as good background information as possible* when evaluating human rights" among the main aid-partner countries.[69] The Norwegian Agency for Development Cooperation (NORAD) and Ministry of Development Cooperation (MDC) have funded an annual yearbook on human rights in developing countries, which assesses the human rights performance of the main-partner countries. This is a courageous step because, as the Sri Lanka's case demonstrated, developing countries may not believe that the yearbook gives an independent rather than official evaluation. Norway's willingness to live with the possibly adverse repercussions of the yearbook is a testament to the government's commitment to ensure public input in the policy arena. By contrast, the Dutch government distanced itself from the Netherlands Institute of Human Rights' participation in the yearbook because Dutch Foreign Minister van den Broek felt that recipients would link negative evaluations in the yearbook to official Dutch perceptions. The minister thus declined to give assistance, through the aid budget, to the institute's collaboration.[70]

BUREAUCRATIC INNOVATIONS: SMOKE AND MIRRORS

One way to enhance the salience of human rights is to ensure that diplomats and aid officials understand the relevant international law and U.N. machinery and know how to gather and evaluate human rights data. Formal training is a useful way of acquiring these skills and is one index of a state's commitment to integrate human rights in foreign policy. The Netherlands was a pioneer in the field and still has the most extensive training program. Canada, in 1986 and 1987, added human rights to the training of new diplomats and aid officials going on a posting. Norway appears to pay only cursory attention to human rights training (a few hours in a general foreign-service training program). Significantly, participation is obligatory for Dutch officials but not for all Canadian bureaucrats.[71]

The Dutch program began after the 1979 memorandum *Human Rights and Foreign Policy*, though it was not a specific recommendation of the memorandum. The program was expanded after 1984, when the government agreed with the Human Rights and Foreign Policy Advisory Committee that the existing training was "not commensurate with the importance attached to ... human rights in Dutch foreign policy."[72] Canada's program grew out of a parliamentary recommendation that External Affairs "follow the example of the

Netherlands Ministry for Foreign Affairs in establishing in-service training and refresher courses *for all its officers.*"[73] The government accepted the joint committee's broad recommendation but not the specific recommendation that all officers be trained. Only officers being posted abroad and those administering export controls policy are required to attend the course.[74] Training can help build institutional knowledge and embed a sensitivity to human rights in diplomatic and aid personnel. It is impossible to gauge with any precision whether the Dutch and Canadian programs are breaking down bureaucratic inertia.[75] But training remains, in principle, a useful way to strengthen the constituency for human rights among state officials.

Dutch, Canadian, and Norwegian statecraft will be only as good as the human rights data that the policy makers possess. The smaller Western states do not have the resources to gather data on all rights, nor can they treat all rights equally without inviting policy paralysis. Accordingly, the way data are collected and the types of right that are given priority may suggest the kinds of human rights situations that our three states will act on. Human rights coordinators in all three states underline the importance of civil and political rights. These rights underpin their resolution diplomacy at the U.N. High Commission on Human Rights. So far, there has been little effort to gather data on social and economic rights. For example, the Norwegian policy makers in the foreign ministry seem not to have taken much notice of the yearbook or its emphasis on social and economic rights.[76] They seem to have emphasized – besides freedom from extrajudicial killing, arbitrary arrest, and torture – some civil liberties such as freedom of expression, assembly, and association. This focus on civil and political rights may have the adverse effect of encouraging policy makers to ignore the systemic neglect of human rights such as the absence of land reform, or the social and economic impact of externally imposed austerity programs on the poorest of the poor.

Canada, the Netherlands, and Norway are all now enhancing their human rights monitoring systems. The Netherlands benefits from a new European Union monitoring system, in addition to its own in-house reporting system. Norway is adapting the U.S. *Country Report* system, which emphasizes civil and political rights.[77] In Canada, the monitoring manual of the Department of Foreign Affairs calls on the reporting officer to look for gross, persistent, and systematic human rights abuses but also to consider evidence of improvement. For the first time, Canada will report on some economic rights, particularly nutritional status. Finally, Canadian officials must now consider trends in the level of abuse and must assess state responsibility for the violations, covering acts of omission as well as commission.[78] Similarly,

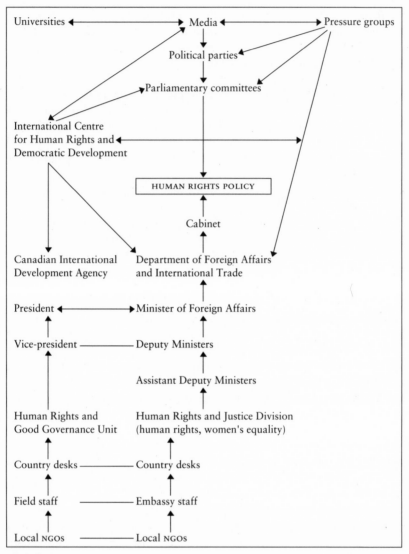

Figure 8.1
Canadian Human Rights Structures

CIDA has produced an extensive list of human rights indicators to inform its long-term programming. They include minority and women's rights, land rights, and the rights of indigenous peoples.[79]

All three states have similar systems for collecting and transmitting human rights data, as figures 8.1, 8.2, and 8.3 show. Information flows from an embassy, which may have drawn on local sources or aid personnel, to a geographic desk at headquarters. In a country-specific

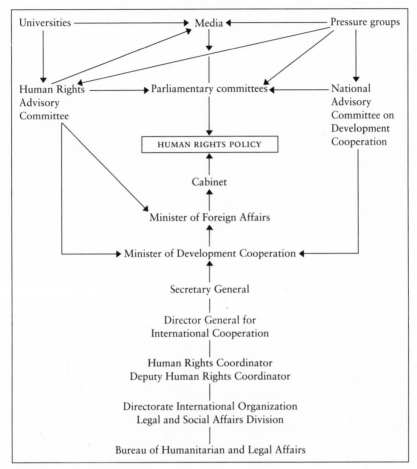

Figure 8.2
Dutch Human Rights Structures

human rights problem, the geographic desk will be responsible for drawing the human rights picture, but it may also liaise with the human rights unit or division. Each foreign ministry has a human rights coordinator. Norway's coordinator has ambassador rank, attesting to the importance of the role. In the Netherlands, the coordinator is the gatekeeper who receives all the pertinent information coming from the geographic desks. It is her task to collate this data for annual human rights reviews or for specific policy discussions by the intradepartmental human rights coordinating group, a formal structure that meets monthly and includes the director general for development cooperation, the director general of the political wing of the foreign ministry and, when necessary, the foreign minister and development aid minister. In

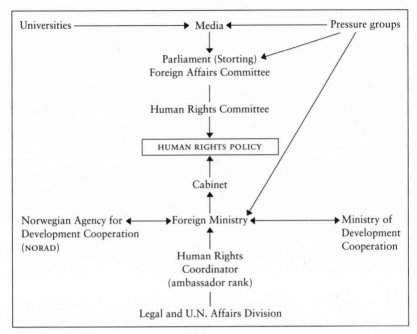

Figure 8.3
Norwegian Human Rights Structures

the Netherlands, summaries of the foreign ministry's perception of human rights in developing countries, called *memorie van toelichten*, had formerly been published with the budget debate, but they were discontinued in the mid-1980s, to the chagrin of human rights groups. They are now found in the foreign ministry's yearbook. The only Canadian government summaries are in a handbook accompanying the annual External Affairs-NGO consultations prior to the meeting of the U.N. Commission on Human Rights. They are cursory treatments of often complex situations, and only those countries likely to be the focus of Western Group attention under item 12 are discussed.

Despite efforts to improve monitoring and to allow some public scrutiny of government policy, there remain obstacles, in all three states, to a stronger bureaucratic constituency for human rights.[80] First, in contrast to the U.S. experience, in each state the human rights units are staffed by career bureaucrats, who may avoid pushing controversial positions on country-specific policies for fear of losing promotion oppportunities. Second, the human rights bureaus appear to carry most weight on multilateral human rights statecraft and to have less clout on bilateral statecraft, where the geographic desks take the lead. Third, there are no permanent structures for interdepartmental consultation on human rights such as the Christopher Committee in the United

States during the Carter administration. The Dutch advisory committee requested a formal relationship between departments other than the foreign ministry, but Foreign Minister van den Broek declined this on the grounds that it would "complicate" the committee's work.[81] An unacknowledged concern is that the formal input of departments, such as Economic Affairs and the Ministry of Justice, would loosen the Ministry of Foreign Affairs' grip on the issue area. Finally, the integration of human rights in the three aid bureaucracies remains precarious. For several years, CIDA's much-lauded "human rights unit" – a recommendation of the Winegard Report – consisted of a single individual. In 1992, CIDA established a four-person "Good Governance and Human Rights" unit to consult all stakeholders and to develop a new agency blueprint on rights, democracy, and good governance. While this should confirm the value of new institutions, it is not clear that there will be any supervision of the implementation by the policy division to ensure coherence across the geographic divisions.[82]

Moreover, the organizational complexities of implementing aid put a premium on continuity, which acts as an in-built brake on attempts to condition aid on human rights grounds. Aid agencies may thus be at odds with their foreign ministries, as in the case of Canadian and Norwegian policy towards Sri Lanka. This combination of forces may perpetuate bureaucratic conservatism rather than human rights activism. Peter Baehr, for example, underlined the differences in the way the Netherlands government and Amnesty International assessed the human rights performance of countries that were recipients of Dutch aid.[83] Baehr claimed that because officials wished to preserve the continuity of aid, "either the human rights criterion is less strictly applied, or the facts are presented in a ... more optimistic fashion" by the government.[84] A similar conclusion emerges from Canadian government and NGO assessments of human rights in El Salvador and Guatemala in the late 1980s. While they agreed on egregious violations, the government was more optimistic than the Inter-Church Committee on Human Rights in Latin America about the overall human rights record and prognosis in these two countries.

CONCLUSION

Canada, the Netherlands, and Norway now have a number of institutions and practices to enhance democratic participation and foster a bureaucratic human rights constituency. Participatory structures include advisory committees, structured consultations, and institutes and centres. Bureaucratic innovations include improved monitoring, coordination, and training. The institutional framework is perhaps weakest in Norway.[85] Egeland reports a "consistent failure to allocate resources for a build up of [bureaucratic] expertise, which limits policy implementation."[86]

Institutional arrangements may be seen as policies, but will they "affect the flow of history"? It is doubtful whether new structures, ipso facto, will institutionalize a bureaucratic constituency for human rights or will guarantee activism. The foreign ministry units are active on multilateral questions but appear to lack influence on bilateral policy. And there are no permanent structures for interdepartmental coordination. However, there may be grounds for more optimism about the participatory structures. That each state has agreed to establish, with government funds, independent voices capable of criticizing government is at least *prima facie* evidence that governments are responsive to the pressures for democratic participation.[87] On the other hand, while parliaments and pressure groups have set policy agendas and persuaded governments to create new institutions, they have substantially failed to constrain executive discretion in policy implementation. Calls for advisory committees (Canada), annual human rights reviews, restrictive policy formulas, and clearer priorities on the range of which rights to promote and defend have been either refused or evaded.

The governments of all three states are reticent because annual reviews and rigid policy formulas impair the state's flexibility, undermine its autonomy, and potentially damage carefully nurtured relations with countries of commercial or strategic interest. None of the institutional innovations negate the continuing primacy of *raison d'état*, particularly in policy implementation. In each state, the limits of democratic participation have been reached or soon will be. Calls for greater "policy transparency" will not be answered because statesmen believe that diplomacy requires secrecy. As the chairman of Canada's Winegard Committee observed, the committee "cannot be effective if we remain uninformed by government ... [but] there is no question that if you want [bureaucrats] to be brutally honest, you cannot have the media [present]."[88]

The achievements of parliaments and the public should not be underestimated, however. While new structures will not necessarily ensure activism or assertive policies, the new institutions are not merely cosmetic. There will always be an uneasy relationship between state and society in the human rights field. Activists are almost by definition "troublemakers" and "idealists."[89] Politicians must always consider interests beyond morality. But this essential and creative tension is needed to build traditions and expectations that will be difficult for governments to ignore.

9 Between Principle and Practice: Ends and Means of Human Rights Statecraft

Our central finding and source of apprehension is that there [is] a serious *lack of coherence and consistency* between many of Canada's aid, trade and financial assistance relationships with other countries, on the one hand, and our human rights commitments on the other. Canada ... seems often to be ... piously condemning human rights abuses "on Sundays" and then carrying on business as usual ... with human rights abusing countries, during the rest of the week.

Human Rights Considerations, 1990[1]

Is a consistent human rights policy feasible? It is what activists and parliamentarians want. But governments are reticent, saying that conventional diplomacy needs more flexibility than such policies would allow. This chapter takes up the issue of consistency, particularly as it affects the linkage of human rights and development aid. Canada, the Netherlands, and Norway hold much the same position on the purpose of human rights statecraft, but the practical integration of human rights and development aid is still unfinished.

The question of policy coherence is behind the seemingly endemic conflict between governments and an informed public in the human rights field. Human rights activists often argue that moral imperatives should trump other concerns in determining responses to severe abuses. According to this view, Western governments should be consistent across the range of their relations with repressive regimes. The moral force of U.N. condemnation may be lost if states continue to trade with and aid egregious human rights violators. Idealists argue that inconsistency compromises credibility and dilutes the effectiveness of Western statecraft.

Parliaments generally have endorsed this view. For example, a committee reviewing Canada's aid program was "convinced" that "a consistent, considered approach to the human rights conditions of development assistance can be in Canada's long-term foreign policy interests" and that these human rights criteria should "be applied in a universal, consistent and transparent manner."[2] Governments, by contrast, are less sanguine about the prospect of consistency. The Netherlands government, in a reply to calls for policy coherence from the Dutch Human Rights and Foreign Policy Advisory Committee, observed that "although consistency should be the aim in every policy ... responses to human rights should always be geared to the requirements and possibilities of the situation in hand ... Such an approach should be judged, not by the moral force of the arguments used, nor by the system of criteria applied, but on its effective contribution to a lasting improvement in a particular human rights situation."[3] A Norwegian white paper sounded a similar note of caution: "Experience has shown that it is difficult to pursue a [human rights] policy which is both consistent and to the purpose, and which at the same time is attuned to Norway's general foreign policy interests."[4]

In the context of development aid, the official endeavour to be consistent has spurred attempts in Canada (by Parliament) and in the Netherlands (by activists) to limit executive discretion with guidelines prompting action according to the human rights performance of aid recipients. The Winegard Report on Canada's aid program recommended a "grid," or index, in which developing nations would be ranked on the basis of whether their human rights record was judged to be improving, satisfactory, worsening, or egregious. These rankings could then be used to assess aid eligibility, channels, and volume.[5] The government, however, was not persuaded of the utility of the grid:

The Government believes that the establishment of a grid, and especially the classification of countries according to such a grid, would not serve the overall interests of Canadian development assistance or of Canadian foreign policy. The judgments implicit in the use of such a grid are too subjective. The grid would not adequately take into account the vast number of situations where violations of human rights are worrisome but where they are at the same time unequal ... The impact of such a grid would be essentially punitive and judgmental rather than positive and developmental. The Government prefers to support positive programs which assist the poorest and those most victimized by violations of fundamental rights.[6]

This exchange underlines the central rift between governments and activists in all Western countries. It is not simply that a grid or index is inherently subjective, for policy makers cannot avoid making judgments. The key issues are (1) that states must balance moral interests with equally valid and often contradictory commercial or political interests; (2) that the criterion of effectiveness is paramount; and (3) that activists are sometimes driven by a retributive moral system (the "punishment" must fit the crime) which the policy makers instinctively reject. Hence, as the Dutch government has pointed out, "it is not feasible to indicate in general formulas how the relationship between human rights and other policy considerations should take shape in specific cases. The promotion of human rights is one of the important aims of foreign policy, but it cannot be its predominating aim. The Government makes every effort to contribute to the promotion of human rights without doing unacceptable damage to other values and interests which it must promote."[7] Accordingly, when the Dutch Human Rights and Foreign Policy Advisory Committee called for a policy index, the government remained opposed: "We feel that the use of objective criteria as a basis for dictating policy ... is untenable ... [and we] do not regard as feasible a cut-and-dried formula whereby violations of human rights automatically invite a response appropriate to their gravity."[8]

If governments are not convinced that a consistent, formula-driven policy is either plausible or desirable, what are their views on the utility of the assorted policy levers outlined in the "human rights hierarchy"? Chapter 2 argued that, other things being equal, Western states prefer unassertive instruments to more coercive or intrusive sanctions, because the latter may cause "unacceptable damage" to other national interests. The case studies tested this claim and largely substantiated it. This chapter shows how official statements predispose statecraft towards caution and minimal assertiveness.

HUMAN RIGHTS AND TRADE: A CASE OF DIPLOMATIC IMMUNITY

Should Western governments minimize trade with repressive regimes? Few states are disposed to do so. As well as it being a reflex not to incur immediate commercial costs for uncertain moral gains, policy makers say that unilateral action has no impact, that trade sanctions should be undertaken only through the auspices of the United Nations or the European Community,[9] and that sanctions rarely alter behaviour. Moralists, by contrast, favour trade sanctions as an effective way of bolstering domestic opposition and punishing or coercing recalcitrant regimes. They are dismayed when countries give "confused signals" – as when Canada, for example, suspended aid to El Salvador and Guatemala while extending export credits and supporting IFI loans to both repressive regimes.[10] In fact, Canadian, Dutch, and Norwegian official export-credit institutions have almost no links to human rights diplomacy. A Canadian parliamentary subcommittee lamented that "current ... policy and practice allow our governments to approve loans to, and encourage trade with, states whose human rights records we condemn. This does not serve the cause of human rights or Canada's overall interests."[11] Empirically, however, it is not clear whether trade with repressive regimes reinforces abuses. An axiom of economic liberalism is that trade fosters interdependence, opens societies, and transmits Western values, including human rights and democracy.[12] That is why Canada decided not to disrupt significantly its trade links with China after the Tiananmen Square killings.

When should trade sanctions be used, then? The Dutch are relatively specific: "Grave and systematic violations may under certain conditions constitute grounds for [economic] restrictions: [when] other methods of improving the human rights situation have proved clearly inadequate, [when] economic restrictions can be genuinely expected to lead to improvements, [or] when ... maintaining these relations would contribute towards a continuation or increase of the human rights violations. Finally, the measures must not disproportionately damage Netherlands interests."[13] On the other hand, the government "cannot subscribe to the view that it is desirable to withhold all Government support from export promotion measures and export transactions [with] countries which infringe generally accepted human rights. The Government's responsibility for the ... economy, including the balance of payments and employment, does not permit it as a general rule to refrain from export-promoting actions ... to uphold ... human rights."[14]

On the basis of these guidelines, economic levers are virtually ruled out in Dutch human rights statecraft. Norway, at least, concedes that sanctions might have an important demonstration effect and could in some circumstances be pursued unilaterally: "Boycott[s] require a high degree of international coordination if they are to be effective. Unilateral boycott[s] which are not authorized by U.N. decisions may also be contrary to international rules and provisions ... Although the direct economic effect of unilateral boycott[s] will be limited, in some cases such actions may have a certain political effect as an expression of solidarity with the oppressed."[15] But in juxtaposition to this concession is the pragmatic question of "whether it is justifiable to impose on the

Norwegian labour market and ... economy the ensuing burdens and losses."[16] Although Canada is also reticent about disrupting trade for human rights criteria, it has kept its options open by voting against a 1979 resolution of the U.N. Commission on Human Rights that was critical of adding human rights criteria to trade policies.[17]

The one clear instance of each state using trade as an instrument of human rights statecraft is that concerning apartheid in South Africa. In the mid-1970s, Norway stopped providing export guarantees for trade with South Africa. It also supported a proposed international oil embargo, and in 1987, in the absence of consensus, it imposed a unilateral ban on the sale of Norwegian oil to South Africa.[18] Similarly, the Dutch helped persuade the European Community to use sanctions against South Africa. A 1986 EC decision banned imports of iron, steel, and gold coins from, and exports of oil to, South Africa. Canada, while acknowledging "sanctions as the only really meaningful and potentially effective measure against repressive regimes,"[19] backed away from coercive trade brinkmanship. The Mulroney government's threat to impose "total sanctions" in 1985 and to "end our relations [with South Africa] absolutely" was subsequently found to be empty rhetoric.[20]

Our three internationalists have been less disposed to disrupt trade with other "gross and persistent" rights-violating regimes. Canada, for example, suspended a tiny aid program in Chile after the Pinochet coup of 1973, but it actually increased Export Development Corporation export credits and loan insurance.[21] Similarly, in its desperate effort to sell the CANDU reactor, the Canadian government seemed ready to ignore human rights abuses among potential buyers in Argentina, South Korea, and Romania. With Romania, media reports allege that Canadian nuclear energy officials knew that the Ceausescu regime was using forced labour to build the nuclear plant.[22] Finally, Canada suspended its minimal aid program to Myanmar in 1989 for human rights considerations but allowed Petro-Canada, a crown corporation, to develop projects and work directly with the military authorities who were illegally running the country.

In May 1995, Foreign Affairs Minister André Ouellet matter-of-factly unlinked human rights and trade. It happened at a Vancouver meeting of the Association of Southeast Asian Nations (ASEAN). Ouellet told his ASEAN counterparts that Canada intended to launch a series of commercial initiatives with certain countries "without regard to their records on the issue of their respect for human rights."[23] In the government's view, trade was the best way in which to promote human rights and democratic development. Ouellet subsequently informed the House of Commons that while Canada was willing to be part of a U.N.-sponsored embargo against rights-violating countries, trying "to be a Boy Scout on your own, when indeed, nobody else is following [trade sanctions] is absolutely counterproductive."[24] The government has made up its mind that commerce must trump conscience in any contest between trade and human rights: "Il faut absolument que nous résolvions la contradiction permanente entre nos engagements en faveur des droits de la personne et les objectifs de la politique commerciale canadienne."[25] Whereas under Prime Minister Mulroney, sanctions were a prominent part of Canada's human rights diplomacy towards apartheid South Africa, they have been all but dropped from the human rights instruments deployed under Prime Minister Chrétien.

The implications of this retreat from human rights conditionality are serious. The new policy gave Canada *carte blanche* to try to sell fighter jets to Turkey just as that government launched an incursion against Turkish and Iraqi Kurds. This was not what most pundits understood by the concept of a peace dividend. The retreat from conditionality has also put Canada's policy towards Myanmar in question. Canada appears to have effectively abandoned any former concept of "benchmark diplomacy" in favour of the less demanding "constructive engagement" policy of ASEAN. Foreign Affairs Minister André Ouellet has said that Canada would be guided by the countries closer to Myanmar. Canada, meanwhile, will act as a mouthpiece for the ASEAN bloc in meetings of the Group of Seven. Raymond Chan, the former human rights activist who is secretary of state for Asia-Pacific, has hinted that Canada may abandon its policy of not supporting Canadian companies seeking to trade in Myanmar: "If Japan and the United States go into Burma, we'll have to go too."[26]

In the Netherlands, responses to the Pinochet coup and the ensuing repression in Chile were initially more coherent than the Canadian reaction. The Dutch suspended bilateral aid, protested IFI loans to Chile, and restricted the reinsurance of export credits. However, the restrictions on export credits were relaxed after 1983 despite pressure from the Dutch parliament. Similarly, in the early 1980s, the Dutch government granted export-credit insurance to Boskalis Westminster to build a gas pipeline in Argentina valued at 4.1 billion guilders, despite concerns that this ostensibly endorsed a rights-repressive junta which the Dutch had vilified in U.N. forums.[27] Similarly, economic interests prevailed over human rights concerns in the sale of two Dutch warships (corvettes) to Indonesia. A Dutch centre-left government had reduced bilateral aid to Indonesia on human rights criteria between 1974 and 1977. The government was principally concerned about the continued detention of political prisoners from the 1965 suppression of communists and about the 1975 invasion of East Timor, but this did not stop it from granting an arms export licence to sell corvettes to Indonesia in 1975. The government subsequently promised to reconsider the licence in an effort to appease Development Cooperation Minister Jan Pronk, who had opposed the sale. But in the end the sale went through, despite reports of mass killings of Timorese by Indonesian security forces and despite the risk that the corvettes would be used in "continuing acts of war around East Timor" in contravention of the criteria used for granting arms export licences.[28]

Most of the debate has centred on using trade as a punitive lever. There has been little discussion of the use of trade as a positive lever to promote human rights by enhancing economic growth in developing nations by, for example, removing import tariffs and offering preferential terms of trade.[29] This would impose unacceptable costs on the domestic economy. The issue of trade and human rights will be taken up in more detail in the final chapter.

THE INTERNATIONAL FINANCIAL INSTITUTIONS

Much of the debate on human rights and development aid has focused on bilateral official development assistance (ODA). But the Netherlands, Canada, and Norway are also generous contributors to multilateral aid agencies, principally to international financial institutions (IFIS) such as the World Bank Group and to specialized U.N. agencies such as the U.N. Development Programme and UNICEF. Less attention has been given to whether human rights criteria should also underpin multilateral ODA.[30] This is surprising, given the centrality of the IFIS in the development of Third World economies.[31]

As with bilateral ODA, there are two issues involved in adding human rights considerations to IFI activity. One is whether or not to lend to repressive regimes. The other is the potentially adverse social effects of IFI adjustment packages. Most public and parliamentary interest has fixed on withholding loans to repressive governments. For example, a Canadian parliamentary committee recommended that Canada "use its voice and its vote at [IFI] meetings to protest systematic, gross and continuous violations of human rights."[32] Similarly, the Winegard Report recommended that "Canada work for changes to allow human rights concerns to be put openly on the agendas of [IFIS] and, in addition, examine very critically multilateral loans to countries deemed 'human rights negative' or 'human rights watch.'"[33]

The governments of all three countries have largely rejected such proposals, precedents notwithstanding. Each donor has pointed to the dangers of politicization and to IFI articles of agreement that require loan and project decisions to be based on economic criteria. Norway, for example, has been cautious and noncommittal in its approach to rights conditionality in the IFIS, undertaking vaguely that it would "more often propose that multilateral aid should promote the full range of internationally accepted human rights."[34] The Dutch, too, have had doubts about taking a punitive approach to human rights conditionality in IFIS.[35] But this position contradicts their actions elsewhere, which do in fact link human rights conditionality to multilateral aid. Against doubts from other EC donors and hostility from Third World states, the Dutch succeeded in adding a human rights component in the European Community's contractual aid obligations with Asian, Caribbean, and Pacific states under the Lomé Convention. The diluted provision added to the convention ensured that EC contractual obligations would end "at the point where the providing of aid would lead to complicity in grave violations of human rights."[36]

But although the IFI's articles of agreement officially prohibit political considerations in loan agreements, they are in fact already politicized. Moreover, human rights have influenced each state's voting on IFI loans. From the late 1970s, the Dutch and Nordic governments opposed World Bank loans to Chile.[37] In 1987, Canada briefly joined other donors when it abstained on World Bank and Inter-American Development Bank loans to Chile on human rights criteria. However, Joe Clark, then external affairs minister, described the Chile abstentions as "unique occasions" and "exceptional actions," and he remained unconvinced "of the effectiveness of such measures on a regular basis." Accordingly, he said, "Our regular practice will continue to be to consider loans on their developmental, economic and technical grounds."[38]

While our internationalists have officially resisted politicizing IFI lending, all three governments recognize that "adjustment packages" may carry negative social costs, and they are willing to "use their voice" to "apply stringent criteria ... to ensure that [IFI] aid particularly benefits the poorest sectors."[39] Canada now faces a test of its commitment to cushion the social and economic fallout from IFI adjustment packages. CIDA is leading an International Monetary Fund (IMF) "support group" to help Guyana manage its adjustment package in return for up to US$2 billion in credit. Meanwhile, a Canadian parliamentary committee remains sceptical: "The [IMF] model of debtor adjustment ... is not working. Canada cannot continue to support in the 1990s policies in the name of adjustment with the disastrous effects on the welfare of the poor, of women, children and other vulnerable groups, that have been observed with such distressing repetition in the 1980s. [We] are disturbed by a discredited colonial model to deal with delinquent countries ... and prescribe the form of political system."[40] In view of these adverse effects, the parliamentary committee recommended that "actions to reduce [Third World] debt neither be done across-the-board nor necessarily linked to [adjustment programs] ... Respect for human rights, including the right of popular participation in policy decisions, should also be a factor in determining [debt relief] eligibility. Debt reduction should not end up rewarding elites, and even less should it be tied to measures that make the poor worse off."[41]

In fairness, the Canadian government has shown some willingness to consider arguments for greater IFI conditionality: "The government would welcome a detailed study of the issues involved" by a parliamentary committee.[42] It is likely that the subcommittee on international human rights will at least "pursue study of the possible human rights abuses that flow from massive development schemes, and examine ways to avoid such unwanted consequences of shared development."[43] A more recent review of Canada's engagement with the international financial institutions again called for the "IFIs to take into account in their lending policies and programs the obligation to respect universal human rights, including those of democratic expression, and also ... [reduce] military budgets."[44]

Is the reticence of Dutch, Canadian, and Norwegian governments on conditioning IFI lending on human rights performance still justified? It will be recalled that human rights abuses were a factor in the consensus among OECD states to withhold new IFI loans to China after Tiananmen Square. This decision was justified on economic grounds, but at the same time there was a de facto recognition of the interdependence between political and economic conditions. While the China freeze is the most striking example of recent IFI human rights conditionality, the World Bank is now drawing a more overt connection between politics, economic stability, and IFI lending. The bank's current credo is "good governance." On a narrow reading, this means new attention to non-economic phenomena such as the rule of law, and the accountability and transparency of state institutions. The governance agenda stems from the inadequate rate of return of many World Bank programs and is aimed primarily at reforming state administrative capacities to create a sound enabling environment for development. It is aimed largely at Africa. On a broader reading, good governance also implies respect for human rights and political pluralism. As the former bank president Barber Conable observed, "Allow me to be blunt: the political uncertainty and arbitrariness evident in so many parts of Sub-Saharan Africa are major constraints on the region's development. This is not advocating a political stance, but an increased transparency and accountability in government respect for human rights and adherence to the rule of law."[45]

This rhetoric has sometimes been backed by action. At the Paris meetings of the consultative groups, the bank has been drawn into political conditionality by default through the coordinated aid reductions of the bilateral donors. Moreover, as chair of these meetings, the bank has served as a political messenger. In Nepal, the bank warned King Mahendra that monetary aid might be cut off if he tried to halt the pro-democracy movement.[46] In Kenya, the bank press release of the 1991 consultative group spoke of conditionality in scarcely veiled terms. Delegates "emphasized that there was growing competition for increasingly scarce donor resources, and that aid programmes were being reexamined with a view to ensuring the most effective use of these resources." Moreover, "delegates underlined that good governance would be a major factor influencing aid allocations and stressed the need for early implementation of political reform to reinforce the benefits of economic structural change." Despite World Bank prohibitions on political interference, the resident representative was obliged to inform President Moi that the consultative group had frozen new aid to Kenya pending improvements in governance and human rights.

HUMAN RIGHTS CONDITIONALITY: A HARD ROAD

The concept of conditionality, as it has been used regarding IFI adjustment packages, has acquired a pejorative or at least controversial connotation. Critics complain that macroeconomic conditionality is a new form of neocolonial coercion of the South by Western institutions. The implications of human rights conditionality for development aid are just as controversial. The policy debate has centred on two themes: using aid as a coercive or punitive lever when gross and persistent abuses prompt a reconsideration of support to a repressive regime; and using aid as a positive lever, as a catalyst to build democratic institutions and foster the participation of target groups. The first could be called negative conditionality to defend human rights, while the second would be positive conditionality, or political aid, to promote human rights and democratic development. A third aspect, as yet scarcely considered by donors, is the human rights implication of major development schemes. As the case of Canada's Maduru Oya project underlined, donors ignore this aspect at their peril, for they may become unwitting accomplices to human rights abuses.[47]

Understandably, Canada, the Netherlands, and Norway are more comfortable promoting human rights and institutional development than punishing governments when rights are abused. For example, a

Norwegian white paper on human rights and development aid notes that "the experience of other donor countries shows that it is more important to concentrate on specific issues to protect human rights rather than punitive action against violators. Assistance must not be seen as a tool for 'rewarding' some governments and 'punishing' others."[48] Similarly, the Dutch "government rejects the idea that aid should be used to reward countries which respect human rights and conversely withheld to punish countries which disregard those rights. Aid should relate to the needs of people and not to the conduct of governments."[49]

In Canada, the principal government reservation about negative conditionality is the "double penalty" dilemma. In the words of a former Canadian secretary of state for external affairs, "our principal aid objective is to deliver assistance to the poorest people of the poorest countries. Should we doubly penalize them by cutting [aid] because their governments abuse them?"[50] CIDA has reflected the same ambivalence: "It is clear that gross violations should not be endorsed by the maintenance of a substantial ODA programme. On the other hand, populations already suffering because of these violations should not be doubly penalized by the withdrawal of ODA programmes."[51]

Despite having an aversion to punishing recalcitrant regimes, each state agrees that in certain circumstances aid may have to be terminated, reduced, or otherwise modified. The lowest common denominator is a pattern of "gross and persistent" violations in which there is good evidence of state complicity in, or perpetration of, abuses. For example, Norway recognizes that "a modification, reduction or cessation of Norwegian assistance may ... take place when the government of a country takes part in, tolerates or directly executes violations of human rights; when these violations are systematic and government efforts to end the abuse and bring the violators to justice are absent; and when the violations are gross and extensive."[52]

The Dutch, although they refer to aid suspension as "an extreme measure," recognize that "in cases where abuses derive directly from government policy, one should take care at any rate to ensure that aid does not contribute to the perpetuation of repression."[53] Avoiding complicity with Desi Bouterse was an important part of the Dutch decision to withhold aid to Suriname. Similarly, a "basic principle" underpinning the reduction or termination of Canadian government-to-government aid "is to ensure that repressive regimes are not legitimized."[54] Since the Dili fiasco and the signs at the World Human Rights Conference of a growing conflict between Western donors and Asian states, the Netherlands has acknowledged the importance of "joint approaches" by donors, who should apply human rights criteria in a consistent way but should reserve the right of unilateral action: "Nothing prevents individual donors, however, from pursuing their human rights principles."[55] An additional Canadian concern was whether CIDA could "deliver an assistance program to the most deserving people" in "those extreme situations where the violations of human rights are so flagrant that they call into question" our rationale for being there.[56] It will be recalled that it was safety issues and not human rights abuses per se that prompted a "downsizing" of Canadian aid to Sri Lanka in the late 1980s and the suspension of new aid to Guatemala and El Salvador in 1981.[57]

There is a significant number of cases of human rights conditionality, especially on the part of Canada and the Netherlands, although most examples are very recent, as tables 9.1, 9.2, and 9.3 show. Canada's decision to condition its development aid to Peru in the wake of President Fujimori's "constitutional coup" is an interesting and early example of principled action to defend democracy, rather than concentrating on a narrow conception of individual human rights. Barbara McDougall, then secretary of state for external affairs, stated, "Canada is committed to democracy and human rights in this hemisphere and we will take every possible action, in concert with the Organization of American States, to support these essential values."[58] Canada subsequently backed an OAS resolution calling for the return to constitutional democracy in Peru, and it suspended direct aid support to the government of Alberto Fujimori "until full democracy is restored." As McDougall announced, "It will not be business as usual with this President."[59]

The surprisingly large number of cases of conditioned aid do not, however, detract from the basic argument developed in this book, which points to a reluctance to employ assertive policy instruments such as a major aid or trade sanction when the core interests of the donor are threatened or at stake. The clearest exception to this assessment was the Dutch suspension of new aid to Indonesia after the 1991 Dili incident in East Timor. Just as revealing are the cases where no core economic interests were at stake (Fiji, in the case of Canada), and where aid was not used as a sanction against rights-repressive regimes (for example, Norwegian aid to Kenya and Pakistan in the 1980s, and Canadian aid to El Salvador, Guatemala, and Honduras since 1987). In the suspension of Canadian aid to Vietnam and Kampuchea in 1979 and to Afghanistan in 1980, political and security concerns (punishing communist aggression) were "interwoven with human rights considerations."[60]

As already noted, all three donor countries were active in their opposition to apartheid in South Africa. And all three have made

Table 9.1
The Netherlands: Human Rights and Development Aid Conditionality (selected cases)

Western states' conditions	Less-developed country	ODA action	Human rights
NEGATIVE	Chile, 1973	Suspended	Negative (coup)
	Indonesia, 1974–77	Threatened	Worsening (detainees)
		Reduced	Negative (E. Timor annexed)
	Suriname, 1982	Suspended	Negative (coup)
	China, 1989	Suspended	Negative (massacre)
	Sri Lanka, 1990	Reduced	Worsening (project safety)
	Sudan, 1990	Reduced	Worsening
	Indonesia, 1991	Suspension (new ODA)	Negative (East Timor)
	Malawi, 1991	Suspended	Worsening
POSITIVE	Philippines, 1986	New program	Improving (democratization)
	Suriname, 1988	Restored	Improving (democratization)
	Chile	Restored	Improving (democratization)
	Namibia	New program	Improving (democratization)
	South Africa, 1994	New program	Improving (democratization)

Table 9.2
Norway: Human Rights and Development Aid Conditionality (selected cases)

Western states' conditions	Less-developed country	ODA action	Human rights
NEGATIVE	Chile, 1973	Suspended	Negative (coup)
	Sri Lanka, 1985	Reduced/modified	Negative (state culpable)
	Pakistan, 1984–86	No action	Worsening
	Kenya, 1985–89	No action	Worsening
	China, 1989	Suspended	Negative (massacre)
POSITIVE	South Africa, 1994	New program	Improving (democratization)

significant investments to bolster democratic development in post-apartheid South Africa. Norway, for example, was part of a near-total Nordic trade embargo against South Africa, but by 1995 it had allocated 75 million kronor to the promotion of political stabilization in the republic, an investment bigger than some bilateral ODA country programs. In 1994, Canada provided technical assistance and support for voter education in South Africa's first multiracial, democratic elections. Three brief vignettes, those of Haiti, Kenya, and Sudan will serve to illustrate how and why donors choose to use (or not use) aid as an instrument of human rights statecraft.

Table 9.3
Canada: Human Rights and Development Aid Conditionality (selected cases)

Western states' conditions	Less-developed country	ODA action	Human rights
NEGATIVE	Chile, 1973	Suspended	Negative (coup)
	Suriname, 1983	Suspended	Negative (coup)
	Sri Lanka, 1985–87	Project "on hold"	Worsening (land equity)
	Fiji, 1987	Terminated	Negative (coup)
	Haiti, 1988	Modified/reduced	Negative
	Haiti, 1991	Suspended	Negative (coup)
	Sudan, 1989	Threatened	Worsening (food withheld)
	Myanmar, 1989	Suspended	Negative (coup)
	China, 1989	Token suspension	Negative (massacre)
	Zaire, 1991	Suspended	Worsening
	Rwanda, 1993–94	Reduced	Worsening (ethnic violence)
	Peru, 1993–94	Modified	Worsening (autogolpe)
POSITIVE	El Salvador, 1986	Program resumed	Improving (democratization)
	Haiti, 1986	Program resumed	Improving
	Philippines, 1986	New program	Improving (democratization)
	Guatemala, 1987	Program resumed	Improving
	Suriname, 1989	Token resumption	Improving (democratization)
	South Africa, 1994	Increased funding	Improving (democratization)

Dictator Proofed: Canadian Aid to Haiti

Human rights conditionality presents donors with a "damned if you do, damned if you don't" conundrum. Haiti is an extreme example of this dilemma. A political and developmental nightmare, Haiti seems incapable of breaking free from the legacy of Duvalierism, with its endemic corruption in state institutions (kleptocracy), its culture of violence and intimidation (Tontons Macoutes), which remains immune to regime changes or democratic values, and its state elites, who are absolutely uninterested in improving the well-being of the poor.[61]

The United States and Canada, both major donors to Haiti, have used aid in very different ways. The United States has used it as a political lever to try to induce change, whereas Canada has avoided complicity by "dictator proofing" its aid program, bypassing the state, and strengthening popular institutions. In the early 1980s, Canada faced a dilemma. Aid was perceived as legitimizing the Duvalier regime; yet as the most impoverished country in the Western hemisphere, Haiti was an obvious candidate for increased Canadian aid to alleviate poverty and strengthen civil and state institutions. The United States cut off or substantially reduced aid to Haiti three times during the Duvalier dictatorship.[62] The Canadian media, NGOs, missionaries, and the large immigrant Haitian community pressed for similar action by Canada. CIDA initially resisted such an extreme proposal, though it did acknowledge that corruption was undermining the effectiveness of Canadian aid. In 1981 it withdrew from a massive integrated rural development project in Haiti. Other donors reported improved cooperation with the Haitian government after this action by Canada.[63] A hoped-for democratic transition in Haiti after Duvalier's ouster in February 1986 proved ephemeral. Canada resumed development assistance to Haiti and announced an $80 million five-year program, with an emphasis on rural development and humanitarian assistance. Canada also provided technical assistance and observers to the election of 29 November 1987, which was rescheduled to 17 January 1988. The election was violent and was regarded by the international community as neither free nor fair.

The Canadian government had in any case established a parliamentary group to review all relations between Canada and Haiti. The group's report recommended maintaining diplomatic relations and continuing development aid, but closely monitoring human rights and democratic processes and including both items in the aid dialogue between the two governments.[64] In fact, since a 1982–83 country program review, Canada had been quietly "dictator proofing" its aid to Haiti by concentrating on small-scale poverty alleviation and human resource development projects, which largely bypassed the central government. Canada was thus well placed when the aborted elections and renewed human rights violations forced a reconsideration of aid to Haiti. On 13 September 1988, the minister of state for external affairs, Monique Landry, announced that Canada would not consider any new government-to-government aid to Haiti and that future aid would be channelled through NGOs and multilateral agencies. The minister directly linked human rights abuses to the modification of Canada's aid to Haiti: "Le gouvernement canadien entend marquer ainsi fermement sa réprobation face aux nombreuses atteintes aux droits fondamentaux qui se multiplient depuis l'arrivée au pouvoir de l'actuel régime."[65]

By 1989, the aid program to Haiti had been subjected to an intensive review. The future emphasis was to be economic development geared towards the achievement of social priorities and the "evolution of the social system." This meant additional programming to support human rights and democratic development.[66] After the election of Jean-Bertrand Aristide, in a vote judged by OAS and United Nations monitors to be broadly free and fair, Canada's government-to-government aid was restored on the basis of new prospects for an improvement in human rights. The decision was short-lived. In October 1991, Canada, acting in concert with other OAS members, suspended ODA as part of a range of economic sanctions, including participation in an international embargo. This time Canada also suspended bilateral aid implemented by NGOs – a decision taken without consulting the NGO community. As part of its disengagement from the illegal junta, Canada permitted only food and humanitarian assistance and $2.5 million for a joint OAS/United Nations human rights monitoring mission.[67] CIDA subsequently added democratic development programs to assist Haitian civil society in its struggle against the Cedras junta.[68] Canada, notably through the International Centre for Human Rights and Democratic Development (ICHRDD), has also been a strong supporter of the Truth Commission process in Haiti, an idea originally proposed by then president-in-exile, Jean-Bertrand Aristide, at the ICHRDD office in Montreal in 1993. The Truth Commission and the strengthening of the judiciary and the police force are key elements by which Canada has tried to consolidate the democratic transition that was made possible by President Aristide's return to power in 1994.

There is little in these policy gymnastics to suggest that aid leverage has improved human rights or democratic development. Suspending both government and NGO aid was a dubious option in Haiti because it has penalized the poor, who may face increased taxes by a state seeking to make up for the revenue shortfall, and because there are few civil institutions capable of mobilizing against a repressive state. Donors must work in uncongenial circumstances and try to develop civil institutions. But while the state is a major reason for the ineffectiveness of the aid, bypassing it is not a viable long-term policy for donors.

Kenya: The Quietude of Terror

Kenya, once viewed as the African exemplar of a stable, capitalist state, came under increasing international scrutiny in the 1980s. Kenya has long been dependent on Western largesse, and in 1987 it received US$687 million in ODA, of which US$83 million was bilateral ODA from Canada, the Netherlands, and Norway.[69] One of eleven of Norway's "main partner" aid recipients, Kenya was its fourth-largest recipient in 1986–87, accounting for 3.7 per cent of total Norwegian aid.[70]

Kenya's drift towards a repressive autocracy began in earnest after an abortive coup attempt in 1982. President Daniel arap Moi declared Kenya a *de jure* one-party state that same year. Economic recession, mounting foreign debt servicing, rising unemployment, and shrinking welfare services have fed open dissent and armed underground opposition by groups such as Mwa Kenya. President Moi responded by augmenting his personal power while restricting civil and political freedoms and circumscribing the independent rule of law. Public opposition to government policy is now restricted, and breaches, such as the possession of "seditious" literature, are cause for incarceration and persecution. Since 1987, incommunicado detentions, disappearances, and deaths in police custody have increased. Lack of progress in the investigation of the deaths of Bishop Muge and Robert Ouko, Kenya's former foreign minister, have cast suspicion on Moi's government. One Kenyan dissident has described the populace as gripped by the "quietude of terror."[71] Kenya has drifted from what Canada's Winegard Report called a "satisfactory" rights performance to a worsening, or "watch" pattern.[72]

Most aid donors ignored the mounting evidence of repression. Only the United States publicly condemned Moi's suppression of all forms of dissent and threatened to tie aid to human rights improvements. In 1987, President Moi cut short his visit to the United States after adverse press and congressional publicity. Other donors, such as the United Kingdom, the former West Germany, Canada, and the Nordic states, have been muted in their criticism. For example, a 1985 joint Nordic *démarche* to the Kenyan government, expressing concern about an alleged massacre by state security forces of two hundred Somali tribesmen at Wajir in northeastern Kenya, did not affect aid. Although, in Norway, conditionality was considered "in-house" as a response to the massacre, it was not pursued because it would only have hurt the aid program's beneficiaries while benefiting no one.[73]

In May 1987 Kenyan Minister for Foreign Affairs Elijah Mangwale visited Norway and Sweden in preparation for President Moi's planned visit later that year. The minister responded to negative Nordic press coverage of Kenya's human rights record by labelling it "inaccurate, malicious, and biased," and he accused the Norwegian and Swedish governments of complicity in "tarnishing Kenya's image."[74] Moi's trip to Oslo was subsequently cancelled on the Norwegian government's advice; the Norwegians expected more critical domestic media coverage of Kenya.[75] In Kenya, large and ostensibly government-organized demonstrations protested the Nordic media's criticism, while pro-Moi newspapers vilified the Norwegian government and questioned the need for further Norwegian aid.[76] The state's control of the media enabled Moi to communicate his views indirectly but with certain effect.

Bilateral relations quickly deteriorated. The Kenyan government appears to have informed Norway that it would not tolerate sustained criticism of Moi, and it implied that Norwegian aid would no longer be needed or welcome in Kenya.[77] In turn, in 1988 Norway refused to grant a small mixed-credits power sector project.[78] The Kenyan authorities also criticized Norway for harbouring the "fugitive" Koigi wa Wamwere, founder of the Kenya Patriotic Front, a banned underground movement.[79] Kenya accepted neither wa Wamwere's status as a political refugee nor his freedom while in Norway to publish in the Norwegian press letters critical of the Moi regime.[80]

Norwegian officials' marked reticence about Kenya is indicative of the two countries' strained relations between 1987 to 1989.[81] The Norwegian officials claimed that bilateral relations improved after the visit of Kenyan Foreign Minister Robert Ouko in December 1989 – just two months before his murder.[82] Reportedly, human rights were privately discussed and the Norwegians made it understood that continuing adverse trends might affect the volume and modalities of Norwegian aid. The Kenyan authorities were keen to increase Norwegian balance-of-payments support. But in fact, in the 1990 budget, undisbursed "pipeline" funds were allowed to lapse, effectively reducing Norway's 1990 aid budget to Kenya by 30 million kroner.[83] On 22 October 1990, Norway's ambassador to Kenya was given just seven days to leave. The Moi government accused Norway of supporting Koigi wa Wamwere, who, on his return to Kenya on 19 October, had been arrested with two others on the allegation that they had assault rifles for subversive use.[84]

Kenya's case illustrates the risks small donors run when they try to act alone. With a regime as insecure as Daniel arap Moi's, any criticism, no matter how constructive, is intolerable. The impact of Norway's departure may have a demonstration effect on other donors, especially the Nordic states. But the volume of Norwegian aid (us$26 million per year) is too small to be taken seriously. In these circumstances, who needs whom?

Sudan: Food, War, and Conditionality

Civil war has been waged in Sudan on and off for almost twenty-five years. It is a war based on ethnic, geographic, and material disputes. Sudan is a major international aid recipient, but in recent years donors have been alarmed by the inability of successive governments to introduce structural reforms, repay International Monetary Fund debts, or find a durable solution to the conflict. Human rights violations and civilian victims in the civil war have been increasing. Moreover, food has been used as a weapon by both state and rebel forces in southern

Sudan. Attempts to deliver food to famine-endangered regions (Operation Lifeline) have been disrupted by the military. These actions constitute a violation of what has been described as a "core" right in this study – the right not to be deprived of access to food or the means of producing food.[85]

Sudan is a main Dutch aid partner (*concentratieland*) and is thus subject to regular aid consultations with the Netherlands government. In 1989 the Dutch aid delegation noted: "The fact that a democratically elected government was replaced by a military [g]overnment has caused serious concern. The existence of democratic structures constituted the basis for [Dutch aid] since 1975." The Dutch issued an implicit threat when they reminded the Sudanese that reports of human rights violations might "lead to a gradual erosion of the public support for the development cooperation programme."[86] The delegation was concerned about "cases of arrest without proper indictment, cases of violations of the right of due process and cases in which punishments would seem extreme in relation to the offences."[87]

The Netherlands normally keeps reserve funds for additional or "special programs." These were withdrawn from Sudan for 1990. Instead, a disbursement ceiling of 60 million guilders was imposed. The Dutch have always insisted that their aid should be evenly split between the north and the south of the country. In the current climate of war in southern Sudan, this is impossible. The Dutch have thus been quietly reducing their aid package to the north and cutting commodity aid such as Royal Dutch Shell base oils. It is not clear whether this aid reduction signalled concern about the lack of progress in structural economic reforms or whether it was meant as a sanction against state tolerance of human rights violations. The Dutch delegation noted that "in the absence of a comprehensive plan for structural economic reforms, the Netherlands ... deems it necessary to limit new allocations for import support to a maximum of 20 per cent of programmable resources."[88] A Dutch official described these funding decisions as a "symbolic commentary" on the possible future of Dutch aid to Sudan. In 1990 the Dutch foreign ministry actively discussed whether Sudan should be demoted from a main partner to a sectoral aid recipient.

Canada also took a tough line. Francis Filleul, who was Canadian ambassador-designate to Sudan, told an audience that included Prime Minister Sadiq Mahdi, "The situation [in southern Sudan] stands as an affront to the conscience of the international community ... In the absence of a settlement and national reconciliation, we will consider seriously whether continuing assistance of other than a purely humanitarian nature can be justified."[89] Canadian ODA reached a peak of

$38 million in 1986–87 but had declined to just $21.7 million by 1988–89, mostly because of delivery problems.[90] West Germany, the United Kingdom, and Denmark also reduced aid.

Sudan's case is an interesting example of joint donor action in which concern about human rights has been used to reinforce macroeconomic conditionality in a country where even humanitarian assistance is dangerous and where structural economic reforms are blocked by an uncooperative government. Conceivably, this blend of both economic and political conditionality may be used more often in the 1990s.

STRENGTHENING HUMAN RIGHTS AND DEMOCRATIC DEVELOPMENT

All three donors are more comfortable promoting human rights than punishing the poor for the sins of their rulers. All three supported participatory institutions and human rights organizations before their principal policy guidelines were formulated.[91] But a more overt linkage between human rights, development aid, and democratization is germinating. For example, the former Dutch development cooperation minister, P. Bukman, observed, "Only development with participation is sustainable ... Our development [aid] policy is based on the firm conviction that it should contribute to a just society. Development cooperation should create possibilities for people, both men and women, to involve themselves actively in shaping the structure of their own society. I would like to call this fundamental democratization."[92]

Chapter 1 described the similar stirrings in intergovernmental organizations such as the Development Assistance Committee and the World Bank. Canada, the Netherlands, and Norway have also begun to develop new institutions and special funds for fostering rights and participatory development. The Dutch have singled out the Philippines and Central America for sectoral funding to support "young" or "budding" democracies.[93] They also created, at the suggestion of a Dutch parliamentarian, the so-called Aarts Fund to provide direct support to human rights organizations and the victims of rights abuses. In 1993, Dutch ODA support to human rights and democratic development was approximately US$6.5 million, mostly channelled through NGOs, with another US$10 million disbursed through country and regional programs. In fact, the Dutch now define the central goal of their aid program for the 1990s as "government of, for and by the people."[94]

Norway helps finance the NGO-run Human Rights Fund. In 1989 the Norwegian parliament announced a "Democracy Fund" as part of the ODA budget and disbursed 989,330 kroner to human rights and institutional development projects.[95] That same year, the Norwegian government also established an "independent" Norwegian Human Rights Fund, which is nevertheless 80 per cent state funded.[96] A Norwegian resource bank of experts concerned with democracy and human rights was compiled in 1992.

A 1993 white paper reiterated Norwegian support for democratization and human rights. It identified six main areas for Norwegian ODA: sustainable development; economic growth; social development and human resources; women in development; children in the development process; and democracy and human rights.[97] The white paper served notice that the government would integrate human rights in the planning and implementation of all operational development cooperation; strengthen efforts to promote the rights of women, children, ethnic minorities, and indigenous peoples; promote popular participation; support peace processes and the peaceful resolution of conflicts at national and regional levels; support the development of free and independent trade unions to strengthen workers rights; and develop an active and informed dialogue on human rights and democracy in the context of bilateral and multilateral negotiations. Norway has supported elections and voter particpation in Mozambique, Zambia, Nicaragua, and Cambodia. The government has also supported, inter alia, programs on women's constitutional rights, the Inter Press Service to promote freedom of opinion and the press in Africa, and study tours in Norway for members of the constitutional committee of Tanzania and the Supreme Court of Mozambique. The Democracy Fund has been used in Chile to build new independent democratic NGOs, in Nicaragua to support the demobilization of soldiers, and in Ethiopia to strengthen the National Assembly. Finally, Norway has expressed concern about military spending and has made reduced defence spending a condition of supporting rural development in Mozambique.[98]

Arguably, the most ambitious promotion initiative is Canada's International Centre for Human Rights and Democratic Development. The centre had an interesting genesis. It was first proposed by the Hockin-Simard Report in 1986.[99] The government endorsed the idea and appointed two special rapporteurs to tap domestic opinion and consider the centre's mandate. Senior bureaucrats in the Department of External Affairs and CIDA apparently did not support the idea; they were concerned that a quasi-independent institution dealing with sensitive isssues overseas could damage Canada's diplomatic relations. Political will may have made the difference. Ed Broadbent, the centre's first president, underscored that it "wouldn't have come into being if [Secretary of State for External Affairs] Joe Clark hadn't gone against the advice of some people in External."[100]

In the House of Commons, Bill c-147 made the proposal official, and royal assent was given in September 1988. Based in Montreal, the centre was funded by CDN$15 million from the ODA budget for its first five years. In contrast to its Dutch and Scandinavian counterparts, it was at first largely project based rather than research based. Its initial mandate was a broad commitment to strengthen democratic institutions and promote human rights in the Third World: "The objects of the Centre are to initiate, encourage and support cooperation between Canada and other countries in the promotion, development and strengthening of institutions that give effect to the rights and freedoms enshrined in the *International Bill of Rights*."[101] Bill c-147 also enabled the centre to "foster research and education, discourse, the exchange of information and collaboration among people and institutions in Canada, developing countries and elsewhere."

During the bill's passage through Parliament, the Senate had made several amendments to ensure greater precision in the centre's mandate and to allow the centre to seek funds from private sources and to develop beyond the Third World – in Eastern Europe and the former Soviet Union, for example. The key amendment was the inclusion, among the centre's objectives, of a statement about "the right to vote and be elected at periodic and genuine elections in pluralistic political systems."[102] This means that there could be more Canadian technical assistance to elections in Third World countries, along the lines of aid given to Haiti in 1988. Other rights singled out in the Senate amendments were protection against torture or cruel, inhuman, or degrading punishment, the rights of freedom of opinion and of expression, and the right to an adequate standard of living.[103] Liberal Senator Allan MacEachen, a former secretary of state for external affairs, mused wryly on the government's discomfort about the possibly paternalistic tenor of the centre: "It was somewhat disconcerting to me that the minister said ... that it was certainly not the intention of the Centre to promote Canadian-style democracy and human rights. That provoked the thought in my mind: whose democracy and human rights if not Canada's?"[104]

There are grounds for both scepticism and optimism about the centre's potential as a focal point of Canada's activism on international human rights. First, the Mulroney government's appointment of Ed Broadbent, the former leader of the New Democratic Party, as the centre's first president was politically astute. The centre risks being too closely identified with the government, but Broadbent's record as a social democrat made him well placed to establish its independence and, on occasion, to criticize official Ottawa. While this has not happened often, the centre did depart from Ottawa in supporting

Myanmar's democratic government in exile; in calling for the linkage of trade and human rights in the NAFTA and World Trade Organization negotiations; and, most controversially, in calling for armed intervention to restore the democratically elected government of Jean-Bertrand Aristide in Haiti.

Second, the centre was created because people matter. The democratization of Eastern Europe, Latin America, and parts of Asia are compelling proof that "people power" works. The centre's budget may be trifling, but it is not for underwriting megaprojects. Small sums are often enough to ensure that a trade union, a legal aid group, or a newspaper survives as a critic of questionable state policies. The government knows that the centre may be controversial and may complicate Canada's foreign policy. But as an aide to the secretary of state for external affairs observed, "There are advantages to having an independent agency do the work that the diplomatic corps cannot."[105] The secretary of state evidently felt that the centre should "play a somewhat aggressive role" in promoting human rights and in leading Canadian policy in this area.[106]

In practice, the centre has positioned itself as a "donor advocate." Its early strength lay in providing financial support to grass-roots human rights NGOS, particularly in Latin America. It then gradually expanded its programming to include Africa and Asia, and by 1995 it was concentrating on thirteen countries and several thematic issues, one being women's rights. By then, too, the all-party parliamentary agreement that had established the centre was a thing of the past. The political map had been redrawn. The Liberals were in power, the New Democrats and Conservatives had been all but wiped out, and two regional parties, the Bloc Québécois and Reform, represented the opposition voice of Quebec separatists and dicontented westerners. In a domestic climate that is inward-looking and fiscally conservative, the centre must reinvent itself and carve out a niche that is distinctive from government in order to counter the harsh parliamentary scrutiny that followed a mixed evaluation of its performance.[107] An increased emphasis on advocacy, applied research, and intellectual leadership may be the centre's best hope of survival, given declining aid budgets and CIDA's growing financing of human rights, good government, and democratic development.

The centre's real value-added may be in calling international and domestic attention to intractable human rights problems. In 1992 it organized a unique mission of Nobel peace laureates, including the Dalai Lama and Archbishop Desmond Tutu, to travel to Thailand to press for the release of the Burmese political detainee, Aung San Suu Kyi. The centre has conducted human rights monitoring missions to

Rwanda and also to Chiapas, Mexico. It has been active in the global women's rights movement and has played a key supporting role to Canada's successful call for a U.N. special rapporteur on violence against women, its causes and consequences. The centre has also played a key role in helping President Arisitide develop a truth commission to examine human rights violations in Haiti's recent past.

Like other quasi-independent crown institutions, the centre is in an ambiguous position. It must be sensitive to the sometimes conflicting interests of the government, the public, and Parliament. Finding the right balance between welcome advice and unwelcome advocacy will take time and experience. Because the centre is government funded, it was initially prudent to build its credentials through projects that enhance human rights instead of inviting controversy at home and abroad by assertive and controversial advocacy. Some parliamentarians have questioned the centre's role, arguing that it duplicates much that CIDA is already doing. The government, however, has given it a ringing endorsement, "applauding its excellent work around the world."[108] In future, the centre's role as advocate and opinion leader may come to dominate as part of a strategy to ensure its long-term survival.

While the centre is a Canadian flagship for promoting human rights, it is not the only institution to undertake such work, and it may in future be in competition with both government and Canadian NGOs as increased funding is identified by CIDA for human rights, good government, and democratic development. In fact, CIDA was quietly supporting human rights and democratic development projects as early as 1982, well before the creation of the centre. A recent inventory of CIDA experience in this field underscores the breadth of Canada's action. Funds for small projects are often disbursed quickly to local NGOs through the Canada Fund, which is administered by Canadian diplomatic missions. The real project growth in the rights, democracy, and governance field appears to date from 1988, however.[109]

CIDA has been active in strengthening women's rights through its Women in Development Program (for example, with paralegal training, the development of regional networks of women lawyers, and legal aid clinics).[110] CIDA has also supported the International Ombudsman Institute, which was established in 1978 in Alberta, and Peace Brigades International in Guatemala and El Salvador. Canada has been very active in certain countries, notably Sri Lanka and South Africa. In Sri Lanka, ODA was used to fund the bar association, an ethnic studies think-tank, and a $500,000 human rights fund; it also provided support to the media, the human rights training of the armed forces and police, and human rights cases in the courts. In South Africa, ODA supported legal advice centres, small presses, human rights lawyers and monitors, black community centres, think-tanks, women's organizations, and union umbrella groups. Canada was also active in supporting the training of future black leaders and in creating the Macro-Economic Research Group, which linked Canadian universities and the policy makers of the African National Congress in their planning for a nonracial government.

CIDA is not the only Canadian institution playing a role in the international promotion of human rights and democratic governance. Elections Canada has established an international reputation for excellence in the technical assistance it has provided for monitoring elections as far afield as South Africa and Cambodia, Mozambique and El Salvador. The federal Human Rights Commission has been active in supporting the development of national human rights commissions around the world. Finally, in a multilateral context, Canada was instrumental in the establishment and funding of the Unit for the Promotion of Democracy and Good Governance in the Organization of American States and a human rights unit (the Agency for Cultural and Technical Co-operation) in La Francophonie.

FROM PRINCIPLE TO PRACTICE: TOWARDS AN OPERATIONAL AID/RIGHTS FRAMEWORK

While all three donors say they are at the forefront of progressive thinking on linking human rights and development aid, there is still a large gulf between principle and practice. Progress to date is at the lowest common denominator. Donors agree that:

- human rights considerations should inform cabinet decisions about aid eligibility, volume, and disbursement channels, but that the reasoning underpinning these decisions will be confidential;[111]
- ODA suspension is a measure to be used only *in extremis* against "gross and persistent violators";
- human rights are just one of several criteria for determining aid eligibility; others include a recipient state's commitment to participatory development and poverty alleviation, political and economic relations, absorptive capacity, and macroeconomic policies;[112]
- the poor should not be penalized in any conflict between the alleviation of poverty and human rights concerns;
- aid should concentrate on promoting human rights and strengthening democratic institutions, not on punishing governments.

However, the issues considered inadequately or not at all underline how far Canada, the Netherlands, and Norway are from translating principles into practice. First and most worrisome is the absence of any concrete guidelines for balancing eligibility criteria, which may mean that human rights lose out in policy trade-offs. Canada, for example, includes a recipient's "commitment" to "improve" its economic policies among CIDA's aid-eligibility criteria.[113] This veiled endorsement of International Monetary Fund (IMF) and World Bank economic orthodoxy may rest uneasily alongside human rights. How will Canada react to a country that is following a structural adjustment package while systematically violating fundamental rights – perhaps in order to maintain law and order that has been threatened by the social and economic fall-out of IMF conditionality? And what will Canada do to ensure that its endorsement of structural adjustment does not lead to the loss or abuse of the social and economic rights of the poorest?[114] The worst cases are simple to identify and can easily justify tough action such as trade or aid sanctions. But this still leaves a large group of Third World countries where an assessment is less clear cut – where rights may be structurally violated (Central America), where civil and political freedoms deteriorate over several years (Kenya), or where egregious abuses persist in so-called budding democracies (the Philippines under President Aquino). Should complexity simply mean business as usual? The record to date suggests that it does.[115]

Second, donors have made no firm commitment routinely to put large infrastructure aid projects through a human rights filter to ensure that aid does not inadvertently worsen the social and economic rights of the poorest or inflame ethnic conflict by unwitting discrimination. All three donors do, however, now profess to include human rights issues in the annual or cyclical "aid dialogue" with recipients.[116] Third, which rights will be promoted through development aid? Vague references to the International Bill of Rights beg the question of priority. In practice, donors appear to equate traditional development goals, such as poverty alleviation, with progress towards social and economic rights. They seem unwilling to spell out the policy implications of an expanded definition of development – one that recognizes political empowerment and self-determination as necessary components in the struggle to escape poverty. For example, a Dutch Human Rights Advisory Committee recommendation that the Netherlands view "the promotion of civil and political rights as a development policy objective *in its own right*"[117] was rejected because "by isolating ... civil and political rights ... and explicitly elevating it [*sic*] to an aim in itself ... [there are] risks of the development issue becoming undesirably politicized."[118] This is a strange and contradictory position given that the

Netherlands, like other Western states, puts civil and political rights at the forefront of its U.N. diplomacy. The statement also contradicts a Dutch government commitment to support "budding" democracies. Can democratization be strengthened *without* stressing civil and political rights? Moreover, rights are, ipso facto, a political issue, as the Dutch discovered in their efforts to use development aid to support institution building in the Philippines.

Until these gaps in donor discussions of human rights and development aid are addressed, the integration of these issues will remain partial at best. Each aid agency's most urgent task is to work out an aid/rights framework. At a minimum, this framework must consider four issues. First, under what circumstances should aid be reduced, modified, or suspended in response to a rights-repressing regime? Second, how should a recipient's human rights record be raised as a routine part of the aid dialogue, and to what extent should donors seek the approval of recipient states before developing governance or rights programs? So far, only the conditions governing aid suspension have been adequately discussed. Donors need to be clear on the objectives that underpin decisions to reduce, modify, or terminate aid. If punishment is the aim, suspension may be justified as long as humanitarian aid continues to reach the poorest people or the victims of armed conflict. If the donor wants to improve human rights, threats to reduce aid or withdraw from prestigious projects coupled with a timetable for specific imrovements could be considered, preferably in the company of "like-minded" donors. If safety and aid delivery are at issue, reducing or shifting to more commodity aid may be the answer. If the intention is to avoid complicity and to "dictator proof" ODA, suspending government-to-government commodity and balance-of-payments support should be balanced by greater use of NGOs where conditions permit. A consistent, principled signal can be sent by ensuring that regimes culpable of gross violations are also ineligible for debt relief or adjustment loans.[119] Donors must determine just how steep and enduring the deterioration in human rights is. They must then decide whether to respond to the exigencies of the moment or to stay on and work towards an improved political and human rights environment.

The third issue to be considered is, what potentially adverse effects might development projects have on the human rights of target groups and how could they be minimized? Fourth, how can donors help disadvantaged or oppressed groups participate more effectively in the official political process? This minimal agenda ensures that human rights conditionality is not just a one-way street; conditionality should impose obligations on the donor as well as on the recipient.

Participation should be behind all development planning. As a human right, applicable to both individuals and groups, participation implies more than voting; it allows people(s) "to take part in the conduct of public affairs, *directly* or through freely chosen representatives."[120] Participation is the thread stitching together human rights, social justice, and democratic development. Democracy is all about political participation; the essence of human rights is control of one's destiny. Development aid may have a modest role in helping disadvantaged groups empower themselves to participate in or protest against decisions affecting their lives.

What do these lofty goals imply in practice? First, beneficiaries should have a say in the design and implementation of aid projects. Second, if donors take rights seriously, they should expand the now token funding available for "institutional" or "democratic" development. Ideally, such aid should command a fixed portion of the ODA budget. In view of the long gestation of these small-scale projects, institution-building funds should be immune from the lapsing conditions that propel the money-moving syndrome of aid bureaucracies.[121] Third, donors should acknowledge more frankly that strengthening civil institutions is inherently political; it cannot be neutral. Programming will call for difficult decisions on where the emphasis should be put. The key choices are:

- primary support to state institutions or programs, e.g., ombudsman, human rights commissions, witness protection schemes, land reform schemes;
- primary support to civil institutions, e.g., trade unions, church groups, media organizations, legal aid clinics, and "first line of defence organizations" such as human rights monitors and advocacy groups;
- a mixed strategy.

These choices are not simply academic. The recipient state's attitude to non-governmental organizations will be decisive, and donors should carefully assess how much leeway they have to work independently of the recipient government. Some countries, such as Indonesia, have a very restrictive and controlling policy; NGOs must be "chartered" and are barred from most forms of political activity. Fragile, emerging democracies, such as the Philippines, may also have a restrictive policy on civil interest groups, especially those the state views as fronts for subversive armed elements.

Countries emerging from repressive rule may establish democratic institutions such as human rights commissions, but their independence and effectiveness vary. The human rights commission in a military-ruled Uganda appears effective, whereas its counterpart in a democratic Philippines is criticized as cosmetic. If donors support such institutions, are they legitimizing a "façade democracy?" In some countries, principally African, civil society is weak and institutions have to be built from the bottom up. This will require a larger, more sustained, and probably more direct concentration of financial and administrative resources. In other countries, such as the Philippines, there is already a rich diversity of NGOS. The key issue here becomes which groups to support and how much control to exert over their activities. Should donors support politicized "people's organizations" or should they confine their aid to relatively apolitical development NGOS? Arm's-length delivery mechanisms, such as Canada's International Centre on Human Rights and Democratic Development, and the co-financing NGOS in Holland may allow official donors to reduce the risks and confine their primary attention to relatively apolitical NGOS. With human rights, an organization's attitude to violence may be decisive.

TOWARDS GOOD PRACTICE IN HUMAN RIGHTS PROGRAMMING

Operational guidelines to build human rights and democratic development into Canadian, Dutch, and Norwegian project and country program planning are still not fully in place. Canada has perhaps gone farthest in deriving systematic lessons learned from its experience in human rights programming.[122] Lessons from donor aid to the Philippines, Sri Lanka, and Suriname may provide additional insights, pointing the way towards a more precise operational framework.

Some of the pitfalls of "political aid" are also common to poverty-alleviation projects. In both cases, donors should guard against replicating patron-client relationships, particularly in rural communities; taking the mega-dollar approach, which may entrench dependency, corruption, and disunity; and strengthening "cronyism" or local bosses who use aid to place loyal followers in organizational positions.[123] Projects to build or strengthen peasant organizations must contain a substantial economic component. Without services or reforms designed to increase production, projects built around sophisticated concepts of community development will fail. And without material incentives, peasants will have little reason to participate.[124]

Other pitfalls are unique to political aid. The Dutch and Canadian experience in the Philippines shows that aid to strengthen human rights and civil institutions is a political and not a neutral activity. The temptation to build large programs rapidly and to throw money at civil institutions in "emerging democracies" should be resisted. Without a detailed assessment of national and local politics at the planning stage, donors may be vulnerable to manipulation by groups at either end of a political spectrum and to hostility from the recipient government. A "see no politics, hear no politics" donor approach may be counterproductive in fragile, internally divided democracies. Mistakes can be minimized by a careful assessment of the political links of the prospective recipient NGOs and their attitude to political violence. For instance, do human rights groups monitor opposition as well as state human rights abuses? Aid to civil groups linked to armed insurgents, secessionists, or liberation movements must be weighed carefully. Such support may be at odds with the non-violent underpinnings of human rights and the democratic process.

CIDA's decision to rechannel more aid to the Philippines via NGOs was made possible by building a "partnership" with Canadian and Filipino NGOs. Developing a dialogue with groups across the political spectrum helped repair the damage done on Negros. This is a potentially fruitful approach for other donors to take. But indirect political aid through NGOs does not solve all the problems. First, the donor government loses some control, which may be problematic for heavily bureaucratized aid agencies. Second, it is not clear, at least in the Philippines, whether ODA can be a vehicle for empowerment. CIDA's Negros Rehabilitation and Development Program was essentially a poverty-alleviation project that apparently deepened power and material inequalities and perpetuated dependency instead of transforming the project's "targets" into "stakeholders" with a say in production and management decisions. However, CIDA had little "political space" in which to disburse ODA to the "people's organizations" that were experimenting with a more radical development model, because the Aquino government labelled these groups subversive, and because several organizations were ambivalent about or hostile towards official aid donors.

Canada's Maduru Oya project in Sri Lanka underlines the fact that human rights must be incorporated into project planning. Donors ignore this dimension at their peril. The failure to do so may worsen communal tensions. Ideally, a human rights "gatekeeper" in the donor agency should assess the human rights implications of large aid projects. At a minimum, the target groups should be notified of the project proposal, have access to information about it, be helped to form their own self-managed associations, and have access to legal resources where necessary. In short, human rights conditionality is a two-way street; it imposes obligations on the donor as well as on the recipient.

A roster of the basic premises underpinning "good practice" in the design and delivery of human rights and democratic development projects would require donors to:

- work with groups which the poor have themselves created, and link rights and gender projects to the material struggles of the disadvantaged;
- involve local beneficiaries in the design and implementation of projects, and ensure that the projects do not put the rights of affected populations at risk;
- nurture national or regional NGO coalitions in the South;
- ensure that the groups supported are internally democratic;
- use gender-disaggregated data;
- assist women who are competing for political office, and support public-interest litigation and reforms of gender-discriminatory laws and practices;
- support the educational and solidarity work of women's organizations;
- explore ways to devolve funding for human rights and democratic development to North-South NGO coalitions;
- increase donor human and financial resources for building civil-society institutions;
- conduct independent or DAC-supervised "peer reviews" of official donor support for human rights, gender justice, and democratic development.

Finally, Canada, the Netherlands, and Norway might find their greatest impact as opinion leaders in intergovernmental organizations such as the EC Development Fund, the OECD's Development Assistance Committee, and the United Nations Development Programme, where they could use their voices to persuade larger donors to develop institution-building programs and establish a common approach to human rights and development aid.[125]

By 1994, CIDA had begun to articulate a more comprehensive policy on rights, democracy, and governance. The new policy is far-sighted and extends the discussion well beyond the funding criteria approach of *Sharing Our Future* into uncharted waters, which potentially implicate CIDA in tackling the full range of rights and democracy challenges – from the strengthening of formal democratic procedures and institutions, such as ombudsmen and parliaments, to civic education and the institution building of civil society NGOs. The final component, good governance, is defined as strengthening the "will of leaders to respect rights, rule democratically and govern effectively" and "the competence of the public sector to promote the effective, honest and accountable exercise of power."[126]

In some remarkably blunt language on conditionality, CIDA stated that it "does not accept that there is a justifiable trade-off between respect for rights and democratic principles and the pursuit of economic growth. Lasting prosperity is not built on continued abuses of rights, disregard for democratic process and poor governance." CIDA called for consultation with Canadian public stakeholders before punitive action; it proposed multilateral coordination where possible, suggested that "constructive initiatives" be used alongside punitive measures, and recommended achievable spelled-out targets and results for maximum effectiveness. Two additions to the policy statement called for CIDA to investigate and consult with affected groups where there are alleged negative rights impacts of individual projects; and for the integration of a "democratic analysis" in the consideration of all CIDA initiatives. The ultimate fate of this "interim" policy was dependent on the recommendations of the parliamentary committee reviewing Canada's foreign policy and on the government's subsequent white paper. In the meantime, CIDA established regional or country-specific funds for human rights and democratic development. This was implemented in francophone Africa, and similar funds have been planned for Peru, East Africa, and El Salvador.

The discussion on human rights and democratic development in the 1994 parliamentary review of Canadian foreign policy was in some respects disappointing.[127] In a document giving highest priority to trade, little new ground was broken to deepen Canada's commitment to human rights or democratization or to offer guidelines for programming or policy dialogue. The only important innovation concerned good governance; it called on Canada to reconsider levels of aid expenditures to countries that spend large sums on arms rather than on social development priorities.

For its part, the government underlined effectiveness as the litmus test of action: "The essential challenge is to decide how we can best influence other governments' respect for human rights. Our ultimate aim is not to punish countries and innocent populations whose governments abuse human rights but rather to change behaviour."[128] The government's response appeared to be a retreat from earlier Canadian positions, which showed a willingness to go it alone on aid and trade conditionality to defend human rights. The government acknowledged that "high profile aid and trade measures may play a role in responding to gross, systematic, and persistent violations of ... human rights standards. Canadian assistance, for example, must not give the impression of rewarding such government behaviour." But it added, "Punitive bilateral action in isolation from other countries, however, usually presents the least effective means of achieving results. In the case of trade, it may hurt Canada more than it will change the behaviour of offending governments."[129] These nuanced shifts in emphasis were a precursor for the government's confident and blunt unwillingness to use trade as a sanction for human rights violations, an issue that is taken up in more detail in chapter 10.

CONCLUSION

The conundrum of "consistency" was used to discuss the link between human rights and development aid. Canada, the Netherlands, and Norway have substantially similar positions on the modalities of human rights statecraft. None is willing to be captive to a rigid, formula-driven policy premised on retribution. All are wary of applying more assertive trade sanctions or pressing for human rights criteria to be added to IFI loan decisions. Each takes a lowest-common-denominator approach to using aid as a sanction. Effectiveness is a key criterion in considering which policy lever to apply, but there is also a pragmatic recognition that smaller players have limited scope for unilateral action and should always explore joint action with "like-minded" states.

The imperative of "effectiveness" and the need to reconcile moral interests with other national interests demand executive discretion in the implementation of policy. A case-by-case approach is thus unavoidable, and the ideal of "consistency" will be difficult to achieve in practice. Complexity, should not, however, be a reason to endorse the status quo. Lessons learned from the case studies in this book and other donor experiences suggest some guidelines for best practice in the management of human rights conditionality. These include clarity of aims and objectives; transparency of purpose; consistency of application; a strategic grasp of the political environment in aid-recipient countries; and a shrewd targeting of conditions linked to modest but feasible changes, which bolster rather than undermine the friends of political reform in rights-violating regimes.[130]

While all three donors now have programs for institution building, the planners have barely begun to translate principles into practice. Taking Canada as a proxy, I looked in some detail at CIDA's plans to develop a coherent aid/rights policy. What are the prospects that a workable policy will emerge? On an optimistic view, adding human rights to aid programming and broad policy decisions will become a standard operating procedure, and a more coherent policy will emerge with time and practice. But sceptics point to three hurdles that may impair the integration of human rights in development aid planning. First, aid is susceptible to fads and fashions. Are human rights simply "the flavour of the month," as basic needs were in the 1970s? The Dutch experience suggests not, but it is by no means certain that their experience will be replicated by the other donors. Second, most aid agencies' agendas are now impossibly broad. How will human rights fare among other aid objectives, such as structural adjustment, sustainable development, export promotion, and industrial development?

Third, the bureaucracy may resist such a policy. For example, sceptics say that Canada's foreign policy bureaucracy is driven by an operational code inimical to human rights.[131] Cranford Pratt has argued that "when a strong lead is given politically for a more forceful human rights policy, there is a recurrent tendency for the bureaucracy to minimize its significance."[132] CIDA's in-house discussion of the new rights and good governance framework makes it clear that some senior management will resist agency-wide coherence and controls to implement the policy. This bureaucratic tendency is clear from other facets of Canada's Third World policy. For instance, the government's code of conduct for Canadian businesses operating in South Africa was "rendered totally useless by the haphazard and disinterested way in which it was implemented."[133] The 1976 basic-needs aid blueprint was largely unrealized as the program shifted to a greater commercial emphasis in the 1980s.[134] The jury is still out on whether a similar fate lies in store for human rights in Canada's aid program. In fact, as the next chapter explains, it is the politicians who seem most likely to downplay human rights. Under the new Liberal government of Jean Chrétien, the focus on "jobs, jobs, jobs" points to trade rather than rights as the driving force of Canadian foreign policy.

10 Between Ethics and Interests: Human Rights in North-South Relations

If the resolve to defend human rights abroad is gauged by a state's willingness to incur costs to other important national interests, then the evidence in this study suggests that Canada, the Netherlands, and Norway are seldom disposed to let human rights considerations trump more self-serving interests, even though all three states profess ethical duties beyond their borders. The tension between human rights and foreign policy is manifest at three levels of analysis: system, state, and society. At the systemic level, states must negotiate the tension between, on the one hand, the norms of sovereignty and non-intervention – which reify states as the principal global actors – and, on the other, customary human rights law, which makes individuals the central legal entities and compels international scrutiny of domestic human rights performance. At the level of state behaviour, human rights diplomacy shifts uneasily between global ethics and national interests. States must constantly weigh the trade-offs among moral, commercial, and political interests, and must gauge their effectiveness in assertively defending human rights. At the domestic level, governments defend executive discretion against public pressure for greater public input and for "transparent" and "consistent" human rights policies.

Politicians insist that human rights are a "fundamental" Canadian foreign policy interest, a "main pillar" of Dutch diplomacy, and an "important" part of Norway's international relations. Are they? "National interest" is notoriously diffuse, but security and wealth – the bases of national power – are paramount goals. Human rights are not a vital interest; they are a lower priority goal, on a par with other vague values, such as peace and a clean world environment. Yet Canada, the Netherlands, and Norway have a reputation as principled defenders of global human rights. Their reputation is largely built on their actions in such international forums as the United Nations, the Commonwealth, and the European Union. This study contains examples of each state's U.N. activism. Norway and Canada initiated the first successful U.N. Commission on Human Rights resolution against Sri Lanka, and Canada also attempted a resolution against the Philippines and used its good offices at the Security Council on the Tiananmen issue. The Netherlands tried to use a thematic U.N. resolution as an indirect sanction against the Beijing leadership.

Standard setting and roll-call diplomacy are not, however, an adequate test of a state's determination to defend human rights abroad. They are relatively unassertive and low-cost instruments in politicized U.N. forums. As this study's "human rights hierarchy" suggests, resolve is more visible when states shift to bilateral and economic levers that potentially compromise other national interests. When these more assertive channels are considered, the reputation of Canada, the Netherlands, and Norway as human rights entrepreneurs is not as convincing as is commonly supposed. Granted, there are examples of all three states taking moral action that potentially threatened other national interests. In 1990, for instance, Norway defied Chinese pressure and sent its leaders to meet the Nobel Prize–winning Dalai Lama. Norway also acted on principle in modifying its aid to Sri Lanka, and Canada insisted that resettlement along the Maduru Oya river be equitably shared among Tamil and Sinhalese communities. The Dutch suspended ODA to Suriname when fifteen opinion leaders were murdered in December 1982, and it did so again in December 1990 when the democratic government was overturned in a bloodless coup. In the Philippines, the Netherlands risked souring bilateral relations by funnelling aid to NGOs and "people's organizations" that were suspected of links with the communist insurgents. Moreover, principles did influence the Netherlands' suspension of all new government-to-government aid to Indonesia after the Dili killings. But it will be recalled that The Hague was poised to relax this sanction just two months later. It was a diplomatic error (to seek the European Union's intercession before hearing the findings of the commission of inquiry) rather than any disposition to harm important interests that may have sealed the fate of Dutch development aid to Indonesia.

Nevertheless, most of the cases examined here suggest that Canada, the Netherlands, and Norway typically view human rights as a long-term goal, an interest often sacrificed in the trade-off among competing interests. States can and do call on many "saving lies"[1] to legitimize a "do nothing" approach to human rights, arguing that they are too small to act alone, that joint action is elusive, that publicity endangers the oppressed, that trade promotes human rights, that alliances preclude assertive action, that preserving bilateral relations requires quiet diplomacy, that states have different cultural values, that sovereignty must be respected, that repressive order may be preferable to instability … and so on.

The empirical evidence in this study validates realist scepticism about the ethical conduct of states. A hypothesis linking assertiveness to perceived costs was tested by selecting cases which, on *prima facie* evidence, would be most likely to disprove realist assumptions. Canada, the Netherlands, and Norway combine a vocation of internationalism and a professed commitment to human rights with no overriding geopolitical interests and with only modest commercial interests in the developing world. These attributes make them well placed to adopt a relatively more assertive human rights diplomacy than the U.S. superpower or economic giants such as Japan and Germany. By showing that Canada, the Netherlands, and Norway are disinclined to adopt assertive policies at the expense of competing national interests, I have demonstrated that these internationalists are states like any other, driven principally by self-interest and prudence, not altruism. This finding qualifies Lumsdaine's broad interpretation of the foreign aid regime as being driven overwhelmingly by benign humanitarian principles.

Unquestionably, there is a growing donor consensus among the OECD's Development Assistance Committee to the effect that "new style" participatory development efforts to promote human rights and independent civil societies can play a vital role in sustaining economic development. This is reflected in coordination at the level of norms and evaluation. But there is a more equivocal story when it comes to defending human rights. Hard-nosed language justifying human rights conditionality has not been matched by consistent or coordinated donor action. The tactic of coordinated political pressure through the consultative groups continues to be applied unevenly for some very instrumental reasons. Donor leverage is greatest in aid-dependent countries. By contrast, in countries that pose significant commercial or political problems for the donor, the consultative groups have largely been silent on human rights. While the groups have proved to be a useful mechanism for defending human rights in weak African states such as Kenya and Malawi, they have been all but silent against powerful countries such as Indonesia. Although some small states, such as Canada, the Netherlands, and Denmark, were prepared to go it alone in tying aid to improved human rights in East Timor, the major players were not. Contrary to Lumsdaine's view, countries are not often "swayed to do what is right by pressure of international opinion."[2] What is true at the level of multilateral aid coordination is also substantially true at the level of government-to-government diplomacy.

Realist premises help explain why the Dutch suspended aid to Suriname in 1982 and 1990. Dutch trade and investment was modest, whereas aid accounted for nearly 20 per cent of Bouterse's budget. Moreover, few countries were interested in Suriname's fate, and there were not many others that could have been threatened by punitive Dutch actions as well as the economically weak and diplomatically isolated Suriname. In fact, other bilateral donors backed the Netherlands by freezing their small aid programs. These unique circumstances gave the Dutch political leverage and the policy independence to put moral considerations at the top of their priorities list. They were free to use a relatively assertive human rights instrument. Suriname is thus a rare instance in which realist calculations combined with idealist convictions to produce a morally principled diplomacy.

Dutch and Canadian aid to the Philippines illustrates the vicissitudes of promoting human rights and democratic development. Aid is not neutral in a protracted armed conflict. Shifting aid through NGOs does not solve this problem; it merely transfers it to another setting. In a deeply polarized environment, donors face criticism whichever end of the political spectrum they support. The Philippines government criticized Dutch NGO aid to human rights monitors on the grounds that it was strengthening groups who were biased in their reporting and were linked to communist insurgents. The Netherlands Ministry of Development Cooperation may have colluded with its "co-financing" partners to downplay domestic and Filipino criticism. Similarly, some NGOs and Filipino people's organizations criticized Canada's Negros program for perpetuating dependency and supporting planter groups with vigilante connections. CIDA's difficulties stemmed principally from inexperience and from disbursement pressures, which prevented a detailed appraisal of Negros' complex politics. The Negros experience led to some institutional learning (suggested by CIDA's decentralizing its activities to Manila) and to increasing the funding for NGOs while relaxing control of them through a "partnership" mechanism with Canadian and Filipino aid groups. For his part, Jan Pronk, the Netherlands minister of development cooperation, wanted to work with more centre-left Filipino groups, and the Dutch looked at Canada's "partnership" mechanism as a possible way to coordinate their programs in the Philippines.

In Sri Lanka, human rights were only occasionally salient in Norwegian and Canadian diplomacy. Although commercial and security interests were negligible, giving each donor a relatively free hand to craft a principled response, neither Norway nor Canada could galvanize other donors into coordinated action that would pave the way for assertive, unilateral measures. Norway modified its aid program to avoid complicity with a repressive regime. Canada initially appeared to be more agnostic on human rights violations, though it did attach equity conditions to its Maduru Oya project in an attempt to prevent discriminatory land settlement ratios from further inflaming ethnic hostility. By the late 1980s, project viability and personnel safety, not human rights, had led to the reduction of Norwegian and Canadian aid to Sri Lanka.

China was the most searching test of the Canadian, Dutch, and Norwegian resolve to defend human rights abroad. Intense commercial interests, trade-driven aid programs, sensitivity to China's geopolitical significance, the demands of international coordination, and concern about reprisals were the competing interests that were likely to trump domestic pressures for an assertive human rights diplomacy. Tiananmen Square produced, nevertheless, the most wide-ranging human rights statecraft by Canada, the Netherlands, and Norway among the cases considered here. Moreover, each actor pulled several moderate and high-assertiveness levers – a finding apparently at odds with realist predictions. A closer reading shows, however, that the economic or political sacrifices for such resolve were not exacting.

The danger of Chinese reprisal was reduced by collective action, such as the OECD and G7 freeze on IFI credits, and the European Community's freeze on export credits. Canada closed down three aid projects with a minimal loss to Canadian exports. External Affairs Minister Clark's three criteria meant that the Export Development Corporation was not subjected to a comprehensive freeze on new credits as were the Dutch and Norwegian export-credit agencies. Before 4 June 1989, Dutch aid to China had been mostly mixed credits, and compliance with the EC policy thus led to minimal earnings or job losses because the mixed-credit allocation for China had largely been used up. Norway did not have to follow the EC policy but chose to anyway. While this resolve did result in immediate losses, even here domestic pressures led to some relaxation of the mixed-credit restrictions by the new Syse government.

In sum, it is doubtful whether Canada, Norway, and the Netherlands would have taken such a range of actions against China without the security of knowing that they were in good company. On Tibet, however, these internationalists were substantially silent. Tibetans have suffered no less than the students in Tiananmen Square, but they have not caught the media's attention with the same intensity. Treaty obligations and the potential costs of unilateral action to commercial interests mark the limits of Canadian, Dutch, and Norwegian altruism.

These internationalists are not poised to transcend "the paradox of unrealized power" in defending human rights abroad. To project convincingly a "responsible radicalism," Canada, the Netherlands, and Norway would have to accept costs to other national interests and be more routinely assertive against repressive Third World states. Nothing in this study suggests that they are consistently prepared to do so. Indeed, the fact that Sri Lanka is the only example of Norwegian willingness to use aid as a punitive lever and that Suriname is the principal example of Dutch resolve on human rights conditionality is indicative of the perceived weakness, not power, of these states. Small states are perhaps more dependent on good bilateral relations than larger powers. Vulnerability does not, ipso facto, disqualify assertive action, but it does raise the costs.

Until 1991, all three Western donors had avoided unilaterally assertive action against repressive states that had the capacity or proclivity to retaliate (Indonesia, in the case of the Netherlands and Canada; Kenya, in the case of Norway). Each assertively defended human rights only against weak states such as Haiti (Canada), Sri Lanka, (Canada and Norway), Suriname (the Netherlands), and Sudan (Canada and the Netherlands). Each acted assertively against powerful states only in the company of larger Western allies (as in the case of China). What do these findings say about the explanatory power of political realism?

REALISM, ETHICS, AND HUMAN RIGHTS

Realists contend that "government is an agent, not a principal. Its primary obligation is to the interests of the national society it represents, not to the moral impulses that individual elements of that society may experience."[3] However, it is one thing for realists to caution that moralism may be interest in disguise, but quite another to disregard morals altogether. Ethics are, in fact, a subject of "enormous *practical* import; [they help] us to clarify ... convoluted and agonizing problems; to offer solutions; ... to offer grounds or reasons for the justification of actions or omission; and [they help] to determine ... the values we choose to live by."[4]

In short, traditional realists are hiding from complicated problems behind claims to empiricism. The essential claim of ethical international relations is not that there is a universal truth, a harmony of interests, or an irreversible movement towards global community. Plainly, no such millennium approaches. Grotians and Kantians simply assert that morality is a vital aspect of the study of world politics. The differences between them concern the implementation of solutions to world problems. Grotians are system reformers seeking an international society undergirded by rules, norms, and customs. Kantians are system transformers who argue that the claims of individuals take precedence over the claims of sovereign states. Realists, by contrast, are system maintainers, justifying an opportunistic approach to international law and an ends-means logic to ethics. The divide between realism and its rivals is less a matter of empirical validation than a disagreement about what forces ought to drive international relations. The issue is not so much morality or immorality, ethics or politics (realists are notoriously driven by dichotomies); the rift is normative at root. Realists have little to contribute in managing such global problems as the unbridled arms bazaar, Third World debt, famine, environmental degradation, and human rights violations. Robert Keohane justly argues that "complacency in the face of [such problems] is morally unacceptable. No serious thinker could, therefore, be satisfied with Realism," even if its explanatory power were unassailable.[5]

That the human rights diplomacy of Canada, the Netherlands, and Norway seldom matches their lofty ideals does not mean that Kantian and Grotian claims are irrelevant. It is the Grotian "quest," not the solution, that is important. Grotians search for a morally justifiable statecraft that advances ethical values without risking unacceptable damage to legitimate national interests. In the late twentieth century, realism and idealism are not mutually exclusive. Accepting the inescapable tension between ethics and interests and living with this moral ambiguity is a perennial condition of the Grotian quest. What is needed is a realism refined at a minimum by an ethics of consequences.

The realist tradition's resilience stems from its power to explain why states fail to cooperate, why cooperation is limited or breaks down, and why internationalist objectives are only fitfully pursued by egoistic states. Yet realism is weak in accounting for change in anything other than structural terms, such as hegemonic decline, or new power balances. Transnational issues such as managing the oceans, Third World development, democratization, and human rights call for international cooperation. Realists seldom grasp that international relations are driven as much by norms, customs, and opinions as by power and force. Although Louis Henkin wrongly supposes that human rights are the idea of our time (why not peace, the environment, or development?), rights are an ethical issue that is here to stay. Contrary to the realists' beliefs, the International Bill of Rights and the global explosion of human rights pressure groups have meant a shift in the agenda if not yet in the practice of states. As R.J. Vincent argues,

What this international law of human rights suggests is that foreign ministers no longer have a choice about the inclusion of human rights. They cannot escape the tension between human rights and foreign policy simply by declaring that the former have no place in the latter. They are obliged to pay attention to human rights whether they like it or not. They are bound, according to the conventions of positivist international law, by their explicit agreements and by custom and practice. This body of doctrine forms part of their social world. There is some latitude in its interpretation, but it is not open to foreign offices to look the other way.[6]

The practice of human rights diplomacy is, nevertheless, still overwhelmingly shaped by power, interest, and contingency – "factors and forces familiar to the student of international politics."[7] Activists are thus "condemned to work within a system that remains fundamentally inhospitable to the kinds of claims and challenges [they] represent."[8]

As chapter 8 underlined, the tension between human rights and foreign policy is also played out in the struggle between activists calling for greater policy participation and bureaucrats defending executive control and *raison d'état*. Both in making and in implementing policy, executive discretion is firmly entrenched in Canada, the Netherlands, and Norway. While activists have opened the policy system somewhat, the limits of participation have probably been reached. Norway has had the courage to fund an independent public reporting system, but Canada and the Netherlands have resisted such an initiative. None has adopted U.S.-style legislation to curb government aid and export promotion or private trade and investment to repressive regimes.

While each government has occasionally criticized IFI loans to repressive regimes, none appears willing to condition IFI loans consistently on human rights considerations that go beyond "damage limitation" to ensure that "adjustment" does not deepen the impoverishment of a developing nation's citizens. Donors are normally reluctant to include human rights considerations in aid consortia meetings. Norway was among the few to do so consistently at the Sri Lanka Aid Group, whereas Canada waited until 1990 before going public. The Dutch used their voice at the Philippines aid consortium, but they consistently refused to raise Indonesia's human rights record at the Inter-Governmental Group for Indonesia, which the Netherlands had traditionally chaired.

There is no better illustration of the unwillingness of most Western democracies to link human rights and trade relations than the Canadian government's decision to trade with certain Asian countries "without regard to their records on the issue of their respect for human rights."[9]

As has been argued throughout this book, a willingness to go it alone with assertive policies that may run counter to national interests is a clear marker of a state's resolve to defend human rights beyond its borders. This latest retreat from hard-won principles is simply the final step in the process, taken by a Liberal government that is at ease with a realist view on international relations (no longer the Boy Scout), coupled with an unambiguous focus on trade and job creation.

In some ways, more disturbing than the headlong retreat from principle was the absence of any effective challenge to the government, and the flawed logic, bordering on misinformation, that underpinned the retreat. The effectiveness of sanctions as an instrument to change another state's behaviour has long been questioned. However, as chapter 1 has underlined, there is no automatic connection between economic growth, human rights, and democratic opennness. The case studies of Indonesia and China acknowledged the achievements made by both countries in tackling poverty. Yet both these development dictatorships have remained politically closed and have at times been brutally repressive even as their economies have expanded. It is thus incorrect to suppose that freer trade in the 1990s will lead automatically to more open governance. Moreover, one reason why trading democracies like Canada should use their leverage to foster democratic development in emerging markets is that the security of property rights and enforcement of contracts that underpin a free-enterprise system is best constructed under democratic governance.[10]

On the related issue of military sales, guidelines on military exports also have loopholes that permit states to disregard their precepts when commercial interests are paramount, as the Dutch did in selling corvettes to Indonesia after Suharto invaded East Timor. Similarly, Canada's arms-sales controls are premised on a dubious claim that there is a difference between, on the one hand, weapons and repression technology and, on the other, military equipment for "non-lethal" purposes. Moreover, deciding when there is a "reasonable risk" that arms will be used against the civilian population is widely open to interpretation.

The Canadian diplomat John Holmes once said that "while moral values may be eternal, their application in international politics must be *ad hoc*. There is no alternative to grappling with complexity, looking at both sides of every argument and at the step-by-step consequences of each policy."[11] This is wise counsel. Nevertheless, this book has tried to show that "grappling with complexity" means, in practice, that executive discretion and competing national interests condemn states to inconsistency and unassertiveness on human rights.

HUMAN RIGHTS IN NORTH-SOUTH RELATIONS

What do the particular findings on middle-power human rights diplomacy say of the larger place of human rights in North-South relations? Recent quarrels – such as the United States' anger over Singapore's corporal punishment of an American teenager or Suharto's ouster of the Dutch – signal rights as an unwelcome irritant for emerging economies in Southeast and East Asia. At the multilateral level, the rights agendas of the North, particularly on workers' rights, are intruding on regional and global trading arangements. For the OECD democracies, rights are now a legitimate and enduring foreign policy concern. By contrast, Asian states that are industrializing under authoritarian auspices are more prepared to challenge the Western human rights lobby. Regimes in Indonesia, Malaysia, and China, for instance, have struck back to defend their sovereignty and their grip on power. A prime example was Malaysian President Mahathir's blunt refusal to consider the tenders of several British enterprises after the British media criticized his human rights record and style of governing.

At the United Nations, rights are an ideological battleground. Rhetorical consensus framed around lowest-common-denominator "declarations," "conventions," and "resolutions" do not a community of values make. And getting states to comply with human rights conventions is an even more distant aspiration. With the passing of the Cold War, the fundamental conflicts on human rights have shifted from East-West to North-South. Each camp uses the language of rights as a weapon in an ideological power struggle. The South says that socio-economic rights must prevail over civil and political liberties, and it has used its voting strength to entrench this doctrine at the United Nations.[12] The North largely emphasizes civil and political rights. As chapters 8 and 9 show, this bias applies also to Canada, the Netherlands, and Norway. But the issue goes deeper than disagreements about priorities among rights. Southern elites proclaim a "right to development," not as an individual right but as a slogan of national empowerment, a call for national self-determination free from external interference. Such slogans were used first in struggles against colonial rule, then against racial oppression, and now against economic dependence.[13] These radical restatements of the doctrine of non-intervention contradict law legitimizing international scrutiny of domestic human rights performance. Western critics see the collective "right to development" as freeing despots and dictators to trample their citizens in the name of forced-march industrialization.

Sovereignty is jealously guarded by the Third World elites precisely because it is often a legal fiction when set against the realities of "soft states" and economic and military dependence on the North. Most developing countries are a long way from resolving the crises of modernization – of state building, nation building, political participation, and economic growth. Moreover, the elites complain that the North's unwillingness to reform an unequal global economic order perpetuates material impoverishment. They blame the North for the absence of human rights in most of the developing world.

The image of a stark North-South divide must be nuanced by at least two observations. First, the South does not speak with a single voice on human rights. In Asia, countries such as South Korea, Thailand, and Taiwan are slowly democratizing. Africa also is experimenting with multiparty democracy, though democracy tethered to poverty is much more precarious. Latin America is now largely governed by democratic regimes. Through initiatives such as the Santiago Commitment to Democracy, the region is reviving a once moribund Organization of American States as a vehicle for collective security to defend democracy. The Santiago commitment calls on OAS member states to "adopt efficacious, timely, and expeditious procedures to ensure the promotion and defense of representative democracy." It has been invoked in responding to democratic crises in Haiti and Peru.

Second, governments typically reject rights, but citizens do not. Few Third World societies are immune from the idea of democracy. One positive trend is the estimated 100 million people across the South who participate in citizens' groups. As we saw in the last chapter, official donors are now taking this explosion of people power more seriously. Thus, the North-South divide is really a series of rifts between the OECD democracies, some Islamic theocracies, and emerging Asian powers such as China, Indonesia, and Malaysia.[14]

I now want to look at three arenas where some OECD democracies have clashed with the emerging economies of Asia. Two focus on multilateral settings – the 1993 World Conference on Human Rights and the question of labour rights in trade negotiations. The third arena is bilateral. The quarrel between China and the United States on human rights and the restoration of Canada's relations with China underlines how shifts in the global balance of power are being driven by rapid changes in the international political economy.

COMMON LANGUAGE, CLASHING VALUES

For an issue that is so central to the United Nations' mission, human rights have rarely been at the cutting edge of its agenda. Vienna was the first intergovernmental conference on human rights in twenty-five years. The only previous congress was held in Teheran in 1968. The World Conference on Human Rights that was held in Vienna in June 1993 was attended by more than 1,500 NGOs and led to a declaration and action plan signed by more than 180 states. The Vienna Declaration is the bell-wether of human rights today. The world conference was in part a stocktaking of the effectiveness of U.N. human rights machinery. It was also meant to reaffirm and strengthen fundamental principles and to develop an action plan to enhance the United Nations' capacity to promote and defend rights.

The four preparatory conferences leading to Vienna were marred by wrangling over the conference agenda and disagreements over the draft text and NGO access to the process. Roadblocks over procedure reflected deeper differences on substance. The draft document for Vienna was riddled with contested language on such issues as "indivisibility," "universality," and "conditionality." A community of values remained elusive. Western conceptions of human rights broadly prevailed, despite a clear fault line between the OECD democracies and a group of Asian and Islamic states. The final text says that "all human rights are universal, indivisible and inter-dependent and inter-related." It describes the "universal nature" of all human rights as being "beyond question." And it recognizes "democracy, development and respect for human rights" as "interdependent and mutually reinforcing." In a significant victory over the views of some Asian states, the Vienna Declaration affirms that "the lack of development may not be invoked to justify the abridgement of internationally recognized human rights." The quid pro quo for these concessions by such states as China, Indonesia, Iran, and Malaysia was the removal of language justifying aid conditionality and a grudging Western acknowledgment of the right to development. By insisting that "the human person is the central subject of development," the industrial democracies could live with their worry that the right to development was a code-word for non-interference that justified state repression. The Asian states also succeeded in ensuring that the Vienna Declaration qualified universality by reconciling it with national cultures: "The significance of national and regional particularities and various historical, cultural and religious backgrounds must be borne in mind." Finally, the Vienna Declaration "reiterates the need to consider the possibility of establishing regional and sub-regional arrangements for the promotion and protection of human rights where they do not already." This is a reference to Asia, the only region without an intergovernmental human rights mechanism. Asian NGOs, however, see this project as a double-edged sword, since Asian states could co-opt such machinery to reinforce "cultural particularities" and undermine the reach of "universal" human rights.[15]

In a sideshow that underlined the conflict between Asian governments and their citizenry, China tried to stop the Dalai Lama from attending the conference. But Tibet's spiritual leader confounded the Chinese by speaking at the Amnesty International tent near the conference site. In his deceptively simple manner, he mocked the distortions of those Asian governments that denied a common human condition and proclaimed a thinly disguised cultural chauvinism to justify repressive, forced-march industrialization. In his words, "It is not enough to provide people with food, shelter and clothing. The deeper human nature needs to breathe the precious air of liberty." He thus saw "no contradiction between the need for economic development and the need for respect of human rights," and he emphasized that "the rich diversity of cultures and religions should help to strengthen the fundamental principles that bind us all as members of the same human family."[16]

HUMAN RIGHTS AND TRADE: THE NEW CONDITIONALITY?

OECD countries, including Canada, have begun to condition decisions on how much aid is given to which countries and by what means on a growing list of concerns: good government, human rights and democracy, the environment, and military spending. Similar debates on conditionality now affect trade. Trade agreements are already used to control trade in hazardous waste, to reduce the use of chlorofluorocarbons, and to impose sanctions for infringing agreements on intellectual property. There is thus no logical reason why trade should not be linked to human rights.

The potential clashes between trade and human rights will take centre stage as the world solidifies into one global economy. In the United States, "increasingly, the thrust of the debate in foreign policy is economics versus human rights" rather than security.[17] As a major trading nation with growing exports and investments in many Third World markets, Canada will not be immune from the trade-offs between trade and rights. Canada's 1993 exports to Asia ($15.1 billion) exceeded the goods it sold in Western Europe ($12 billion). Promising markets in China, Indonesia, Iran, and Saudi Arabia are all in countries with atrocious human rights records. What should Ottawa do? Jean Chrétien's Liberal Party, when in opposition, had recognized the problem: "Il faut absolument que nous résolvions la contradiction permanente entre nos engagements en faveur des droits de la personne et les objectifs de la politique canadienne."[18]

Although we live in a market-driven world, the economic consequences of markets are ambiguous. They give rise to demands for democracy. They prompt a rational framework for commerce, which helps entrench the rule of law. They help rid societies of bloated, inefficient bureaucracies that stifle economic and human creativity. They hasten the growth of cities and expand communications from which emerging middle and working classes make demands for democracy. But markets also create winners and losers. Left on their own, they increase disparities in power and income. Markets can survive quite well without democracy and can be disastrous for rights.

Consider Thailand, one of the world's fastest-growing economies. In May 1993, nearly two hundred women burned to death in a Bangkok factory. They were locked inside the factory with no means of escape because domestic labour standards are simply not enforced. The victims' families have still not received compensation. Or consider Chiapas, in southern Mexico, where Mayan Indians invoked NAFTA in their bloody uprising against the government. Earlier amendments to the Mexican constitution which appeared to threaten indigenous land rights were linked by the Zapatista rebels to the Mexican government's preparations for NAFTA. Consider South Korea, where two hundred trade unionists were arrested and almost five thousand dismissed between 1988 and 1992. Many of those dismissed were from transnational companies trading in Europe and North America – Hyundai and Daewoo, for example. And consider Malaysia, whose government, with full support from foreign-owned multinational employers, has for more than twenty years refused to allow electronics workers the right to organize unions of their choice. Located largely in export zones, 85 per cent of the 130,000 electronics-sector workers are women. Malaysian Prime Minister Mahathir has denounced as traitors those trying to organize.

Consider, finally, Indonesia, where in 1992 a young woman unionist was raped and murdered after she organized a strike at an East Java factory. In 1993 a twenty-six-year-old worker was pulled from a river two days after he took part in a strike at a rubber factory. A few days later, a woman was found drowned in a pool of effluent near a West Java textile factory. The marks on her body strongly suggested her wrists had been bound and that she had been tortured.[19] Third World workers, particularly women, children, migrants, and those in the informal and rural sectors, experience these deplorable conditions in large part because they have little freedom to speak out, to organize, or to exercise genuine political choice. In 1993 alone, 4,500 trade unionists were arrested and imprisoned worldwide for trade union activity. In dozens of countries, lax or unenforced domestic standards permit foreign multinational companies to exploit those workers least able to defend themselves. These companies are able to do abroad what domestic standards no longer permit at home.

It is not clear that human rights and labour standards can be effectively reconciled with the imperatives of trade, free markets, and profits. Good corporate citizenship and responsible global governance should require trade practices that do not thrive on human rights abuses. Should profits be made by turning back the global clock to the 1930s? On one view, rich countries and their citizens have the right and duty to reject products made under cruel or inhumane working conditions. If trade agreements are used to protect property, water, trees, and air, surely it is time they are used to protect people? Yet even among concerned governments there is neither consensus nor clarity about what is at stake. The United States is the only country willing to take a clear bilateral approach to the problem. It has labour standards locked into the legislation dealing with its generalized system of preferences. As chapter 7 underlined, labour rights have been raised in U.S. trade negotiations with Indonesia. Labour rights have also been part of the larger quarrel between America and China over most-favoured-nation status.

Multilateralism is another tack, particularly for the less powerful players. Because domestic legislation is frequently wanting or simply ignored, enforceable *international* standards might help ensure that corporations do not practise abroad what they can no longer do at home. Multilateralism would be a realistic approach to defending workers' rights as the world moves towards regional trading blocs (the European Union, NAFTA, and APEC) and as the General Agreement on Tariffs and Trade is poised to evolve into the World Trade Organization. But there is no consensus on what is at stake. Some countries focus on child labour and forced labour. Others invoke minimum wages and democratic institutions or see lax labour standards as an unfair trade practice, a form of social dumping that should prompt sanctions. For their part, several Third World countries see the rights issue as a pretext for protectionism. At the July 1994 ASEAN meeting in Bangkok, the governments of the region avoided any mention of human rights in their communiqué save to note that concern for labour rights was an argument for protectionism. By contrast, the parallel Southeast Asian NGO meeting, while conceding that protectionism was a concern, nevertheless emphasized "that the ASEAN governments should be held primarily responsible for the continued violations of workers' rights, the undermining of labour standards and the degradation of the environment in their respective countries." They stated, "We believe that as long as such violations persist, then there should be considerations of human rights provisions in any trade agreement."[20]

France and the United States want to integrate labour standards into negotiations for the new World Trade Organization. The British are opposed. Canada seems comfortable sitting on the fence. Speaking in Marrakesh, Canadian International Trade Minister Roy MacLaren argued that any integration must be "based on mutual consent or it simply will not work." MacLaren was, however, clear that "the use of trade penalties to impose standards of conduct is not the answer. We must not let the World Trade Organization be recruited into such a misguided effort."[21]

HUMAN RIGHTS IN BILATERAL DIPLOMACY: BRINKMANSHIP AND ENGAGEMENT IN U.S. AND CANADIAN RELATIONS WITH CHINA

In May 1993, President Clinton kept good on a pre-election theme by issuing an executive order conditioning the renewal of China's most-favoured-nation (MFN) status "on overall progress on seven aspects of its human rights performance."[22] So began a year of heated domestic debate and bruising bilateral diplomacy. It led, in the end, to a humiliating defeat. The president not only restored MFN status without exacting the full human rights concession he had pressed for, but he also permanently unlinked rights from MFN considerations. Scarred by Somalia, baffled on Bosnia, and newly chastened on China, Clinton, by this MFN flip-flop, once again appeared to the public as a president with a fumbling, incoherent foreign policy. But it is worth remembering that Secretary of State Warren Christopher did not come away completely empty-handed. He had made progress on two issues specified in President Clinton's executive order. First, the United States and China signed a joint declaration to end Chinese exports to the United States of goods produced by prison labour. Second, China agreed to begin talks with Red Cross officials leading to their access to prisoners of conscience.[23] Beijing also agreed to provide a list of Tibetan political prisoners. These concessions would probably not have been won without the threat of sanctions.

The MFN debate provoked an odd constellation of forces in which the American Chamber of Commerce was allied to the Communist Party of China in opposition to Congress. For the business community, revoking MFN would have been, in the words of one Democratic senator, "the trade equivalent of a nuclear bomb."[24] While Beijing stood to suffer most from a curtailment of the two-way trade of US$42 billion in 1993, the prospect of retaliation would have put at risk US$9 billion of goods produced by an estimated 200,000 American workers. Some U.S. rights groups, such as Asia Watch, applauded the president's resolve, but the Chinese dissident community was divided. Writer Liu Binyan spoke in favour of sanctions. The exile group, Federation for a Democratic China, called for *permanent* MFN status to be linked to immediate action on rights. The dissident Dai Ching argued for no linkage, and so did Minxin Pei, who saw trade as promoting pluralism. Wang Dan thought the trade-rights linkage was essential but opposed the withdrawal of MFN.

The American brinkmanship on rights in China is plausibly the high-water mark of an aggressive human rights diplomacy by the OECD democracies. In fact, the abrasive and unilateral U.S. diplomacy may have done a profound disservice to human rights in China and in the Asia-Pacific region, for it strengthened the hand of the Chinese author-ities looking to blame domestic problems on the cultural imperialism of the West. It will be recalled that President Suharto used a similar strategy in getting Indonesian domestic opinion behind him when he threw out the Dutch. The limits and lessons of an assertive and unilateral human rights diplomacy were driven home to the new Liberal government in Canada, which took a very different tack on human rights as part of a larger strategy to restore good relations with China.

Jean Chrétien's government lost no time in getting Sino-Canadian relations back on track. One week after being sworn in as international trade minister, Roy Maclaren was in Vancouver speaking to the Canada-China Business Council. He then returned to Ottawa to wel-come the Chinese foreign trade minister, Wu Yi. This high-level contact signalled that Canada was finally putting Tiananmen Square behind it. "We're back in the loop," remarked Earl Drake, Canada's ambas-sador at the time of the massacre.[25] In 1994, Canada launched a major diplomatic offensive with a flurry of trade-driven, high-level visits to China: by Bob Rae, premier of Ontario; by a Quebec trade delegation; by Raymond Hnatyshyn, Canada's governor general; and by Raymond Chan, the Chinese emigré and rights activist who had been appointed a junior minister for Asia. In July 1994, Foreign Minister André Ouellet visited China as the prelude for Prime Minister Chrétien's visit in November 1994.

The Liberals see their China policy as one based on constructive engagement. Others see it as a retreat from rights and principled diplomacy. Sidney Jones of Asia Watch called it the "roll-over-and-play-dead position," complaining that "its absolutely irresponsible for Canada not to exert pressure on countries to respect human rights."[26] Whichever way you cut it, there is no doubt that trade is in the driving seat. André Ouellet complained that for too long after the massacre, Canada publicly lectured Beijing on human rights while "other countries have been much quicker to forget Tiananmen Square and ... reestablish diplomatic, friendly, cordial relations."[27] Market share was clearly on Ouellet's mind. While Canadian trade with China quietly increased by 23 per cent from 1990 to 1992, over the same period the Japanese increased their China exports by 82 per cent, the Germans by 50 per cent, and the Americans by 47 per cent.

The fundamentals of the new China policy spring from an acknowledgment of complexity. The foreign minister says that Canada's "relationship with China goes far beyond the trade versus human rights argument."[28] It must also consider China's key role in regional security issues (North Korea, the regional arms spiral, the Spratly Islands, nuclear nonproliferation, Myanmar), and the global and regional environment. The four pillars of national interest in China thus comprise "economic partnership, sustainable development, peace and security, and human rights and the rule of law." This requires a constant balancing of "mutually reinforcing" objectives.[29] While Foreign Minister Ouellet proclaimed that "we will not sacrifice one [objective] at the expense of another," there is no question that the new credo on human rights is not outspoken public criticism; it is quiet diplomacy in high-level meetings, coupled with ways of promoting good governance and the rule of law through the development aid program. As the minister observed, "The question we must now ask ourselves is this: what can Canada do to promote dialogue rather than confrontation?"[30] And he put to rest the sanctions issue: "It is our view that conditionality of trade on respect for human rights is not a fruitful path to follow." Instead of sanctions, he implied a multilateral linkage – China's entry into the World Trading Organization – "which will have standards and codes of conduct which would bind China ... [because] membership brings obligations, not just benefits."[31]

The Liberals are right to set their China policy on a new course, one that emphasizes dialogue and constructive engagement across a range of complex international issues. They are also right to explore ways in which aid can be used to promote human rights. But the Liberal government has retreated from its commitment to defend human rights, and it is wrong in supposing that its actions will have no impact. As the former secretary of state for external affairs, Barbara McDougall, put it, "Do we then abandon the field because we cannot predict a clear-cut victory, a direct cause-effect, an immediate result?

... We cannot adopt a policy of parking our principles at the border when we pick up our passport."[32]

The China business lobby in Canada and the United States vociferously peddles the dubious argument that expanded trade will "guarantee a more pluralistic society" and a decline in human rights abuses.[33] This may be true in the very long run. But by this counsel, the West should keep silent for a generation or two while China modernizes under brutally authoritarian auspices. Why anyone thinks China will be more humane once it is richer is not clear. As U.S. Secretary of State Warren Christopher, put it, "We must not assume that a free market in goods will produce a free market in ideas."[34] Nor will the cause of human rights be helped by consigning it, as a Canadian Foreign Affairs spokesman disingenuously suggested, to the quiet waters of the U.N. Commission on Human Rights. As we saw in chapter 6, Beijing has adroitly prevented any meaningful initiative on human rights at Geneva by the Western Europe and Others Group.[35]

No one is saying that the ordinary Chinese do not enjoy more freedom today than they did in the dark days of the Cultural Revolution. The larger point is that such freedoms remain tenuous; they are granted to the Chinese at the whim of their masters and can be withdrawn at any time. There are, besides, several human rights issues that require immediate and sustained attention by the OECD democracies. These include the situation in Tibet, the release of prisoners of conscience, the predicament of Christian and Muslim minorities, and the persistence of widespread torture and executions. Freedom of association is very restricted in China. And while Western governments are slowly succeeding in getting Beijing to establish commercial law as the enabling environment for market-driven growth, criminal law reform lags far behind.

In the short to medium term, there is much that responsible internationalists such as Canada can do to advance human rights in China. Near the top of this agenda should be a sustained and coordinated campaign to get Beijing to sign the international covenants on civil and political rights and on economic, social, and cultural rights. Ottawa might also explore with its business community the development of a voluntary set of principles based on international labour standards so that Canadian firms could play a constructive role in the emergence of humane working conditions in China.[36] This should be coupled with vigorous action to promote the inclusion of a minimum set of human rights in the new World Trade Organization.[37] The 1995 World Conference on Women, held in Beijing, was an important opportunity to try to expand women's rights and their freedom of speech, association, and assembly. The Chinese government showed its true colours by moving the site of the parallel NGO conference and by trying to restrict the number of women activists attending. But "the thorniest problem" in Sino-Canadian relations is "the management of value differences." Recognizing the cultural differences between Chinese and Western views on human rights, Canada should foster closer dialogue among intellectuals, artists, and business leaders. This would be a modest Canadian contribution to shaping the institutional and attitudinal framework that will underpin the Pacific order in the next century. It is "in Canada's interests that the future be shaped along Asia-Pacific rather than continental lines."[38]

At all costs, Canada must avoid a hard-nosed indifference to rights and the blind pursuit of profits. Prime Minister Chrétien's flip and unfortunate comments about Canada being "a small country" will only embolden the hardliners in Beijing. As Roger Clark, secretary general of Amnesty International Canada, stated, "Canada's public silence about human rights violations is interpreted by Chinese government officials as recognition that they were justified in crushing the democratic opposition in 1989."[39] To the question "Who can stand up to China?" we must answer, "Canada and the world."

These three narratives – on China, on the World Conference on Human Rights, and on labour standards – show that human rights are a growing irritant in North-South relations as the idea of conditionality is taken up in new arenas, such as trade and labour standards. The prospect of retaliation and brinkmanship is especially great when the OECD democracies try to challenge the new emerging Asian economies. Canada, the Netherlands, and Norway have not been immune from this North-South conflict, despite their excellent credentials in the developing world. Sri Lanka complained bitterly about the biased human rights reporting of "independent" institutes, which it took to reflect official Norwegian policy. The Philippines complained about subversive Filipino propaganda groups in Holland and about Dutch NGOs supporting legal-left groups that had links to the communist insurgents. The Aquino government saw Dutch ODA as aiding and abetting this unholy alliance. Kenya warned Norway not to make waves about the Moi regime's human rights record; it organized the Kenyan media and public opinion against Norway and obliquely threatened to close down Norwegian aid programs; and a diplomatic impasse about the political dissident Koigi wa Wamwere came to a head when Kenya broke diplomatic relations with Norway, the first country to do so in peacetime. Similarly, the Suharto government turned the tables on the Dutch, removing Holland from the chair of the Inter-governmental Group on Indonesia and closing down its bilateral ODA program. A Dutch aid program in Indonesia may not be restored in Suharto's lifetime. Although Jakarta tolerated Canada's decision to freeze planned aid projects after Dili, Suharto shut down a CIDA-funded project when the University of Guelph conducted an independent human rights audit of the project.

However, human rights conditionality is not, strictly speaking, intervention. There are no legal grounds to prevent donors from reviewing aid allocations and reducing, modifying, or withdrawing aid according to their foreign policy priorities. In fact, at a time when the aid budgets of most Western donors are shrinking, adding human rights to planning and funding decisions may be essential in order to maintain domestic support for ODA. Political aid to promote human rights is more intrusive, though such actions amount more to interference than to intervention. Nevertheless, among the cases examined here, it is striking that each donor prevailed to defend or promote human rights despite risky bilateral actions and despite diplomatic turbulence, program disruptions, and the risk of retaliation.

Western states seeking to strengthen global human rights face a fourfold predicament: the legal network is weak; the gulf between norms and practice is wide; the crises of modernization dim the prospects for internal improvement in most developing nations; and the impact of international action is modest at best. The struggle for human rights is fundamentally a domestic struggle. International action will always be supplementary to domestic struggles. But the international community can influence human rights in the Third World. To suppose otherwise would be to counsel passivity, not action.[40] For several reasons, it is a mistake to be too pessimistic. Granted, compliance cannot be enforced, the universal nature of many rights is contested, and the legal weight of most rights is notoriously "soft." I have argued, however, that two nonderogable rights, freedom from torture and freedom from extrajudicial killings, have special legal and moral force. They must be preserved at all times, even during national emergencies. Their systematic and persistent violation validates assertive responses by the international community against culpable state elites. In some circumstances, the effectiveness of a trade or aid sanction should not be judged by its ability to improve human rights immediately; its larger purpose and impact may be to undermine a government's legitimacy, to strengthen the opposition, and to serve as a precedent for subsequent international action against other rights-repressive regimes. Such assertive actions can be as much a standard setter as conventional U.N. diplomacy.

CONCLUSION

Comparative foreign policy research makes it clear that the "issue is not which paradigm operates but in what areas each is an adequate conceptualization of reality."[41] Dutch, Norwegian, and Canadian aid policies still reflect their domestic political culture of humane internationalism. But their North-South trade policies are said to be increasingly driven by commercial self-interest and are only marginally receptive to equity considerations.[42] Canada, the Netherlands, and Norway claim that human rights are central to their international relations. The evidence in this study qualifies such assertions. Their search for moral opportunity is most visible in the growing use of political aid to *promote* human rights and democratic development. But the ethical imperative to *defend* human rights beyond national borders is undermined again and again by realism's cost-benefit reasoning. Despite the leaders' claims to the contrary, human rights remain substantially a subordinate part rather than a "fundamental pillar" of the North-South policies of Canada, the Netherlands, and Norway.

This book has focused on Dutch, Canadian, and Norwegian human rights policies and practices up to the early 1990s. Since the late 1980s, there have been momentous changes in the intellectual and international landscape which have strengthened the normative global appeal of human rights and democratic governance[43] and have emboldened Western donors to attach political strings to aid giving. This constellation of influences includes (1) an erosion of the principles of state sovereignty and non-intervention; (2) the collapse of socialism in Eastern Europe; (3) the shift to democratic governance in Latin America, and pressures for multiparty democracy in parts of Africa and Asia; (4) the rethinking of "development" to incorporate sustainability and the enhancement of human potential; and (5) the normative conviction that human rights are a *sine qua non* of legitimate governance. Such immense changes had not been fully registered in the practice of the major aid donors or the "like-minded" smaller donors that have been under examination here. The case studies, set in the 1980s and early 1990s, underline the ambivalence of individual aid donors in withholding aid to governments that are culpable of endorsing systematic and persistent human rights abuses. They also reveal the dilemma of small states, which may have had little impact when acting alone, but which found it difficult to persuade other donors to act in concert with them.

By the early 1990s, the consultative groups – the gatherings of major bilateral and multilateral donors who combined to coordinate aid financing to some twenty-five less-developed countries – had evolved from forums strictly confined to economic issues and were prepared to tackle political phenomena that adversely affected the rate of returns on aid investments. In the new agenda of "good governance," the aid donors have increasingly appreciated that economic reforms may not succeed unless attention is paid to the political climate in which they are undertaken. Smaller donors such as Canada, the Netherlands, and Norway have found themselves in good company with most other OECD aid donors in temporarily withholding aid to such repressive regimes as Malawi (under President Banda), Kenya, and Zaire. A singular exception to this trend was the decision by Canada, Denmark, and the Netherlands to make symbolic reductions in their aid to Indonesia following the Santa Cruz killings in East Timor in late 1991. None of the major aid donors did so.

This principled action must be qualified by the observation that all three donors looked to the results of the Indonesian government's "independent" commission of inquiry as the signal to restore normal relations. By then, however, the Netherlands' development cooperation minister, Jan Pronk, had sufficiently antagonized the Indonesian government with the bluntness of his views that the Dutch were told to pack up and go home and to relinquish their seat as chair of the Intergovernmental Group on Indonesia, the major donor forum. The unity of the consultative groups in dealing with Kenya and Malawi and the absence of donor coordination on Indonesia simply confirms that, notwithstanding the collapse of the Berlin Wall, most donors will not deal away their trade interests by quixotic adventures to tie aid to human rights. In essence, political conditionality and indeed the entire governance agenda is written largely with Africa in mind.

These developments in the international environment do not therefore alter the broad conclusion of this study. While human rights appear as a new irritant in relations between rising Asian economies and the OECD democracies, the signs are that the West will not push this agenda too hard or too consistently. The U.S.-Chinese quarrel on most-favoured-nation status may turn out to have been the high-water mark of an aggressive human rights diplomacy. Canada clearly heeded the lesson and went out of its way to unlink rights and trade in restoring its relations with China. Moral sceptics such as Hedley Bull are thus substantially correct in their assessment that ethical claims represent a "muted voice" in a still predominantly state-centric world. While Canada, the Netherlands, and Norway are among the more activist Western states on human rights, instrumental calculations based on realist assumptions frequently undermine the prospect of there being consistent, principled diplomacy to defend the human rights of oppressed citizens and groups in the South.

Notes

1 "Declaration on China" (Paris: Summit of the Arch Communiqué, 15 July 1989).
2 "World Bank Denies Aid," *Globe and Mail*, 14 May 1992.
3 Joan M. Nelson with Stephanie Eglington, *Encouraging Democracy: What Role for Conditioned Aid?* (Washington, D.C.: Overseas Development Council 1992).
4 See Anthony Ellis, ed., *Ethics and International Affairs* (Manchester: Manchester University Press 1986); Charles Beitz et al., *International Ethics* (Princeton, N.J.: Princeton University Press 1985); and Stanley Hoffman, *Duties beyond Borders: On the Limits and Possibilities of Ethical International Relations* (Syracuse, N.Y.: Syracuse University Press 1981).
5 Fred Halliday, "Three Concepts of Internationalism," *International Affairs* 64, no. 2 (1988): 187–98. Internationalism has four variants: humane, liberal, reform, and radical. See Cranford Pratt, ed., *Internationalism under Strain: The North-South Policies of Canada, the Netherlands, Norway, and Sweden* (Toronto: University of Toronto Press 1989).
6 Note, for example, the dissonance between aid and trade relations in Dutch, Nordic, and Canadian policies towards the South. Humane internationalism is embedded in aid policy, but the reformist rhetoric on trade relations, particularly Dutch and Nordic, was insubstantial and facile in practice because the larger northern states were never likely to

endorse middle-power proposals. See Pratt, *Internationalism under Strain*, 200–7.

7 Two classics are E.H.Carr, *The Twenty Years' Crisis 1919–1939* (London: Macmillan 1951), and Hans Morgenthau, *Politics among Nations* (New York: Alfred A. Knopf 1966). Neorealist accounts include Robert Gilpin, *War and Change in World Politics* (New York: Cambridge University Press 1981), and Kenneth Waltz, *Theory of International Politics* (Reading, Mass.: Addison-Wesley 1979). A good overview is Joseph M. Grieco, "Anarchy and the Limits of Cooperation: A Realist Critique of the Newest Liberal Institutionalism," *International Organization* 42, no. 3 (1988): 485–507.

8 Ralf Dahrendorf, *Class and Conflict in Industrial Society* (Palo Alto, Calif.: Stanford University Press 1959).

9 Robert Gilpin, "The Richness of the Tradition of Political Realism," *International Organization* 38, no. 2 (1984): 290.

10 Kenneth N. Waltz, *Man, the State and War* (New York: Columbia University Press 1959).

11 Morgenthau, *Politics among Nations*, 5.

12 Compare, for example, the Canadian government's green paper *Competitiveness and Security* (1985) with the parliamentary committee's *Independence and Internationalism* (1986). Both review Canadian foreign policy and consider future priorities. The green paper, however, was produced by bureaucrats in the Department of External Affairs and is replete with realist assessments of the constraints and opportunities confronting Canadian diplomacy. The committee's work, by contrast, is more attentive to the internationalist themes historically associated with Canada's international role.

13 "Assertion" denotes a hierarchy among a large repertoire of human rights instruments. "Costs" are opportunity losses to other values or interests (Carr, *The Twenty Years' Crisis*, 159). See chapter 2 of this study for details.

14 Realists fall along a moral continuum. Cynical realism justifies international immorality. Amoralism argues that ethics are an interpersonal, not an interstate, issue. Moral sceptics such as Hedley Bull concede that ethical claims are a "muted voice" in a state-centric world. Prudentialism is an ethics of consequences. See Constantine Melakopides, "Ethics and International Relations: A Critique of Cynical Realism," in David G. Haglund and Michael K. Hawes, eds., *World Politics: Power, Interdependence and Dependence* (Toronto: Harcourt Brace Jovanovich, 1990), 511–18.

15 See, for example, Robert O. Keohane, *Neorealism and its Critics* (New York: Columbia University Press 1986).

16 For a qualified "no," see George F. Kennan, "Morality and Foreign Affairs," *Foreign Affairs*, 1985–86, 205–18; for a qualified "yes," see

Stanley Hoffman, "Reaching for the Most Difficult: Human Rights as a Foreign Policy Goal," *Daedalus* 112, no. 4 (1983): 19–50.

17 Louis Henkin, *The International Bill of Rights* (New York: Columbia University Press 1981), 1.

18 The call for rights was a key element in the unravelling of repressive East European regimes.

19 R.J. Vincent, *Human Rights and International Relations* (Cambridge, U.K.: Cambridge University Press 1986), 129.

20 Lars Schoultz, *Human Rights and United States Policy toward Latin America* (Princeton, N.J.: Princeton University Press 1981); Michael Stohl, David Carleton, and Steven E. Johnson, "Human Rights and U.S. Foreign Assistance from Nixon to Carter," *Journal of Peace Research* 21, no. 3 (1984): 215–26.

21 David B. Dewitt and John J. Kirton, *Canada as a Principal Power* (Toronto: John Wiley and Sons 1983).

22 In a large literature see, for example, Irving Brecher, ed., *Human Rights, Development and Foreign Policy: Canadian Perspectives* (Halifax, N.S.: Institute for Research on Public Policy 1989), and R.J. Vincent, ed., *Foreign Policy and Human Rights* (Cambridge, U.K.: Cambridge University Press 1986).

23 See, for example, David P. Forsythe, "Human Rights in U.S. Foreign Policy: Retrospect and Prospect," *Political Science Quarterly* 105, no. 3 (1990); James M. McCormick and Neil Mitchell, "Is U.S. Aid Really Linked to Human Rights?" *Social Science Quarterly* 70, no. 4 (1989); Steven C. Poe, "Human Rights and the Allocation of U.S. Military Assistance," *Journal of Peace Research* 28, no. 2 (1991); and Abraham F. Lowenthal, *Exporting Democracy: The United States and Latin America: Part One* (Baltimore: Johns Hopkins University Press 1991).

24 Edward S. Herman and Noam Chomsky, *The Political Economy of Human Rights*, 2 vols. (Boston, Mass.: South End Press 1979).

25 James Mayall, "The United States," in Vincent, *Foreign Policy*, 165.

26 For a comparison of U.S. and Norwegian policies, see Jan Egeland, *Impotent Superpower – Potent Small State: Potentials and Limitations of Human Rights Objectives in the Foreign Policies of the United States and Norway* (Oslo: Norwegian Universities Press 1988).

27 See, for example, Terry Nardin, *Law, Morality and the Relations of States* (Princeton, N.J.: Princeton University Press 1983); Robert C. Johansen, *The National Interest and the Human Interest* (Princeton, N.J.: Princeton University Press 1980); and John Holmes, "Morality, Realism and Foreign Policy," *International Perspectives*, 1977, 20–4.

28 Hoffman, *Duties beyond Borders*, 23.

29 Vincent, *Human Rights and International Relations*, 113.

30 Ibid.

31 Hedley Bull, "The Grotian Conception of International Society," in Herbert Butterfield and Martin Wight, eds., *Diplomatic Investigations* (London: Allen and Unwin 1966); and Richard A. Falk, "The Grotian Quest," in Richard A. Falk, Friedrich Kratochwil, and Saul H. Mendlovitz, eds., *International Law: A Contemporary Perspective* (Boulder, Colo.: Westview Press 1985), 25–31.

32 Stephen Hall, cited in Hersch Lauterpacht, "The Grotian Tradition in International Law," in Falk et al., *International Law*, 17.

33 Charles R. Beitz, *Political Theory and International Relations* (Princeton, N.J.: Princeton University Press 1979); Richard A. Falk, Samuel Kim, and Saul H. Mendlovitz, eds., *Towards a Just World Order* (Boulder, Colo.: Westview Press 1982).

34 David Lumsdaine, *Moral Vision in International Politics* (Princeton, N.J.: Princeton University Press 1993).

35 Ibid., 272, 273.

36 Ibid., 30.

37 Richard Claude and David Davis, "Political Legitimacy at Risk: The Emergence of Human Rights in International Politics" (paper presented at the Fourteenth World Congress of the International Political Science Association Convention, Washington, D.C.), 1988.

38 See Amy Gutmann, *Liberal Equality* (Cambridge, U.K.: Cambridge University Press 1980), 171, and Robert Tucker, *The Inequality of Nations* (New York: Basic Books 1977).

39 Hoffman, *Duties beyond Borders*, 20.

40 *Independence and Internationalism: Report of the Special Joint Committee of the Senate and the House of Commons on Canada's International Relations* (Ottawa: Queen's Printer 1986), 99.

41 Jan P. Pronk, "Human Rights and Development," *Review of the International Commission of Jurists* 18 (1977): 33–9.

42 Kal J. Holsti, "National Role Conceptions in the Study of Foreign Policy," *International Studies Quarterly* 14 (1970): 233–309. Middle powers traditionally have voted together in U.N. forums. For empirical evidence, see Thomas F. Keating and T.A. Keenleyside, "Voting Patterns as a Measure of Foreign Policy Independence," *International Perspectives*, May–June 1980, 21–6.

43 Carsten Holbraad, "The Role of Middle Powers," *Co-operation and Conflict* 7, no. 2 (1971): 77–90.

44 With the relative decline of U.S. global power, international regimes are the liberal institutionalist's prescription to cure the leadership vacuum.

45 Consider Norway's key role in bringing together Palestinians and Israelis in the secret meetings in Oslo that preceded the historic accord between Israel and the PLO.

46 Canada, in the Cairns group of agricultural producers trying to reduce farm subsidies through GATT; Norway, on international cooperation on the environment; both, in U.N. peacekeeping.

47 John Holmes, "What Role for Middle Powers?" (paper presented at the Third Mexico-Canada Colloquium, Mexico City, September 1984), mimeo.

48 Bernard Wood, *The Middle Powers and the General Interest* (Ottawa: North-South Institute 1988), 1.

49 Ibid., 17.

50 See Jock Finlayson, *Limits on Middle Power Diplomacy: The Case of Commodities* (Ottawa: North-South Institute 1988).

51 Stephen D. Krasner, *Structural Conflict: The Third World against Global Liberalism* (Berkeley: University of California Press 1985), 268.

52 Andrew Cooper, Richard Higgott, and Kim Nossal, *Relocating Middle Powers* (Vancouver: University of British Columbia Press 1993).

53 A possible contender might be "like-minded countries." The term is less compelling now, as Dutch policy moves closer to European political cooperation and as Canada arguably moves closer to the United States.

54 An African case – Norwegian policy towards Kenya – was planned, but official reluctance to discuss the case in depth precluded a full case study. A brief discussion of Kenya appears in chapter 8 of this study.

55 For example, Amyn B. Sajoo, "International Human Rights and Canadian Foreign Policy: Principles, Priorities and Practices in the Trudeau Era and Beyond" (unpublished DCL dissertation, McGill University, 1987), and Frances Arbour, "America's Backyard: Central America," in Robert O. Matthews and Cranford Pratt, eds., *Human Rights in Canadian Foreign Policy* (Kingston and Montreal: McGill-Queen's University Press 1988) 221–45.

56 The only exception in the Universal Declaration of Human Rights is the right of peoples to self-determination, a collective right. I have drawn here on Jack Donnelly, *Universal Human Rights in Theory and Practice* (Ithaca, N.Y.: Cornell University Press 1990), 9–27.

57 Alison Dundes Renteln, "The Unanswered Challenge of Relativism and the Consequences for Human Rights," *Human Rights Quarterly* 7, no.3 (1985): 514.

58 Verbatim comments from a public speech at the Amnesty International tent, Vienna, 15 June 1993. See also his written text, "Human Rights and Universal Responsibility," 15 June 1993.

59 For interesting differences in rich-country conceptions of democratization, compare James D. Baker, "Democracy and American Diplomacy" (address to the World Affairs Council, Dallas, Tex., 1990), Douglas Hurd, "Promoting Good Government" (article by the British foreign

secretary for the Bow Group Party Conference Special, 30 September 1990), and Joe Clark, "Human Rights and Democratic Development" (notes for a speech by the secretary of state for external affairs to the International Conference on Human Rights, Banff, Alta., November 1990).

60 Bernard Crick, *In Defence of Politics* (Harmondsworth, Middx.: Penguin Books 1964), 140–60; Robert Dahl, *Democracy and Its Critics* (New Haven and London: Yale University Press 1989).

61 Ronald Dworkin, *Taking Rights Seriously* (Cambridge, Mass.: Harvard University Press 1977), 272–3. This is not to reify liberalism; equality of condition remains elusive in all democracies.

62 In an aggregate measure of the civil and political rights performance of 120 countries, the scores of Western democracies ranged from 86 per cent (Spain) to 98 per cent (Netherlands, Sweden, Finland, and Denmark). Similarly, Third World democracies such as Botswana (78 per cent), Venezuela (88 per cent), and Costa Rica (98 per cent) compared favourably with authoritarian regimes such as Chile (35 per cent), Haiti (33 per cent), and Ethiopia (13 per cent). See Charles Humana, *World Human Rights Guide* (New York and Oxford: Facts on File Publications 1986).

63 Rhoda E. Howard and Jack Donnelly, "Human Dignity, Human Rights and Political Regimes," quoted in Donnelly, *Universal Human Rights*, 67. Their categoric assessment seems too strong, hence my qualifier.

64 For this argument, see Michael Doyle, "Kant, Liberal Legacies and Foreign Affairs," *Philosophy and Public Affairs*, 12, no. 3 (1983).

65 *Human Rights Tribune*, November 1993.

66 Consider the military's resilience in Myanmar, Thailand, Argentina, Algeria, and Pakistan, the fragility of the coup-prone Philippines, the democratic decay of Sri Lanka, and the "constitutional coup" in Peru.

67 In essence, Schumpeter's conception of democracy.

68 These distinctions are developed in Gerald J. Schmitz and David Gillies, *The Challenge of Democratic Development* (Ottawa: North-South Institute 1992)

69 For reviews, see Robert E. Goodin, "The Development-Rights Trade-Off: Some Unwarranted Economic and Political Assumptions," *Universal Human Rights* 1, no. 1 (1979): 31–42; and Donnelly, *Universal Human Rights*, pt. 4.

70 The prediction of the Kuznets curve.

71 The classic statement of this view remains Samuel P. Huntington, *Political Order in Changing Societies* (New Haven: Yale University Press 1968).

72 See the essay by Harold Crouch and James Morley on the "Dynamics of Political Change" in J. Morley, ed., *Driven by Growth: Political Change in the Asia-Pacific Region* (New York: M.E. Sharpe 1993), 277–310.

73 A notable example of such a disaster was President Nyerere's *Ujamaa* policy of forced "villagization," which trampled on rights only to see the collapse of Tanzania's agricultural sector.

74 Seymour Martin Lipset saw economic growth as a prerequisite – a necessary but not sufficient condition for democracy. Democracies are sustained by building legitimacy. See Lipset's "Some Social Requisites of Democracy: Economic Development and Political Legitimacy," *American Political Science Review* 53 (1959): 69–105.

75 Douglas A. Hibbs, Jr, "On the Political Economy of Long-Run Trends in Strike Activity," *British Journal of Political Science* 8, no. 2 (1978): 153–75. Bismarck, at any rate, took this proposition seriously.

76 Mancur Olsen, "Dictatorship, Democracy and Development," *American Political Science Review,* 1993.

77 Robert D. Putnam, *Making Democracy Work: Civic Traditions in Modern Italy* (Princeton, N.J.: Princeton University Press 1993).

78 Larry Sirowy and Alex Inkeles, "The Effects of Democracy on Economic Growth and Inequality: A Review," in A. Inkeles, ed., *On Measuring Democracy* (New Brunswick and London: Transaction Books 1991), 125–56.

79 Atul Kohli, "Democracy and Development," in Valeriana Kallab and John P. Lewis, eds., *Development Strategies Reconsidered* (New Brunswick, N.J., and Oxford, U.K.: Transaction Books 1987), 153–82. This is not to deny that newly industrializing countries such as Brazil have achieved rapid growth, albeit at the cost of state repression and extreme income inequalities.

80 See Paul Sieghart, "Economic Development, Human Rights – and the Omelette Thesis," *Development Policy Review* 1, no. 1 (May 1983): 95–104.

81 Zehra Arat, "Human Rights Trade-Offs in Developing Countries: A Comparative Study of Declining Democracies" (paper prepared for the meeting of the International Political Science Association, Washington, D.C., 1988).

82 See United Nations Development Programme, *Human Development Report, 1991* (New York and Oxford: Oxford University Press 1991). This, of course, is not to deny the considerable methodological difficulties in measuring freedom.

83 Ernst Michanek, "Democracy as a Force for Development and the Role of Swedish Assistance," *Development Dialogue* 1 (1985): 56–85; Robert Miller, *Canada and Democratic Development* (Ottawa: International Development Research Centre 1985).

84 *Development Co-operation in the 1990s: Policy Statement by DAC Aid Ministers and Heads of Agencies* (Paris: OECD 1989). The assumed synergy among these variables needs closer scrutiny, as do some of the policy

prescriptions. For a welcome (though belated) recognition that political variables may decide the fate of economic reforms, see World Bank, *Sub-Saharan Africa: From Crisis to Sustainable Growth* (Washington, D.C.: World Bank 1989); for a searching critique of the bank's "twin panaceas" of democracy and the market, see Richard Sandbrook, "Taming the African Leviathan," *World Policy Journal* 5, no. 4 (1990): 673–701.

85 Paul Streeten, "Basic Needs and Human Rights," *World Development* 8 (1980): 107–11; Frances Stewart, "Basic Needs, Human Rights and the Right to Development," *Human Rights Quarterly* 11, no. 3 (1989): 349–73; and Katarina Tomasevski, *Development Aid and Human Rights* (London: Pinter Publishers 1989).

86 Rhoda E. Howard, "The Full-Belly Thesis: Should Economic Rights Take Priority over Civil and Political Rights? Evidence from Sub-Saharan Africa," *Human Rights Quarterly* 5, no. 4 (1983): 467–90; and Jack Donnelly, *Universal Human Rights*, pt. 4.

87 P. Bukman, "The Role of Non-Governmental Participation in the Netherlands [Development] Cooperation Policy," *Informatie no. 13* (The Hague: Ministry of Foreign Affairs 1989).

88 This ethic underpins the UNDP's attempt to measure "human development." See its *Human Development Report 1990* (New York and Oxford: Oxford University Press 1990).

89 UNDP, *Human Development Report 1992* (New York and Oxford: Oxford University Press 1992).

90 The bank's focus is on enhancing state administrative capacities for "sound development management" and fostering an "enabling environment" for a market economy. See "Governance: The World Bank's Experience" (Washington D.C., 1993); "Managing Development: The Governance Dimension" (Washington D.C., 1991); and David Gillies, "Human Rights, Democracy and Good Governance: Stretching the World Bank's Policy Frontiers," in *Essays on Human Rights and Democratic Development*, no. 2. (Montreal: International Centre for Human Rights and Democratic Development 1993).

91 Compare, for example, the Arusha Charter on Popular Participation by African NGOs, the Manila Declaration on People's Participation in Sustainable Development, the Covenant on Philippines Development, and the pamphlet *Put Our World to Rights* by a group of largely Southern-based Commonwealth NGOs.

92 See Howard, "The Full-Belly Thesis," 467–90.

93 See, generally, Robert E. Goodin, "The Development Rights Trade-Off: Some Unwarranted Economic and Political Assumptions," *Universal Human Rights* 1 (1979): 31–42.

94 See Human Rights Watch, "Indivisible Human Rights: The Relationship of Political and Civil Rights to Survival Subsistence and Poverty" (New

York: Human Rights Watch September 1992), and Amartya Sen's classic *Poverty and Famines: An Essay on Entitlement and Deprivation* (Oxford: Clarendon Press 1981).

95 Joan Nelson, *Encouraging Democracy: What Role for Conditioned Aid?* (Washington: Overseas Development Council 1992).

96 On military spending, the World Bank favours a proactive approach to assist with demobilization and the conversion of military industries. Mozambique, Angola, and Ethiopia have asked the bank for assistance with demobilization.

97 See, for example, the annual *Report to CIDA: Attitudes to International Development Assistance* (Ottawa: Decima Research).

98 Nelson, *Encouraging Democracy*.

99 See, for example, Lynda Chalker, "Good Governance and the Aid Programme" (speech given at the ODI conference, Chatham House, 1990), and "Governance Working Paper," Africa Bureau Democracy and Governance Program (Washington: US AID 1992).

100 *Financial Times*, 1 October 1990.

101 Mark Robinson, "Governance, Democracy and Conditionality: NGOs and the New Policy Agenda," in A. Clayton, ed., *Governance, Democracy and Conditionality: What Role for NGOs?* (Oxford: INTRAC Publications 1994), 47.

102 For details, see Demetrios James Marantis, "Human Rights, Democracy and Development: The European Community Model," *Harvard Human Rights Journal* 7 (1994): 1–32.

103 OECD, "DAC Orientations on Participatory Development and Good Governance" (Paris: OECD 1993), 9.

104 Ibid., 23.

105 André Newberg, "Economic Development and Human Rights: The Role of the European Bank for Reconstruction and Development" (address to the Association of the Bar of the City of New York, 1 November 1991).

106 United Nations, "Secretary General's Address at the University of Bordeaux" (New York: United Nations 1991).

107 Dunstan M. Wai, "Governance, Economic Development and the Role of External Actors" (paper delivered at Queen Elizabeth House, Oxford University, May 1991).

108 Javier Pérez de Cuéllar, "Address to the University of Florence" (New York: United Nations, 22 November 1991).

109 For a development of this argument, see David W. Gillies, "Evaluating National Human Rights Performance," *Bulletin of Peace Proposals* 21, no. 1 (1990): 15–27.

110 Nelson, *Encouraging Democracy*, 62–3.

111 See Gerald J. Schmitz and David Gillies, *The Challenge of Democratic Development* (Ottawa: North-South Institute 1992).

112 Nelson, *Encouraging Democracy.*

113 Ibid., 64.

114 For example, the World Bank was forced to suspend its involvement in the Mahaweli dam and irrigation project as a result of the intensification of the Sri Lankan ethnic conflict in the early 1990s.

115 The previous option is more likely, since consensus is the modus operandi of the World Bank's loan deliberations. It is rare for votes to be cast on any particular loan, and voting is usually a sign of serious conflict among the executive directors of the bank.

116 Nelson, *Encouraging Democracy,* 90. Nelson includes many African development dictatorships and also one-party-dominant states such as Mexico and Tunisia.

CHAPTER TWO

1 A version of this section was published as "Evaluating National Human Rights Performance: Priorities for the Developing World," *Bulletin of Peace Proposals* 21, no. 1 (March 1990): 15–27.

2 These include conventions on genocide, on the elimination of all forms of racial discrimination, on slavery and forced labour, torture, and children, and declarations on the right to development and on the rights of women, workers, the mentally retarded, and the disabled. See *Human Rights: A Compilation of International Instruments* (New York: United Nations 1978).

3 "Human Rights in the 1980s: Revolutionary Growth or Unanticipated Erosion," *World Politics* 35, no. 2 (January 1983): 291 (emphasis in the original).

4 Overviews are provided by Richard P. Claude and Thomas Jabine, "Editor's Introduction: Symposium on Statistical Issues in the Field of Human Rights," *Human Rights Quarterly* 8, no. 1 (1986): 551–6; and David L. Banks, "Measuring Human Rights," in Irving Brecher, ed., *Human Rights, Development and Foreign Policy: Canadian Perspectives* (Halifax, N.S.: Institute for Research on Public Policy 1990), 539–62. An innovative framework is developed by Jack Donnelly and Rhoda E. Howard in "Assessing National Human Rights Performance: A Theoretical Framework," *Human Rights Quarterly* 10, no. 2 (1988): 214–48.

5 See Judith Innes de Neufville, "Human Rights Reporting as a Policy Tool: An Examination of the State Department 'Country Report,'" *Human Rights Quarterly* 8, no. 1 (1986): 681–99; and the annual "Critique" of the Country Reports by the Lawyers' Committee for Human Rights.

6 Bard-Anders Andreassen and Asbjorn Eide, eds., *Human Rights in Developing Countries 1988* (Copenhagen: Akademisk Forlag 1988).

7 The breadth of international human rights makes comprehensive reporting virtually impossible. Most reporting systems opt for a reduced but representative list.

8 Nonderogable rights' normative status derives from a claim that they are essential for human dignity. See, generally, Joan F. Hartman, "Derogation from Human Rights Treaties in Public Emergencies," *Harvard International Law Journal* 15, no.1 (1981).

9 W.P. Gormley, "The Right to Life and the Role of Non-Derogability: Peremptory Norms of *Jus Cogens*," in B.G. Ramcharan, ed., *The Right to Life in International Law* (Dordrecht: Martinus Nijhoff 1985), 122–5.

10 *Development Co-operation and Human Rights* (The Hague: Human Rights and Foreign Policy Advisory Committee 1987), 15.

11 Ibid.

12 Ibid. (emphasis added).

13 Ibid., 26.

14 de Neufville, "Country Report," 685.

15 Donnelly and Howard, "Assessing National," 22. See also Asbjorn Eide, *Report on the Right to Adequate Food as a Human Right* (U.N. doc. E/CN.4/sub.2/1987/23).

16 In 1990 a rapporteur for the U.N. Working Group on Indigenous Populations examined Canadian policies towards its native peoples.

17 Donnelly and Howard, "Assessing National," 228.

18 Theo van Boven has used this term for "rights whose validity is not dependent on their acceptance as subjects of law but which are at the foundation of the international community." See his article "Distinguishing Criteria of Human Rights," in Karel Vasak and Philip Alston, eds., *The International Dimension of Human Rights* (Westport, Conn.: Greenwood Press 1982), 1:43.

19 Theo van Boven, *People Matter: Views on International Human Rights Policy* (Meulenhoff: Amsterdam 1982), 181.

20 Gormley, "The Right to Life," 146. The U.N. human rights program was established "in reaction to some of the most outrageous assaults on human life ever committed in the history of mankind" (van Boven 1982, 78). The primacy of the right to life is also evident in the panoply of international instruments that attempt to safeguard it. These include the Convention against Genocide, the Nuremberg Principles, and the Geneva conventions and protocols on humanitarian law.

21 The trend, however, is to narrow the scope for derogation. See, for example, the Siracusa Principles, "Symposium: Limitation and Derogation Provisions in the International Covenant on Civil and Political Rights," *Human Rights Quarterly* 7, no. 2 (1985).

22 *For Whose Benefit? Report of the Standing Committee on External Affairs and International Trade on Canada's Official Development*

Assistance Policies and Programs (Ottawa: Queen's Printer 1987), 27–30, hereinafter called the Winegard Report.

23 In Charles Humana's ranking system, the Western democracies ranged from a human rights rating of 87 per cent (Italy, the Irish Republic) to 98 per cent (Sweden). See *World Human Rights Guide* (New York and Oxford: Facts on File Publications 1986).

24 Robert Dahl, *Polyarchy: Participation and Opposition* (New Haven: Yale University Press 1971).

25 Bernard Crick, *In Defence of Politics* (Harmondsworth, Middx.: Penguin 1964), 141.

26 Adam Przeworski, *Democracy and the Market* (Cambridge: Cambridge University Press 1991), 14.

27 Dahl, *Polyarchy*.

28 Guillermo O'Donnell and Philippe C. Schmitter, eds., *Transitions from Authoritarian Rule* (Baltimore and London: Johns Hopkins University Press 1986), 9.

29 Ibid., 71.

30 Ibid., 23.

31 Alex P. Schmid, *Research on Gross Human Rights Violations* (Leiden, Netherlands: Center for the Study of Social Conflicts 1988), 9, table 3.

32 *For Whose Benefit?* 28.

33 Ibid., 28.

34 There is no need to rehearse this well-known debate. For opposing views, see Alison Dundes Renteln, "The Unanswered Challenge of Relativism and the Consequences for Human Rights," *Human Rights Quarterly* 7 (November 1985): 514–40; and Jack Donnelly, *Universal Human Rights in Theory and Practice*, pt. 3 (Ithaca: Cornell University Press 1990).

35 Social anthropologists consider reciprocity and retribution (*lex talionis*) to be fundamental elements of human societies.

36 Johan Galtung, "On the Meaning of Non-Violence," *Journal of Peace Research* 3 (1965): 251.

37 Richard Falk, "Evolution of American Foreign Policy on Human Rights, 1945–1978," in Jorge I. Dominguez et al., eds., *Assessing Human Rights Conditions* (New York: McGraw-Hill 1979), 27; Evan Luard, "Human Rights and Foreign Policy," *International Affairs* 56 (1981): 579; Amyn B. Sajoo, "Towards a Systematic Appraisal of Human Rights Orientation in Foreign Policy," in Brecher, *Human Rights*, 115–43; Robert O. Matthews and Cranford Pratt, eds., *Human Rights in Canadian Foreign Policy* (Kingston and Montreal: McGill-Queen's University Press 1988), 14–15.

38 David Baldwin, *Economic Statecraft* (Princeton, N.J.: Princeton University Press 1986); Gerald Schmitz and Victoria Berry, *Human Rights in Developing Countries* (Ottawa: North-South Institute 1988), 8.

39 Baldwin, *Economic Statecraft*, 104.

40 Sidney Weintraub, ed., *Economic Coercion and U.S. Foreign Policy: Implications of Case Studies from the Johnson Administration* (Boulder, Colo.: Westview Press 1982), 11.

41 Cranford Pratt, "The Limited Place of Human Rights in Canadian Foreign Policy," in Brecher, *Human Rights*, 171.

42 United Kingdom. *British Policy towards the United Nations*. Foreign Policy Documents no. 26 (London: HMSO 1978), 14–26.

43 *Human Rights and Foreign Policy. Memorandum Presented to the Lower House of the States General of the Kingdom of the Netherlands on 3 May 1979 by the Minister of Foreign Affairs and the Minister for Development Co-operation* (The Hague: Ministry of Foreign Affairs 1979), 134 (emphasis added).

44 Sheldon Wolin, "Max Weber: Legitimation, Method and the Politics of Theory," *Political Theory* 9, no. 3 (1981): 406.

45 Arnold Wolfers uses the terms "possession" and "milieu" goals to describe self-interested and ethical objectives. See "The Goals of Foreign Policy" in his *Discord and Collaboration: Essays on International Politics* (Baltimore: Johns Hopkins University Press 1962), chap. 5.

46 Intervention and non-intervention may also reflect power capabilities and/or foreign policy traditions.

47 In consensus-oriented Norway, only six decision-making structures have a say in human rights policy. In the United States there are at least fifteen such structures, with conflict endemic among some. See Jan Egeland, *Impotent Superpower – Potent Small State* (Oslo: Norwegian University Press 1988), 181–2. The classic study of bureaucratic politics is Graham Allison, *Essence of Decision: Explaining the Cuban Missile Crisis* (Boston: Little, Brown 1971).

CHAPTER THREE

1 This account is from an eyewitness reconstruction. See *SIM News Letter* 2 (April 1983): 28–34. SIM is the Netherlands Institute of Human Rights.

2 Ibid.

3 Ibid., 33.

4 T.A. Keenleyside, "Development Assistance," in Robert O. Matthews and Cranford Pratt, eds., *Human Rights in Canadian Foreign Policy* (Kingston and Montreal: McGill-Queen's University Press 1988), 201.

5 This overview draws on Manfred Nowak and Theresa Swinehart, eds., *Human Rights in Developing Countries 1989* (Kehl and Strasbourg: N.P. Engel 1989), 352–75; and International Alert, *Suriname: An International Alert Report* (London: International Alert 1988).

6 An analysis of the "sergeants' revolution" is provided by a former Suriname army officer, Hugo Fernandes Mendes, in "Militair en Samenleving in Suriname," *Internationale Spectator* 43, no. 2 (1989): 91–7 (with English summary).

7 In this chapter, "core rights" are freedom from arbitrary killing and torture.

8 Nowak and Swinehart, *Human Rights*, 355.

9 *Supporting Human Rights: Human Rights in Suriname* (The Hague: Human Rights and Foreign Policy Advisory Committee 1984), 8.

10 Cited in ibid.

11 See *Amnesty International 1981 Report* (London: Amnesty International 1982), 181–2.

12 *Supporting Human Rights: Suriname*, 9.

13 Alex P. Schmid, *Research on Gross Human Rights Violations* (Leiden: Center for the Study of Social Conflicts 1988), 9–12.

14 *Report on the Situation of Human Rights in Suriname* (Inter-American Commission on Human Rights, OAS/ser.L 11.61 doc. 6, rev. 1, 5 October 1983).

15 *Amnesty International Report, 1983* (London: Amnesty International 1984), 193.

16 International Labour Organization, "Committee on the Freedom of Association, 230th Report" (GB 224/9/17, 224th session, Geneva, 15–18 November 1983, case no. 1160), 107–31.

17 *Annual Report of the Inter-American Commission on Human Rights, 1986–87* (Washington, D.C.: Organization of American States 1987), 262.

18 ACP refers to the Africa, Caribbean, and Pacific countries that participate in the EC's development fund under the Lomé Convention. Suriname was a potential addition to the group, with aid eligibility partly dependent on the restoration of democratic rule.

19 U.S. State Department, *Country Reports on Human Rights Practices for 1988* (Washington D.C.: U.S. State Department 1989), 607.

20 Ibid., 614.

21 Ibid., 608–9.

22 Ibid., 608.

23 Ibid., 611.

24 International Alert, *Suriname*, 27. For a description of the army raids on Maroon villages, see Amnesty International, *Suriname: Violations of Human Rights* (London: Amnesty International, series AMR 48/02/1987).

25 U.S. State Department, *Country Reports*, 611.

26 *Bosnegers* are "bush negroes," the Dutch term for the Maroons.

27 *Overeenkomst tussen het Koninkrijk der Nederlanden en de Republiek Suriname betreffende Ontwikkellingssamenwerking.* Paramaribo, 25

November 1975. Other treaties were also signed on police and military issues.

28 *Supporting Human Rights: Suriname*, 16.

29 Article 5 of the *Tractenblad*.

30 Interview with a Dutch official, 12 May 1989.

31 The material in this section draws heavily on interviews with Dutch foreign ministry and aid officials and with Jan Nico van Overbeeke, Foreign Affairs Committee, Netherlands Parliament, October 1989.

32 Cited in *Supporting Human Rights: Suriname*, 1.

33 "Recent Events in Suriname" (report of a discussion, Lower House of Parliament, 1982–83 session, 17 723, no. 1), 2.

34 Interview with a former Canadian high commissioner to Guyana, Ottawa, 6 February 1990.

35 Ibid.

36 See the letter dated 23 February 1983 from the representative of the Netherlands to the 39th session of the U.N. Commission on Human Rights (U.N. doc. E/CN.4/1983/55).

37 Interview with a Dutch foreign ministry official, 12 May 1989.

38 Written communication from a retired Dutch foreign ministry official, 5 June 1990.

39 As outlined in an internal document, *Suriname: A Proposal for Economic Reform* (Washington, D.C.: World Bank Report no. 7635-Sur, 31 August 1989).

40 *Development Cooperation Budget 1989. Informatie no. 25* (The Hague: Ministry of Foreign Affairs 1989).

41 Interview with Dutch aid official, The Hague, October 1989.

42 Interview with Jan Nico van Overbeeke, The Hague, October 1989.

43 Interview with a foreign ministry official, 5 May 1989.

44 Overbeeke interview, 1989.

45 Telephone interview with a US AID official, Washington, D.C., 26 February 1990.

46 A favourite example among a number of Canadian policy makers whom I interviewed.

47 In 1978, Suriname produced about 6 per cent of the world's bauxite. By 1987, it produced less than 2 per cent. See *CRB Commodity Yearbook* (New York: Commodity Research Bureau 1989), 13.

48 Mendes, "Militair en Sameleving," 1989.

49 Interview with a foreign ministry official, 5 May 1989.

50 Overbeeke interview, 1989.

51 This point was stressed by a high-ranking Dutch official who was closely involved in the suspension decision, and it is noticeably at odds with the scepticism of more junior foreign ministry officers. Interview at The Hague, October 1989.

52 Tweede Kamer (Lower House of Parliament), 1978–79 session, 15571, nos. 1–2, 81.

53 See, for example, the assessment of the 1982 killings by Amos Wako, the U.N. rapporteur on summary executions (U.N. doc. E/CN.4/1985/17, annex V, "Visit by the Special Rapporteur to Suriname").

54 Human Rights and Foreign Policy Advisory Committee, *Development Co-operation and Human Rights* (The Hague: Human Rights and Foreign Policy Advisory Committee 1987), 15 (emphasis added).

55 *Supporting Human Rights: Suriname,* 16.

56 *Latijns Amerike,* 18 March 1987, 4–6.

57 Netherlands Ministry of Foreign Affairs, *Netherlands Development Co-operation Yearbook* (The Hague: Ministry of Foreign Affairs 1988), 126.

58 Ibid.

59 *Verslag Delegatie Suriname* (The Hague: Tweede Kamer, 9 December 1988), mimeo.

60 Monetary reserves were 68 million guilders compared with 400 million in 1981. Gross national income had dropped from 500 million guilders in 1980 to just 85 million in 1988. Foreign debt stood at US$1.5 billion with a debt burden of 17 per cent of national income (*Verslag Delegatie Suriname,* 9).

61 Human Rights and Foreign Policy Advisory Committee, *Development Co-operation Yearbook* (The Hague, 1988), 127.

62 Ibid.

63 Interview with a Dutch official in Montreal, 10 May 1989.

64 This view was strongly asserted by a now retired Dutch official who was involved in the decision to suspend the treaty.

65 *Latijns Amerike,* 18 March 1987, 5.

66 "Military Officers Take Control in Suriname," Associated Press and Reuters, 26 December 1990.

CHAPTER FOUR

1 The study examines the 1986–89 Aquino era. Funding constraints prevented fieldwork for an analysis of Dutch CARP (a land reform support program). A published version of this chapter appeared in David Gillies, "The Philippines: Foreign Aid and Human Rights in an Uncertain Democracy," in Bard-Anders Andreassen and Theresa Swinehart, eds., *Human Rights in Developing Countries, 1990* (Kehl and Strasbourg: N.P. Engel 1990).

2 For a mainstream analysis, see John Bresnan, ed., *Crisis in the Philippines: The Marcos Era and Beyond* (Princeton, N.J.: Princeton University Press 1986). For a grass-roots view, see Lester Edwin J. Ruiz, "A

People's Quest for Authentic Polity: The Philippines' Case," in Saul H. Mendlovitz and R.B.J. Walker, eds., *Towards a Just World Peace: Perspectives from Social Movements* (London: Butterworths 1987).

3 The coalition included the Roman Catholic bishops represented by Cardinal Sin, the former Marcos defence minister Juan Ponce Enrile, the chief of the armed forces Fidel Ramos, and a diverse group of "people's organizations" covering the political spectrum: business groups, legal advocates, human rights and electoral monitoring groups, mainstream development NGOs, "legal-left" trade unions such as the National Federation of Sugar Workers, and peasant groups such as BAYAN and KMP.

4 A good analysis of the Marcos era is David Wurfel, *Filipino Politics: Development and Decay* (Ithaca: Cornell University Press 1988).

5 In 1981 arrests numbered 1,377, in 1982 there were 1,911, and by 1983 there were 3,038. Similarly, there were 321 recorded extrajudicial killings in 1981, 210 in 1982, 368 in 1983, and 445 in 1984. In 1983 the Task Force for Detainees documented 644 torture victims, 163 massacre victims, and 102 victims of military strafing. See the figures quoted in Richard Pierre Claude, "The Philippines," in Jack Donnelly and Rhoda Howard, eds., *International Handbook of Human Rights* (New York: Greenwood Press 1987), 283–4.

6 See, for example, Amnesty International, *Report of a Mission to the Republic of the Philippines, 1982* (London: Amnesty International 1982), and William T. Butler, John P. Humphrey, and G.E. Bisson, *The Decline of Democracy in the Philippines* (Geneva: International Commission of Jurists 1977).

7 The Philippines senate later ratified the Optional Protocol of the civil and political covenant.

8 Amnesty International, *Report of a Mission*, 261.

9 *Philippines Country Report* (London: Economist Intelligence Unit no. 2, May 1989).

10 For an acute analysis of the government's land reform program, see John Cunnington and James Putzel, *Gaining Ground: Agrarian Reform in the Philippines* (London: War on Want Publications 1989).

11 Guillermo O'Donnell and Philippe C. Schmitter, *Transitions from Authoritarian Rule: Tentative Conclusions about Uncertain Democracies* (Baltimore and London: Johns Hopkins University Press 1986); see also David Wurfel, "The Philippines' Precarious Democracy: Coping with Foreign and Domestic Pressures under Aquino," *International Journal* 64, no. 3 (1989): 676–97.

12 Canada-Asia Working Group, *Annual Report 1988*, 35.

13 The Bush administration asked Congress to authorize a $658 million aid package for the Philippines for fiscal year 1990, of which $200 million would be for the Military Assistance Program. See *Foreign Assistance*

and Related Programs Appropriations Fiscal Year 1989 (hearings before the Senate Committee on Appropriations, 100th Cong. 2nd session, 244–54).

14 Vincente A. Santos, et al., *Report of the Citizens' Mendiola Commission* (Manila, 27 February 1987), mimeo.

15 Figures taken from Laurie S. Wiseberg, "Philippines Revisited: Plus ça change, plus ça reste la même," *Human Rights Internet* 13, no. 1 (1989): 22.

16 *Annual Report 1988* (Toronto: Canada-Asia Working Group 1988), 36; *Report of a Mission* (London: Amnesty International 1988), 176.

17 Lawyers' Committee for Human Rights and Asia Watch, *Lawyers under Fire: Attacks on Human Rights Lawyers in the Philippines* (New York: Asia Watch 1988), 6–7.

18 Bryan Johnson, "Atrocity at Philippine Barrio Haunts Teen-age Survivor," *Globe and Mail*, 11 July 1989. Johnson says the massacre "exposed the leftist leanings of the prominent ... Task Force for Detainees, which refused to label the Binaton massacre a human rights violation – on the grounds that it was not committed by any government agency." The task force's biased reporting was condemned by the Catholic bishops of the Philippines. See Bryan Johnson, "Bishops Condemn Rights Group's Tactics," *Globe and Mail*, 16 July 1989.

19 See Human Rights Watch, *The Persecution of Human Rights Monitors, December 1987 to December 1988* (New York: Human Rights Watch 1988), 4.

20 Hamletting is a mass evacuation, either by direct military orders or as a panic response to counterinsurgency operations. Internal refugees are casualties of the AFP's low-intensity conflict, a strategy borrowed from the United States in dealing with guerrilla insurgencies throughout Southeast Asia.

21 Cited in Canada-Asia Working Group, "Urgent Action: Massive Evacuation in Negros Occidental," *Update*, June 1989.

22 Ibid.

23 Ibid.

24 The military subsequently indicted nine of its personnel for the 1986 murder of trade union leader Roland Olalia (Lawyers' Committee and Asia Watch, *Lawyers under Fire*, 165).

25 Bautista also claimed that there was no torture in the Philippines "for the simple reason that it is prohibited by law." See Manfred Nowak and Theresa Swinehart, *Human Rights in Developing Countries 1989* (Kehl and Strasbourg: N.P. Engel 1989), 307.

26 Ironically, the Supreme Court later overruled President Aquino's discretionary power to dismiss Bautista.

27 Quoted in Canada-Asia Working Group, *Annual Report, 1988*, 32.

28 Quoted in Lawyers' Committee and Asia Watch, *Lawyers under Fire*, 143.
29 "Cory Backs Alsa Masa," *Manila Chronicle*, 24 October 1987.
30 Nowak and Swinehart, *Human Rights in Developing Countries 1989*, 297.
31 Armed, in this context, refers to standard military weapons, such as machine guns and rifles. It does not include the bolo knife, the "weapon of choice" among groups such as Alsa Masa, NAKASAKA, and the Tadtad. The bolo's handiwork is graphically illustrated in photographs of decapitations and eviscerations.
32 Guidelines on Civilian Volunteer Self-defense Organization, article 4, 30 October 1987.
33 In practice, freedom of association was circumscribed. In 1987 the president enforced the unrepealed labour laws of the Marcos regime, which virtually banned strikes. Moreover, the military considered practically all strikes illegal (Nowak and Swinehart, *Human Rights in Developing Countries 1989*, 317).
34 Amnesty International, *Report on Unlawful Killings by Military and Paramilitary Forces* (London: Amnesty International 1989), 49.
35 Lawyers Committee for Human Rights, *Vigilantes in the Philippines* (New York: Lawyers' Committee for Human Rights 1988), 165.
36 *For Whose Benefit? Report of the Standing Committee on External Affairs and International Trade on Canada's Official Development Assistance Policies and Programs* (Ottawa: Queen's Printer, 1987), 28 (Winegard Report).
37 This is the view of Roy L. Prosterman and Jeffrey M. Riedinger, *Land Reform and Democratic Development* (Baltimore and London: Johns Hopkins University Press 1987).
38 For an optic on the NDF, see "Inside the Revolution," *South*, November 1988, 20–3, and "Movement without Momentum," *South*, February 1989, 53–4.
39 A point repeatedly stressed by Canadian officials defending a lacklustre record on human rights diplomacy. See, for example, CIDA *Philippines Briefing for NGOs* (Hull: CIDA 1989).
40 In 1988, Canada was the twelfth-largest trading partner of the Philippines. Exports valued at $131.016 million were offset by Philippine imports valued at $178.351 million, producing a negative trade balance of –$47.335 million. Canada's market share increased from 0.84 per cent in 1986 to 1.05 per cent in 1988. The principal Canadian business opportunities were in power, communications and informatics, agriculture, and mining (Asia-Pacific Foundation *Backgrounder* and External Affairs data).
41 The trade balance was in the Philippines' favour. Canadian exports were $50 million in 1986, climbing to $131 million by 1988. Philippine

exports to Canada were $109 million in 1986, climbing to $178 million in 1988.

42 Her retinue consisted of seven senior ministers and thirty-five top Philippine business leaders.

43 This is the common denominator revealed by interviews with officials at CIDA, the Department of External Affairs, and the Department of Finance.

44 Both objectives were outlined in CIDA's aid strategy, *Sharing Our Future* (Hull: CIDA 1988).

45 The normal planning cycle is about two years.

46 CIDA, *Sharing Our Future*, 30.

47 The priorities of the government, as articulated by the National Economic and Development Authority, are (a) economic recovery; (b) alleviation of poverty; (c) generation of employment; and (d) equitable distribution of income and wealth. Emphasized are decentralized, small-scale job creation, and income generation projects, particularly in the rural areas.

48 CIDA's submission to cabinet recommending category 1 status noted that "respect for human rights and the restoration of democratic freedoms are major elements in President Corazon Aquino's programme." See CIDA, *Interim Strategy: Canada-Philippines Development Cooperation Programme* (Hull: CIDA 1986), 6.

49 *For Whose Benefit?* 28.

50 The other members were the International Monetary Fund, the World Bank (IBRD), Australia, Japan, Germany, and the United States.

51 CIDA, *CIDA Philippines Briefing for NGOs*.

52 CIDA, *Interim Strategy*, 13.

53 Ibid.

54 I am grateful to David Wurfel for explaining the political impact of changing sugar prices.

55 See Peter Laurie, "Canad-Aid: Who's Our Money Working for in the Philippines?" *This Magazine* 22, no. 5 (1988): 23–9.

56 Landowners chose the crops to be planted, organizing was discouraged, loans were to be repaid in two years instead of the customary ten, and land allocations were a minuscule quarter of a hectare per peasant. See Laurie, "Canad-Aid," 25.

57 According to Laurie, $1.7 million was allocated to planter groups and $625,000 for state agencies ("Canad-Aid," 24).

58 For example, a letter from a National Federation of Sugar Workers representative to CIDA's Philippine program manager Nita Cherniguin "wondered how you would feel if you were in the sugar worker's shoes? Would you feel that your dignity has been preserved? Would you be able to retain your self-respect if your basic needs ... were to be placed in the

hands of ... planters who have exploited you for such a long time?" (confidential letter dated 9 April 1987).

59 Caesar A. Espiritu and Clarence J. Dias, "Project Sarilakas: A Philippine Experiment in Attempting to Realize the Right to Development," in *Development, Human Rights and the Rule of Law* (Oxford: Pergamon Press for the International Commission of Jurists 1981), 207–20.

60 This criticism has come largely from legal-left organizations, such as the National Federation of Sugar Workers, and their Canadian NGO partners, including Inter-Pares and the Canada-Asia Working Group.

61 The material in this paragraph is drawn from an "in-house" CIDA study obtained through the Access to Information Act, *Philippines Case Study: Negros Rehabilitation and Development Fund* (Hull: CIDA 1989).

62 Canadian Council for International Cooperation. See *Partnership: The Philippine-Canadian NGO Consultation for CIDA's Country Program Review*, Report Submitted by the Steering Committee for the Philippine-Canadian NGO Consultation (Tagaytay, Philippines, 12–15 June 1988).

63 This line was taken consistently by officials interviewed at CIDA and External Affairs.

64 The study, prepared by an Australian official seconded to CIDA, is highly critical of the agency's role in Negros.

65 CIDA's sensitivity about NRDF links to right-wing planter groups led to the suppression of the "in-house" study on the NRDF, which was originally commissioned as a case study for a CIDA human rights training course. The study examined the NRDF "from a human rights perspective." A CIDA vice-president, in a letter to this writer, disowned the study as "not consistent" with "the firm requirement and position of the agency." He meant that the study had no mandate to examine the NRDF from a human rights lens, since Canada's human rights legislation was enacted *after* the NRDF began, and that rights were never a programming issue for the NRDF. Naturally, the study was never used as a case study for the human rights training course.

66 *For Whose Benefit?* 136. Decentralization offers more scope for local decisions on projects and could, in theory, lead to more responsive and participatory small-scale projects.

67 Canadian Council for International Cooperation, *Partnership: NGO Consultation,* n.p.

68 Interview with an External Affairs official, 14 July 1989.

69 See "Country Briefs," in *Consultations in Preparation for the 44th Session of the U.N. Commission on Human Rights* (Ottawa: Department of External Affairs 1988).

70 From a submission by the Canadian Council of Churches to the House of Commons Standing Committee for External Affairs and International Trade, cited in *For Whose Benefit?* 29.

71 Dr P. Bukman, Netherlands minister of development cooperation, "Out of the Fortress and Onto the Bridge: Interdependency and Third World Development" (address to the American Overseas Development Council, Washington, D.C., 3 April 1989).

72 Ibid.

73 The material in this section is based on interviews with Dutch aid and foreign ministry officials and with Dutch NGOs.

74 *Development Aid Yearbook 1988* (The Hague: Ministry of Foreign Affairs 1988), 186.

75 Randolf David, "The Role of International Agencies in the Philippines," in NGO *Consultation* (Ottawa: Canadian Council for International Cooperation 1989), 67–75.

76 Sison was among some five hundred Marcos-era political prisoners released by the Aquino government.

77 The *groep* is the only full-time office for the broad leftist coalition called the National Democratic Front (NDF), the political wing of the Philippine communist movement. The Utrecht-based *groep* was led by Luis Jalandoni, priest turned rebel.

78 But according to Bert Everts of the Filipijnen groep, the Dutch government did not grant political asylum to any Filipinos during Aquino's administration. Allegedly, the U.S. government pressured the Dutch to ensure that full asylum was not granted.

79 This recounting is derived from Dutch foreign ministry officials and from the Dutch foreign ministry's internal records.

80 ICCO supports the EMJP, though NOVIB supports FLAG (granting it approximately 50,000 guilders) and TFD (granting it 800,000 guilders through a consortium in which NOVIB provides 50 per cent of the funding). NOVIB also supports BATAS, a small advocacy group providing "bare-foot" legal help to farmers fighting for land access claims.

81 In contrast to Canada, Dutch development aid is handled by the foreign ministry. There is no separate aid agency like CIDA.

82 Interview with Hermann Abels, NOVIB, The Hague, October 1989.

83 Kilusang Mayo Uno means "First of May Movement" in Tagalog.

84 Letter of 5 July 1989. The KMU statement of 11 June 1989 said that it was "bothered by the aggressive media hype" and "malicious" imperialist and reactionary forces; and that despite these efforts to distort "what is really happening in China, ... the CCP [Chinese Communist Party] and PLA [People's Liberation Army] have been able to *moderate* the conflict and are now moving towards resolution of the underlying issues" (emphasis added).

85 Willem Wolters, "Marginal Notes to the Report 'Philippine People's Organizations and the Struggle for Democracy,' of the DGIS/ICCO Evaluation Team," mimeo. DGIS is the development aid component of the

Netherlands Ministry of Foreign Affairs. ICCO is the main Protestant co-financing agency.

86 Bernard Crick, *In Defence of Politics* (Harmondsworth, Middlesex: Penguin Books 1964), 141.

87 With the exception of Inter-Pares and the Canadian Catholic Organization for Development and Peace, which remain sceptical of CIDA's agenda and programs in the Philippines.

88 Australia appears to be the only government to have funded the National Federation of Sugar Workers. Private groups in Europe and Japan have also funded the trade union.

89 "CIDA Philippines Briefing for NGOs," (Hull: CIDA, 26 September 1989).

90 Interview with Hermann Abels, NOVIB, The Hague, October 1989. See also "A Situation Report on the Cordillera, North Luzon, Philippines," prepared for NOVIB by R. Reyes-Boquiren, G. Nettleton, Ma. Regalpa and R. Torres, 30 April 1988, mimeo.

91 Guilermo L., a Filipino working for PCHRD, went into hiding after receiving threats. The PCHRD steering committee met with External Affairs officials to try to ensure Mr L.'s safety. Philippines members of the steering committee noted more "fishing expeditions" by the military as part of a "trend of activities of harassment of NGOs" (PCHRD Steering Committee Meeting minutes, 24 November 1989; and an interview with Ian Filewod, the Canadian Council for International Cooperation, 15 January 1990).

CHAPTER FIVE

1 A version of this chapter has been published as "Canadian Aid, Human Rights, and Conflict in Sri Lanka," in Robert Miller, ed., *Aid as Peacemaker* (Ottawa: Carleton University Press 1992), 51–70.

2 For a detailed discussion of the roots of political violence in Sri Lanka, see David Gillies, "Between Ethics and Interests: Human Rights in the North-South Relations of Canada, the Netherlands and Norway" (doctoral dissertation, Department of Political Science, McGill University, 1992). See also James Manor, ed., *Sri Lanka in Crisis and Change* (New York: St Martin's Press 1984); S.J. Tambiah, *Sri Lanka: Ethnic Fratricide and the Dismantling of a Democracy* (Chicago: University of Chicago Press 1985); Robert Oberst, "Political Decay in Sri Lanka," *Current History*, December 1989, 425–9; and John Bray, "Things Fall Apart," *The World Today*, August–September 1989, 154–6.

3 The material in this section is largely drawn from the Nordic human rights yearbooks, *Human Rights in Developing Countries* (Kehl and Strasbourg: N.P. Engel [various years]), and *Cycles of Violence* (New York: Asia Watch 1987).

4 Joan Hartman, "Working Paper for the Committee of Experts on the Article 4 Derogation Provision," *Human Rights Quarterly* 7, no. 1 (1985): 89–131.

5 Ibid.

6 *Storting Meld*, 94 (1974–75). Ironically, it was the centre-right Christian Peoples Party rather than the Social Democrats who lobbied for Sri Lanka's status as a main-partner country. See also Jan Egeland, *Impotent Superpower – Potent Small State* (Oslo: Norwegian University Press 1988), 200.

7 *Arsmelding*, 1983–84 (Oslo: NORAD), 67.

8 Cited in Egeland, *Impotent Superpower*, 76.

9 "Willoch: Hjelpen til Sri Lanka fortsetter," *Aftenposten*, 5 August 1983.

10 The position is equivalent to deputy minister status in Canada. Saeter served as state secretary until May 1986.

11 This section is based on an interview with Saeter in Oslo on 10 December 1989. Saeter noted that NORAD, the aid agency, was also pervaded by a "non-interventionist" attitude and that the aid program was traditionally defined in technical terms, insulated from political considerations.

12 Saeter commissioned human rights activist Jan Egeland and scholar Asbjorn Eide to prepare a pilot study on human rights and development aid. Their study formed the basis of the subsequent white paper on the subject.

13 *Vart land*, 15 November 1983.

14 A senior official said that the Ministry of Foreign Affairs preferred that Norway adopt a nonjudgmental approach or at least send a clear message that abuses were committed by both sides. The official sympathized with the Sri Lankan government's position. He recognized that excesses were committed but asked if the Norwegian government "would have done any better in the same position." He was also upset that the Ministry of Development Cooperation was tackling a sensitive *political* issue, which normally would be in the foreign ministry's domain (interview at the Ministry of Foreign Affairs, Oslo, 14 December 1989).

15 Recalled verbatim by a Ministry of Development Cooperation official, Oslo, October 1989.

16 *Observations on Report Entitled "Human Rights in Norway's Main Aid Receiving Countries – 1985,"* Chr. Michelsen's Institute (Stockholm: Sri Lankan Embassy, April 1985).

17 Ibid. (emphasis added).

18 *Sri Lanka Country Study and Norwegian Aid Review* (Bergen: University of Bergen, Centre for Development Studies 1987), 2.

19 Statement of Hans Chr. Bugge, deputy development cooperation minister, 24 October 1986 (emphasis added).

20 Ibid. (emphasis added).

21 See Olav Fagelund Knudsen and Maurice A. East, "Leeway for Personal Impact: The Case of Foreign-Policy Making in Norway," *Scandinavian Political Studies* 8, no. 3 (1985): 207–21.

22 The Sri Lankans were furious about the resolution, describing it as a "Tamil-sponsored" initiative. The delegation was nonetheless confident that European governments would not sponsor a resolution which their newly acquired Tamil communities might invoke to claim refugee status. The Sri Lankans also underestimated Leandro Despouy, the leader of the Argentinian delegation, who had endured torture and imprisonment during the Galtieri military junta. See *Sri Lanka Human Rights News Letter No. 1* (Oslo, 1987).

23 United Nations, Commission on Human Rights 1987, draft report of the commission, chapter 12 (E/CN.4/1987/L.10/Add.12), 28–31.

24 Interview with a senior NORAD official, 12 December 1989.

25 See *Political Killings in Southern Sri Lanka* (London: International Alert 1989).

26 *Sri Lanka Aid Group*, mote 1, Paris, 17 October 1989. *Norsk Hovedinnlegg*, mimeo.

27 *Sri Lanka Landprogram, 1990–1993* (Oslo: NORAD/MDC, 16 November 1989), mimeo.

28 Egeland, *Impotent Superpowers*, 82.

29 *Landanlayse*, 34.

30 James C.N. Paul, "International Development Agencies, Human Rights, and Humane Development Projects," in Irving Brecher, ed., *Human Rights, Development and Foreign Policy: Canadian Perspectives* (Halifax: Institute for Research on Public Policy 1990), 275–328.

31 This perception was a strong and consistent theme in interviews with Canadian diplomats and aid personnel.

32 In 1989, there were about 11,000 Sri Lankan refugees in Canada.

33 Sheldon Gordon, "A Test for Sri Lanka," *Globe and Mail*, 7 April 1986.

34 Telephone interview with A. Tsui, World Bank official, 5 April 1990.

35 CIDA, *Country Profile: Sri Lanka* (Hull: CIDA 1989).

36 Interviews in Ottawa, January and April 1990.

37 The narrative here draws on several unusually open interviews with Canadian diplomats based in Sri Lanka between 1982 and 1987 (interviews in Ottawa, February and March 1990).

38 In 1981, the ethnic distribution in Batticaloa was Sinhalese 3.2 per cent, Sri Lankan Tamils 70.9 per cent, Muslims 23.9 per cent, and others 1.9 per cent (Colombo: Department of Census and Statistics and Ministry of Plan Implementation 1982), 32.

39 Interview in Ottawa, 17 February 1990.

40 Ibid.

41 Ibid.

42 Ibid.

43 Interview with Canadian diplomats, Ottawa, 17 February 1990.

44 The differences between the endemic bureaucratic conflicts in the U,S. system and the more muted Canadian conflicts are explored by Kim Richard Nossal in "Allison through the (Ottawa) Looking Glass: Bureaucratic Politics and Foreign Policy in a Parliamentary System," *Canadian Public Administration* 22, no. 4 (1979).

45 One External Affairs official bluntly asked, "Why the hell were we emptying $125 million a year down a rat hole like Sri Lanka?" (interview in Ottawa, 26 March 1990).

46 Ibid.

47 Ibid.

48 Interview with External Affairs officials in Ottawa, 17 February 1990.

49 Interview with a CIDA official, 9 January 1990.

50 Interview at External Affairs, 29 March 1990.

51 Ibid.

52 Ibid.

53 Interview with a government official, Ottawa, 17 February 1990.

54 Interview at External Affairs, Ottawa, 17 February 1990.

55 Ibid. CIDA began to work with Sarvodaya – a Gandhian grass-roots organization – and with South Asia Partnership, a group of Canadian NGOs active in Sri Lanka.

56 Interview at External Affairs, Ottawa, 17 February 1990. Commodity aid subsidized Canadian potash producers and helped CIDA approach – if not entirely meet – its annual disbursement quotas. While potash and food aid have developmental benefits, they are not, strictly speaking, a poverty-alleviation mechanism. The potential *non-developmental*, and possibly repressive, use of the counterpart funds seems to have been of less concern to CIDA than to the Norwegians.

57 *Consultation in Preparation for the 44th Session of the UN Commission on Human Rights* (Ottawa: Department of External Affairs, 25–26 January 1988), no pagination.

58 Speech by Ambassador Andreychuk, representative of Canada at the UNCHR, Geneva, 26 February 1990 (item 12), 10, mimeo. The speech did, however, acknowledge the "recent decision to revoke several emergency regulations, including 55FF, as contributing to an improved human rights situation." Clause 55FF permitted senior security officials to dispose of bodies without a post-mortem.

59 David Housego, "Death Toll in Sri Lanka May Be as High as 30,000," *Financial Times* (London), 17 January 1990.

60 This section draws on interviews with officials in the Humanitarian and Social Affairs Division of External Affairs, Ottawa, 30 March 1990.

61 Canada's delegate noted, however, that raising human rights might have been easier here than at IFI meetings, because the financial pledging at the aid group is made by individual donor governments using bilateral funds. The World Bank simply supervises the meeting (interview in Ottawa, 10 March 1990).

62 *Sri Lanka Aid Group Meeting: Statement by Canada* (Paris, 30 June 1988).

63 *Statement by the Canadian Delegation, Sri Lanka Aid Group* (Paris, July 1989).

64 Ibid.

65 Interview in Ottawa, 19 March 1990.

66 This list is reproduced verbatim from Government of Canada files (interview with an External Affairs official, Ottawa, 29 March 1990).

67 An internal telex, from the Canadian High Commission in Colombo to Ottawa, noted that the Sri Lankans had accepted the pull-out. "We were not left feeling we were seen by the Sri Lankans as [project] killers," the telex observed. ("Telex on Subject of Mahaweli," 2 January 1990).

68 Interview with Richard Harmston, executive director of South Asia Partnership, Ottawa, 14 February 1990. The victims were Mr M.I.M. Cassim and Mrs W.L. Fernanda. Cassim reportedly contacted SAP headquarters fearing a threat on his life just days before his murder. Fernanda is thought to have been killed for her local political work and membership of the UNP.

69 Interview in Ottawa, 29 March 1990.

70 Canadian Human Rights Commission, *Annual Report 1989* (Ottawa: Minister of Supply and Services 1989).

71 Interview in Ottawa, 27 March 1990.

72 Ibid.

73 Telephone interview with a World Bank official, 2 April 1990. The bank had allocated US$42 million to the fund from the IDA, its soft-loan window.

74 *Financial Times* (London), 1990.

75 Interview with a Canadian official at External Affairs, Ottawa, 10 March 1990.

76 Interview with a Dutch official, The Hague, 11 April 1990.

77 *Country Report: Sri Lanka*, Economist Intelligence Unit, report no. 1 (London, 1990), 21. The debt burden is partially lightened because 65 per cent of it is on concessional terms.

78 Ibid.

79 *Financial Times* (London), 1990.

80 Uganda is perhaps another example, although personnel safety, rather than rights per se, may have been a more salient factor in the departure of Norwegian and other aid donors.

81 The Sri Lankans think that India has designs on Trincomalee, the deepest harbour in the Indian Ocean. The Indians in turn are "paranoid" that the Sri Lankan's will tempt the United States to consider "Trinco" should the Philippines not renew the Subic Bay facilities. This security dimension was dismissed by a former Canadian high commissioner, who observed that both Indian and Sri Lankan policy makers have "a remarkable capacity for self-delusion" (interview in Ottawa, 17 February 1990).

82 Interview at the Department of External Affairs, 30 March 1990.

CHAPTER SIX

1 For analyses of why it happened, see Huan Guocang, "China After Tiananmen: The Roots of Political Crisis," *World Policy Journal* 6, no. 4 (1989): 609–20, and Anita Chan, "China's Long Winter," *Monthly Review* 41, no. 8 (1990): 1–14. On the lag between economic and political reforms, see Robert Benewick and Paul Wingrove, eds., *Reforming the Revolution: China in Transition* (London: Macmillan 1988), and Benedict Stavis, "Contradictions in Communist Reform: China Before 4 June 1989," *Political Science Quarterly* 105, no. 1 (1990): 31–52.

2 Hu had been among the leading reformers but fell from grace in 1987.

3 International Commission of Jurists, *The Review* 43 (December 1989): 1. This list shows that the term "pro-democracy movement" is misplaced. Multiparty democracy was not the main focus of the demonstrations; corruption and party reform were.

4 *The Review*, 2.

5 United Nations Economic and Social Council, "Information Received from Amnesty International on Violations of Human Rights in China" (U.N. doc. E/CN.4/1990/52), 5.

6 *For Whose Benefit? Report of the Standing Committee on External Affairs and International Trade on Canada's Official Development Assistance Policies and Programs* (Ottawa: Queen's Printer 1987), 28.

7 This account is drawn from archival material, from interviews with "China hands" at the Netherlands and Norwegian foreign ministries, and from J. Colijn and P. Rusman, "Arms Trade Policies (1): Submarines for Taiwan," in Ph. P. Everts, *Controversies at Home: Domestic Factors in the Foreign Policy of the Netherlands* (The Hague: Martinus Nijhoff 1985), 269–87.

8 Colijn and Rusman, "Arm Trade Policies," 274.

9 Data from the Norwegian Export Council.

10 See Asia Watch, *Human Rights in Tibet* (New York and Washington, D.C.: Asia Watch 1988). For evidence of continued abuses in Tibet, see

the report by the Dutchman, P. Kooijman, "Report of the Special Rapporteur on Torture" (U.N. doc. E/CN.4/1990/17).

11 In 1987 and 1988 he visited the Nordic countries, the United Kingdom, West Germany, Switzerland, Austria, Greece, and the United States.

12 By the late 1980s, however, the Dalai Lama had renounced any goal to secede from the People's Republic of China. The material in this section is drawn from an interview on 25 June 1990 with Dr Jens Braavig of the University of Oslo and member of the Norge-Tibet *Komite*, and two discussions with a senior Norwegian foreign ministry official, Oslo, October 1989 and June 1990.

13 "China Warns Norway," *Dagbladet*, 3 October 1988.

14 Officials declined to provide precise details, but, reportedly, several joint ventures in the shipping and oil industries were implicated.

15 Response to a question by MP Kare Kristiansen, *Storting Debates*, 12 October 1988.

16 *Aftenposten*, 11 October 1988; the quotation is from the question by Kare Kristiansen, *Storting Debates*, 12 October 1988.

17 "The Voice of China," *Dagbladet*, 6 October 1988.

18 Canada had been preceded by French recognition of the People's Republic in the late 1950s. A study of Canada's recognition of China is Francis Conrad Raabe, *The China Issue in Canada: Politics and Foreign Policy* (PH D dissertation, Pennsylvania State University, 1970). See also John Holmes, "Canada and China: The Dilemmas of a Middle Power," in Abraham M. Halpern, ed., *Policies towards China: Views from Six Continents* (New York: McGraw-Hill 1966); and John Harbron, "Canada Recognizes China: The Trudeau Round," *Behind the Headlines* 33 (1974).

19 On 20 November 1970, the General Assembly voted to give China's seat to the People's Republic, not to Nationalist China (Taiwan). Canada voted for the resolution, which passed by two votes with twenty-five abstentions (*International Canada* 1970, 202–3).

20 *International Canada*, October 1973, 262.

21 Quoted in *International Canada*, October 1973, 262–3.

22 Communiqué of 16 May 1972, *Jaarboek van het Ministerie van Buitenlandse Zaken 1971–72*, 86. Similarly, the Sino-Canadian Joint Communiqué reads, in part: "The Government of Canada and the Government of the People's Republic of China, in accordance with the principles of mutual respect for sovereignty and territorial integrity, and non-interference in each other's internal affairs ... have decided upon mutual recognition and the establishment of diplomatic relations." And point 3 reads: "The Canadian Government recognizes the Government of the People's Republic of China as the sole legal government of China."

23 The Netherlands, for example, only raised the issue of Tibet at UNCHR when a Dutch national was injured and detained during the 1987 clashes between monks and Chinese security forces in Lhasa.

24 Prime Minister Mulroney preferred to raise human rights concerns privately on a 1986 visit to China.

25 "China and Canada: The Months Ahead," press statement by the Right Honourable Joe Clark, MP, Secretary of State for External Affairs, Ottawa, 30 June 1989.

26 Ibid.

27 *Statement of the Twelve on China*, 27 June 1989, reproduced in Kingdom of the Netherlands, *Foreign Affairs Yearbook, 1988–1989* (The Hague, 1989), 82b–83b.

28 According to Lundestagt, the director of the Nobel Institution, the decision to give the award to the Dalai Lama was based partly on his "creed of non-violence" and his attitude to the peaceful resolution of Tibet's problems. Lundestagt also observed that the "growing [public] interest in China and Tibet took nothing away from the decision" (telephone interview, Oslo, 2 July 1990).

29 The subcommission is an independent expert body. Government delegations are normally present in a non-voting, observer capacity.

30 Theo van Boven, a former director of the U.N. Human Rights Centre, and Asbjorn Eide, director of the Norwegian Institute of Human Rights.

31 U.N. doc. E/CN.4/sub.2/1989/L.11/Add.1, 37th Meeting, Geneva, 31 August 1989.

32 Discussion with Norwegian expert Asbjorn Eide, Oslo, 26 June 1990. The Chinese actions at the subcommission are described by the Dutch expert Theo van Boven in *Netherlands Human Rights Quarterly*, winter 1989.

33 U.N. doc. A/C.3/44/1.50/rev.1, 21 November 1989.

34 Statement by P. van Wulften Palthe, representative of the Kingdom of the Netherlands, in the third committee of the General Assembly on agenda item no. 98 (International Covenant on Human Rights, New York, 21 November 1989).

35 "XINHUA Roundup Views Interference 'Plot' at U.N.," FBIS, Chi-89-229, 30 November 1989. See article 2 (7) in the U.N. Charter on the principle of non-intervention.

36 Paul Lewis, "China Draws Fire for Effort to Curb U.N. on Rights," *New York Times International*, 17 December 1989.

37 *XINHUA* is an official Chinese government publication.

38 *New York Time International*, 17 December 1989.

39 The resolution was supported by all Western states and by Costa Rica, Fiji, Guatemala, Honduras, Hungary, Malta, Israel, and Turkey. There

were "no" votes from virtually all other developing countries and from the USSR.

40 FBIS, Chi-89-229, 30 November 1989.

41 There are forty full-member states in the commission, with an allotted number for each region of the globe. Membership is by election, for three years, and is followed by observer status.

42 Interview with a member of the Norwegian delegation at UNCHR, Oslo, 26 June 1990.

43 One NGO arranged for a leader of the June movement to make an oral intervention – to the intense anger of the Chinese delegation. Exercising the right of reply, a Chinese delegate branded the student leader a wanted criminal.

44 Interview with a member of Canada's UNCHR delegation, Ottawa, 30 March 1990.

45 The Chinese delegation reportedly questioned the legality of an unsigned text.

46 This is permissible under rule 65, section 2, which stipulates, "A motion requiring that no decision be taken on a proposal shall have priority over that proposal." See the rules of Procedure of the Functional Commissions of the Economic and Social Council (U.N. doc. E/5975/Rev.1, New York, 1983).

47 Interview at the Ministry of Foreign Affairs, Oslo, 2 July 1990.

48 A confidential memorandum, dated 21 February 1990, from the foreign ministry to the Dutch delegation at Geneva, referred to the Australian draft as being "to our conviction rather mild" and stated, "You can co-sponsor this [text] taking into account the apparently wide support in the Commission. In the light of the previous co-ordination of the Twelve, a common co-sponsorship is logical."

49 Interview with a member of the Dutch UNCHR delegation, The Hague, 19 June 1990.

50 The argument that observer status implies passivity is weak. Observer status did not constrain the Australians from playing a lead role as "master of the text" on the China resolution.

51 Statement by Ambassador Raynell Andreychuk, representative of Canada, on item 12: "Violations in All Parts of the World" (UNCHR, 46th session, Geneva, 26 February 1990).

52 Interview with a Canadian official, Asia-Pacific Division, Department of External Affairs, Ottawa, 10 March 1990.

53 Interview with a member of Canada's UNCHR delegation, Ottawa, 30 March 1990.

54 Ibid.

55 See article 2 (7) and chapter 7 of the U.N. Charter.

56 *Proceedings of the Standing Committee for External Affairs and International Trade* 8 (22 June 1989): 912.

57 Ibid., 8 (20 June 1989): 24–5.

58 Press statement by the Right Honourable Joe Clark, 30 June 1989.

59 Interview with an External Affairs official, 6 June 1990. The Bank of China president has the rank of senior Politburo member and is a state councillor.

60 "Reforms Called Key to Canada-China Relations," *Globe and Mail*, 20 July 1990.

61 In 1983, China had the ninth-largest voting share in the IMF, just behind Canada (seventh) and ahead of India (tenth) and the Netherlands (11th).

62 As of 31 December 1988, the Asian Development Bank had approved US$416 million in cumulative loans to China.

63 Loans decisions were due by 30 June, the end of the bank's fiscal year.

64 Article 4, section 10 states: "The Bank and its officers shall not interfere in the political affairs of any member, nor shall they be influenced in their decisions by the political character of the member or members concerned. Only economic considerations shall be relevant to their decisions and these considerations shall be weighed impartially ..."

65 Renate Pratt, "Human Rights and International Financial Lending: The Advocacy Experience of the Taskforce on the Churches and Corporate Responsibility," Working Paper no. A15 (Toronto: Development Studies Program, University of Toronto 1985).

66 That is, voting for loans to "friendly" dictators but against loans to Soviet surrogates such as Nicaragua – the Kirkpatrick doctrine.

67 Interview at External Affairs, Ottawa, 8 June 1990.

68 Voting, however, is the exception, not the rule.

69 This is always a possibility against less powerful players. For example, Chile threatened to renege on debts owed to Canadian banks if Canada voted against a proposed World Bank loan to that country. For details, see David Gillies, "Do Interest Groups Make a Difference? Domestic Influences on Canadian Development Aid Policies," in Irving Brecher, ed., *Human Rights, Development and Foreign Policy: Canadian Perspectives* (Halifax: Institute for Research on Public Policy 1989), 435–66.

70 *Declaration on China* (Paris: Summit of the Arch, 15 July 1989).

71 For example, when the Chinese representative at an Asian Development Bank meeting lobbied his Canadian counterpart, he added the sweetener that China would not ask for a further expansion of its borrowing rights at the Asian Bank (interview with an External Affairs official, Ottawa, 6 June 1990).

72 This perspective was offered by a Norwegian official, who also noted that "there are limits to how far a small nation can take the lead on an issue like this" (interview in Oslo, 19 June 1990).

73 The Nordic group accounts for 5.02 per cent of the voting share in IDA, the bank's soft-loan facility, and 3.37 per cent of the voting share in IBRD. Canada accounts for 4.46 per cent of the voting share in IDA and 4.65 in IBRD. The Netherlands accounts for 3.15 per cent of the voting share in IDA and 3.65 per cent in IBRD. Both the Netherlands and Canada cast votes for a larger bloc of countries (*Europa Yearbook 1989*, 72).

74 U.S. policy seems to have shifted from opposition to normal lending to supporting "basic human needs" loans to China on a case-by-case basis, and finally to outright support for a return to normal lending. The initial U.S. position was based on section 701(f) of the International Financial Institutions Act. For an optic on the evolution of the State Department's position, see the statement by John M. Niehus, senior deputy assistant secretary of state, before the U.S. Congressional Subcommittee on International Development, 8 May 1990.

75 The investment market also registered the economic downturn. China's risk assessment was sharply downgraded from 7.6 on a ten-point scale to 5.6 by the Japan Bond Research Institute. China thus fell from a class B "little risk" country to a class C "some risk" category. See "China's Risk Rating Worsens," *Financial Times* (London), 12 September 1989.

76 Thus, a Canadian official referred to the separation as "mythical." A Dutch official said that economic liberalization in China was doubtful without more political freedom and he feared that hardliners, intent on recentralization, were "undoing" earlier reforms. A Norwegian official agreed, observing that the World Bank loan "postponements" were "not done according to the book, but we also live in a political environment" (interviews in Ottawa, 6 June; at The Hague, 19 June; and in Oslo, 28 June 1990).

77 "World Bank Lends to China Again," *Globe and Mail*, 9 February 1990.

78 Interview with an External Affairs official in Ottawa, 6 June 1990.

79 A Canadian official said that the emergency loan "does not alter our perception of the [poor] state of the Chinese economy" (interview in Ottawa, 6 June 1990).

80 Interviews with officials at The Hague, 21 June 1990, and in Ottawa, 6 June 1990.

81 One Canadian official was visibly irritated with this perception, aggressively stating that Canada was "not playing footsie with [the U.S.] Congress, we are just trying to be consistent" (interview in Ottawa, 6 June 1990).

82 "Curbs to Ease against China, Diplomats Say," *Globe and Mail*, 12 September 1990.

83 Charlotte Montgomery, "Amnesty Decries China Executions," *Globe and Mail*, 13 September 1990.

84 Data supplied by the Export Council of Norway.

85 From Department of External Affairs data.

86 Data supplied by Ministry of Economic Affairs, The Hague, 13 February 1990.

87 *China's Customs Statistics No.1 (1989)* (Hong Kong, April 1989), table 4. China held a US$382 million trade surplus in its two-way trade with the Netherlands in 1988.

88 External Affairs data.

89 Interview with a Canadian trade official, Ottawa, 26 March 1990.

90 It was approved in Storting (*Innst. S. nr. 253*, 1982–83).

91 *Jaarverslag Ontwikkelingssamenwerking* (Development Cooperation Yearbook) (The Hague: Ministry of Foreign Affairs), various years.

92 In Canada, parallel financing is used more extensively than mixed credits and consists of separately funded and administered EDC and CIDA "soft-loan" packages.

93 For a discussion of these issues as they apply to Canada and Norway, see David Gillies, "Commerce over Conscience? Export Promotion in Canada's Development Aid Program," *International Journal* 44 (Winter 1988–89): 102–33; and Stein Hansen, Peter. G. Bohm, Finn O. Bjerke, and Odd K. Ystgaard, *Parallel Financing and Mixed Credits: Evaluation Report 1.89* (Oslo: Royal Norwegian Ministry of Development Cooperation 1989).

94 The argument that primarily "industrial" ODA complements Chinese national development priorities does not negate the commercial spinoffs to the donor. At best, an argument of complementary donor and recipient goals can be advanced. At worst, a deliberate "commercialization" of development aid is at work in China.

95 Unfortunately, Dutch officials were not willing to provide details about the funds committed in China through this or other export-credit mechanisms.

96 Interview with a Ministry of Economic Affairs official, The Hague, 22 June 1990.

97 Interview with a CIDA official, Ottawa, 19 March 1990.

98 CIDA Corporate Memory database, 13 March 1990.

99 Ibid.

100 Interview with a CIDA official, Ottawa, 19 March 1990.

101 This argument has been corroborated by several officials, both in CIDA and at External Affairs (interviews in Ottawa, 20 March 1990). In fairness, small items of engineering being undertaken by the Chinese were affected by Canada's decision.

102 The Right Honourable Joe Clark, Secretary of State for External Affairs, *Press Statement*, 30 June 1989.

103 Interview with a senior EDC official, Ottawa, 24 March 1990.

104 "Cabinet Agrees to Lend China $100 million," *Toronto Star*, 2 August 1989; "Canada Gives Loans to China," *Globe and Mail*, 3 August 1989.

105 "Government Quietly Approved Huge China Loan," *Ottawa Citizen*, 12 September 1989.

106 Data from the Canada-China Trade Council show that "grandfathered" export-credit approvals after 4 June included Swedish and Spanish telephone systems valued at US$12 million and US$15 million, respectively, a West German subway construction project for Shanghai valued at DM460 million, and a U.S. Exim Bank credit of US$26 million for signalling equipment (*Newsletter*, January 1990, 3).

107 *Ottawa Citizen*, 12 September 1989.

108 Ibid.

109 Ibid.

110 Norway's officially supported export-financing system is managed by the Guarantee Institute for Export Credits, an institution similar to the U.S. Exim Bank and Canada's Export Development Corporation.

111 As of 4 June 1989, six mixed-credit projects "under consideration" were immediately frozen. A further six were closer to final approval. The grant element in these was later approved (written communication, from NORAD official, 1 August 1990).

112 The government official was not prepared to name the company (interview in Oslo, 4 July 1990).

113 An agreement could then be made at a lower bureaucratic – instead of ministerial – level between Norway and the partner government. So, in the Chengdu case, Exportfinans, Norway's export-credit agency, and FOTEC, an affiliate of the Bank of China, could seal the contract. The Chengdu mixed-credit component was valued at 150 million kroner, 85 per cent of the project's total value.

114 The ODA concessional component was 15 million kroner. Alcatel and its subsidiaries were the Norwegian contractors.

115 The reports are unsubstantiated, but the concern is a real one, and rumours are contagious in the export-credit arena.

116 Interview with a trade ministry official, Oslo, 5 July 1990.

117 According to a senior Dutch Ministry of Finance official, five cabinet ministers were involved in the policy to register disapproval of World Bank loans to Chile (interview at The Hague, 21 June 1990). In Canada, discussion regarding whether or not to abstain on a 1987 World Bank loan to Chile led to a dispute between the Departments of Finance and External Affairs, which were only finally resolved by the ministers concerned.

118 This assessment is drawn from interviews with foreign service officials in Canada, the Netherlands, and Norway. Because Western policy on

Tiananmen Square was still evolving at the time of writing, it has not been possible to explore the policy process in detail.

119 It is also evident in the muted response of each actor to human rights abuses in Tibet.

120 For example, the "peripheral-dependence" model argues that Canada's penetration by, and dependence on, the United States limits the possibility of an autonomous foreign policy. See David B. Dewitt and John J. Kirton, *Canada as a Principal Power* (Toronto: John Wiley and Sons, 1983), 28–36. In the case of China, however, international action strengthened rather than inhibited Dutch, Norwegian, and Canadian policies.

121 See the testimony of Minxin Pei of Harvard University and Holly Burkhalter of Asia Watch, before the U.S. House Subcommittee on International Development, Finance, Trade and Monetary Policy, House Banking Committee, 8 May 1990; and Marie Gottschalk, "China after Tiananmen: The Failure of American Policy," *World Policy Journal* 6, no. 4 (1989): 667–84.

122 This was the Canadian government's position at its meetings with domestic NGOs before the 1990 UNCHR meeting. See *Consultations in Preparation for the 44th Session of the U.N. Commission on Human Rights*, 22–23 January 1990, n.p.

123 The Philippines' New Peoples Army, for example.

124 For a review of the transformation of Chinese foreign policy in the 1980s, see Michael B. Yahuda, "The People's Republic of China at 40: Foreign Relations," *China Quarterly* 119 (1989): 519–39.

125 While the opportunity to do so inside China is obviously circumscribed, lobby and media groups are now active in the United States, Hong Kong, and Europe. The Hong Kong–based journal *China Spring* is one example of an opposition organization that could be aided by Western governments – though at considerable potential cost after the Chinese government became aware of it.

126 The Spanish and French were rumoured to have circumvented the EC's Madrid Declaration.

127 Data compiled from Colina MacDougall, "Partial Rehabilitation Unlikely to Halt China's Slide," *Financial Times* (London), 11 January 1990; A.M. Rosenthal, "U.S. Actions on China a Litany of Shame," *Globe and Mail*, 16 January 1990.

128 And key regional economies, such as Japan, South Korea, and Taiwan, were less prepared to follow the OECD economic sanctions. See, for example, Robert Thomson, "Japanese Banks Lend to China," *Financial Times* (London), 17 January 1990.

129 Iain Hunter, "Government Won't Meet Dalai Lama," *Ottawa Citizen*, 13 September 1990.

130 Interview at the Ministry of Trade, 28 June 1990.

131 Andrew Nathan, *Chinese Democracy* (New York: Knopf 1985).

CHAPTER SEVEN

1 *Statement of the Government of Indonesia on the incident in Dili on 12 November, 1991* (U.N. General Assembly doc. 07/PR/111491, 14 November 1991).

2 *Fact and Fiction: Implementing the Recommendations of the UN Commission on Human Rights* (London: AI Index, ASA 21/05/94, 16 February 1994).

3 In September 1993 security forces fired on 500 people who were protesting the construction of a dam on the island of Madura. Four were killed, three injured. In May 1993 a woman was murdered for leading a strike for higher wages at a watch-making factory in East Java. In October 1993 a woman was imprisoned for ten months for organizing a protest against a real estate and golf course development.

4 Terence Keenleyside, "Aiding Rights: Canada and the Advancement of Human Rights," in Cranford Pratt, ed., *Canadian Development Assistance Policies: An Appraisal* (Montreal and Kingston: McGill-Queen's University Press, 1994), 246.

5 Interview with Susan Davies, director, CIDA Indonesia Program, Ottawa, 22 July 1994.

6 See the testimony of John Tennant, Department of External Affairs, and Jean-Marc Métivier, CIDA's acting vice-president for Asia, at the 9 December hearing of the Standing Committee on External Affairs and International Trade.

7 Two of the three projects were also in a very early planning stage. All three were finally terminated by the new foreign minister, André Ouellet, on 17 November 1993.

8 Hansard, 18 November 1991.

9 Hansard, 6 February 1992.

10 Hansard, 2 October 1991.

11 As told in a meeting at the International Centre for Human Rights, Montreal, 23 June 1994.

12 On 18 September 1991, Minister McDougall had told the House of Commons, "Canada considers that Indonesian sovereignty over East Timor is a fact recognizing that there has never been a history of independence or self-determination or self-government in that territory."

13 Interview with Marius Grenius, director, South Asia Relations Division, Department of Foreign Affairs, Ottawa, 7 July 1994.

14 Ibid.

15 The IGGI was established in 1966 under Dutch chairmanship to provide balance-of-payments support in the wake of the 1966 Indonesian balance-of-payments crisis. Over the years, membership expanded, and the IGGI coordinated development aid packages.

16 Interviews with Ruud Treffers, acting director, International Cooperation, and J.J.P. de Jong, head, South Asia and Indonesian Relations Division, Ministry of Foreign Affairs, The Hague, 23 and 24 March 1994. Much of this narrative on Dutch diplomacy is drawn from de Jong and Treffers. Interpretations are my own.

17 See, for example, the debate following the presentation by Foreign Minister Hans van den Broek on 20 November 1991 in the Tweede Kamer, and the all-party debate on 21 November 1991.

18 Ruud Treffers claimed that Pronk managed to outmanouevre van den Broek to persuade cabinet to allow the statement to be made in a European Union context (interview at The Hague, 28 March 1994).

19 This view was strongly asserted by senior Dutch bureaucrats. Interviews with Ruud Treffers and J.J.P. de Jong, Ministry of Foreign Affairs, The Hague, 28 March, 1994.

20 *Jakarta Post*, 31 December 1991.

21 Ibid.

22 This section is based on interviews with Herman Abels of NOVIB, at The Hague on 23 March 1994, and with Peter van Tuijl of INGI, at Schipol on 26 March 1994.

23 Interview with Ruud Treffers, The Hague, 28 March 1994.

24 The Dili killings pale alongside those occurring in Kashmir at about the same time. Yet J.J.P. de Jong could not recall a single Tweede Kamer question on human rights in Kashmir (interview at The Hague, 24 March 1994).

25 Interview with de Jong, The Hague, 24 March 1994.

26 Professor Peter Baehr (interview at Leiden University, 25 March 1994).

27 Yaysan Pijar (Glowing Light Foundation), press release, 8 April 1992.

28 Paul Baylis, "Linking Canadian Aid to Human Rights in Asia: Vietnam, Indonesia and China" (School of Journalism, Carleton University 1993).

29 Private communication to the International Centre for Human Rights and Democratic Development.

30 Private communication to the author.

31 Christopher Dagg, "Linking Aid to Human Rights: A Canadian Perspective," *Issues* (Vancouver: Asia-Pacific Foundation), 7, no. 1 (Winter 1993).

32 Personal communication by Ian Hamilton, a staff member of the International Centre for Human Rights and Democratic Development who attended the NGO meeting in Bangkok.

33 Canadian Press newswire, 4 July 1994. An official at the International
Centre for Human Rights and Democratic Development was asked to
co-author the human rights audit, *Information on the University of
Guelph's Involvement in the Sulawesi Regional Development Project*
(January 1994). The report highlighted the "centralized dominance" of
the Indonesian government in project design and found "nothing in the
arrangements that would imply or lead to meaningful non-state participation" (60). It raised questions about Guelph's involvement in Sulawesi
in the context of the university's ethical guidelines for its international
development work. For its part, Jakarta was angry that the report went
beyond its remit to describe the Sulawesi project and that it included an
appraisal of national human rights (interview with Susan Davies, director of the Indonesia Program, Ottawa, 22 July 1994).
34 Davies interview.
35 Reuters, 18 February 1994.
36 See the "Review of Advocacy" (The Hague: INGI Secretariat, August
1992). At the first meeting of the reconfigured Consultative Group for
Indonesia, held in Paris in July 1992, only the U.S. delegation raised
human rights in its statement. The British chair of the European Community organized a private discussion on human rights with the Indonesian delegation. The Indonesian minister of the interior forbade
Indonesian NGOs from participating in the consultative group meetings
and attempted unsuccessfully to dissolve the INGI.

CHAPTER EIGHT

1 *Independence and Internationalism. Report of the Special Joint Committee of the Senate and the House of Commons on Canada's International Relations* (Ottawa: Minister of Supply and Services 1986), 6
(Hockin-Simard Report).
2 *Canada's International Relations. Response of the Government of
Canada to the Report of the Special Joint Committee of the Senate and
the House of Commons* (Ottawa: Minister of Supply and Services 1986),
71; *Human Rights and Foreign Policy. Memorandum Presented to the
Lower House of the States General of the Kingdom of the Netherlands
on 3 May 1979 by the Minister of Foreign Affairs and the Minister for
Development Co-operation* (The Hague: Ministry of Foreign Affairs
1979); *Norway and the International Protection of Human Rights.
Report to the Storting (Parliament), no. 93 (1976–77)* (Oslo: Royal
Ministry of Foreign Affairs, 1977).
3 Cranford Pratt, ed., *Internationalism under Strain: The North-South
Policies of Canada, the Netherlands, Norway, and Sweden* (Toronto:
University of Toronto Press 1989), 16, 195.

4 Ibid., 4, 198. Canadian ODA as a percentage of GNP has been declining progressively since the mid-1980s, a victim of pressures to reduce the national deficit and of growing scepticism about effectiveness and the return on investments. ODA was set at 0.34 per cent of GNP in 1995, and some analysts fear that it may drop as low as 0.27 per cent of GNP by 1997, the lowest level since 1965. See *The Reality of Aid* (London: Earthscan Publications 1995). Note also that social and economic rights find no place in Canada's Charter of Rights and Freedoms.

5 Philippe Leblanc, "Canada's Experience with United Nations Human Rights Treaties" (Ottawa: Canadian Committee for the Fiftieth Anniversary of the United Nations, November 1994).

6 Kal J. Holsti, "National Role Conceptions in the Study of Foreign Policy," *International Studies Quarterly* 14, no. 3 (1970): 233–309.

7 J.J.C. Voorhoeve, *Peace, Profits and Principles* (The Hague: Martinus Nijhoff 1979). For a brilliant discussion on the Dutch "obsession" with the "moral ambiguity of good fortune" (7), see Simon Schama, *The Embarrassment of Riches: An Interpretation of Dutch Culture in the Golden Age* (Berkeley and Los Angeles: University of California Press 1988).

8 Hans Daalder, "The Mould of Dutch Politics: Themes for Comparative Inquiry," *West European Politics* 12, no. 1 (1989): 17.

9 Helge Hveem, *International Relations and World Images: A Study of the Norwegian Foreign Policy Elites* (Oslo: Universitetsforlaget 1972), 51.

10 Ibid., 49.

11 Johan Jorgen Holst, "Lilliputs and Gulliver: Small States in a Great Power Alliance," in Gregory Flynn, ed., NATO's *Northern Allies: The National Security Policies of Belgium, Denmark, the Netherlands, and Norway* (London: Croom Helm 1985), 261. In 1992, as Norwegian foreign minister, Holst was to demonstrate this point by secretly convening meetings in Oslo betweeen Palestinian and Israeli leaders. This diplomatic breakthrough began a negotiating process that culminated in the historic peace accords in 1993.

12 Kumar Rupesinghe, "Norway in the Year 2000: The Future of Development Assistance Policies," in Rupesinghe, ed., *Development Assistance in the Year 2000* (Oslo: Institute for Social Research 1987), 9.

13 Although social democrats have ruled provincially and were catalysts in the emergence of the Canadian welfare state.

14 In the summer of 1990, experts at the U.N. Subcommission on the Prevention of Discrimination and the Protection of Minorities took the unprecedented step of asking Canadian government observers to report daily about events at Oka, Quebec, the site of a stand-off between armed Mohawks and the Canadian army. Stephen Lewis, former Canadian representative at the United Nations, described Canada's treatment of aboriginal peoples as an "Achilles' heel."

15 Tom Hockin, "Foreign Affairs: Canada Abroad as a Measure of Canada at Home," in John H. Redekop, ed., *Approaches to Canadian Politics* (Scarborough, Ont.: Prentice-Hall 1978), 87.

16 David. B. Dewitt and John J. Kirton, *Canada as a Principal Power* (Toronto: John Wiley and Sons 1983), 17.

17 Dennis Stairs, "The Political Culture of Canadian Foreign Policy," *Canadian Journal of Political Science* 15, no. 4 (1982): 685

18 Pratt, *Internationalism under Strain*, 195.

19 David R. Protheroe, *The United Nations and Its Finances: A Test for Middle Powers* (Ottawa: North-South Institute 1988), 8–9; Robert Angell, "National Support for World Order: A Research Report," *Journal of Conflict Resolution* 17, no. 3 (1973): 429–54.

20 Jan P. Pronk, "Human Rights and Development Aid," *ICJ Review* 18 (1977): 33–9.

21 Kjell Goldmann, Sten Berglund, and Gunnar Sjostedt, *Democracy and Foreign Policy: The Case of Sweden* (Aldershot: Gower Publishing 1986).

22 John Locke, *Two Treatises on Government*, ed. Peter Laslett (New York: Mentor 1988): 411–12.

23 Cited in Goldmann et al., *Democracy and Foreign Policy*, 2.

24 Ibid., 3.

25 James Rosenau, "The Opinion-Policy Relationship," in A.M. Scott and Raymond H. Dawson, eds., *Readings in the Making of American Foreign Policy* (New York: Macmillan 1965), 79.

26 Gabriel Almond, *The American People and Foreign Policy* (New York: Praeger 1965), 5.

27 Baehr, "The Dutch Foreign Policy Elite," 225.

28 Goldmann et al., *Democracy and Foreign Policy*, 5–9.

29 Goldmann et al., *Democracy and Foreign Policy*, 14–24. See also Walter Carlsnaess, "Foreign Policy and the Democratic Process," *Scandinavian Political Studies* 4, no. 2 (1981): 81–107.

30 James Rosenau, "A Pre-Theory Revisited: World Politics in an Era of Cascading Interdependence," *International Studies Quarterly* 28 (1984): 245–305.

31 Saul H. Mendlovitz and R.B.J. Walker, eds., *Towards a Just World Peace: Perspectives from Social Movements* (London: Butterworths 1987).

32 *Report to CIDA: Public Attitudes toward International Development Assistance* (Ottawa: Decima Research 1988), 16.

33 "Fighting Different Wars: Canadians Speak Out on Foreign Policy," *Review '87/Outlook '88* (Ottawa: North-South Institute 1988), 11–12.

34 *Competitiveness and Security: Directions for Canada's International Relations* (Ottawa: Minister of Supply and Services 1985).

35 Cathal Nolan, "The Influence of Parliament on Human Rights in Canadian Foreign Policy," *Human Rights Quarterly* 7 (1985): 373–90. Pratt describes the views of human rights activists and aid NGOs as a "counter-consensus" at odds with the realist assumptions of foreign ministries, but with marginal influence. See his "Dominant Class Theory and Canadian Foreign Policy: The Case of the Counter-Consensus," *International Journal* 39 (Winter 1983–84): 99–135.

36 James G. March and Johan P. Olsen, *Rediscovering Institutions* (New York: Free Press 1989). The tradition draws on the theory of organizations and is distinct from the state-autonomy literature. See also Ernst B. Haas, *When Knowledge Is Power: Three Models of Change in International Organizations* (Berkeley: University of California Press 1990).

37 March and Olsen, *Rediscovering Institutions*, 739.

38 Edwin S. Maynard, "The Bureaucracy and Implementation of U.S. Human Rights Policy," *Human Rights Quarterly* 11, no. 2 (1989): 175–248; Victoria Berry and Allan McChesney, "Human Rights and Foreign Policy-Making," in Robert O. Matthews and Cranford Pratt, eds., *Human Rights in Canadian Foreign Policy* (Kingston and Montreal: McGill-Queen's University Press 1988), 59–78.

39 Judith Innes de Neufville, "Human Rights Reporting as a Policy-Tool: An Examination of the State Department 'Country Report,'" *Human Rights Quarterly* 8, no.1 (1986): 681–99.

40 Lars Schoultz, *Human Rights and United States Policy toward Latin America* (Princeton, N.J.: Princeton University Press 1981), 119–20.

41 Goldmann et al., *Democracy and Foreign Policy*, 182.

42 R.J Vincent, *Human Rights and International Relations* (Cambridge: Cambridge University Press 1986), 133.

43 Everts, *Controversies at Home*.

44 This account draws on Peter R. Baehr, "Human Rights, Development, and Dutch Foreign Policy: The Role of an Advisory Committee," in David P. Forsythe, ed., *Human Rights and Development* (London: Macmillan 1989), 154–70.

45 Baehr, "Advisory Committee," 156 (emphasis added). The committee's terms of reference are explained in a memorandum by Minister H. van den Broek to the Dutch Parliament's Standing Committee on Foreign Affairs. See *Human Rights and Foreign Policy: Establishing an Advisory Committee* (The Hague: Ministry of Foreign Affairs 1982).

46 Speech by Foreign Minister H. van den Broek at the inauguration of the provisional Advisory Committee on Human Rights and Foreign Policy, The Hague, 21 April 1983 (emphasis in the original).

47 Baehr, "Advisory Committee," 157.

48 *Establishing an Advisory Committee*, 11.

49 Baehr, "Advisory Committee," 159.

50 Ibid., 164–5. The foreign ministry attempted, unsuccessfully, to block the committee on procedural grounds (interview with Peter Baehr, Leiden, October 1989).

51 Reconciling differences between, on the one hand, defence and foreign ministry officials and, on the other hand, activists proved almost impossible during the cruise missile debate. There were hints that the government might try to dismantle the council (interview with council member Prof. Ph. P. Everts, Leiden University, October 1989).

52 The terms of reference encourage the committee to give "further attention to the instruments of human rights policy" and to "consider whether it is possible to state criteria or priorities [to] clarify the relationship between human rights and other aspects of government policy" (*Explanatory Memorandum*, 10–11). A committee study on trade and human rights has also been undertaken.

53 *For Whose Benefit? Report of the Standing Committee on External Affairs and International Trade on Canada's Official Development Assistance Policies and Programs* (Ottawa: Queen's Printer, 1987), 119 (Winegard Report).

54 *To Benefit a Better World. Response of the Government of Canada to the Report by the Standing Committee on External Affairs and International Trade on Canada's Official Development Assistance Policies and Programs* (Ottawa: Minister of Supply and Services 1987), 78.

55 *Independence and Internationalism*, 101.

56 *Canada's International Relations*, 72.

57 "Proposal to Establish a Parliamentary Mechanism for Review of the Interrelationship between Canadian Foreign Policy and International Human Rights" (brief for the Special Committee on Reform of the House of Commons by the Task Force on the Churches and Corporate Responsibility, May 1985).

58 Ibid.

59 *Independence and Internationalism*.

60 Ibid., 101–2.

61 *Canada's International Relations*, 73.

62 *For Whose Benefit?* 30.

63 *To Benefit a Better World*, 54.

64 Ibid., 53.

65 Howard McCurdy, MP (NDP), subcommittee hearings, 29 April 1990.

66 *Human Rights Considerations and Coherence in Canada's Foreign Policy. Third Report of the Standing Committee on Human Rights and the Status of Disabled Persons (Subcommittee on International Human Rights)* (Ottawa: Minister of Supply and Services 1990), 2.

67 John W. Foster, "The U.N. Commission on Human Rights," in Robert Matthews and Cran Pratt, *Human Rights in Canadian Foreign Policy*

(Kingston and Montreal: McGill-Queen's University Press 1992), 79–100.

68 Jan Egeland, *Impotent Superpower – Potent Small State*, (Oslo: Norwegian Universities Press 1988), 192n12.

69 *Report no. 36 (1984–85) to the Storting on Certain Major Questions Related to Norwegian Development Assistance* (Oslo, n.p.), 3.

70 Interview with the foreign ministry human rights coordinator, October 1989.

71 Allan McChesney, "Teaching Human Rights to Foreign Service Officers and Other Public Servants: Developments in Canada and Abroad," in Irving Brecher, *Human Rights, Development and Foreign Policy: Canadian Perspectives*, (Halifax: Institute for Research on Public Policy 1989), 187.

72 Human Rights and Foreign Policy Advisory Committee, *On an Equal Footing* (The Hague, 1984), annex 4–8, 11–12n16.

73 *Independence and Internationalism*, 101 (emphasis added).

74 *Canada's International Relations*, 72.

75 The Dutch Advisory Committee, for example, pointed to greater resistance among older foreign ministry officials (*On an Equal Footing*, 6).

76 Discussion with a Norwegian foreign ministry official, 19 June 1990.

77 Interview with a Norwegian foreign ministry official, Oslo, 29 June 1990.

78 Rhoda E. Howard, "Practical Problems of Monitoring Human Rights Violations" (paper presented at a conference at Leiden University, 26 April 1990).

79 "Human Rights, Democratization and Good Governance" (draft CIDA policy statement, 1994).

80 David Gillies, "Human Rights and Foreign Policy: We've Only Just Begun," *Policy Options* 11, no. 2 (March 1990): 7–9.

81 *Establishing an Advisory Committee*, 16.

82 Interview with Doug Williams, Good Governance and Human Rights unit, CIDA, in Montreal, 14 July 1994. When the new blueprint was debated in-house, Williams observed a spilt among senior CIDA management, with some of the older vice-presidents wanting to ensure that their fiefdoms retained the power to implement the blueprint as they saw fit.

83 Peter R. Baehr, "Concern for Development Aid and Fundamental Human Rights: The Dilemma as Faced by the Netherlands," *Human Rights Quarterly* 4 (1982): 39–52.

84 Ibid., 49.

85 In Norway, advisory committees on human rights, for example, are used when an issue area is still disorganized (interview with Jon Bech, research officer, Storting Foreign Affairs Committee, Oslo, October 1989).

86 Egeland, *Potent Small State*, 183.

87 This finding is at odds with Pratt's harsh judgment on the "counter consensus" and is in accord with Dennis Stairs's view that public influence will be most evident in setting agendas. See Stairs's article "Public and Policy Makers: The Domestic Environment of Canada's Foreign Policy Community," *International Journal* 26 (1970–71): 246–7.

88 William Winegard, "Winegard on the Winegard Report and on Parliamentary Committees," in Brecher, *Human Rights*, 394–5.

89 Gerald Schmitz, "Between Political Principle and State Practice: Human Rights 'Conditionality' in Canada's Development Assistance," in Brecher, *Human Rights*, 475.

CHAPTER NINE

1 *Human Rights Considerations and Coherence in Canada's Foreign Policy. Third Report of the Standing Committee on Human Rights and the Status of Disabled Persons* (Ottawa: Minister of Supply and Services 1990), 2.

2 *For Whose Benefit? Report of the Standing Committee on External Affairs and International Trade on Canada's Official Development Assistance Policies and Programs* (Ottawa: Queen's Printers 1987), 23, 25 (Winegard Report).

3 Human Rights and Foreign Policy Advisory Committee, *Development Cooperation and Human Rights* (The Hague: Human Rights and Foreign Policy Advisory Committee 1987), annex 2, 70.

4 *Norway and the International Protection of Human Rights. Report to the Storting no. 93 (1976–77)* (Oslo: Royal Norwegian Ministry of Foreign Affairs 1977), 5.

5 *For Whose Benefit?* 27–9. The committee's categories are human rights "positive," "satisfactory," "watch," and "negative."

6 *To Benefit a Better World: Response of the Government of Canada to the Report by the Standing Committee on External Affairs and International Trade on Canada's Official Development Assistance Policies and Programs* (Ottawa: Minister of Supply and Services 1987), 52.

7 *Human Rights and Foreign Policy: Establishing an Advisory Committee* (The Hague: Ministry of Foreign Affairs 1982), 72.

8 Human Rights and Foreign Policy Advisory Committee, *Development Cooperation and Human Rights*, annex 2, 66.

9 *Establishing an Advisory Committee*, 135.

10 Frances Arbour, "'America's Backyard': Central America," in Robert O. Matthews and Cranford Pratt, eds., *Human Rights in Canadian Foreign Policy* (Kingston and Montreal: McGill-Queen's University Press 1988), 221–45.

11 *Human Rights Considerations*, 3. A rare instance in which rights conditionality restricted EDC activity was a 1980 cabinet decision to remove
newsprint from the list of commodities eligible for purchase under a line
of credit to Guyana because newsprint was not made available to the
opposition media (T.A. Keenleyside, "Development Assistance," in Matthews and Pratt, *Human Rights*, 203).

12 This tradition stretches back at least to Kant, Smith, and Cobden. The
corollary of a commitment to free markets and minimal state intervention is a commitment to individual liberty. See Robert Gilpin, *The Political Economy of International Relations* (Princeton, N.J.: Princeton
University Press, 1987), 26–31.

13 *Establishing an Advisory Committee*, 135.

14 Ibid.

15 *Norway and International Human Rights*, 32.

16 Ibid.

17 Martin Rudner, "Human Rights Conditionality and International Development Co-operation" (Hull: Canadian International Development
Agency 1983), 55.

18 Jan Egeland, *Impotent Superpower – Potent Small State*, (Oslo: Norwegian University Press 1988), 99. The Norwegian merchant marine, however, evaded government restrictions on supplying South African ports
by selling through third parties.

19 "Human Rights, One of the Most Complex Foreign Policy Issues," statement by the Honourable Don Jamieson, Secretary of State for External
Affairs, reprinted in *Human Rights and Canada's Foreign Policy*.

20 Kim Richard Nossal, "Out of Steam? Mulroney and Sanctions," *International Perspectives*, November/December 1988, 13–15.

21 Keenleyside, "Development Assistance," 200.

22 "MPs Demand Probe at CANDU Site," *Globe and Mail*, 23 May 1990.

23 Lise Bissonnette, "Une morale hors commerce," editorial, *Le Devoir*,
16 May 1995.

24 "Canada Is No Longer the World Boy Scout," *Gazette* (Montreal),
16 May 1995.

25 Cited in the *Liberal Party Foreign Policy Handbook*, May 1993 ("It is
fundamental that we resolve the permanent contradiction in our actions
to support human rights with our Canadian political objectives"). In the
same document, the then opposition Liberals affirmed that trade and
rights were not linked issues: "Il n'en reste pas moins que les questions
commerciales et celles qui ont trait aux droits de la personne sont consi-
dérées séparément lorsque le Canada fait affaire avec des pays réputés
pour leur intolérance."

26 Daphne Bramham, "Activists Chide New Trade Policy," *Vancouver Sun*,
13 May 1995.

27 See Ph. P. Everts, *Controversies at Home: Domestic Factors in Dutch Foreign Policy* (Dordrecht: Martinus Nijhoff 1985), 231–49.

28 Ibid., 251–67.

29 Parliaments have called for the liberalization of imports from less-developed countries (see, for example, *For Whose Benefit?* 43), but the trend of all three governments is in fact towards more protectionism against such imports. See the essays by Pratt, Cooper and van Themaat, and Hveem in *Internationalism Under Strain: The North-South Polices of Canada, the Netherlands, Norway, and Sweden*, ed. Cranford Pratt (Toronto: Toronto University Press 1989).

30 For details on Canadian policy, see Renate Pratt, "International Financial Institutions," in Matthews and Pratt, *Human Rights*, 159–86.

31 In 1985 the seventeen countries of the OECD's Development Assistance Committee contributed US$7.5 billion to multilateral institutions. See *Development Co-operation* (Paris: OECD 1986), 236.

32 *Independence and Internationalism: Report of the Special Joint Committee of the Senate and the House of Commons on Canada's International Relations* (Ottawa: Minister of Supply and Services 1986), 103 (Hockin-Simard Report).

33 *For Whose Benefit?* 29. Similar proposals were made by the Dutch Human Rights and Foreign Policy Advisory Committee and the Norwegian Standing Committee on Foreign Affairs and the Constitution. See the advisory committee's *Development Cooperation and Human Rights*, 6–7; and *Recommendation the Storting no. 186 (1986–87)* (Oslo: Standing Committee on Foreign Affairs and the Constitution).

34 *Report no. 36 (1984–85) to the Storting on Certain Major Questions Related to Norwegian Development Assistance.* (Oslo, 1984–85), 118.

35 *Establishing an Advisory Committee*, 140.

36 Ibid.

37 This alliance unravelled when dissent among the Nordic states (some of whom wanted to improve trade with Chile) left the Netherlands isolated (interview with a Dutch foreign ministry official, The Hague, May 1990).

38 Cited in David Gillies, "Do Interest Groups Make a Difference? Domestic Influences on Canadian Development Aid Policy," in Irving Brecher, ed., *Human Rights, Development and Foreign Policy: Canadian Perspectives* (Halifax: Institute for Research on Foreign Policy 1989), 444.

39 *Establishing an Advisory Committee*, 140.

40 *Securing Our Global Future: Canada's Stake in the Unfinished Business of Third World Debt. Report of the Standing Committee for External Affairs and International Trade* (Ottawa: Minister of Supply and Services, 1990), 39.

41 Ibid., 37.

42 *Canada's International Relations. Responses of the Government of Canada to the Special Joint Committee of the Senate and the House of Commons* (Ottawa: Minister of Supply and Services, 1986), 74.

43 *Human Rights Considerations*, 10.

44 *From Bretton Woods to Halifax and Beyond. Report of the House of Commons Standing Committee on Foreign Affairs and International Trade on the Issues of International Financial Institutions Reforms for the Agenda of the June 1995 G-7 Halifax Summit* (Ottawa: House of Commons Publications Service 1995), 39–40.

45 Barber B. Conable, address to a meeting with African governors of the World Bank, Washington, D.C., September 1990.

46 "Nepal Faces Loss of Foreign Aid If Pro-Democracy Forces Impeded," *Ottawa Citizen*, 19 April 1990.

47 Another Canadian ODA project with a negative human rights impact concerns the land and cultural rights of patoralists in northwest Tanzania, where CIDA has worked with the Tanzanian government to transform traditional range and herding land into commercial wheat farms. After pressure from local pastoralist NGOs, Canada eventually persuaded the Tanzanian government to set up an inquiry – the so-called Kisanga Commission. This led to a CIDA-funded community development fund for the pastoralists.

48 *Storting meld no. 36 (1985–86)*, 118.

49 *Establishing an Advisory Committee*, 138.

50 Jamieson, "Human Rights," 7.

51 CIDA, *Elements of Canada's Official Development Assistance Strategy* (Hull: CIDA 1984).

52 *Storting meld no. 36 (1984–85)*, 118.

53 *Establishing an Advisory Committee*, 139.

54 *To Benefit a Better World*, 51.

55 OECD, "Update of the Survey of DAC Members' Policies and Programmes in Participatory Development and Good Governance" (Paris: OECD, DCD-DAC [93], 23, 31 August 1993), 36.

56 Ibid., 50–1.

57 Keenleyside, "Development Assistance," 201.

58 Department of External Affairs and International Trade Canada, "McDougall Concerned by the Situation in Peru" (news release no. 66, 7 April 1992).

59 Department of External Affairs and International Trade Canada, "An Address by the Honourable Barbara McDougall, Secretary of State for External Affairs, to the 22nd Annual General Meeting of the Organization of American States," Nassau, Bahamas, 19 May 1992.

60 Ibid., 198–9.

61 For a review of human rights abuses, see *Report on the Situation of Human Rights in Haiti* (Washington, D.C.: Organization of American States, Inter-American Commission on Human Rights 1988).

62 Roger C. Riddell, *Foreign Aid Reconsidered* (Baltimore and London: Johns Hopkins University Press 1987), 258.

63 E. Philip English, *Canadian Development Assistance to Haiti* (Ottawa: North-South Institute 1984), 135.

64 *Rapport du groupe parlementaire sur Haïti* (Ottawa, 1988), mimeo.

65 CIDA, *Communiqué*, 13 September 1988 ("The Canadian government wants to state clearly its disapproval regarding the numerous violations of fundamental human rights that have multiplied since the beginning of this regime").

66 Philip Rawkins and Monique Bergeron, "Lessons Learned in Human Rights and Democratic Development: A Study of CIDA's Bilateral Programming Experience," (Hull: CIDA 1994), 42.

67 Le centre canadien d'études et de coopération internationale was selected as the Canadian executing agency for a $5 million five-year human rights program to support human rights organizations and assist the victims of violations.

68 Rawkins and Bergeron, "Lessons Learned," 43.

69 *Human Rights in Developing Countries 1989 Yearbook*, (Kehl and Strasbourg: N.P. Engel 1989), 183.

70 *Development Co-operation* (Paris: OECD 1988), 217.

71 Gitobu Imanyara, as quoted by Jonathan Manthorpe, "Political Powderkeg," *Ottawa Citizen*, 29 October 1990.

72 For evidence of growing suppression of dissent, see the 1986 to 1989 yearbooks on *Human Rights in Developing Countries* (Copenhagen: Akademisk Forlag).

73 Interview with a senior Norwegian foreign ministry official, Oslo, June 1990.

74 As quoted in Bard-Anders Andreassen and Asbjorn Eide, eds., *Human Rights in Developing Countries 1987–88* (Copenhagen: Akademisk Forlag 1988), 45.

75 The bad press stemmed in part from the Amnesty International Report, *Kenya: Torture, Political Detention and Unfair Trials* (London: Amnesty International 1987, AI Index AFR/32/17/87). The Norwegian government stressed that the domestic media were free to comment negatively and were likely to do so should Moi visit (interview with a foreign ministry official, Oslo, October 1989).

76 The *Weekly Review* published a survey of Norwegian aid to Kenya under the title "Norwegian Aid: What Cost the Souring Relations?" (*Weekly Review*, 4 September 1987, 9–10).

77 Interview with a senior official, Ministry of Development Cooperation, Oslo, 29 June 1990.

78 The grant element was 18.5 million kroner (interview with a Norwegian official, Oslo, June 1990).

79 In 1989, Koigi, a former Kenyan MP, published *Kenya: selvstre uten frihet* (Kenya: Independence without Freedom). The book asks why Norway and other aid donors insist that democratization is a condition for aid to Eastern Europe but not for aid to African states. When I interviewed Koigi in Oslo in December 1989, he claimed that his life was in danger, and when he returned to Kenya in 1990 he was detained in custody. The Kenyan government was similarly critical of the United States for harbouring Gibson Kuria, a leading human rights lawyer and government critic.

80 In response to a question about an alleged assassination attempt on wa Wamwere, a Norwegian foreign ministry official replied that it is "well known" that Kenya has a good intelligence service (interview in Oslo, 23 October 1989).

81 Kenya was actively discussed *in camera* in the "expanded" Foreign Affairs Committee – i.e., in the presence of the prime minister. Committee staff were not, however, prepared to divulge information about Kenya in view of the issue's sensitivity.

82 Interview with a foreign ministry official, Oslo, June 1990.

83 *Innst S. nr. 255*, 4. A senior aid official insisted the cut was made for administrative and not political reasons.

84 "Kenya: Norwegians under the Bed," *Economist*, October/November 1990, 46.

85 A useful overview is K.K. Prah, "Ethnicity, Politics and Human Rights in the Southern Sudan," in David P. Forsythe, ed., *Human Rights and Development* (London: Macmillan 1990).

86 *Agreed Minutes of Consultations on Development Co-operation between Delegations of the Republic of Sudan and the Kingdom of the Netherlands for the Year 1990* (Khartoum, 25 January 1990).

87 Ibid.

88 Ibid.

89 *Globe and Mail*, 9 March 1989.

90 CIDA computer database, April 1989.

91 The Dutch have aided human rights victims and channelled funds through their co-financing NGOs since pioneering human rights work by NOVIB in the mid-1970s. For Canadian examples, see Gisèle Côté-Harper and John Courtney, *International Cooperation for the Development of Human Rights Institutions. Report to the Right Honourable Joe Clark and the Honourable Monique Landry* (Ottawa, 1987). For Norway, see Arne Arneson, Norwegian state secretary for development

cooperation, "Norwegian Assistance to Non-Governmental Organizations," in *Assistance to Third World Human Rights Groups* (Oslo: Norwegian Red Cross 1989): 22–3.

92 "The Role of Non-Governmental Participation in the Netherlands [Development] Cooperation Policy" (speech by Dr P. Bukman, minister for development cooperation, Jakarta, 1 May 1989), printed in *Informatie no. 13* (The Hague Ministry of Foreign Affairs 1989).

93 "1988 Budget: Extra Aid for Emergent Democracies," *Informatie no. 20/E.15* (The Hague: Ministry of Foreign Affairs 1987).

94 OECD, "Update of the Survey of DAC Members' Policies and Programmes in Participatory Development and Good Governance" (Paris: OECD, DCD-DAC [93] 23, 31 August 1993), 34.

95 Internal Ministry of Development Cooperation data.

96 OECD, "Review of the Survey of DAC Members' Policies and Practices in Participatory Development/Good Governance" (Paris: OECD, DCD-DAC [92] 11, April 1992).

97 OECD, "Update on the Survey of DAC Members' Policies and Programmes in Participatory Development and Good Governance" (Paris: OECD, DCD-DAC [93] 23, 31 August 1993), 42.

98 Ibid., 21–2.

99 *Independence and Internationalism*, 105. But the centre owes much to ideas in Robert Miller, *Canada and Democratic Development* (Ottawa: International Development Research Centre 1985).

100 Quoted in Mark Abley, "Trying to Make a Difference," *Gazette* (Montreal), 18 February 1995.

101 House of Commons, *Bill C-147, An Act to Establish the International Centre for Human Rights and Democratic Development*.

102 *Senate Debates*, 30 September 1988, 4560.

103 Ibid.

104 Ibid., 4557–60.

105 Interview in Ottawa, 10 May 1990.

106 An assessment by Edward Broadbent, president of the International Centre for Human Rights and Democratic Development (interview in Ottawa, April 1990).

107 Several members of the Standing Committee on Foreign Affairs and International Trade, including the chairman Jean-Robert Gauthier, took aim at the allegedly high administrative overheads and the "duplication" or "overlap" with CIDA's mandate (Hansard, 12 April 1994). Speaking before the committee that same day, CIDA's president, Huguette Labelle, seemed to point to advocacy as a distinguishing feature of the centre's work: "Its current mandate ... does not include implementing programs: rather its role is to promote human rights in developing countries." She suggested that the committee help define and distinguish the respective

mandates of the centre and CIDA. The external review of the centre criticized it for poor internal communication, excessive hierarchy, and the tardy development of a strategic plan.

108 *Canada in the World* (Ottawa: Canada Communication Group 1995), 34.

109 "List of Approved CIDA Bilateral Projects between 1982 and 1992 with a Significant Civil-Political and-or Democratization Component" (Hull: CIDA Policy Branch 1994).

110 Ibid., 12–13.

111 Canada will, however, publish an "excluded list" of countries deemed ineligible for Canadian aid for human rights or other considerations.

112 See *Sharing Our Future: Canadian International Development Assistance* (Ottawa: Minister of Supply and Services 1988), 30; Hermann von Hebel, "The Netherlands," and Hugo Stokke, "Norway," in Nowak and Swinehart, *Human Rights in Developing Countries 1989* (Kehl and Strasbourg: N.P. Engel 1990).

113 *Sharing Our Future*, 30.

114 An internal CIDA review of its supports for rights and democratization in El Salvador saw a potential contradiction between CIDA support for small-scale rural cooperatives and Canada's endorsement of the economic reform packages that favoured private agribusiness and put the future of the rural cooperatives in question. I am grateful to CIDA's Policy Branch for sharing this review with me.

115 An empirical study of the relationship between Canadian aid and the human rights record of recipients confirmed that an "inordinate proportion of Canadian aid was flowing to countries in which the basic rights of individuals were being violated in a serious way" (T.A. Keenleyside and Nola Serkasevich, "Canada's Aid and Human Rights Observance: Measuring the Relationship," *International Journal* 45 no. 1 [Winter 1989–90], 165).

116 Norway's 1976 white paper made a weak commitment that "increasingly, a dialogue on human rights questions should be started with recipient countries." The 1984–85 white paper on aid and rights agreed that NORAD/MDC should "raise human rights when discussing further cooperation, [but only] *when there is a reason to do so*" (emphasis added).

117 Human Rights and Foreign Policy Advisory Committee, *Development Cooperation and Human Rights*, 1982, 64.

118 Ibid., 64–5.

119 *Securing Our Global Future*, 56.

120 Article 25 of the International Covenant of Civil and Political Rights.

121 Judith Tendler, *Inside Foreign Aid* (Baltimore and London: Johns Hopkins University Press 1975).

122 See Phillip Rawkins and Monique Bergeron, "Lessons Learned in Human Rights and Democratic Development: A Study of CIDA's Bilateral Programming Experience" (Hull: CIDA 1994). The report underscored the absence of helpful guidelines for programming and the tendency for programming decisions to predate data collection and analysis. It also highlighted the importance of a strong field presence and the need to build a strong stakeholder consensus for long-term programming.

123 Ralph M. Goldman, "The Donor-Recipient Relationship in Political Aid Programs," in Ralph M. Goldman and William A. Douglas, eds., *Promoting Democracy: Opportunities and Issues* (New York: Praeger 1988), 51–73.

124 Richard L. Hough, "Peasant Organizations in Democratic Development," in Goldman and Douglas, eds., *Promoting Democracy*, 185–205.

125 At the DAC, the Dutch and Danes are spearheading donor thinking on human rights, the Norwegians will focus on decentralization, while Canada will, together with the United Kingdom, focus on public-sector management.

126 "Human Rights, Democratization and Good Governance" (draft CIDA policy statement, Good Governance and Human Rights, Policy Branch, July 1994).

127 *Canada's Foreign Policy: Principles and Priorities for the Future. Report of the Special Joint Committee Reviewing Canada's Foreign Policy.* (Ottawa: Government Printer 1994).

128 *Government Response to the Recommendations of the Special Joint Parliamentary Committee Reviewing Canadian Foreign Policy* (Ottawa: Government of Canada 1995).

129 Ibid., 4, 5.

130 Peter Burnell, "Good Government and Democratization: A Sideways Look at Aid and Political Conditionality," *Democratization* 1, no. 3 (1994): 485–503.

131 Victoria Berry and Allan McChesney, "Human Rights and Foreign Policy-making," in Robert Matthews and Cranford Pratt, *Human Rights in Canadian Foreign Policy* (Kingston and Montreal: McGill-Queen's University Press 1988), 59–78. The four axioms of the code are the primacy of Cold War perspectives, the centrality of the U.S. relationship, a bias to business, and alliance commitments.

132 Cranford Pratt, "The Limited Place of Human Rights in Canadian Foreign Policy," in Brecher, *Human Rights*, 173.

133 Ibid.

134 Glynn R. Berry, "Bureaucratic Politics and Canadian Economic Policies Affecting the Developing Countries: The Case of the 'Strategy for International Development Co-Operation'" (PH D dissertation, Dalhousie University, 1981).

CHAPTER TEN

1 The "saving lie" is the central theme of Henrik Ibsen's play *The Wild Duck*. It refers to the belief in something that is known to be untrue.

2 *Moral Vision in International Politics* (Princeton, N.J.: Princeton University Press, 1993), 67.

3 George F. Kennan, "Morality and Foreign Policy," *Foreign Affairs*, Winter 1985, 206.

4 Constantine Melakopides, "Ethics and International Relations: A Critique of Cynical Realism," in David G. Haglund and Michael K. Hawes, eds., *World Politics: Power, Interdependence and Dependence* (Toronto: Harcourt Brace Jovanovich 1990), 506 (emphasis in the original).

5 Robert Keohane, ed., *Neorealism and Its Critics* (New York: Columbia University Press 1986), 198.

6 R.J. Vincent, *Human Rights and International Relations* (Cambridge: Cambridge University Press 1986), 130.

7 John Gerard Ruggie, "Human Rights and the Future International Community," *Daedalus* 112 (Fall 1983), 93–109.

8 Ibid., 107.

9 Foreign Affairs Minister André Ouellet, as cited in Lise Bissonnette, "Une morale hors commerce," *Le Devoir*, 16 May 1995.

10 See Mancur Olsen, "Dictatorship, Democracy and Development," *American Political Science Review*, September 1993, and "Democracy and Growth," *Economist*, 27 August 1994.

11 John Holmes, "Morality, Realism and Foreign Affairs," *International Perspectives*, September/October 1977, 20–4.

12 Particularly through the Declaration of Teheran and Resolution 32/130 of the General Assembly.

13 Vincent, *Human Rights and International Relations*, 183.

14 For a good evocation of these differences, see Bilhari Kausikan, "Asia's Different Standard," and Aryeh Neir, "Asia's Unacceptable Standard," both in *Foreign Policy* 92 (Fall 1993).

15 See the NGO Bangkok Declaration for a prescription on how an Asian regional rights mechanism should be configured.

16 "Human Rights and Universal Responsibility" (text of a talk by His Holiness the 14th Dalai Lama of Tibet at the Non-Govermental Meeting, U.N. World Conference on Human Rights, Vienna, 15 June 1993).

17 Winston Lord, assistant secretary of state for East Asian and Pacific Affairs, U.S. State Department, quoted in Thomas L. Friedman "Trade vs. Human Rights," *New York Times*, 6 February 1994.

18 *Liberal Party Handbook*, May 1993 ("It is fundamental that we resolve the permanent contradiction in our actions to support human rights with our Canadian political objectives").

19 These examples are taken from data compiled by the International Confederation of Free Trade Unions.

20 "Response to the ASEAN Foreign Ministers Communiqué" made by a coalition of Asian NGOs, Bangkok, 25 July 1994. The Indonesian government tried to pressure the Thai government to prevent the NGO parallel meeting from taking place at all. Note that Asian NGOs do not speak with a single voice on this issue. See Martin Khor, "Why GATT and WTO Should Not Deal with Labour Standards," Penang, Malaysia, *Third World Network*, July 1994, mimeo.

21 Notes for an address by the Hon. Roy MacLaren, minister for international trade, to the GATT ministerial conference in Marrakesh (Marrakesh, Morocco, 12 April 1994).

22 Bill Clinton, "To Advance the Common Interest in a More Open China," *International Herald Tribune*, 1 June 1994.

23 Warren Christopher, "The Important Message I Carried to China," *International Herald Tribune*, 23 March 1994.

24 Quoted in "Colliding with China," *Economist*, 12 March 1994.

25 Warren Carragata, "A Change of Heart," *Maclean's*, 21 March 1994.

26 Quoted in Shawn McCarthy, "Giving Trade Policy Black Marks," *Toronto Star*, 19 May 1994.

27 Ibid.

28 Notes for an address by the Hon. André Ouellet, minister of foreign affairs, to the Canadian Institute for International Affairs (Ottawa, 31 May 1994).

29 Ibid.

30 Ibid.

31 Ibid.

32 Barbara McDougall, "When Trading with Tyrants," *Toronto Star*, 17 June 1994.

33 Henry A. Kissinger and Cyrus R. Vance, "America's China Policy Is Back on Course," *International Herald Tribune*, 8 June 1994.

34 *International Herald Tribune*, 23 March 1994.

35 Robert Peck, letter to the *Globe and Mail*, 12 June 1994.

36 President Clinton proposed the same compact with U.S. business after he unlinked rights from MFN (*International Herald Tribune*, 1 June 1994). In Canada the precedent for this idea is the 1978 voluntary code of conduct for Canadian firms operating in South Africa. The code covered trade union rights and racial equality in hiring.

37 Edward Broadbent, president of the International Centre for Human Rights and Democratic Development, has proposed three rights: free trade unions, free speech, and free association.

38 Paul M. Evans, "Canada's Relations with China Emergent," *Canadian Foreign Policy*, Spring 1993, 28.

39 Jeff Sallott, "Trade 'Stampede' to China Condemned," *Globe and Mail*, 1 June 1994.

40 Jack Donnelly comes perilously close to advocating passivity; see *Universal Human Rights in Theory and Practice* (Ithaca, N.Y.: Cornell University Press 1990), chap. 13. Stephen D. Krasner takes the realist position that Western human rights policies "will be politically barren" given the "endemic" conflict between North and South; see *Structural Conflict: The Third World against Global Liberalism* (Berkeley: University of California Press 1985), 268, 294.

41 Bengt Sundelius, "Interdependence and Foreign Policy," *Cooperation and Conflict* 15, no. 4 (1980): 187–208.

42 Olav Stokke, ed., *Middle Powers and Global Poverty: The Determinants of the Aid Policies of Canada, Denmark, the Netherlands, Norway and Sweden* (Uppsala: Scandinavian Institute of African Studies 1988); Cranford Pratt, ed., *Internationalism under Strain: The North-South Policies of Canada, the Netherlands, Norway, and Sweden* (Toronto: University of Toronto Press 1989).

43 See Gerald J. Schmitz and David Gillies, *The Challenge of Democratic Development* (Ottawa: North-South Institute 1992).

Index